Clinical and Counseling Practice

Clinical and Counseling Practice

A Case-Guided Approach

Peter Sturmey

Queens College and Graduate Center
City University of New York

Michael D. Gaubatz

University of the Incarnate Word

Boston   New York   San Francisco
Mexico City   Montreal   Toronto   London   Madrid   Munich   Paris
Hong Kong   Singapore   Tokyo   Cape Town   Sydney

Series Editor: Kelly M. May
Series Editorial Assistant: Marlana Voerster
Executive Marketing Manager: Wendy Gordon
Editorial-Production Administrator: Beth Houston
Editorial-Production Service: Walsh & Associates, Inc.
Composition Buyer: Linda Cox
Manufacturing Buyer: Andrew Turso
Cover Administrator: Kristina Mose-Lisbon

Library of Congress Cataloging-in-Publication Data

Sturmey, Peter.
    Clinical and counseling practice / Peter Sturmey, Michael D. Gaubatz.
      p. cm.
    Includes bibliographical references and index.
    ISBN 0-205-33219-6
    1. Psychotherapy—Practice. 2. Psychotherapy. 3. Counseling.
I. Gaubatz, Michael D. II. Title
RC467.S848 2002
616.89'14'068—dc21   2002026117

To Bill and Julie, for all their support and understanding

CONTENTS

PREFACE

Many psychotherapy students and beginning practitioners face the daunting task of integrating diverse information about diagnosis, treatment, and ethical and multicultural issues into their actual work. Like experienced clinicians, they often find that key issues with which they were once familiar seem just out of reach when facing a clinical situation. Such students face the challenge of integrating information from coursework and supervision cases they experienced sequentially over the course of several years. Unfortunately, no current resource distills this information into a single readily accessible volume. This book aims to do just that.

We believe there is a need for a concise book that integrates the most important aspects of working with clients using concrete clinical material. Assuming a basic knowledge of abnormal psychology and the theories of psychotherapy, we designed this book to address the most common issues beginning clinicians and counselors face.

The key strategy of this book is to simplify common situations into smaller numbers of options. To focus the reader on the essentials of clinical situations, we have used a standard format for treatment plans that includes three common elements: immediate concerns, short-term goals, and long-term goals, including ongoing strategies for enhancing clients' developing strengths. Finally, we have provided, throughout each chapter and for every clinical issue, illustrative examples of the application of this format to diverse clinical concerns.

This book is described as a case-guided approach. We have chosen this approach because we believe there is a gap between the classroom and actual clinical and counseling practice. When novice clinicians begin working with clients, they often struggle with situations that do not neatly fit their class notes. They may see a client with both a mood disorder and an anxiety disorder. They may work with parents who inadvertently contribute to their children's behavior problems. They may see a client with a fear of heart attacks, who has actually has had a heart attack in the past and justifiably fears having another one. We believe that, as a teaching tool, case studies best highlight such issues early in students' training. We therefore did not design this book to be a comprehensive review of the field of counseling and clinical psychology. We designed it to be a concise, case-based resource for the student or beginning clinician facing the challenges of actual clinical work.

Acknowledgments

We would like to thank John Velasquez, Kasey Songy, Adrienne Robek, and Howie Reyer for editorial assistance with this book.

We would also like to thank the following reviewers for their time and input: Leonard M. Bohanon, Our Lady of the Lake University; Elizabeth Vera, Loyola University-Chicago; Ray Miltenberger, North Dakota State University.

PART ONE

Diagnosis, Assessment, and Treatment Planning

1 Diagnostic Assessment and Treatment Planning

CHAPTER OVERVIEW

1. DSM-IV diagnosis is the outcome of over one hundred years of development of classification schemes for psychiatric disorders. Its development is responsive to both scientific and sociocultural pressures. Over the years the number and range of psychiatric diagnoses have expanded considerably. In response to criticisms that earlier versions of DSM were unreliable, DSM-IV included checklists of signs and symptoms. It is characterized by polythetic categories, multiaxial classification, and recognition of gender and cross-cultural issues in psychiatric diagnosis.

2. Assessment is undertaken for many purposes. These purposes include determining client eligibility for services, guiding treatment, determining etiology, making statistical returns, communication among professionals, and treatment planning. Assessment may be undertaken using interviews with the client or third parties, reviews of collateral information, psychometric assessment, behavioral assessment, medical assessment, psychiatric consultation, and neuropsychological consultation. Professionals should be sensitive to the ethical aspects of assessment. Specifically, practitioners should only undertake assessments that are in the best interests of their clients and that they are competent to perform.

3. Treatment planning includes three phases: (a) immediate concerns, such as risk of harm to self or others; (b) short-term goals, such as teaching coping skills; and (c) long-term plans, such as personal and vocational life goals, relapse prevention, and enhancement of the client's developing strengths.

4. Intervention today takes place in an environment characterized by managed care, cost containment, and evidence-based practice.

LEARNING OBJECTIVES

The student will:

1. Describe the history of the development of DSM-IV diagnosis.
2. Describe four characteristics of DSM-IV diagnoses.
3. Name and describe the six purposes of classification.
4. Name and describe six methods of assessment.
5. Apply three types of treatment goals to a given case study.
6. Describe three characteristics of the current environment of practice.

History of DSM-IV

The Diagnostic and Statistical Manual, fourth edition, text revised (American Psychiatric Association, 2000) is the official psychiatric nomenclature of the American Psychiatric Association and the most recent version of a continually developing stream of psychiatric classification systems. DSM-IV is part of a larger effort to classify all kinds of illness, both physical and psychological, in the United States and worldwide. A parallel diagnostic system, the *International Classification of Disease and Related Health Problems* (World Health Organization, 2001), ICD, is used primarily outside the United States.

The DSM-IV derives from a long history of attempts to classify mental illness. In the nineteenth century, U.S. censuses included categories of mental illness. In 1840 there was only one diagnostic category, idiocy, which included insanity. By the 1880 census there were seven kinds of mental disorder: mania, melancholia, monomania, paresis, dementia, dipsomania, and epilepsy. In the early part of the twentieth century, the U.S. government, primarily interested in monitoring public expenditures in mental hospitals, asked psychiatrists to develop a more extensive psychiatric classification system. Ironically, many psychiatrists were reluctant to do so, citing the complexity of the task. Nevertheless, between 1918 and 1942 ten editions of the *Statistical Manual for the Use of Institutions for the Insane* were published. This classification system used twenty-two categories of mental illness, which primarily referred to organic etiology, such as strokes, tumors, and infections of the brain. It generally was assumed that mental disorders reflected some form of organic pathology of the brain or nervous system.

In 1952 the American Psychiatric Association published what is now referred to as DSM-I, which differed significantly from its diagnostic predecessors. First, DSM-I was firmly based in psychoanalytic rather than organic explanations for mental illness. This reflected psychiatrists' experiences in World War II, during which many observed that battle neuroses appeared to be reactions to trauma rather than to diseases of the brain or nervous system. Coupled with the ascendance of psychoanalysis in the United States, these observations led to a psychoanalytic bent in the development of the DSM-I, an orientation that was further reflected in the DSM-II.

Published in 1968, the DSM-II expanded the number and breadth of psychiatric disorders and added several sections dealing with childhood and adolescent disorders. By the 1970s, however, several studies had questioned its reliability. Even when psychiatrists used very crude categories, such as "psychopathic personality" or "neurosis," the inter-rater reliability of specific diagnoses was sometimes close to zero. DSM-II was also attacked for including homosexuality as a mental illness. Although consistent with psychodynamic theory of the time, this classification had little empirical basis and was changed in 1980 with the publication of the DSM-III (later revised to form DSM-III-Revised). DSM-IV was published in 1994 (American Psychiatric Association, 1994), and recently the text, but not the diagnostic criteria, has been revised (American Psychiatric Association, 2000).

Throughout the revisions of the DSM several trends can be observed. First, the psychodynamic term *reaction*, a keystone of the early DSM editions, was dropped. Later editions adopted a more theoretically neutral stance by referring only to specific symptoms, such as "elevated, expansive or irritable mood" or "repeated nightmares involving the theme of separation." Second, DSM revisions reflected (and continue to reflect) an ongoing attempt to address the unreliability of psychiatric diagnosis. This was done in two ways: The collection of information on individual symptoms was made explicit by listing and defining the symptoms associated with a particular disorder, and the number and type of symptoms necessary to diagnose each disorder were explicitly enumerated.

In addition to these internal changes, the external processes by which new editions of DSM were developed became more elaborate and time consuming. Whereas DSM-I had been assembled in just one year, DSM-IV was the outcome of a five-year process. First, a web of thirteen committees was developed covering each major diagnostic area, each of which conducted extensive literature reviews (cf. Widiger et al., 1996; Widiger et al., 1998). Multicenter field trials of proposed diagnostic categories were then conducted in order to assess the reliability of proposed new categories, and hundreds of experts, including experts outside the field of psychiatry, were called upon to evaluate the utility of the emerging system. This process resulted in a hefty manual encompassing hundreds of diagnoses, thousands of diagnostic criteria, weighty appendices addressing cross-cultural aspects of mental health practice, and twenty-two pages acknowledging the contributions of mental health researchers and practitioners.

Despite these efforts, critics of DSM-IV remain, including many physicians, psychiatrists, psychoanalysts, psychologists, behavior analysts, and sociologists. Some practicing psychiatrists view DSM-IV diagnoses as an administrative inconvenience that does little to aid their treatment of patients. Some psychologists criticize DSM-IV for poor reliability, while others criticize its sacrifice of validity to its effort to obtain reliability at any cost (cf. Beutler & Malik, 2002). Behavior analysts are dissatisfied that psychiatry continues to explain observable behavior by referring to unobservable causes, such as illnesses of the brain or dysregulated neurotransmitters. Many feminist, multicultural, and social constructionist critics argue that DSM-IV pathologizes minority cultural norms while codifying ever-enlarging forms of "psychopathology" that may actually be rooted in social causes (e.g., Ani, 1994; Flax, 1990; Foucault, 1954/1987; Gergen, 1994; Gonzalez, Biever, & Gardner, 1994; Hines & Hare-Mustin, 1978; McWhirter, 1998; Prilleltensky, 1989, 1995, 1997; White & Parham, 1990).

Despite these and many other criticisms, DSM-IV continues to be the primary reference for psychiatric diagnosis in the United States. It also remains highly influential on the refinement and development of the International Classification of Diseases. Furthermore, over the past two decades the DSM-IV has become a primary gatekeeper for determining access to, and research about, mental health services in the United States. A person today probably could not be admitted to an American mental hospital without a DSM-IV diagnosis. Insurance claims are not honored without it. Researchers would find it hard to publish papers or obtain research grants without reference to DSM-IV, and replicating published research would be difficult without referring to its categories. Psychotropic medications and various psychotherapies are developed, evaluated, and disseminated as being appropriate for certain DSM-IV categories, and there is a large industry of developing psychometric measures that are based and marketed explicitly on DSM-IV criteria. Finally, of course, books such as this one are written and marketed to students and professors with the cachet of being "based on DSM-IV." Despite its many critics, the DSM approach is likely to occupy a central place in mental health practice and research for the foreseeable future.

DSM-IV Definition of Mental Disorder

DSM-IV defines a mental disorder as follows:

> . . . A clinically significant behavioral or psychosocial syndrome or pattern that occurs in an individual and that is associated with present distress . . . or disability . . . or with a significantly increased risk of suffering death, pain, disability, or an important loss of freedom. . . . this syndrome or pattern must be not merely an expectable or cultural sanctioned response to a particular event . . . it must be considered a manifestation of a behavioral, psychological, or biological dysfunction in the individual. . . . Neither deviant behavior . . . between the individual and society are mental disorders unless the deviance or conflict is a symptom of a dysfunction in the individual as described above. (APA, 2000, p. xxxi)

This definition is necessarily broad. Because it must encompass everything from transient mood disorders to lifelong, refractory schizophrenia, and from male erectile dysfunction to compulsive shoplifting, it avoids addressing many important issues surrounding the definition of abnormality and mental illness. Although the DSM-IV acknowledges some of these issues, it does not resolve them. One of the problems is that the distress a client experiences must be "clinically significant." But how can such significance be objectively judged? If a client presents with a chronic, moderately depressed mood and subjective "unhappiness," but can work and fulfill most of his or her family roles, is that distress clinically significant? To some extent, such a definition merely deflects "macro" cultural constructions of abnormality to the "micro" level assessments made by individual clinicians (cf. Prilleltensky, 1995).

Another problematic aspect of the definition is the requirement that a given disorder must be "not merely an expectable . . . response" (APA, 2000, p. xxxi).

Here again, personal judgment on the part of the client and clinician is necessarily involved. For example, criteria for a Major Depressive Episode call for symptoms lasting at least two weeks, but many people experience two weeks of depressed mood or other symptoms in response to a variety of situations. Would two weeks of depressive symptoms be expectable for the loss of a job, the death of a spouse, or the death of a pet? Reasonable clinicians would disagree with each other about these judgments. DSM-IV also specifies that conflict between the individual and society should be excluded unless it is "a symptom of a dysfunction in the individual" (p. xxxi). But how can a clinician distinguish distress due to a conflict between an individual and society versus distress that is symptomatic of dysfunction? Does a transvestite performer who drinks to calm her nerves on stage meet DSM-IV criteria for Social Anxiety Disorder, or do her symptoms reflect a conflict between her unusual role and society? Should we see her as mentally ill or as a social rights activist experiencing understandable, reasonable distress in the face of her efforts?

Finally, many mental health professionals struggle with the cultural specificity of diagnosing "abnormality" with any psychological diagnostic system. A wide variety of sexual, relational, and personal behaviors that have been regarded as normal within 100,000 years of human cultural variation would be judged abnormal by Western standards today. Culturally sensitive clinicians have little problem accommodating behavioral variations among agricultural and postagricultural societies, such as preferences for nonreflective treatments or identification with extended family members. However, the diversity of behaviors exhibited by hunting and gathering cultures throughout history, including infanticide, bestiality, human sacrifice, clitoridectomies, obeisance to deceased spirits, and strong forms of anti-acquisitionism, are more philosophically challenging (Barstow, 1999; Diamond, 1992; Herdt & Stoller, 1990; Sahlins, 1982). As several critics have argued, these issues subtly, and perhaps insidiously, underlie the diagnosis of alternative and/or minority cultural practices in modern cultures as well, including judgments about S&M sexual practices, drug use, antimonetarism, and assisted suicide, among other issues (e.g., Berlin, 2000; Foucault, 1976/1978; Leenaars et al., 2001; Silverman, 1997; Tsang, 1995; Weil, 1972; Weinberg, 1995). Because DSM-IV does not resolve these issues, an unreflective use of its nosology contradicts current trends toward heightened multicultural awareness in both counseling and psychology (see Chapter 2).

General Features of DSM-IV

Descriptive and Atheoretical Categories

As noted above, earlier versions of DSM were criticized for their unreliability. This was believed to be partly due to the vague, inferential descriptions of symptoms early versions of DSM offered. In response, DSM-IV was designed to describe symptoms of a disorder in as clear and operational a way as possible. For example, DSM-IV defines a Panic Attack as "a discrete period of intense fear or discomfort in which four or more of the following symptoms developed abruptly and reached a peak within 10 minutes: (1) palpitations, pounding heart, or accelerated heart rate; (2) sweating . . . [etc.]" (APA, 2000, p. 432). By specifying that a panic attack lasts for a discrete period with peak anxiety within 10 minutes of onset, DSM-IV attempts to distinguish panic attack from high levels of general anxiety. By enumerating the symptoms that must be present for diagnosis, it reduces clinical judgment to deciding whether to interpret a client's complaints as symptoms of a panic attack. In other words, DSM-IV provides very clear decision rules: Four symptoms must be present to diagnose panic attack; three would be insufficient.

It also should be noted that this description of a panic attack includes no suggestion of a particular cause for a panic attack. The DSM-IV definition does not refer to psychodynamic, physiological, conditioning, or any other psychological mechanisms that could be the cause of a panic attack. In this sense, DSM-IV is atheoretical.

Categorical, Polythetic Classification

Some diagnostic classifications assume that psychopathology is continuously distributed along one or more dimensions. These models hold that individuals fall on a continuum from normal to pathological, an assumption DSM-IV does not make. Instead, DSM-IV assumes there is a relatively clear distinction between mental illness and mental health. This approach also assumes that clients who meet the diagnostic criteria for a particular disorder are similar to each other in important ways, such as in their response to specific treatments.

Clients, however, are not identical just because they share specific symptoms. DSM-IV recognizes this reality (arguably) by employing polythetic classification. Thus, for the majority of disorders it requires no one single symptom for a diagnosis. Instead, for each diagnosis, some minimum number of symptoms from a list of possibilities is required to meet diagnostic thresholds. For example, in the diagnosis of a Major Depressive Episode, five or more of the following symptoms are required: depressed mood; diminished interest or pleasure; weight loss or gain when not dieting; insomnia or hypersomnia; psychomotor agitation or retardation; fatigue or loss of energy; feelings of worthlessness or guilt; poor concentration or indecisiveness; and thoughts of death, suicidal ideation, or suicidality (APA, 2000).

In addition, as in this example, the list of symptoms is usually only one part of DSM-IV's total diagnostic criteria. Other commonly used criteria include the duration of disorder, change in functioning, and the exclusion (or "ruling out") of other potential explanations for the client's symptoms. For example, in a Major Depressive Episode the symptoms must be present for at least two weeks. The client must not meet other diagnostic criteria, such as a Mixed Mood Episode (which consists of symptoms of both depressed and manic episodes) and must suffer distress or impairment in her or his occupational or social functioning. Physiological causes, such as drug abuse, medication, or a general medical condition such as hypothyroidism, must also be excluded as explanations for the client's distress and symptoms.

Multiaxial Classification

In early classification schemes only one primary diagnosis was recorded. Multiaxial classification was developed to present a more holistic assessment of the client. It was also developed to assess factors that might contribute to the client's clinical formulation, such as social support and concurrent general medical conditions, and to assist in treatment planning.

DSM-IV includes five treatment axes. Axis I, "Clinical Disorders," records common acute psychiatric disorders, such as Depressive Disorder and most of the diagnoses one thinks of in association with psychological concerns. Axis II, "Personality Disorders and Mental Retardation," records more lifelong problems, such as developmental disabilities, personality disorders, maladaptive personality traits that fail to meet the criteria for personality disorders, and maladaptive habitual defense mechanisms. Axis III, "General Medical Conditions," records medical conditions related to diagnoses on Axes I and II. For example, if a client's hypothyroidism exacerbates her or his mood disorder symptoms, it would be recorded on Axis III, as would a physical illness, such as skin cancer, that worsens a client's Obsessive-Compulsive Disorder. Axis IV, "Psychosocial and Environmental Problems," records both positive and negative factors that impact the client's well-being, such as poverty, lack of social support, or an upcoming marriage. Finally, Axis V, the "Global Assessment of Functioning" scale (GAF), records the client's overall level of adjustment on a 100-point scale. Whereas a rating of 100 represents a nearly unobtainable level of "superior" adjustment (e.g., command over a wide range of activities; absence of life problems), a rating of 5 to 10 represents imminent danger of hurting someone else, a persistent inability to maintain minimal personal hygiene, or serious suicidal acts. GAF scores are used in various ways in mental health settings. They are sometimes used as a crude screen to ensure that only people who are severely impaired are admitted to services and are sometimes used to measure a client's response to treatment by comparing his or her GAF scores at admission, discharge, and follow-up. (Examples of simple and complex DSM-IV multiaxial diagnoses may be found in Table 1.1). A nonaxial format is often used in practice, in which diagnoses are simply listed in the order of the five DSM-IV axes. Examples of this format can also be found in Table 1.1.

TABLE 1.1   Examples of DSM-IV multiaxial classification.

Example 1

Axis I:	300.4 Dysthymic Disorder
Axis II:	None
Axis III:	None
Axis IV:	None
Axis V:	GAF = 60 (Current); potential = 85
"Axis VI":	Solid job performance, positive relationship with partner, social skills, above-average intelligence and insight

Example 2

Axis I:	295.30 Schizophrenia, Paranoid Type
Axis II:	317 Mild Mental Retardation
Axis III:	Chronic asthma
Axis IV:	Hostile relationships with family
Axis V:	GAF = 40 (Current); potential = 55
"Axis VI":	Support from grandmother; access to housing; interest in basic job skills at vocational setting; interest in carved figurines

Example 3

296.23	Major Depressive Disorder
305.0	Alcohol Abuse

Example 4

300.3	Obsessive-Compulsive Disorder
296.23	Major Depressive Disorder
GAF = 45 (Current)	

Examples 1 and 2 use the full "six-axis" format. Examples 3 and 4 use the nonaxial classification format. (Note that Axis VI is not a formal part of DSM-IV.)

"Axis VI"

From a counseling psychology perspective in particular (Gelso & Fretz, 2001), but also from emerging strength-based clinical perspectives such as constructional behaviorism (Goldiamond, 1974) and solution-focused therapy (DeShazer,

1985; DeShazer & Berg, 1992), it is important to recognize the strengths the client brings to his or her initial contact with the therapist. Although a client's presenting strengths are easily overlooked in a clinical focus on presenting concerns, they may be important springboards for resolving current difficulties and enhancing the client's life after treatment. To promote the clinician's recognition of the client's strengths, an additional axis may be used to record them: an "Axis VI" (Gaubatz, in process). Although such a record obviously would not be recognized in many, if not most, institutional settings, it arguably would help clinicians utilize the positive traits and experiences their clients bring to treatment.

Gender, Age, and Multicultural Issues

DSM-IV attempted to reduce previous diagnostic biases related to gender, age, and culture by adding an extensive appendix to address Culture Formulation and Culture-Bound Syndromes (APA, 1994, pp. 843–49). As this appendix notes, there are many culture-specific forms of mental disorders. For example, Coro, a disorder specific to certain Asian cultures, is a morbid fear that one's penis will retract into one's abdomen. (A range of mechanical devices is available to prevent this problem.) Similarly, certain psychotropic stimulants are specific to particular cultures, such as the use of coca leaves in South America to enhance the user's physical endurance or the chewing of the khat plant leaf by some Middle Eastern people to obtain a mildly euphoric mood.

A Cultural Formulation should include five elements. First, the client's cultural identity should be noted to record his or her ethnic and cultural reference groups and degree of involvement with his or her culture of origin and host cultures. Second, potential cultural explanations of the client's illness should be noted, in addition to the client's culturally based preferences for professional or informal sources of care. In South Texas, for example, one of the authors of this text often encountered Mexican nationals and Mexican Americans who believed that a mother of a mentally retarded child was receiving punishment for her past sins. Similarly, among some South Texas Hispanic and Mexican national cultures, a suitable source of help for some forms of distress might be a local botanico, where a *curandero* (healer) might prescribe an appropriate herbal tea (e.g., Alegria et al., 1977).

A third element of a DSM-IV Cultural Formulation is an evaluation of the client's psychosocial environment, including his or her level of social support from family, religious, or other institutions. Cultural factors affecting the client's relationship with the clinician should also be recorded, including considerations of potential differences in social status, language, and communication. Finally, an overall evaluation should be made of how cultural considerations might affect diagnosis and the course of treatment. A sample Cultural Formulation and example of Culture-Bound Syndrome is presented in Table 1.2.

TABLE 1.2   Example of a cultural formulation.

Cultural Identity

Mrs. Berkowitz is a Canadian national who has lived in the United States for fifteen years. She rarely visits Canada, and most of her familial and friendship ties to Canada have been severed. Her parents passed away ten years ago and she is an only sibling. She is Jewish and married an orthodox Jewish husband. She is very involved in her local Jewish community and synagogue, but she is conflicted over certain aspects of orthodox Jewish practices that, in her view, limit and diminish the role of women.

Cultural Explanations of Illness

Mrs. Berkowitz has a Dysthymic Disorder and has no culture-specific views on her problems.

Psychosocial Environment

Her husband's family, friends at the synagogue, other Jewish organizations, and her children's school are important sources of support for her. She describes her religious faith as a source of comfort to her.

Cultural Factors Affecting the Relationship between Client and Clinician

The clinician is very unfamiliar with Orthodox Jewish culture. As an atheist, he is somewhat hostile to deeply held religious beliefs. He is aware of these limitations, but feels that it limits his empathy for some aspects of working with this woman. There are no language issues.

How Cultural Issues Affect Diagnosis and Intervention

There are no major issues in how cultural issues affect diagnosis. Interventions may be limited by the clinician's lack of knowledge of Orthodox Jewish culture.

Assessment

Purposes of Assessment

Assessment serves several different purposes. It is important that the clinician be clear about the reason(s) for assessment and design it to meet those purposes. Assessment may be performed for at least five reasons. First, assessment may be carried out to determine whether a client is eligible to receive services. In some states, for example, admission to a psychiatric hospital can be made only for clients who have GAF scores of less than 50 or who present immediate danger to themselves or others. In such a circumstance, an assessment might be directed only at those pieces of information needed to make the admission decision: What is the person's GAF score and is he or she a danger to self or others? Other questions, such as diagnosis and appropriate forms of treatment, must be separated from these immediate questions.

A second purpose for assessment is to determine which diagnoses are appropriate for the client. Ascertaining diagnosis can hide several different questions, and the clinician should be clear about *why* he or she is trying to determine a diagnosis. Sometimes a diagnosis is useful for guiding treatment. For example, a common question when working with older clients who present with possible dementia is whether they suffer from dementia, a mood disorder, or an unrecognized medical problem—all of which may present as memory loss, confusion, and disorientation. In such situations, diagnosis makes an important difference in the selection of treatment. Depending on the diagnosis, a client might be given a cognitive enhancer, be prescribed an antidepressant, or be taken off antihistamines that may be causing her or his sedation and confusion.

In other situations, diagnosis might make relatively little difference in guiding treatment. For example, many clinicians work in settings in which group anxiety management is the typical initial treatment for clients with a wide range of anxiety disorders. An extensive diagnostic workup to determine whether the client meets DSM-IV criteria for Panic Disorder without Agoraphobia or Panic Disorder with Agoraphobia would make little or no difference to these clinicians' decisions about placing a particular client in an anxiety management group and instead may merely delay the client's progress. In such cases, extensive evaluation may actually be harmful to clients while raising liability issues for their clinicians (see Case 1.1).

Diagnostic questions sometimes relate to etiology. For example, knowing that a person is presenting with depression primarily because of a general medical problem, such as hypothyroidism, a deficiency in naturally occurring thyroid hormone, would guide a clinician's intervention to treat the medical problem first. Diagnostic assessments also are used to collate statistical returns. Health insurance companies and state regulatory bodies often use diagnostic data to monitor services and resource allocations and to assess changes in the epidemiology of mental health disorders. School districts, for example, make statistical returns of the number of children in special education with different kinds of diagnoses. Recent findings from these returns that schoolchildren are presenting with higher rates of autism than in previous years (Fombonne et al., 2001; Sturmey & James, 2001) have important implications for services delivery decisions and special education interventions.

Diagnostic evaluation also is used in mental health research, in which it serves as an important means of communication among researchers and practitioners. In a study of effective treatments for mood disorders, for example, it would be important to describe how participants were solicited, screened, included, and excluded so researchers who wished to replicate and extend the study's findings could follow the same selection protocols. This information also would be important for practitioners hoping to determine whether the study's findings apply to the client population with whom they work. Screening the pool

CASE **1.1**

An example of how excessive assessment can cause client harm and raise liability issues for the clinician.

A consultation was referred to one of the authors by a masters-level psychologist working in a publicly funded mental health service. The reason for the consultation was to advise on the most appropriate intervention strategy for a man with mild mental retardation. The man was currently in an admission and assessment unit. He had a long history of sexually acting out with other clients. An incident in which he had attempted to engage in sexual activity with a nonconsenting fellow client had been interrupted by staff three days previously. There was significant concern that this was continuing. The masters-level psychologist was advised to begin sex education with the client that week to ensure that a good-faith effort at treatment had been initiated and to protect other residents of the unit from further harm. The masters-level psychologist wished to complete a comprehensive diagnostic evaluation of the client, going through all possible DSM-IV diagnoses to ensure that no diagnostic stone was left unturned, but was advised not to do so until beginning some form of intervention with the client. A treatment-team meeting two weeks later revealed that the client had been found attempting to engage in anal intercourse with another client with mental retardation. No intervention had taken place, but the diagnostic evaluation was still ongoing. By failing to provide some form of intervention, the masters-level psychologist may have been liable for harm done to other clients that might have been prevented if he had intervened earlier.

of potential participants with a Likert assessment of mood symptoms might yield participants with relatively mild problems. By contrast, the strict application of DSM-IV Major Depression criteria using a clinical interview would restrict the study's participants to those with more severe, clinically significant problems.

Finally, diagnosis can form a useful function for clients and their families. Many clients are perplexed by and afraid of their problems. For some clients, having a disorder that is recognized and familiar to the therapist can be reassuring. This is especially true if the client initially believes he or she has some unknown or unusual problem.

Assessment, then, serves several different purposes. When conducting an assessment, clinicians should be clear about why they are doing so. Assessments should be comprehensive enough to help clients gain effective treatment, but not so extensive as to cause them harm by delaying or denying effective intervention.

Forms of Assessment

There are many forms of assessment, each of which has unique strengths and weaknesses. When developing a diagnosis or treatment plan, reformulating a case, managing relapse, or assessing a client's lack of progress, a clinician must judiciously select among various forms of assessment. In this section we review some of the most common forms of assessment.

Clinical Interview.   Almost all clinicians use some form of an interview. An interview may take place over a single appointment or over several appointments. It may take the form of a telephone call with a teacher, a conversation with a staff member, a phone consultation with a colleague, a meeting with family members, a conference with a treatment team, or a formal one-on-one interview with a client. In a clinical interview, both general concerns and specific matters of interview technique are important. It begins, however, with a demonstration of concern for the client, in which the clinician communicates an interest in the client and a willingness to help him or her work through the presenting problem (if the clinician is competent to do so).

It is important that the client perceive that the clinician has an accurate picture of his or her problem, a perception that begins with trust. Unless the clinician establishes trust with the client, he or she may well have an incomplete formulation of the case. A clinician must do a few basic things to promote client trust. To begin with, the clinician should ensure that the interview is not interrupted by phone calls, electronic devices, or other people. The clinician should also ensure that the client receives his or her full attention. If the interview is interrupted or rushed, or if the clinician seems vague or unfamiliar with the client's information, the therapeutic relationship may be seriously undermined. Although empathy and rapport are important, the clinician also should be aware that clients vary considerably in their preference for intimacy and disclosure. Some clients may be uncomfortable with what they perceive to be excessive prying by an unfamiliar clinician when they merely want help with a presenting difficulty. The clinician should carefully balance the degree of rapport and interpersonal warmth to achieve the main task of helping the client.

When clients come to a first interview, they often bring stereotypical expectations about counseling and psychotherapy. They may expect to lie on a couch or to be hypnotized, given drugs or psychoanalyzed. One important thing clinicians can do is to gain an understanding of clients' expectations and discuss with clients, early on, how they work. Basic information about the frequency and duration of appointments, billing, confidentiality, note-taking, access to records, and the type and length of therapy likely to be offered also should be discussed with the client as early as possible. Clinicians should also be sensitive to culturally related differences both in clients' views of psychotherapy and in the content of clients' presenting concerns (Acosta, 1979; Solberg, Choi, Ritsma, & Jolly, 1994; Sue, 2001; Sue & Sue, 1977; Thompson, Worthington, & Atkinson, 1994). Especially when clients are not self-referred, they may benefit from a relaxed discussion, prior to the beginning of assessment, of the goals and procedures of psychotherapy. Clients also may benefit from a collaborative approach that identifies overlaps between the clinician's view of therapy and the client's (Anderson & Goolishian, 1992).

The form an interview takes depends on its purpose. An initial interview may be used to establish diagnoses, establish eligibility for services, evaluate suitability for treatment, or determine a specific type of intervention. The theoretical orientation and techniques used by the clinician also are important determinants of the questions he or she should ask. A behaviorally oriented clinician, for example, is likely to ask questions about the specifics of a problem behavior, including its frequency, duration, and intensity. The interview will help the client and clinician develop a list of target problems ranked in order of importance, identify triggers for the problem, and evaluate current coping strategies and personal strengths. By contrast, a cognitive therapist is likely to ask questions designed to ascertain the client's core beliefs, attributions, and cognitive style. He or she is also likely to ask questions about the client's current coping strategies and goals for treatment but is less likely to focus directly on the client's behavior.

Structured diagnostic interviews are different in both purpose and character from assessment interviews designed to guide treatment. Structured diagnostic interviews are designed to assess the specific diagnostic criteria a client meets. Intended to enhance the reliability and accuracy of clinical diagnosis, structured diagnostic interviews consist of a series of standard questions that probe for the presence of certain groups of symptoms. If a probe question indicates possible psychopathology within a certain diagnostic category, a series of more detailed questions are asked. If a probe question indicated a client suffered from mood disorder symptoms, for example, the interviewer would follow up with specific questions related to each criterion symptom of mood disorders. By contrast, if the initial probe question failed to indicate mood symptoms, the interviewer would move to the next (unrelated) question in the series. Another characteristic of structured psychiatric interviews is that the clinical information they obtain is combined in a predetermined way in order to eliminate interviewers' judgment. Structured diagnostic interviews require extensive and careful training. Although structured interviews are generally limited to research settings, they sometimes are used as diagnostic screens in clinics that serve large numbers of clients. Self-report checklists, which require less specialized training for clinicians, sometimes serve this function more efficiently.

It is important that clinicians be competent in the interview methods they use. Unfortunately, however, much of the professional training psychologists and counselors receive about interview methods is arguably inadequate. It is often assumed that clinicians learn to conduct interviews by reading books, observing supervisors, receiving mutual support from colleagues, or experiencing some unspecified form of clinical osmosis. Many psychotherapy students receive supervision interviewing clients only once or twice throughout their entire professional training. As findings by Miltenberger and Fuqua (1985) and Miltenberger and Veltum (1988) suggest, students and novice clinicians at minimum should be videotaped conducting clinical interviews and should observe themselves and solicit feedback from fellow students and supervisors about their interview skills.

Interviewing Third Parties. When working with children or adults facing relationally embedded problems, it is often helpful to interview third parties such as partners, family members, or other professionals involved with the client. Important information can be obtained from family members' responses to a client's struggles and from the possible family systems origins of client's presenting difficulties. On a more basic level, a second person's account of the facts can often be surprisingly different from the client's report. Child and adolescent referrals also necessitate family interviews. If parents and/or stepparents are separated, for instance, it may be helpful to evaluate the different strategies each adult uses with the client. It is also useful to explore whether one group of family members may be undermining the strategies used by other family members, as a consequence of family tension, for instance, or of mere lack of communication (Baucom et al., 1998; Becvar & Becvar, 1999; Berg, 1994; Boscolo et al., 1987; Madanes, 1981; Minuchin, 1974).

Interviewing third parties raises additional issues beyond interviewing a single client. First, practical problems such as attending to more people with more information, conversation, body language, and other cues can make these interviews difficult. Group interviews often require special training or supervision. Whereas a single client typically receives the therapist's undivided attention, it is easy for the therapist to become distracted or focus on one main participant at the expense of others when multiple people are present.

Managing and controlling the flow of information and participation pose similar problems in large treatment team meetings. In large case conferences, having a good chairperson is essential to allow all participants and all points of view to be heard. Team meetings lacking an effective chairperson often become unfocused and unruly or break up into a series of parallel, independent conversations. In such situations the clinician should be sufficiently assertive to ensure that his or her important questions are resolved and that the group reaches some consensus about client concerns and immediate goals. With some treatment teams this can be a challenge.

Collateral Information. Collateral information consists of documentation from other sources such as assessments from other professionals, records from previous therapists, school reports, and medical documentation. Collateral information is often useful in designing appropriate treatments or making appropriate referrals. It also can be used to confirm or refine a client's history or to provide baseline data for readministration of psychometric testing. When seeking collateral information, the clinician should always obtain written consent from the client or from his or her legal guardian.

Psychometric Assessment. Psychometric testing may be used for a number of purposes. The most common use of psychometric testing is to compare a person's scores with those of a population of interest. For example, IQ scores are essential for assessing mental retardation, and most state laws require an IQ score two or more standard deviations below the average of a well-normed IQ test in addition to significant adaptive behavior deficits. In such situations the assessment of both IQ and adaptive behavior involves questions of performance relative to the general population. Psychometric tests also can be used to identify children whose development is slower than a typical child, information that can be useful both to obtain early intervention services and to promote the child's development.

Another reason to conduct standardized testing is to compare a client's performance across areas of his or her own ability or behavior. When assessing a person with possible neurological deficits or Alzheimer's disease, for example, a clinician may want to know if the client has a memory deficit compared to her or his baseline intelligence. Similarly, assessments of learning disabilities often involve comparisons of a child's score in a specific area of academic functioning with her or his overall academic performance.

Psychometric assessments also may be used to measure a client's change in performance over time. For example, ongoing assessment of a client with a deteriorating neurological condition, such as a dementia, might compare his or her performance over time with his or her initial performance on a series of tests. Similarly, a person suffering a catastrophic accident or medical condition associated with lost cognitive functions might be evaluated with intellectual, academic, or other tests to assess evidence of residual changes in functioning. Similar assessments might be used to evaluate a client's cognitive performance after a stroke or head trauma.

Counselors and psychologists have developed hundreds of psychometric tests for use (cf. Murphy et al., 1999). A summary of commonly used psychometric tests can be found in Table 1.3.

Psychometric assessment is a relatively specialized area of clinical practice, and it is important that therapists administer and interpret only those instruments for which they have had training and supervised experience. In some states, the administration of certain kinds of tests, such as projective tests, is legally restricted to particular professionals (e.g., psychologists, social workers). All clinicians, however, should have general knowledge and skills that enable them to interpret test results in written reports. Additionally, while recognizing the limits of their own competence, they also should request testing from other professionals when appropriate. Clinicians should be familiar with basic psychometric theory and should understand basic statistical concepts, such as norms, central tendency, spread, error, and bias in test scores. Clinicians also should be aware of the potential cultural biases in standardized tests, especially in tests of putative scholastic aptitudes and cognitive abilities, and the discriminatory effects of their uncritical application to minority students and other clinical populations (Helms, 1992; Reyes & Valencia, 1995; Valencia & Aburto, 1991). Clinicians should be familiar with the tests commonly used in their area of practice and should receive training to become familiar with new tests in their area of practice. If clinicians encounter test reports they are not competently able to inter-

TABLE 1.3 **Some commonly used psychometric tests.**

Function assessed	Population	Tests
Intelligence	Children and adolescents	WPPSI-III (Psychological Corporation, 2002) WISC-III (Wechsler, 1991)
	Adults	WAIS-III (Wechsler, 1998)
Adaptive behavior	Children and adults	Vineland Adaptive Behavior Scales (Sparrow & Cicchetti, 1989)
Maladaptive behaviors	Children and adolescents	Child Behavior Checklist (Achenbach, 1991)
Memory	Adults	WMS-III (Wechsler, 1997).
Academic performance	Children and adolescents	Wide Range Achievement Test (Wilkinson, 1994)
Personality	Adults	Millon Scales (Millon, 1994)
Projective tests	Adults	Rorschach (Aronow et al., 1994)
	Children	Draw-a-Person Test (Naglieri, 1988)

pret (as frequently happens), they should seek consultation from a qualified colleague.

Behavioral and Observational Assessment. Behavioral observation and assessment are used to obtain direct measures of a client's behavior, such as the number of times a student calls out in class, the number of work items an employee completes correctly, or the frequency with which a father speaks to his daughter. Behavioral observations measure specific parameters of the client's observable behavior, such as frequency, duration, proportion of time, latency, intensity, and permanent product. Examples of these assessments are provided in Table 1.4.

Behavioral observation is often used when initially developing a behavioral intervention. For example, if, during the observations described in Table 1.4, a child was observed to be mostly out of her seat during difficult tasks, but worked well when given easy tasks, this information could be used to devise a shaping procedure to teach her to work effectively on hard tasks. She might be assigned a small amount of a difficult task at the beginning of class after which she would be permitted to work on a preferred task for the remainder of the period. Over time, the amount of the difficult task could be increased in small increments, contingent upon successful completion of the hard task for a predetermined amount of time. If such manipulations of task difficulty reduced the child's out-of-seat behavior from 0.25 episodes per minute to 0.05 episodes per minute and increased

TABLE 1.4 **Example of various measures used in behavioral assessment.**

Behavioral parameter	Examples
Frequency and rate	A child gets out of her seat 15 times in an hour of observation and yells 45 times. This yields a rate of out-of-seat behavior 0.25 per minute and a rate of 0.75 per minute for yelling.
Duration and proportion of time	During the hour of observation she spent 35 minutes in her seat. Thus, 58% of the time was spent in her seat.
Latency	On three occasions her teacher asked her to start working. It took her 30s, 120s, and 180s to begin work on each occasion for an average latency of 110s.
Permanent product	At the end of the hour, a review of her workbook indicated that she had written only 30 words in her book. From this we can infer that she wrote at the rate of 0.5 words per minute during the hour.

her rate of writing from 0.5 words per minute to 12 words per minute, the strategy might well be continued. The process of identifying such triggers and consequences of maintaining a target behavior is called functional assessment or, in school settings, functional behavioral assessment (Sturmey, 1996).

Medical Assessment. A significant proportion of clients referred to mental health professionals suffer from coexisting medical problems. Although some of these problems may not be related to the client's presenting mental health concern, others may be directly related. Unresolved medical problems should be referred to a physician for appropriate treatment. As part of a counselor's or psychologist's legal duty of care, she or he is obliged to help clients find help for their medical problems. Failing to do so, an error of omission, may constitute negligence. (See Chapter 2 for further discussion of negligence and the duty of care.)

Psychiatric Consultation. Many clients referred to counselors or psychologists take prescribed psychotropic medications. Many of these clients may not have had a routine consultation for some time, whereas others may receive psychotropic medications from multiple sources, such as a general practitioner, neurologist, and psychiatrist. In these situations a consultation with a psychiatrist may be indicated. A psychiatric consultation also may be indicated if it appears a client might benefit from psychotropic medication but currently is not under the care of a psychiatrist or other prescribing physician, or if a client presents with unresolved diagnostic issues.

Neuropsychological Assessment. Neuropsychological assessment is a relatively specialized area of psychometric evaluation. Clinicians who do not have specialized training in neuropsychological assessment should avoid performing or interpreting neuropsychological tests. All clinicians, however, should be able to recognize situations when a neuropsychological assessment may be indicated and make referrals for a suitable assessment. Clinicians also should know how to read and understand neuropsychological reports and assessment summaries. Recognizing the limits of their competence (e.g., American Counseling Association, 1995; APA, 1992), clinicians should ask for a consultation from a qualified and competent colleague when appropriate.

A variety of organic brain disorders may present as an anxiety or mood disorder in adult mental health. Clients with adjustment, mood, or anxiety disorders following traumatic injuries, for instance, may be at risk for organic disorders. In addition, many older adults referred to counselors or psychologists with mood disorder symptoms actually suffer from Alzheimer's disease or other dementias. If the clinician suspects a client may be suffering from an organic brain disorder, he or she should make a referral for a neuropsychological consultation.

Summary. Several assessment strategies may be useful in developing a formulation of a case. Clinicians should be aware of the benefits and limitations of each strategy and should recognize the limitations of their own competence in conducting or interpreting various assessments. Clinicians also should refer clients to other mental health professionals when appropriate (e.g., neuropsychologists, psychiatrists) and should recognize the appropriate actions to take when issues of competency and ethics arise.

Treatment Planning

Ethical Issues

Treatment planning is one of the most important tasks a clinician performs. Selecting and implementing treatment involves many complex and subtle decisions on the part of both the clinician and the client. It involves clarifying treatment goals in collaboration with the client and decisions about the anticipated time, cost, and effort involved in particular forms of treatment. It also involves weighing the likely benefits and risks of different treatment options.

Issues of time and cost have been made explicit with the growth of third-party cost management. In response to the escalating costs of medical care, including treatment for psychological and psychiatric disorders, government and health insurance providers have developed a range of strategies to contain costs and maximize client benefit from treatment. Collectively, these strategies are referred to as managed care. For many clients who personally pay the cost of treatment, the issue of payment is also very real. Clinicians must resolve important ethical issues surrounding therapy reimbursement. They must ask themselves whether they are selecting the most efficient form of treatment for the client or whether they are meeting their own needs by selecting treatments they find ideologically palatable, personally gratifying, or lucrative.

Managed care has become a more important force in determining the kinds and amount of treatment available under insurance plans. In the context of managed care, clinicians must resolve issues such as which treatments realistically can be implemented in the six to eight sessions permitted under many insurance plans. They must determine whether the person has the resources available to pay for more sessions if more are needed. They also must determine how likely the insurance company may be to extend authorization for payment beyond the number of sessions typical for a given presenting problem.

An especially onerous practice to which many clinicians have resorted under managed care pressures is known as "creaming and dumping" (Keith-Spiegel & Koocher, 1985), in which a clinician takes on a poor client who cannot realistically be treated in The number of sessions allowed by her or his insurance. In this practice, the clinician "creams" the client by performing (and gaining reimbursement for) relatively low-risk assessment procedures before "dumping" her or him to a local mental health agency for referred treatment. This practice is clearly unethical: The clinician harms the client by consuming her or his funded treatment sessions with a useless assessment. "Creaming and dumping" illustrates the potential of even the most benign psychotherapeutic intervention (in this case, treatment planning) to harm clients by preventing them from accessing more appropriate treatments.

Another important ethical question in treatment planning is the selection of an appropriate form and location of treatment. Clinicians are often faced with a dilemma when selecting treatments. First, there is genuine professional disagreement over the effectiveness of different schools of therapy. Some therapists contend, as in *Alice in Wonderland*, that "all have won and all must have prizes." These authors suggest that the common processes underlying therapies, such as a validating therapeutic relationship and the inspiration of hope, eviscerate longstanding arguments over the differences between specific therapies (cf. Ahn & Wampold, 2001; Luborsky, Singer, & Luborsky, 1975; Wampold, 2001). Other approaches, however, especially behavioral therapy (Sweet, Giles, & Young, 1987), cognitive therapy (Beck, 1976; Beck & Freeman, 1990), and biological psychiatry, have claimed specific superiority over other competing treatments. Managed care companies have typically swayed toward the latter side of the argument, partly because these treatments are more time-limited and offer ready empirical evidence to support their effectiveness.

Together, these trends have forced therapists to limit the number of therapy sessions they offer and to critically question the effectiveness of specific treatment techniques. Increasingly, therapists have been forced to answer directly to health insurance plans, clients, and public oversight mechanisms about the services they offer. A clear trend toward more focused and efficient therapy has consequently emerged over the past fifteen years (Goldman et al., 2001; Mace, Moorey, & Bernard, 2001). Although a whole field of research and practice called "evidence-based medicine" or "evidence-based psychotherapy" (see below) has grown to address these issues, controversies remain about the restriction of reimbursement to only those models with enough financial or academic support to offer controlled research evidence for their effectiveness (Chambless & Ollendick, 2000; Stewart, 2001; Webb, 2001).

Treatment Goals

When conducting an initial assessment, it is useful for the client and therapist alike to have clear goals for their work. Treatment goals help to guide both the client and the therapist through the process of intervention. They also offer a useful framework to structure important issues at different stages of treatment and to help clinicians identify important issues that otherwise might not be apparent until things go wrong. For convenience, psychotherapeutic treatment goals can be divided into three developmental stages: immediate concerns, short-term goals, and long-term goals. Questions related to each of these stages are illustrated in Case 1.2.

Immediate Concerns.   Immediate concerns are concerns immediately relevant at the time of the referral and during the first appointment. Immediate concerns relate mostly to the safety of the client and anyone else who may be vulnerable to harm by the client. For many referrals, there will be no immediate concerns. However, there are several situations when clinicians should be alert both to a client's own safety (e.g., suicidal ideation, driving while abusing substances) and to the safety of a client's family members, coworkers, or social contacts (e.g., child endangerment, violence, unsafe sex practices by an HIV-positive client). The appropriate actions to take in these situations will be discussed throughout this book and in various case examples that illustrate these issues. In general, it is useful to recognize that a clinician has a duty of care to his or her clients, defined as "the care an ordinary, average person should exercise in such circumstances" (Bennett et al., 1990, p. 33). In situations in which potential or actual danger threatens a client or others, it is useful to imagine the actions you would expect another therapist to take under similar circumstances. It is especially useful to imagine what a reasonable person might do if the threat of harm were to be realized.

Case 1.3 offers two courses of action, and the outcomes of those actions, by a hypothetical therapist. Although a therapist's actions obviously are vulnerable to critical judgment if they lead to negative outcomes, clinical actions that are similar to those a reasonable person might take in similar situations are more likely to be judged as reasonable and defensible. Two key differences are apparent in the actions of the therapist in Case 1.3. In the first example, the therapist merely noted the problem, an appropriate but insufficient strategy. Few therapists would agree that this was a reasonable action, and fewer yet would do so if

CASE **1.2**

An example of treatment planning using immediate concerns, short-term goals, and long-term goals.

Mike is a 15-year-old adolescent with a poor relationship with his parents. He drinks, steals money, lies, and cuts school. Mike seems to be mixing with dangerous friends, and his grades have dropped over the last two years. He appears to be of average intelligence, but is probably underperforming academically.

Immediate concerns	Are there any immediate dangers to the client or other vulnerable persons?	Yes. Mike may be engaging in dangerous activities, such as stealing, taking drugs, drinking, and engaging in unprotected sex or criminal behaviors. An initial assessment interview with Mike and his parents should explore if these dangers are real or potential. If they are real, a plan to ensure Mike's safety, or at least counseling to Mike and his parents about these dangers, should be developed.
Short-term goals	What goals need to be achieved in the first 2–6 sessions? Are there particular coping skills that can be taught? Are there important personal goals that need to be clarified?	The first 2–6 sessions should be used to negotiate some goals for Mike, such as attending school, completing schoolwork, and finding safer forms of recreation.
Long-term goals	What broad lifestyle changes and other long-term personal, relationship, and career goals need to be achieved over a period of 2–6 months?	Long-term goals for Mike might include graduating from high school, engaging with some form of prevocational training, clarifying vocational and personal objectives, and making a plan to meet these objectives.

they were granted hindsight into the adversity of the outcome (as one may be given on a witness stand, for instance). In the second example, by contrast, the clinician actively intervened to prevent harm to her client (despite the negative outcome of the case). She didn't merely note the client's risk of suicide; she de-

CASE **1.3**

An example of how therapist action and client outcomes can raise or limit liability issues for the therapist.

Ms. Jimenez was a 22-year-old student referred to her university counselor for failing academic grades. Although the referral did not indicate any particular psychiatric problems, Ms. Jimenez revealed during the first interview with her counselor that she had felt depressed for the last two years, that she found the stress of school too great to cope with, and that she felt hopeless about graduating and about life in general. She told her therapist that there had been times when she thought she should put an end to her own misery.

Possible therapist actions	Possible client outcome
The therapist listed suicidal threats in her notes as a problem to work on.	Ms. Jimenez continued to be depressed for several months. From time to time she thought a great deal about killing herself and discussed this with her therapist.

Possible therapist actions	Possible client outcome
The therapist listed suicidal threats in her notes. She worked with Ms. Jimenez to develop a plan to address the problem. The plan included the following elements: (1) actions Ms. Jimenez should take when she thought about suicide; (2) identification of two trigger situations when suicidal thoughts were more likely; (3) whom to contact if she thought that she would kill herself; (4) directions to phone the clinic for an additional appointment if she thought she needed one; and (5) directions to set up an appointment with her psychiatrist, whom she had not seen for three months, to review her psychotropic medications.	Ms. Jimenez skipped her next appointment Two weeks later the therapist was told she had killed herself.

veloped a plausible, reasonable plan to prevent the client from harming herself. Furthermore, the clinician's actions in scenario two were similar to those other therapists might be expected take in such situations. A clear message lies in Case 1.3: If there is a possibility clients may harm themselves or others, the clinician should directly prevent them from doing so. This is the "standard of care."

When seeing a client for the first time, therapists should be aware of actual or potential ethical or legal issues that might emerge. Besides duty of care concerns (discussed above), other legal and ethical issues that commonly emerge in clinical work include confidentiality, child abuse, dual relationship issues, and unique concerns surrounding the treatment of minors.

Therapists should be aware of the need for and limits of confidentiality—and they should communicate both to their clients. Therapists should be able to identify actual or potential child abuse and should know how to report it as required by the law and the regulations of the agency within which they work. (This issue is discussed in more detail below.)

Dual relationships are relationships with a current or former client other than a formally therapeutic one. They include sexual, financial, scientific, or professional relationships. They should be resolutely avoided. Although sexual relationships with current clients are obviously precluded, sexual relationships with former clients are also unadvisable and often present the possibility of harm to the client. On the other hand, ACA and APA ethical codes recognize that more benign types of dual relationships may be unavoidable in limited circumstances (ACA, 1995; APA, 1992). In small rural communities, for instance, therapists often encounter current or former clients socially. When such relationships occur they must be dealt with carefully. The overriding principle is that the situation must be handled in the best interest of the client (APA, 1992; Bennett et al., 1990).

The treatment of minors is a special case that requires unique sensitivity to the roles parents and legal guardians play in consenting to assessment and treatment. Therapists should be aware of who can consent to assessment and treatment. This is especially true in cases of divorce, grandparent guardianship, and reconstituted families. Consent can also be an important ethical and legal issue when working with people who are factually incompetent, such as those with dementia, some clients with mental retardation, and some persons with acute psychoses or chronic mental illnesses. Chapter 2 presents a more detailed discussion of these ethical and legal issues.

Short-Term Goals.   Short-term goals focus on changes in client behaviors and coping skills and the clarification of personal goals in the first few sessions of therapy. Short-term goals may include learning to relax in stressful circumstances, applying a new method to manage a child's behavior, identifying a more satisfying career, changing dysfunctional behavioral patterns, acquiring new study habits, improving interpersonal skills, or changing cognitions underlying a depressed mood. Short-term goals are designed to alleviate distress and make immediate progress on the client's presenting concerns.

Long-Term Goals.   Long-term goals relate to broader outcomes that will support and maintain positive changes in the client's life and prevent the relapse of his or her initial treatment concerns. Examples of long-term goals include obtaining a new job, terminating a problematic relationship, successfully reestablishing a broken relationship, graduating from school, and recognizing and dealing successfully with potential relapse situations. Long-term goals also should promote successful developmental changes in the client's life and build on the client's emerging strengths.

Managed Care and the Cost of Treatment.   A single 45-minute appointment might be sufficient to assess a relatively simple clinical problem with an articulate client who is comfortable with self-disclosure. On the other hand, it might take three to five sessions to disentangle a complex problem or gain the trust of a shy and very suspicious client. For a significant number of clients, two to five sessions of treatment focused on specific techniques may be helpful. Other, more complex client issues may require a greater number of sessions. The achievement of long-term goals necessary to support change, gain a positive and satisfying lifestyle, and prevent relapse may take anywhere from two to twelve months depending on the complexity and nature of the problems at hand.

In the past, some clients underwent psychotherapy, such as psychoanalysis, two to three times weekly for five or more years. Currently, however, few if any managed care companies or publicly funded services support such long-term interventions. Intense, extensive psychotherapy is no longer available for any but the wealthy and those whose lifestyle permits biweekly appointments over the course of several years. The guidelines in Case 1.2 are general and must be tailored to each individual, but they would be stretched significantly to accommodate multiyear interventions.

As previously discussed, most mental health services today are provided within an environment of careful management of resources. When mental health services are provided through health insurance plans, therapists often are forced to keep within the number of sessions typically required for treating similar clients. Therapists also must be aware of the unique restrictions of each client's plan. Similarly, publicly funded mental health services typically have limited resources, and careful discussions must be made about the intensity of support provided to each individual client. Finally, some clients pay for their treatments directly. Whereas some of these self-paying clients may be able to reimburse frequent and extensive counseling, others may be burdened, ironically, by the costs of a treatment intended to alleviate their concerns. Therapists must strive to minimize these forms of harm to clients.

Evidence-Based Practice.   Evidence-based practice is an increasingly important aspect of publicly funded health services. Deriving from evidence-based medicine, evidence-based psychotherapy attempts to demonstrate value for the public dollar, as well as ethical conduct on the part of therapists, by ensuring that the therapies selected and implemented are those most likely to efficiently benefit the client. Basing treatment selection on well-designed, data-based studies of treatment efficacy (and corresponding literature reviews) for the problem at hand

CASE EXERCISE

Mr. Ong, a 56-year-old Asian American man, has been referred to you for help with a chronic mood disorder. Prior to the first appointment, you learn that Mr. Ong complains of vague feelings of lethargy, fatigue, and self-doubt, coupled with physical complaints including chronic back pain, headaches, and other vague pains he cannot specify. Mr. Ong, who works as a supervisor for a security company, has a history of chronic lower back pain for which he takes medication. He has tried physiotherapy over the past three years, but reports that it rarely helps, and he often takes to his bed for several days because of his pains. According to Mr. Ong, his relationship with his wife is poor, partly because he feels guilty for making her endure his problems. Mr. Ong's children live in distant cities and do not visit as often as he feels they should. He does not approve of his children's spouses, the way they manage their own children, or their choice of careers. They call, but infrequently. Family visits are rare, tense occasions. Mr. Ong has taken a variety of antidepressants with only modest benefit. He fears he is going to lose his job, that his wife will divorce him, and that he will be left on his own until he dies alone in his bed. He also fears that he is going to suffer a terrible illness that he cannot specify.

Study Questions

1. What diagnostic issues does Mr. Ong present? What are the most likely DSM-IV diagnoses from which he suffers (i.e., ranked from most to least likely)?

2. Select the most likely diagnostic possibility and write a complete multi-axis DSM-IV diagnosis for Mr. Ong.

3. What assessment strategies would you use with Mr. Ong?

4. Does Mr. Ong present any immediate treatment concerns (e.g., harm to self or others)?

5. How would you develop rapport with a client who views life rather negatively and may be skeptical of your abilities and motivations?

6. Mr. Ong is rather vague and diffuse in his answers to your initial questions in your interview with him. How would you overcome this vagueness to develop specific treatment goals with him?

7. What are your short-term and long-term goals for your work with Mr. Ong? How will you coordinate treatment with the psychiatrist or personal physician from whom he is receiving antidepressants?

8. What ethical challenges Mr. Ong's case might present?

9. What liability issues might you face when working with Mr. Ong?

10. What multicultural issues might be relevant in your work with Mr. Ong?

does this. Evidence-based practice is also implemented by negotiating clear, mutually agreed-upon goals with clients, toward which subsequent progress can be measured.

Chapter Summary

1. DSM-IV diagnoses occupy a central role in clinical practice and research. They have evolved as part of an ongoing effort to refine and develop psychiatric diagnosis over the past one hundred years. Over time, diagnostic systems have become more detailed, encompassing a broader array of human behavior and populations. DSM-IV was developed in response to criticisms that earlier versions of DSM were unreliable and based on a psychoanalytic model of psychopathology. DSM-IV diagnoses are designed to be atheoretical, operationalized, polythetic, and multiaxial.

2. Assessment is performed for many purposes and is undertaken using many different modes of collecting and evaluating information. Clinicians should be aware of the advantages and limitations of each method of assessment, as well as the ethical implications of assessment.

3. Treatment planning involves evaluation of immediate concerns and establishment of both short-term and long-term goals. Important ethical issues surround maximizing the client's benefit from therapy using evidence-based practice.

REFERENCES

Achenbach, T. M. (1991). *Manual for the child behavior checklist 14-18 and 1991 profile*. Burlington: University of Vermont, Department of Psychiatry.

Acosta, F. X. (1979). Pretherapy expectations and definitions of mental illness among minority and low-income patients. *Hispanic Journal of Behavioral Sciences, 1*, 403–410.

Ahn, H., & Wampold, B. E. (2001). Where oh where are the specific ingredients? A meta-analysis of component studies in counseling and psychotherapy. *Journal of Counseling Psychology, 48*, 251–57.

Alegria, D., Guerra, E., Martinez, C., & Meyer, G. G. (1977). El hospital invisible: A study of curanderismo. *Archives of General Psychiatry, 34*, 1354–1357.

American Counseling Association. (1995). *Code of ethics and standards of practice*. Alexandria, VA: Author.

American Psychiatric Association. (1994). *Diagnostic and statistical manual of mental disorders* (4th ed.) *(DSM-IV)*. Washington, DC: Author.

American Psychiatric Association. (2000). *Diagnostic and statistical manual of mental disorders* (4th ed., text revision) *(DSM-IV-TR)*. Washington, DC: Author.

American Psychological Association. (1992). *Ethical principles for psychologists and code of conduct*. Washington, DC: Author.

Anderson, H., & Goolishian, H. (1992). The client is the expert: A not-knowing approach to therapy. In S. McNamee & K. J. Gergen (Eds.), *Therapy as social construction* (pp. 25–39). London: Sage Publications.

Ani, M. (1994). *Yorugu: An African-centered critique of European cultural thought and behavior*. Trenton, NJ: Africa World Press.

Aronow, E., Rezinikoff, M., & Moreland, K. (1994). *The Rorschach technique. Perceptual basics, content interpretation and application* (2nd ed.). San Antonio: The Psychological Corporation.

Barkham, M., Shapiro, D. A., Hardy, G. E., Rees, A. (1999). Psychotherapy in two-plus-one sessions: Outcomes of a randomized controlled trial of cognitive-behavioral and psychodynamic-interpersonal therapy for subsyndromal depression. *Journal of Consulting and Clinical Psychology, 67,* 201–211.

Barstow, D. G. (1999). Female genital mutilation: The penultimate gender abuse. *Child Abuse and Neglect, 23*(5), 501–510.

Baucom, D. H., Shoham, V., Mueser, K. T., Daiuto, A. D., & Stickle, T. R. (1998). Empirically supported couple and family interventions for marital distress and adult mental health problems. *Journal of Consulting and Clinical Psychology, 66,* 53–88.

Beck, A. T. (1976). *Cognitive therapy and the emotional disorders.* New York: International Universities Press.

Beck, A. T., & Freeman, A. (1990). *Cognitive therapy and the personality disorders.* New York: Guilford Press.

Becvar, D. S., & Becvar, R. J. (1999). *Family therapy: A systemic integration* (4th ed.). Boston: Allyn and Bacon.

Bennett, B. E., Bryant, B. K., VandenBos, G. R., & Greenwood, A. (1990). *Professional liability and risk management.* Washington, DC: American Psychological Association.

Berg, I. K. (1994). *Family based services: A solution-focused approach.* New York: Norton.

Berlin, F. S. (2000). Treatments to change sexual orientation. *American Journal of Psychiatry, 157*(5), 838.

Beutler, L. E., & Malik, M. L. (2002). *Rethinking the DSM: A psychological perspective.* Washington, DC: American Psychological Association.

Boscolo, L., Cecchin, G., Hoffman, L. & Penn, P. (1987). *Milan systemic family therapy: Conversations in theory and practice.* New York: Basic Books.

Chambless, D. L., & Ollendick, T. H. (2000). Empirically supported psychological interventions: Controversies and evidence. *Annual Review of Psychology, 52,* 685–716.

DeShazer, S. (1985). *Keys to solution in brief therapy.* New York: Norton.

DeShazer, S., & Berg, K. (1992). Doing therapy: A post-structural revision. *Journal of Marital and Family Therapy, 18,* 71–81.

Diamond, J. (1992). *The third chimpanzee: The evolution and future of the human animal.* New York: HarperCollins.

Flax, J. (1990). *Thinking fragments: Psychoanalysis, feminism, and postmodernism in the contemporary West.* Berkeley: University of California Press.

Fombonne, E., Simmons, H., Ford, T., Meltzer, H., & Goodman, R. (2001). Prevalence of pervasive developmental disorders in the British Nationwide Survey of Child Mental Health. *Journal of the American Academy of Child and Adolescent Psychiatry, 40,* 820–827.

Foucault, M. (1954/1987). *Mental illness and psychology* (A. Sheridan, trans.). Berkeley: University of California Press (Original work published 1954).

Foucault, M. (1976/1978). *The history of sexuality: An introduction.* New York: Random House.

Gaubatz, M. D. (in process). Reaffirming clients' strengths: An argument for a DSM "Axis VI."

Gelso, C. & Fretz, B. (2001). *Counseling psychology* (2nd ed.). Fort Worth: Harcourt.

Gergen, K. J. (1994). *Realities and relationships: Soundings in social construction.* Cambridge, MA: Harvard University Press.

Goldberger, N. R., & Veroff, J. B. (1995). *The culture and psychology reader.* New York: New York University Press.

Goldiamond, I. (1974). Toward a constructional approach to social problems. Ethical and constitutional issues raised by applied behavior analysis. *Behaviorism, 2,* 1–84.

Goldman, H. H., Ganju, V., Drake, R. E., Gorman, P., Hogan, M., Hyde, P. S., & Morgan, O. (2001). Policy implications for implementing evidence-based practices. *Psychiatric Services, 52,* 1591–1597.

Gonzalez, R. C., Biever, J. L., & Gardner, G. T. (1994). The multicultural perspective in therapy: A social constructionist approach. *Psychotherapy, 31,* 515–524.

Helms, J. E. (1992). Why is there no study of cultural equivalence in standardized cognitive ability testing? *American Psychologist, 47,* 1083–1101.

Herdt, G., & Stoller, R. G. (1990). *Intimate communications: Erotics and the study of a culture.* New York: Columbia University Press.

Hines, P. M., & Hare-Mustin, R. T. (1978). Ethical concerns in family therapy. *Professional Psychology, 8,* 165–71.

Keith-Spiegel, P., & Koocher, G. P. (1985). *Ethics in psychology: Professional standards and cases.* New York: Random House.

Leenaars, A., Connolly, J., Cantor, C., EchoHawk, M., He, Z. X., Kokorina, N., Lester, D., Lopatin, A. A., Rodriguez, M., Schlebusch, L., Takahashi, Y., & Vijayakumar, L. (2001). Suicide, assisted suicide and euthanasia: International perspectives. *Irish Journal of Psychological Medicine, 18,* 33–37.

Luborsky, L., Singer, B., & Luborsky, L. (1975). Comparative studies of psychotherapies: Is it true that "everyone has won and all must have prizes"? *Archives of General Psychiatry, 32,* 995–1008.

Mace, C., Moorey, S., & Bernard, R. (Eds.) (2001). *Evidence in the psychological therapies: A critical guide for practitioners.* Philadelphia: Brunner-Routledge.

Madanes, C. (1981). *Strategic family therapy.* San Francisco: Jossey-Bass.

McWhirter, E. H. (1998). Emancipatory communitarian psychology. *American Psychologist, 53,* 322–323.

Millon, T. (1994). *Millon index of personality styles.* San Antonio, TX: The Psychological Corporation.

Miltenberger, R. G., & Fuqua, R. W. (1985). Evaluation of a training manual for the acquisition of behavioral assessment interview skills. *Journal of Applied Behavior Analysis, 18,* 323–328.

Miltenberger, R. G., & Veltum, L. G. (1988). Evaluation of an instruction and modeling procedure for training behavioral assessment interviewing. *Journal of Behavior Therapy and Experimental Psychiatry, 19,* 31–41.

Minuchin, S. (1974). *Families and family therapy.* Cambridge, MA: Harvard University Press.

Mirkin, H. (2000). Sex, science, and sin: The Rind report, sexual politics, and American scholarship. *Sexuality & Culture: An Interdisciplinary Quarterly Special Issue: Consequences of child sexual abuse, 4,* 82–100.

Murphy, L. L., Impara, J. C. & Plake, B. S. (Eds.) (1999). *Tests in print V: An index to tests, test reviews, and the literature on specific tests (serial).* University of Nebraska-Lincoln: Buros Institute of Mental Measurements.

Naglieri, J. (1988). *Draw-a-person: A quantitative scoring system.* San Antonio: The Psychological Corporation.

Padilla, A. M. (1995). *Hispanic psychology: Critical issues in theory and research.* Thousand Oaks, CA: Sage Publications.

Prilleltensky, I. (1989). Psychology and the status quo. *American Psychologist, 44,* 795–802.

Prilleltensky, I. (1995). The politics of abnormal psychology: Past, present, and future. In N. R. Goldberger & J. B. Veroff (Eds.), *The culture and psychology reader* (pp. 652–673). New York: New York University Press.

Prilleltensky, I. (1997). Values, assumptions, and practices: Assessing the moral implications of psychological discourse and action. *American Psychologist, 52,* 517–535.

Psychological Corporation (2002). *Wechsler Preschool and Primary Scale of Intelligence (WPPSI-III).* (3rd ed.). San Antonio: Psychological Corporation.

Reyes, P., & Valencia, R. R. (1995). Educational policy and the growing Latino student population: Problems and prospects. In A. M. Padilla (Ed.), *Hispanic psychology: Critical issues in theory and research* (pp. 303–325). Thousand Oaks, CA: Sage Publications.

Sahlins, M. (1982). The original affluent society. In J. B. Cole (Ed.), *Anthropology for the eighties: Introductory readings* (pp. 219–240). New York: Free Press.

Silverman, M. M. (1997). Current controversies in suicidology. In R. W. Maris, M. M. Silverman, & S. S. Canetton (Eds.), *Review of suicidology* (pp. 1–21.). New York: Guilford.

Solberg, V. S., Choi, K. H., Ritsma, S., & Jolly, A. (1994). Asian-American college students: It is time to reach out. *Journal of College Student Development, 35,* 296–301.

Sparrow, S. S., & Cicchetti, D. V. (1989). The Vineland Adaptive Behavior Scales. In C. S. Newmark (Ed.), *Major psychological assessment instruments* (vol. 2., pp. 199–231). Boston: Allyn and Bacon.

Stewart, R. (2001). NICE guidelines and the treatment of Alzheimer's disease: Evidence-based medicine may be discriminatory. *British Journal of Psychiatry, 179,* 367.

Sturmey, P. (1996). *Functional analysis in clinical psychology.* Chichester, UK: Wiley.

Sturmey, P., & James, V. (2001). Administrative prevalence of autism in the Texas school system. *Journal of the American Academy of Child and Adolescent Psychiatry, 40,* 621.

Sue, D. W. (2001). Multidimensional facets of cultural competence. *The Counseling Psychologist, 29*(6), 790–821.

Sue, D. W., & Sue, D. (1977). Barriers to effective cross-cultural counseling. *Journal of Counseling Psychology, 24,* 420–429.

Sue, D. W., & Sue, D. (1999). *Counseling the culturally different: Theory and practice* (3rd ed.). New York: John Wiley & Sons.

Sweet, A. A., Giles, T. R., & Young, R. R. (1987). Three theoretical perspectives on anxiety: A comparison of theory and outcome. In L. Michelson & L. M. Ascher (Eds.), *Anxiety and stress disorders: Cognitive-behavioral assessment and treatment* (pp. 39–61). New York: Guilford Press.

Thompson, C. E., Worthington, R., & Atkinson, D. R. (1994). Counselor content orientation, counselor race, and Black women's cultural mistrust and self-disclosures. *Journal of Counseling Psychology, 41,* 155–161.

Tsang, D. C. (1995). Policing "perversions": Depo-Provera and John Money's new sexual order. *Journal of Homosexuality Special Issue: Sex, cell, and same-sex desire: The biology of sexual preference: II, 28,* 397–426.

Valencia, R. R. (1991). *Chicano school failure and success: Research and policy agendas for the 1990's* (Stanford Series on Education and Public Policy). Basingstoke, UK: Falmer.

Valencia, R. R., & Aburto, S. (1991). The uses and abuses of educational testing: Chicanos as a case in point. In R. R. Valencia (Ed.), *Chicano school failure and success: Research and policy agendas for the 1990's* (Stanford Series on Education and Public Policy, pp. 203–251). Basingstoke, UK: Falmer.

Wampold, B. E. (2001). *The great psychotherapy debate: Models, methods and findings.* Mahwah, NJ: Lawrence Erlbaum & Associates.

Webb, S. A. (2001). Some considerations on the validity of evidence-based practice in social work. *British Journal of Social Work, 31,* 57–79.

Wechsler, D. (1991). *Wechsler Intelligence Scale for Children (WISC-III)* (3rd ed.). San Antonio: Psychological Corporation.

Wechsler, D. (1997). *Wechsler Memory Scale (WMS-III)* (3rd ed.). San Antonio: Psychological Corporation.

Wechsler, D. (1998). *Wechsler Adult Intelligence Scale (WAIS-III)* (3rd ed.). San Antonio: Psychological Corporation.

Weil, A. (1972). *The natural mind: A new way of looking at drugs and the higher consciousness.* Boston: Houghton Mifflin Company.

Weinberg, T. S. (1995). Sociological and social psychological issues in the study of sadomasochism. In T. S. Weinberg (Ed.), *S and M: Studies in dominance and submission* (pp. 289–303). Amherst, NY: Prometheus Books.

White, J. L., & Parham, T. A. (1990). *The psychology of blacks: An African-American perspective.* Englewood Cliffs, NJ: Prentice Hall.

Widiger, T. A., Frances, A. J., Pincus, H. A., Ross, R., First, M. B., & Davis, W. W. (Eds.). (1996). *DSM-IV sourcebook,* vol. 2. Washington, DC: American Psychiatric Association.

Widiger, T. A., Frances, A. J., Pincus, H. A., Ross, R., First, M. B., Davis, W. W., & Kline, M. (Eds.). (1998). *DSM-IV sourcebook,* vol. 4. Washington, DC: American Psychiatric Association.

Wilkinson, G. S. (1994). *The Wide Range Achievement Test Revision 3 (WRAT 3).* Wilmington, DE: Jastek Associates.

World Health Organization. (2001). *ICD-10. The international statistical classification of disease and related health problems, tenth version.* Geneva, Switzerland: Author.

2 Ethical and Multicultural Issues

CHAPTER OVERVIEW

1. Ethical principles are conventions that guide professional conduct. They are distinct from the law. This chapter focuses on the APA ethical guidelines. They consist of a preamble, six general principles (competence, integrity, professional and scientific responsibility; respect for people's rights and dignity; concern for other's welfare; and social responsibility), and a variety of specific ethical standards.

2. Privilege and confidentiality are common ethical dilemmas. Whereas privilege is a legal term, confidentiality is an ethical obligation. Confidentiality may be broken in a number of circumstances.

3. Other common ethical dilemmas include advertising, use of psychological tests, reporting suspected abuse, and third-party requests for services.

4. Common emergencies include suicide, violence, and hospitalization. In dealing with emergencies, clinicians often must balance one ethical principle against another and ensure the safety of the client and others.

5. Malpractice is a legal tort. Four elements must be present for malpractice: a duty of care, a standard of care, a breach in the standard of care, and legal, proximate cause of injury or other damages.

6. Case formulations should directly address multicultural issues. Clinicians should be aware of their own competencies and limitations and should learn about other cultures. Clinicians also should consider language, acculturation, immigration, gender roles and stereotypes, sexual orientation, work roles, and religious and cultural beliefs issues that may affect treatment. They should be cautious about applying tests for which no culturally appropriate norms exist.

LEARNING OBJECTIVES

Students will:

1. Describe the six ethical principles of the American Psychological Association.

2. Explain the difference between legal and ethical principles, and give two examples of the application of ethical principles and standards to practice.

3. Distinguish privilege from confidentiality and describe three conditions in which confidentiality may be broken.

4. Describe the essential elements of the Tarasoff case.

5. Describe six common ethical dilemmas and how they may be avoided or resolved.

6. Describe three common emergency situations and how each may be appropriately handled.

7. Describe the four essential elements of malpractice and discuss their application to two clinical examples.

8. Describe six common multicultural issues and how they apply to two case studies.

Ethics and the Law

Ethics are principles or conventions that act as a guide for the behavior of a profession. However, they are not laws. Laws refer to statutes passed by a legislative body, such as a state or federal senate, and the administrative rules passed by a state agency, such as a psychology licensing board. Generally, but not always, ethical standards require a higher standard of conduct than the law. Thus, a professional's actions may be legal while failing to meet ethical standards. Ethics and the law usually, but not always, coincide. When ethical demands conflict with legal standards, clinicians attempt to resolve the conflict in a responsible manner, but sometimes are forced into legal but unethical actions. For example, in states that require the reporting of HIV status, clinicians may face a conflict between legal requirements and the APA principle of respect for others. Although ethical standards usually are enforceable only with respect to a therapist's professional conduct, they occasionally may be invoked against her or his private conduct, such as in cases of moral turpitude or behaviors that bring a clinician's profession into public disrepute.

APA Code of Ethics

The APA published *The Ethical Principles of Psychologists and Code of Conduct* in 1992 (APA, 1992). As a condition of their membership in the APA, psychologists voluntarily agree to abide by this code. The ethical principles consist of a preamble, six general principles, and many specific standards. Although the APA has no legal powers, it may conduct its own ethics investigation of members and take actions against them ranging from an educative letter to dismissal from the APA. Many state licensing boards also have adopted or modified the APA ethical principles and standards as the local code of conduct in a particular state—it is very important that clinicians be aware of the legal and ethical standards that apply in their own localities. APA ethical standards also may be cited in cases of alleged negligence as an indication of the professional "standard of care" alluded to in Chapter 1.

The ethical principles include six general principles, such as competence and integrity, which are aspirational and broadly written. In contrast to general principles, ethical standards are more specific and prescriptive. For example, whereas the general principle of competence asserts only that psychologists should be competent to practice and should strive toward competency, Ethical Standard 2.06, "Unqualified Persons," states that "psychologists do not promote the use of psychological assessment techniques by unqualified persons" (APA, 1992). Unlike the principle of competence, which is broadly written, Ethical Standard 2.06 standard forbids a specific, explicit practice that falls under the aegis of professional competence. Despite (or perhaps because of) this clarity, it is possible to meet all applicable APA standards while violating the application of a principle to a situation not specifically described in the standards.

APA Ethical Principle A: Competence.   APA Ethical Principle A (APA, 1992; see also ACA, 1995, C) asserts that clinicians should be competent to render the services they offer and should recognize the limits of their competence. They should protect the public from harm, which necessitates practicing only within the limits of their competence. Clinicians also maintain their competence through continuing education and make appropriate use of scientific and technical resources as necessary to their practice.

Issues of competence and protecting the public from harm underlie the need to recognize when to refer a client or seek consultation or supervision from a more experienced clinician. Recently qualified therapists, especially, should seek frequent consultation from experienced colleagues when facing new and unfamiliar clinical situations. Consultation also may be indicated when a clinician applies a familiar technique to a new clinical problem, for example, using cognitive therapy for an eating disorder.

The ethical principle of competence also asserts that if a clinician delegates work to a supervisee, he or she should ensure the delegate is qualified to do the work assigned. Although it would be inappropriate for a psychologist to delegate psychometric testing to an unsupervised intern, for example, it might be appropriate to delegate test administration and scoring, but not interpretation, to a competently trained psychometrician.

If a therapist realizes that his or her own competence may be impaired due to mental or physical health issues or other factors, he or she has a responsibility to seek treatment or supervision. If necessary, the therapist should help his or her clients find treatment elsewhere.

Clinicians switching areas of practice, such as from counseling psychology to neuropsychology, should seek training equivalent to licensed specialists in that area. Such training may range from brief supervised continuing education to extensive graduate work and clinical rotations. A licensed professional counselor hoping to begin practice in biofeedback, for example, might need only to complete a graduate course and professional certification to meet the standard of practice for biofeedback in his or her state. On the other hand, a counseling psychologist hoping to practice industrial psychology would need to undertake extensive postgraduate coursework and supervised practice equivalent to the training typical of a practicing industrial psychologist.

APA Ethical Principle B: Integrity.   In research, teaching, and practice, psychologists are honest, fair, and respectful of others. They are also honest about their qualification, fees, research, and teaching. While clinicians obviously should not make statements that are false or misleading, they also should be aware of how their own values may affect their work. Clinicians also should avoid dual relationships because they may harm their clients.

Practitioners' representation of their fees, services, and qualifications commonly raise integrity issues. Obviously, advertising oneself as "Dr. Wonder, Ph.D., licensed psychologist, cures all mental problems" raises multiple integrity issues. However, most representation issues are subtler. A licensed professional counselor with a doctorate in accounting, for example, would be acting unethically by introducing himself or herself to a client as "*Dr.* (Whomever)." Another subtle misrepresentation issue concerns the pricing of initial versus subsequent services, as with a clinician who charges $15 an hour for a first consultation and a higher fee for later treatment without revealing this practice to clients ahead of time (ACA, 1995; APA, 1992).

Dual relationships, as discussed in Chapter 1, are relationships in which a clinician has a relationship with a client both professionally and informally, such as a neighbor, friend, student, or current or former sexual partner. Because dual relationships present the potential for exploitation or harm to the client, they should be avoided whenever possible. The relationship between a therapist and a client is inherently asymmetrical: The therapist not only holds direct power over the client but holds indirect power merely by being privy to personal and confidential information about a client that normally would not be divulged to a stranger.

Sexual relationships between clinicians and their patients, which unavoidably are tainted by this power asymmetry, are unfortunately not uncommon. Sexual relationships are the most frequent cause for action by psychology licensing boards against psychologists, for example, and a frequent source of negligence lawsuits and insurance claims among a wide variety of mental health professionals (Herlihy & Corey, 1992). The typical case of sexual exploitation is an older male therapist in his forties with a female patient in her twenties (Peterson, 1992).

Whereas many state laws explicitly prohibit sexual contact between therapists and current patients, APA and ACA guidelines forbid sexual contact between current and former patients for two years after the termination of therapy. Some state licensure regulations specify even longer time period requirements. Even when the professional relationship has been terminated more than two years, professional ethical guidelines squarely place the responsibility on the clinician to demonstrate the absence of harm or exploitation of former clients. Sex between a clinician and a current or former client is inherently dangerous for both. The onus will always be on the clinician to prove that no harm was done to a client and that exploitation did not occur. Such proof may be hard to come by when a former lover in the witness box testifies that she left her husband, her family, and her job for her psychologist before he terminated their relationship.

Fraudulent billing is another common integrity issue. Potential problems include billing for services not rendered, failing to collect copayments, and falsifying diagnoses to obtain higher payment rates. These activities are unethical and almost always illegal. Fee-splitting, a practice in which a referring clinician receives remuneration for providing a colleague with a referral, is also unethical and often illegal.

APA Ethical Principle C: Professional and Scientific Responsibility. Professional ethical principles require that clinicians uphold professional standards for their own behavior and adapt their behavior to the needs of different populations (ACA, 1995; APA, 1992). They cooperate with other professionals in the best interest of their clients. If they have concerns with the ethical conduct of their colleagues, they consult with those colleagues to remediate these problems. If a clinician becomes aware of a potential ethical problem with another practitioner he or she should first attempt to resolve the issue where possible directly with that person. If the issue cannot be resolved in that conversation, the clinician may be obligated to report the matter to the appropriate licensing board. Failure to do so may be unethical and, under some circumstances, illegal.

APA Ethical Principle D: Respect for People's Rights and Dignity. Mental health professionals respect the dignity, rights, and worth of all people. They respect their privacy, confidentiality, self-determination, and autonomy. Counselors and psychologists should be aware of the different needs of different client groups, based on their age, gender, race, ethnic background, immigrant status, national origin, sexual orientation, disability, language, or social class (ACA, 1995; APA, 1992). They work to eliminate bias in their work and do not participate in or condone discriminatory behaviors. Although it is unethical to refuse to work with a client based on his or her membership in one of the above categories, APA rule 1.13 states that practitioners who become aware that a difference between themselves and a client may impair their personal effectiveness should refer the client to other mental health services. (See further discussion under Multicultural Issues, beginning on page 50.)

APA Ethical Principle E: Concern for Others' Welfare. Clinicians contribute to the welfare of their clients, supervisees, and research participants. They are aware of the inequalities and power asymmetries between a psychologist and a client and do not exploit or mislead others.

A common situation in which a client's welfare may be compromised is when a client has been in a therapeutic relationship from which he or she is not benefiting. In these circumstances, clinicians should put the client's best interests ahead of their own and assist the client in finding a more helpful form of therapy. Similarly, clinicians who become aware that their religious, cultural, sexual orientation, lifestyle, or political differences with a client are interfering with the client's progress should help him or her find more appropriate services. These efforts must be balanced, however, with the potential danger of client abandonment, that is, the danger of terminating nonproductive work with a client before referring him or her to an alternative form of help.

APA Ethical Principle F: Social Responsibility.   Mental health professionals recognize their responsibilities to society and use their work and research findings to alleviate human suffering and advance human welfare. Professional standards also encourage clinicians to contribute a portion of their time pro bono, or without charge (ACA, 1995; APA, 1992)

Common Ethical Dilemmas

Privilege and Confidentiality

The confidentiality of information between mental health professionals and their clients is an ethical and legal mandate. Whereas *privilege* is a legal term, *confidentiality* is an ethical obligation. ACA and APA ethical guidelines each devote an entire section to client privacy and confidentiality (ACA, 1995; APA, 1992). Confidentiality applies to both written and verbal information. Neither type of information may be shared with others, including professional colleagues, outside the therapist-client relationship. Client records, including multiclient databases, furthermore must be secured so that no one other than the therapist, including office staff or clinical/counseling interns, may access it without the client's informed consent. Even the deletion of the client's identifying information may be insufficient to protect confidentiality. In some cases, clients may be identified by their demographic or treatment records in combination with other sources of information. In teaching, professional writing, and consultation with colleagues, identifying information should be removed to sufficiently ensure that the client's confidentiality is maintained.

In situations where confidentiality may become an issue, it is important to clarify its limits with clients early on. Records of conjoint and family therapy should not be released without the consent of all parties. A client's spouse cannot consent to the release of the client's mental health records, and vice versa. Similarly, a parent of a legal adult cannot access the adult child's information without the client's consent. This is true even if the parent's intentions are benign, and even if they are paying for the therapy. Stepparents and grandparents acting in the day-to-day role of parents also cannot access a child's information without the written consent of the child's legal guardian. When consent is obtained, it should be written, dated, and time-limited (e.g., "within 3 months of 6/11/03"). Even when clinicians request release of a client's medical or other confidential records, they should do so only with written informed consent.

The confidentiality of client information is not absolute. There are quite a few situations, in fact, in which confidentiality must be broken. Besides those circumstances in which the client's consent permits it, confidentiality may be broken when required or authorized by law. It also may be legal, and ethical, to break confidentiality if there is an imminent danger to the client or others. Confidentiality also may be breached for third-party payment and associated audits, for administrative and judicial hearings (e.g., a license-revocation hearing), or to a client's personal representative after his or her death. Confidentiality also may be breached during mental health commitment hearings after the client has been informed that the process is not confidential.

When confidential information is disclosed, it should be limited only to the information that is required for the purpose of the disclosure. For example, a secretary may know names and addressees for billing and mail communication, but no more. It may be reasonable to provide an insurance company with a client's identifying information, diagnoses, and appointments attended, but, again, with no more information than is necessary to meet the insurance company's requirements.

Tarasoff

In 1976, the parents of Tatiana Tarasoff sued the regents of the University of California after their daughter had been shot and stabbed to death by Prosenjit Poddar, the client of a University of California counseling center psychologist. Concerned that Poddar was dangerous and intended to harm Ms. Tarasoff, the psychologist contacted the police, but did not warn Ms. Tarasoff directly. Upon review of the case, the California Supreme Court ruled that "when a therapist determines . . . that his patient presents a serious danger of violence to another, he incurs an obligation to use reasonable care to protect the intended victim. . . . [He may] warn the intended victim . . . notify the police, or take whatever steps are reasonably necessary" (*Tarasoff v. Board of Regents of the University of California*, 1976).

The Tarasoff decision does not apply under all circumstances or within all states. First, there must be both an imminent danger and a specific, identifiable victim. Revelations by a client of past murders would remain confidential under the parameters of Tarasoff, as would reports of his or her friends' or relatives' homicidal intentions. In such cases, a clinician could (and should) encourage the client to contact the police or warn the victim, but could do so himself or herself only with the client's consent. Tarasoff-based laws vary significantly from state to state. In Texas, for example, the Supreme Court ruled that there is no mandate to break client confidentiality even when a specific victim and imminent harm may be identified.

HIV Status

Clinicians working with HIV-positive clients sometimes encounter a client who is in imminent danger of infecting a specific, identifiable sexual partner. Some mental health professionals have suggested that the Tarasoff principles should apply to this circumstance (i.e., that the clinician has a duty to warn the potential partner). Others, however, including the APA (1991), have suggested that whereas the clinician should strenuously work to ensure that the client warns his or her partners or engages only in safe sexual practices, he or she should not directly warn a client's partners of the client's HIV status. Legally, however, this issue remains temporarily unresolved, and clinicians should recognize that their actions might be subject to civil penalties, even if they act in accord both with prevailing law and with their professional ethical standards. Clinicians are best served, in these instances, by consulting frequently with colleagues and by keeping themselves explicitly aware of (and duly noting) the justifications for their actions.

Third-Party Requests for Services

From time to time, mental health professionals receive requests for services from a third party. A client may request services for his child, for example, or a relative may request service for an older family member. Other common situations are requests by employers to evaluate an employee and court orders to conduct assessment or treatment of a defendant, each of which raises thorny questions of confidentiality. It is important in these circumstances that the clinician be able to clearly identify who the client is. Before beginning evaluation or treatment, the clinician should clarify the nature of his or her relationship with the client and the limits of the confidentiality of their work. For example, if ordered by a court to evaluate a client convicted of sexual assault, the information a clinician receives from the offender is not confidential. In this case, the court is the evaluator's client. Thus, the court is provided full access to the evaluation summary, a fact that should be clarified at the outset with the offender. On the other hand, if a counselor receives a referral from a school to work with a troublesome adolescent, the teachers, principals, or other staff of the school should not be privy to any aspects of the adolescent's progress without informed, written consent from the adolescent's parents or legal guardians. These issues should be discussed up front with the adolescent, his or her parents, and members of the referring institution.

Advertising and Presenting Oneself as a Mental Health Professional

The ethical principle of integrity most commonly relates to advertising and presenting oneself as a psychologist or counselor. Mental health professionals must honestly and accurately present their degrees, affiliations, training, experiences, competence, fees, services, and, where appropriate, the scientific and clinical basis for their services. Their statements must not only be true, they also should not be misleading or deceptive. The degree a therapist lists on professional documents, for example, should be the highest degree that qualified his or her credentials. As described earlier, a masters-level counselor with a doctorate in accounting should advertise only the masters degree when conducting counseling. Similarly, a trainee or a psychological associate should describe his or her supervised status in advertisements and in communication with clients (ACA, 1995; APA, 1992).

Mental health professionals should follow other common sense guidelines in their advertisements and public communications. They should not solicit testimonials from clients. They should make accurate claims about their fees and the efficacy of their treatments and fully disclose the limitations of psychotherapy and available alternative treatments.

When a clinician becomes aware that others have misrepresented his or her qualifications or opinions, he or she should take reasonable actions to correct the misrepresentation. If a clinician conducts a radio interview with a host who describes her as a clinical hypnotist when she lacks that qualification, for example, she should correct the host's error before continuing the interview.

Psychological Tests

Psychological tests should be performed only within a defined professional relationship. Under no circumstances should psychological testing be done casually with friends or acquaintances. Psychological tests should also be administered, scored, and interpreted only by people competent to do so. Test administration cannot be delegated to those who are not competent to administer or score the test. The interpretation of psychological tests should be reserved for psychologists.

Psychological tests are constructed using psychometric principles, and clinicians should take reasonable precautions to maintain their integrity and security. Test items, scoring sheets, and scoring protocols should not be shared with the public since doing so would invalidate the test norms.

Explaining Assessment Results

Test results should be interpreted carefully and with explicit acknowledgment of the limitations of the findings. Diagnoses and psychometric evaluations should be explained using language that the client is reasonably likely to understand. Most clients, for instance, will not understand diagnostic labels or test scores without additional explanation. When working with clients whose first language is not English, it is important that assessment results be given to them in the language they understand best.

APA Standard 2.02 specifically prohibits the release of raw test scores to unqualified persons including the client (cf. ACA, 1995, E4b). Unfortunately, this ethical standard conflicts with laws that give parents access to their children's educational and medical records. It also conflicts with federal laws that give persons over 18 years of age access to their educational records and test results. These discrepancies often present clinicians with a dilemma. In such cases, the clinician should attempt resolve the matter in a responsible manner. He or she might explain to the client why raw scores would not be helpful, for instance, and instead offer the client a detailed summary of the test scores. At the end of the day, however, the client may have a legal right to obtain whatever results he or she likes, including raw scores.

Similar ethical dilemmas emerge when a court mandates the release of raw test scores or when a client requests the release of raw scores to a third party, such as a lawyer or a teacher, who may not be qualified to interpret them. Although it may be possible to adhere to ethical standards by releasing only summaries and not raw scores, courts may order the release of raw information at their discretion.

Personal and Professional Growth and Limitations

Counselors and psychologists should be able to describe their past professional development experiences and their plans for future personal and professional growth. A continuing commitment to competence and familiarity with ever-changing state and federal laws requires continuing education. These experiences should be formally documented through continuing education units, as well as through other evidence that the clinician has kept current with his or her areas of practice.

Psychologists and counselors should be aware of the limits to their personal and professional competence. A clinician who feels uncomfortable working with perpetrators of abuse, with homosexuals, or with people who have Alzheimer's disease, for example, may refer clients of these descriptions to qualified colleagues. Such practices are acceptable as long as the clinician does not engage in discriminatory practices. A clinician who is unable to work with certain groups of clients or with certain clinical problems, in fact, may be acting unethically if he or she does so.

Abuse, Neglect, and Exploitation

Mental health professionals have an ethical and sometimes legal obligation to report abuse, neglect, and exploitation when they become aware of it. Abuse refers to action that causes harm to someone else, such as striking, yelling at, or threatening a victim. Neglect refers to a failure to act or to act sufficiently to care for someone in need such as by leaving an unsupervised child in a hot vehicle, failing to prevent someone from experiencing harm, or failing to care properly for a bedridden relative. Exploitation refers to taking advantage of a vulnerable person, such as by purchasing his or her possessions well below their actual value, or by compelling him or her to perform work without pay.

Mental health professionals are typically required by state law to report suspicions of abuse, neglect, or exploitation that occurs to members of protected classes, such as children and adolescents, seniors, and people with disabilities.

Suspicions of abuse, neglect, or exploitation should be reported to the appropriate state protective agency. Most states require that suspected offenses be reported immediately or within very limited time frames. Some state or agency regulations may require reporting allegations within 24 hours or even one hour of learning the allegation.

If a mental health professional has a reasonable suspicion of abuse, he or she should report it. It is not the clinician's responsibility to investigate cases to confirm that abuse has occurred before reporting it; that is the job of the relevant state agency. Where appropriate, the clinician should document the reports of third parties who present evidence of abuse, neglect, or exploitation. As closely as possible, these notes should stick to the facts (e.g., "brother-in-law stated client was observed shoving mother to floor") rather than clinical speculation or opinions. Professionals should also carefully separate what they observed from what was reported to them. If a clinician observes bruises on her adolescent client, for example, she should note: "At 2:35 P.M. on Sunday in the nurse's station I observed a bluish-green bruise on George's right buttock. It was 2 inches by 1 inch. Nurse Smith was also present and observed this." If someone else reported the same information to the clinician, she instead should note: "At 2:40 P.M. on Sunday, Nurse Smith reported that George had a bruise in the shape of a shoe heel on his buttock. She stated that George's mother said he fell down. Nurse Smith stated she did not believe this account. Nurse Smith and I reported this information to Protective and Regulatory Services at 2:45 P.M."

If a clinician observes (or is informed about) physical evidence that may support suspicions of abuse, neglect, or exploitation, she or he should take reasonable steps to preserve it. This may include asking victims of suspected sexual abuse to refrain from bathing or washing their clothes until examinations have taken place and physical evidence has been collected or photographed.

Failure to report abuse may lead to legal actions against a mental health professional, including malpractice lawsuits compensating the harm that occurred to the victim as a result of the continuing abuse the professional might have stopped by intervening. On the other hand, it is important to be cognizant of damage a client or other vulnerable person might suffer if a clinician frivolously reports abuse with no substantiating evidence or genuine suspicion of harm.

Multiple Therapists

A client who concurrently sees more than one therapist subjects himself or herself to potential harm and raises issues of confidentiality for both clinicians. Despite these concerns, it is sometimes in a client's interest to see more than one therapist. For example, a counselor untrained in behavior therapy may refer a phobic client to a behavior therapist to enhance his treatment of the client's depression. On the other hand, a client diagnosed with hypochondriasis who is already seeing multiple health professionals should be dissuaded from adding treatment professionals to an already growing list. Such a client's interests might be served best by suggesting he or she see only one therapist at a time.

When a client receives treatment from more than one therapist, it may be appropriate for the professionals to receive information about therapy sessions or the results of assessments from each other orally or in writing. However, information sharing like this should be done only with the client's informed written consent.

Consulting and Supervision

Consultation occurs when a clinician confers with a colleague of equal standing about a case, but assumes no responsibility for the clinician's professional conduct. When consulting about a case, the clinician should disguise the client's identifying information and discuss only the information that is required for the purpose of the consultation.

Supervision, by contrast, occurs when a licensed professional assumes responsibility and liability for the actions of a clinician-trainee. Depending on the licensure and training status of the supervisee, supervision should be consistent, timely, and thorough: The supervisor is fully responsible for the conduct of the supervisee. It is essential that supervisees clearly inform clients about their supervised status and provide them with the name of licensed person under whom they are receiving supervision. Clients also should be informed that the clinician's supervisor is given full access to the details of their history, diagnosis, and treatment.

Multiple Patients

Treating couples and families raises ethical issues of confidentiality and potential conflicts of interest between clients. Therapeutic situations complicated by divorce, child custody, or other legal issues can become especially tricky. When working with multiple clients, the clinician should clarify the goals of therapy with all clients very early during treatment. The limits of confidentiality and the privacy of confidences between family members should be discussed during the first meeting. As new situations arise that pose ethical problems, the clinician should immediately clarify the issue with all parties and withdraw from inappropriate roles. If in marital therapy one partner hopes to maintain the marriage while the other wants to obtain a divorce, for example, the clinician should clarify the possible outcomes for all parties and agree on goals both clients can share. Few circumstances would recommend seeing one partner individually while withholding information from the other.

For a variety of reasons, group therapy interventions may also be problematic when combined with concurrent individual work (although not always; see Vinagradov & Yalom, 1989). If a group therapy member asks the facilitating clinician to see him or her in individual therapy, he or she is probably best referred to another therapist while continuing group participation.

Bartering

Although ACA and APA ethics do not prohibit bartering, they strongly discourage it (ACA, 1995; APA, 1992). Bartering presents an ethical problem because of potential client exploitation. In infrequent circumstances it may be in the client's best interests to arrange bartering payment for clinical services. If the client cannot otherwise pay for services and the goods or services exchanged possess a clear and equitable value, bartering may be considered. As a general rule, however, bartering should be avoided whenever possible.

Clinical Records

In accord with ethical and legal demands, clinicians should keep useful, complete clinical records. At a minimum, these records should contain the client's name and address, a record of all treatment contacts including face-to-face appointments and telephone contacts, and a detailed record of assessment and therapy sufficient for another mental health professional to continue treatment without interruption or harm to the client. According to APA standards, clinicians must also maintain business records, including client names and payments, for the IRS for at least seven years. Similar standards apply to the records kept by counselors and other professionals (ACA, 1995). State laws vary as to the requirement of how long records or summaries of records should be maintained.

Dealing with Emergencies

Ethical and Legal Principles

Many beginning therapists dread client emergencies. Emergencies present clinicians with multiple ethical and legal challenges. Long before emergencies arise, clinicians should review APA and/or ACA ethical principles concerning client welfare (e.g., ACA section A.1; APA ethical principle E) and become familiar with the circumstances under which confidentiality may need to be broken to protect a client or someone else (e.g., ACA section B; APA ethical principle D). APA Ethical Principle A, "Competence," for example, becomes especially pertinent when dealing with a potentially violent or suicidal client. Should a client contemplating harm to a friend be referred to someone who can provide more effective, immediate help? Should a client with a bottle of pills or razors in her purse be hospitalized? Should a telephoning client be invited immediately to the office? It is helpful to consider such questions, and to review the relevant ethical guidelines, before they arise in vivo.

In anticipation of emergency situations, many clinicians keep consultation contacts and emergency referrals on hand both at the office and at home, including police, emergency clinic, and hospital phone numbers. Several resources are often needed to help a suicidal or homicidal client.

When dealing with a suicidal or actively psychotic client, it is important to attempt to empower the client to handle life challenges and to ensure that he or she is treated with dignity (APA ethical principle D). This effort requires that clients be given the opportunity to determine their own future, including their immediate future (e.g., whether they may return home, whether they should be involuntarily admitted to treatment), unless they are a danger to themselves or to others. At the same time, a clinician must also be sensitive to liability issues in emergency situations. It is sobering but wise to recognize that one's actions eventually might be reviewed by a licensing board or courtroom jury, where they may be judged against professional standards, commented upon by colleagues, or critiqued by experts who have coolly reviewed the clinical record years after the precipitating events. A jury that has spent hours hearing the testimony of children whose father killed himself, perhaps because of a clinician's negligence, might consider the details of his emergency situation more sympathetically if the clinician took appropriate actions to protect the client from harm. Dealing with emergencies requires negotiating an often tenuous balance between legal, ethical, and practical realities, but it mandates, above all, ensuring the safety of the client and those with whom he or she interacts.

Suicide

Many mental health clients contemplate suicide at one time or another. Research suggests that nearly 40 percent of Americans have considered suicide at some time during their lives and 3 percent have attempted suicide (Clark, 1995; Meehan, Lamb, Saltzman, & O'Carroll, 1992; Rudd, 1989). Beginning clinicians will eventually face clients who are contemplating or actively planning suicide. In such situations, the clinician should conduct a thorough suicide assessment.

An important first step of such assessments is asking the client directly about his or her suicidal intentions. Clients disclosing such intentions should next be asked about the details of their suicidal plans. By assessing whether those plans are vague or specific and by assessing whether the client has access to moderately (e.g., drug overdose, razor blades) or extremely lethal means of self-harm (e.g., firearms, multistory buildings), the clinician can determine the scope of the interventions necessary to prevent the client's efforts.

It is also important to assess the client's history of previous suicide attempts. Past diagnoses of mood disorders, psychotic disorders, or acting-out disorders such as Borderline Personality Disorder are also important risk factors. Many severely depressed clients ironically become greater risks to themselves as they improve, finally gaining enough energy or insight into their situation to motivate their suicidal efforts. Rapid-cycling bipolar clients swaying from depressive to manic episodes may similarly be at risk of self-harm. Disinhibiting factors, such as excessive use of drugs and alcohol, and farewell gestures, such throwing final birthday parties or giving away prized possessions, may also indicate the need for more direct intervention. (See Table 2.1 for a summary of suicidal risk factors.)

TABLE 2.1 Risk factors for suicide.

Risk factors

Previous history of suicide attempts: frequency and seriousness of attempts

Similar situations to previous suicide attempts

High-risk diagnoses: mood, psychotic, and acting out disorders

Hopelessness

Lifting mood in a severely depressed client

Presence of a plan: present or absent; vague or specific

Low-risk versus high-risk methods

Disinhibiting factors (e.g., drugs or alcohol)

Mitigating factors

Coping skills

Children, family, and friends

Hope

Suicide prevention plan

In addition to identifying risk factors, those aspects of the client's life that may be holding her or him back from committing suicide should also be assessed, including the client's religious beliefs; coping skills; hesitance to abandon children, family members, or friends; and hopes for an improved future. (The last of these, especially, may more strongly predict whether clients harm themselves than do such commonly recognized factors as depressed mood; see Keller & Wolfersdorf, 1993). These positive factors may be built on as part of a long-term intervention plan to prevent future suicidal actions.

Suicidal assessments should be carefully documented. If a clinician is not competent to treat the client beyond the initial crisis intervention, she or he should refer the client, and in some situations personally escort the client, to another treatment professional or facility. The bottom line is that the client's safety must be ensured. In an inpatient setting, this may mean placing a suicidal client on a 24-hour watch; in an outpatient setting, it may mean voluntary or involuntary admitting of the client to a hospital or other psychiatric facility (see Psychotic Episodes and hospitalization, p. 48.).

If a client is experiencing some suicidal ideation but is not actively suicidal, a no-harm contract is often used. A no-harm contract specifies agreements between the client and clinician about the frequency of their meetings (usually more frequent until the crisis passes) and the client's commitment to phone the clinician or other treatment professional in the event of increased suicidal ideation.

Short-term suicide interventions also include helping the client identify triggers for suicidal thoughts and helping him or her develop more adaptive strategies for dealing with these triggers. Being able to get through a crisis period one week at a time, or even one day at a time, is the most many clients can manage at the beginning of treatment. Attempting to deal with bigger issues at these times may make things worse, and the clinician may consider delaying some aspects of therapeutic work until the crisis passes. Instead, the clinician should immediately give the client hope and help him or her determine stressors that might be temporarily put on hold until he or she gets beyond the crisis period (e.g., by having a relative look after the children for a week or by taking a week off from work). Many clinicians also give suicidal clients an immediate "reality check" by asking a suicidal client to envision the future implications of his or her death, for example, including the whereabouts of his or her children ten days or years into the future. Suicidal clients may also need temporary supervision from family members or, in inpatient settings, supervision from professional staff, who might be asked to check in on them frequently until their suicidal ideation passes. These strategies, too, may be codified in the no-harm contract.

Violence

Assessments of violence are broadly similar to suicide assessments. The client's previous history, coping skills, disinhibiting factors, and violent reactions to similar situations in the past are all risk factors for violence. In addition, some types of clients, such as those with Antisocial Personality Disorder, may be at a higher risk for violence than others.

As the discussion of Tarasoff issues indicated, mental health professionals in some situations have a duty to break confidentiality, and in some states they have a duty to warn a specific victim or alert the police about the imminent potential of harm. Some states similarly require that mental health professionals break confidentiality when they become aware of the abuse of minors, seniors, or people with disabilities. In general, however, all state laws and civil standards recognize a common reality: If a clinician learns that a client or other person is in imminent danger, he or she must take action to protect the potential victim from harm.

After meeting this immediate responsibility, clinicians may employ a variety of strategies to help clients manage violent behavior. Cognitive-behavioral techniques, such as anger management, relaxation therapies, and problem-solving and social skills training, are often used and are discussed in later chapters of this book.

Psychotic Episodes and Hospitalization

Psychologists and counselors may work with clients who become psychotic. This is a more straightforward issue in inpatient facilities than in community or private practice settings. In an inpatient facility, the clinician should alert the client's psychiatrist and treatment team to ensure that information is available to all team members, to provide side-effect and symptom information for appropriately adjusting medications, and to arrange treatment and relapse prevention services for the client. If an inpatient client becomes a danger to self or others, the treatment team should develop immediate protective measures to ensure everyone's safety.

More challenging issues arise when working with actively psychotic clients in outpatient settings. As with suicide and violence, client safety and the safety of others must be balanced against other ethical principles. An outpatient client who is also actively psychotic (i.e., hallucinating and deluding) should immediately receive a diagnostic evaluation and, if indicated, be referred for psychotropic medications from a psychiatrist. Clients who become agitated for extended periods of time may present a danger to themselves or to others by refusing to eat or drink, by enduring exploitation, by placing themselves in danger, or by threatening harm to someone else. In such cases, hospitalization may be required. It is preferable, when possible, to have the client admitted voluntarily so as to maintain his or her dignity and autonomy (cf. APA ethical principle D). If this is not possible, however, involuntary commitment should be pursued if the person is an imminent danger to self or others. In some states, a court may issue a mental health warrant upon application by any person, including a psychologist or counselor. In other states a law officer may be enlisted to take a person to a state hospital or other treatment facility for assessment and evaluation.

Summary

Most psychologists and counselors will face emergency situations during their professional career. Clinicians should be trained, competent, and prepared to deal with such emergencies when they arise. Negotiating emergencies involves balancing one ethical principle—protecting the client and others from harm—against other ethical principles, such as ensuring the client's dignity, respect and autonomy. Professionals should be familiar with these principles and act within the law when dealing with emergencies.

Malpractice

Malpractice is a legal *tort* or wrongdoing. It has four elements: (1) a professional relationship, (2) a demonstrable standard of care, (3) harm or injury to the client, and (4) a legal, proximate cause of the injury (Bennett, Bryant, VandenBos, & Greenwood, 1990).

Each of these four elements may be considered separately. First, a duty of care exists between a mental health professional and her or his client. Evidence of a duty of care may include a contract between a therapist and client, a bill for services, admission to a facility where the therapist works, entry notes, or other documentation in the client's record. Even without written documentation, certain actions, such as asking a client to come for an appointment, may constitute evidence of a duty of care. By contrast, a duty of care probably does not exist when nonclients ask for general advice. If friends or acquaintances ask for advice, it may be prudent to refer them on to a colleague in order to minimize ambiguity about whether the acquaintance is owed a duty of care.

A standard of care codifies the notion that a clinician's professional services must meet the same quality any other reasonable practitioner would provide. If a clinician undertakes a particular kind of assessment or intervention, for example, he or she should possess the training and skills appropriate for these services. In some circumstances, it may be sufficient to demonstrate that a respectable minority of practitioners would have acted similarly.

Establishing that harm or injury occurred to the client is the third element of malpractice. Harm may be an indisputable injury or death, injuries such as loss of wages or divorce, or subjective injuries such as pain and suffering. Subjective injuries also may include exacerbation of current symptoms, the appearance of new symptoms, the misuse of therapy (for example, resulting in dependence on the therapist), or the client's disillusionment with psychological treatment.

The final element of malpractice is that the therapist's action must be the legal, proximate cause of the client's harm. If other causes are evident, such as the client's own contributory negligence or other intervening events, the clinician may be partially or totally absolved of the claim of malpractice (cf. Bennett et al., 1990).

When analyzing claims of malpractice, each of the four above elements should be assessed independently. A duty of care and harm alone are insufficient for malpractice. There must also be a breach in the standard of care and a proximate, legal cause to meet the legal standard for malpractice. (See Case 2.1 for example analyses of malpractice cases.)

Multicultural Issues

The APA published its *Guidelines for Providers of Services to Ethnic, Linguistic, and Culturally Diverse Populations* in 1990 (APA, 1990b). These guidelines are suggestions to practitioners. Like the APA ethical principles, they are aspirational in nature.

The guidelines recommend that clinicians educate their clients about the nature of the therapeutic relationship, confidentiality, and their theoretical orientation. They should provide this information in writing and orally in a language that the client can easily understand. Clinicians should be aware of relevant research about ethnic and cultural differences and should recognize how ethnic and cultural parameters (e.g., the values, attitudes, behaviors, and epistemic lenses of clients' reference groups) might influence psychological processes. They should be aware of the role family members, community structures, and cultural beliefs play for the client and should respect the client's religious beliefs and val-

---

CASE **2.1**

Examples of key issues of malpractice.

Case 2.1A

A student sues his psychology professor for giving him grades that resulted in the rejection of his application to graduate school. Did the professor owe the student a duty of care? Yes, for which the student paid tuition. Did the student suffer harm? Yes—he did not get admitted to graduate school. Was the professor's action the legal and proximate cause of the harm? This is debatable: It could be argued that the student's failure to study effectively contributed substantially, if not completely, to his receipt of a poor grade, but the professor's actions, too, could be argued to have a significant proximate role in the student's suffering. This case hinges most around the final element of malpractice: standard of care. Did the professor act similarly to what might be expected of other reasonable psychology professors? If she can prove she did by giving accurate, unbiased grades and by providing the additional assistance to the student that would be expected of most psychology professors, she is solidly defended against the charge of malpractice. If she cannot, she is susceptible to an adverse judgment (cf. Bennett et al., 1990).

Case 2.1B

The family of a client who committed suicide sued a psychologist. For several sessions the client, who was severely depressed, discussed suicide increasingly often. One morning the client and his wife appeared at the psychologist's office after he had attempted suicide hours earlier. The psychologist recommended psychiatric admission. After the client consulted with his wife's family physician, the client was admitted to a psychiatric hospital. However, the psychologist failed to adequately inform the hospital's staff about the client's risk of suicide, and the client almost immediately killed himself.

Here, the psychologist clearly had a duty of care to this client, and the client and his family clearly suffered harm. The malpractice claim, therefore, rested on two remaining issues: standard of care and legal, proximate cause. Although the psychologist's hospital notes recorded that the client was severely depressed, they did not record that he was suicidal. As a result, it was argued that the psychologist failed to fully communicate the client's risk of suicide to the hospital staff. When witnesses in the psychologist's malpractice trial reported that most psychologists would have explicitly informed hospital staff about the client's suicidal ideation, the case was decided. Although several other people arguably contributed to the client's harm, most notably including the client himself, the psychologist was found guilty of malpractice (Bennett et al., 1990).

---

ues. Clinicians should interact with the client in a language requested by the client and should make culturally appropriate referrals where indicated. Clinicians also should consider the impact of adverse social, environmental, and political factors on clients, and work to eliminate biases, prejudices, and discriminatory practices that affect their clients. Their clinical records should document relevant factors such as English language fluency, number of years in the country, and acculturation-related stressors. Psychological tests that have not been normed with ethnically or culturally diverse populations should be interpreted cautiously and supplemented with (or supplanted by) more appropriate tests when possible.

Multicultural Issues and Case Formulation

What should clinicians do when working with clients from a different culture than their own? First, they should be aware of their own cultural identity and the implicit cultural biases they bring to clinical practice, including their views of what constitutes mental health, healthy family interaction, appropriate gender roles, and appropriate devotion to remunerated work, among numerous other culturally imbued issues (Betan, 1997; Carter, 1986; Christopher, 1999; Kubacki, 1994; Peterson & Gonzalez, 2000; Prilleltensky, 1997; Sue, 2001; Sue & Sue, 1997; Tjeltveit, 1999; Woolfolk, 1998). In particular, clinicians should not overestimate their own cultural competence. A single multicultural counseling course coupled with a Spanish-language immersion experience, for example, does not qualify a clinician to provide culturally sensitive counseling to Mexican American, Puerto Rican, and all other Hispanic/Latino clients. Clinicians should seek multicultural training and continuing education throughout their careers. If a clinician is unfamiliar with a client's culture, she or he may learn about it to some extent from clients. However, in addition to informal and empirical exposures, clinicians should seek relevant training about their clients' cultural and sociopolitical experiences and consult frequently with culturally competent colleagues or supervisors.

In addition to recognizing their own cultural limitations and biases, clinicians should explicitly consider the impact of cultural issues on their clients. A wide body of research suggests that ethnic minority clients face not only society-wide discrimination but specific institutional barriers and cultural biases within mental health treatment (Katz, 1985; Pinderhughes, 1989; Solberg, Choi, Ritsma, & Jolly, 1994; Sue, 2001; Sue & Sue, 1977, 1999). The clinician should also be sensitive to circumstances, such as racial identity and sociopolitical influences, that affect clients' lives. In some cases, clinicians also should consider making use of or contributing to systemic, "community-as-client" interventions designed to address these underlying issues (West-Olatunji & Watson, 1999).

Clinicians should be aware of specific empirical facets of clients' cultural backgrounds, such as preference for extended family interactions, traditional versus future time-sense orientations, and lineal or collateral social relations. They should also be aware of culturally specific resources such as community social work resources, extended family support and/or interventions, and culturally specific healers from which individual clients might benefit. In so doing, however, they should not tilt too far toward culturally based views of their clients that neglect within-group differences among cultural minorities and the putative transcultural aspects of human living (Atkinson & Thompson, 1992; Carter & Helms,

1987, 1990; Dana, 1993; Gaubatz, 1997; Hare-Mustin & Maracek, 1990; Speight, Myers, Cox, & Highlen, 1991).

Clinicians should also recognize that their clients' religious and cultural backgrounds might influence their beliefs about the etiology and appropriate treatment of mental illness. For example, some research indicates that Hispanic clients are more likely than non-Hispanic clients to hold fatalistic views of disability and mental health issues (although these issues vary between diverse Hispanic American groups; see Fabrega, 1995). Culturally competent practitioners should consider their clients' religious and cultural beliefs when considering treatment options. For example, some research suggests Asian American clients may prefer more directive therapies, with lower expectations about self-disclosure, than many Anglo clients. Clinicians should take these possibilities into account when planning treatment. It may be appropriate, in many circumstances, to include members of clients' social or family systems in treatment sessions and to make extensive referral use of community resources in their treatment (Attneave, 1990).

When conducting assessments, clinicians should recognize that test norms might be invalid with ethnic and cultural groups when tests have not been normed with these groups (see Chapter 1). When possible, clinicians should consider using inventories that have been specifically designed to access the value systems of diverse reference groups (e.g., Culture-Fair Intelligence Test, Hare Self-Esteem Inventories) or instruments that can be adapted for use with ethnically diverse clients (e.g., Peabody Picture Vocabulary Test, Denver Developmental Screening Test). Assessment ideally should acknowledge that clients are best understood within the contexts of both their own reference group values and those of larger community (including mental health profession) discourses (Dana, 1993). Historically, and regrettably contemporarily, the actual practice of psychological assessment has often breached this ideal.

Clients' cultural differences also may factor into clinical formulations in the form of gender roles and stereotypes, sexual orientation, social class, and vocational status. Numerous of these issues often intersect with a given individual client, whose identification with various aspects of his or her cultural background furthermore may vary across time (Gonzalez, Biever, & Gardner, 1995; Helms & Cook, 1999). For instance, a 20-year-old Latina lesbian pursuing a professional degree away from home may face more stress coming out to her family than a 32-year-old Anglo woman with an established relationship and career. Furthermore, her stresses may vary with her family's degree of acculturation. If her family holds strongly traditional religious beliefs and views about women's roles, she may experience greater stress than if her family came to the United States 200 years ago and attends church infrequently. As such examples illustrate, making stereotyped assumptions about clients' issues based only on their nominal ethnic categorizations can compromise the quality of therapy they receive. Clinicians should proceed with an open mind and make an ongoing effort to surmount their own presumptions—arguably a lifelong, continuously evolving process.

Immigration and Acculturation

In addition to other cultural issues, case formulations should consider the effects of language, acculturation, and the process of immigration on the client's history. The client's comfort and fluency with English may initially be assessed informally. If the client prefers a language other than one in which the clinician is fluent, the clinician should consider referring him or her to another clinician or consider obtaining help, if appropriate, from a translator or family member.

Acculturation refers to the degree to which a client identifies with his or her own culture versus a mainstream culture. Whereas some immigrants are highly integrated within their adopted mainstream cultures, others may be linguistically, socially, and culturally isolated. Although the number of years or generations a client's family has lived in the United States may be tied to his or her identification with U.S. culture(s), clinicians should be sensitive to a number of other issues that affect client acculturation. First, cultural identification waxes and wanes over time. Recent research suggests some immigrants experience an initial honeymoon period, then become disenchanted with mainstream cultures as they adjust to the realities of life in the United States (Araujo, 1996). Cultural identification also may become stronger during such religious and socially significant periods as family member deaths, marriages, or other rites of passage. It also may vary for particular ethnic groups as a consequence of political and social events.

An important distinction to be made is whether a client's immigration was voluntary or forced (and possibly traumatic). Clients' legal status and experiences with immigration lawyers or the U.S. Immigration and Naturalization Service may further complicate their immigration experiences, leading to financial and legal worries for both the client and her or his extended family members.

Matching

Research evidence is mixed about whether ethnic minority clients are best matched with clinicians of similar backgrounds. Some research has suggested that clients may do better with matched therapists (e.g., Alladin, 1994). However, other investigators have found that it is the clinician's cultural sensitivity and own cultural awareness, rather than his or her ethnicity, that has most influence on the treatment success of minority clients (Atkinson, 1983; Vera et al., 1999).

CASE EXERCISE

Professional Issues

You graduated from a masters program in counseling two years ago and obtained a counseling license that permits you to practice independently. You have been engaged in typical adult mental health work when you run into a former classmate who now has a lucrative practice conducting psychometric assessments for work rehabilitation and pain evaluations. Your former classmate tells you she has more work than she can handle and is making more money than she can spend. She asks you to join her practice, and you agree. (Time 1)

After working with your former classmate for three weeks, you decide not to continue in her practice after all. However, she tells you that her secretary has booked appointments for you all week and that failing to see those clients (whom you have not yet seen) will constitute abandonment of them. She makes it clear that she will turn you into the licensing board if you do not see them. (Time 2).

Study Questions

1. What ethical issues are raised by your actions at Time 1?

2. When you arrive at your former classmate's practice, you find she has printed a business card for you that states you provide "effective psychological treatments for all forms of pain, with guaranteed results." What ethical and legal issues does this raise and how should you resolve them?

3. What actions should you take at Time 2?

4. Analyze your options at Time 2 in terms of the four aspects of malpractice.

CASE EXERCISE

Multicultural Issues

Mrs. Schumaker is a 54-year-old Anglo-American client with Generalized Anxiety Disorder. You have worked with her for the past twelve weeks and she has always struck you as a conservative person. She attends the same fundamentalist church several times a week that she went to as a child. Today she brings up an issue that has been worrying her for two weeks: A fellow white church member is having an affair with an African American man. Mrs. Schumaker is upset both that the woman is dating an African American and that she is breaking her promise to God to remain faithful to her husband. Mrs. Schumaker's church's view on the latter matter is clear: If the woman does not repent, she should be publicly denounced and shunned by the church community. Mrs. Schumaker wants to know how to use her newly acquired anxiety management skills to confront the woman, who is her friend, in an assertive and relaxed manner.

Study Questions

1. Identify some of the ethical challenges you face as Mrs. Schumaker's therapist.

2. What multicultural issues may be involved in your relationship with Mrs. Schumaker and in her views of her friend's actions?

3. During your next session with her, Mrs. Schumaker expresses racist attitudes toward African American and Mexican American men, as well as discriminatory attitudes towards Catholics and Jews. If you become concerned that you cannot work effectively with Mrs. Schumaker because you find her views repugnant, how should you exercise your duty of care to her?

CASE EXERCISE
Confidentiality

Melissa is a successful counselor practicing in resolution of family disputes, adult disorders, and conflicts between parents and their teenage children. Her practice was going well when she began seeing Mr. Street, a new client. Mr. Street was diagnosed with a mood disorder and alcohol dependency that began after his divorce three years ago. Within six months of working with Mr. Street, Melissa began seeing him conjointly with his two daughters, primarily focusing on resolving conflicts within the home. Later Melissa also began seeing Mr. Street's oldest daughter, Maria, individually to help resolve some of her academic problems. Because Mrs. Street indicated she wanted to support her daughter, Melissa began seeing her jointly with Maria. Uncertain where to file her session notes, she photocopied them and placed them in both Maria's and Mrs. Street's file. Although Melissa found it hard to keep some of the issues separate, she did the best she could.

Then things got nasty. Mr. and Mrs. Street got into a major fight. He drove his two daughters to Mrs. Street's house, where she accused him of being drunk. They got into a fight and the police were called. Mrs. Street said that she was going back to court to prevent Mr. Street from seeing his daughters so often, describing him as an unfit father and a danger to them. Her lawyer wrote to Melissa to sequester all the session notes and any other documentation relating to both daughters. Mrs. Street furthermore indicated she wants Melissa to testify about Mr. Street's psychiatric problems and their impact on the daughters. (The second daughter apparently told her mother that Melissa stated that her father had damaged her development by his coldness and neglect when he was drinking.) Melissa became concerned when she reviewed her notes and found that she had indeed used the word "neglect" in several places in Mr. Street's and his daughter's notes. She also had discussed Mr. Street's feelings of guilt with him over what he described as his neglect of his daughters. Mr. Street's lawyer has written to Melissa forbidding her to disclose any and all notes, since Mr. Street is the children's legal guardian. He says Melissa cannot disclose these records without his written consent, which he refuses to give. Melissa is now expecting a subpoena requiring her to disclose all notes on all participants. She does not know what to do. Mr. Street has called Melissa. He wants to know why Melissa is discussing the confidential material from his sessions with his daughters and probably with his wife.

Study Questions
1. Who is Melissa's client?
2. Analyze the confidentiality issues here.
3. What actions should Melissa have taken to avoid these problems?

CASE EXERCISE
Integrity

You are working in a community mental health clinic. A nurse who works there recently obtained her doctoral degree in nursing. On two occasions she phoned the local mental hospital to arrange admission for a blatantly psychotic patient, without success. Frustrated, she decided to introduce herself on the phone, she tells you later, as "Doctor Auslander from the Newton Community Clinic." It is clear that she deliberately gave the impression she was a psychiatrist. (Time 1)

When you discuss this with the nurse, she becomes upset and angrily states that one of your colleagues, a Mexican national employed in the clinic as a counselor, "probably has fake credentials herself, so why are you fussing at me?" (Time 2)

Study Questions
1. What ethical principles are at stake at Time 1?
2. What actions should you take at Time 1?
3. To what professional standards should the nurse be held, given that she is not a counselor or psychologist?
4. What ethical principles are at stake at Time 2?
5. What actions should you take at Time 2?

Chapter Summary

1. APA and ACA ethical codes describe the code of conduct for counselors and psychologists. These codes include principles, which are broad and aspirational, and standards, which are narrow and specific. Ethics are codes of conduct that can be distinguished from laws.

2. Common ethical dilemmas include confidentiality; misrepresenting one's credentials; using psychological tests; maintaining professional competency; reporting abuse, neglect, and exploitation; concurrent therapies; bartering; maintaining adequate records; and dual relationships.

3. Psychologists and counselors should be competent to deal with emergencies such as suicide or violence in a way that ensures the safety of clients and others. It often is difficult in these circumstances to balance ethical principles against one another.

4. Malpractice is a legal tort and involves four key elements, each of which must be present for malpractice to be found. Psychologists and counselors should be able to analyze practice situations for each aspect of malpractice and identify preventive or corrective actions to take to avoid malpractice.

5. Multicultural aspects of practice require that practitioners explicitly explore cultural issues, such as language, acculturation, gender, and other roles, and culture-specific beliefs about mental health, with their clients. Clinicians should be aware of their own tacit biases and should seek continuing education and supervised experiences to maintain, and recognize the limits of, their cultural competence.

REFERENCES

Alladin, W. J. (1994). Ethnic matching in counseling: How important is it to ethnically match clients and counsellors? *Counselling Psychology Review, 9,* 13–17.

American Counseling Association. (1995). *Code of ethics and standards of practice.* Alexandria, VA: Author.

American Psychological Association. (1990a). Ethical principles for psychologists. *American Psychologist, 45,* 390–395.

American Psychological Association. (1990b). *Guidelines for providers of services to ethnic, linguistic, and culturally diverse populations.* Washington, DC: Author.

American Psychological Association. (1991). *American Psychological Association AIDS-related policy statement.* Washington, DC: Author.

American Psychological Association. (1992). *Ethical principles for psychologists and code of conduct.* Washington, DC: Author.

Araujo, Z. A. (1996). Portuguese families. In M. McGoldrick & J. Giordano et al. (Eds.), *Ethnicity and family therapy* (2nd ed., pp. 583–594). New York: Guilford Press.

Atkinson, D. R. (1983). Ethnic similarity in counseling psychology: A review of research. *Counseling Psychologist, 11,* 79–92.

Atkinson, D. R., & Thompson, C. E. (1992). Racial, ethnic, and cultural variables in counseling. In S. D. Brown & R. W. Lent (Eds.), *Handbook of counseling psychology* (2nd ed., pp. 349–382). New York: John Wiley & Sons.

Attneave, C. L. (1990). Core network intervention: An emerging paradigm. *Journal of Strategic & Systemic Therapies, 9,* 3–10.

Bennett, B. E., Bryant, B. K., VandenBos, G. R., & Greenwood, A. (1990). *Professional liability and risk management.* Washington, DC: American Psychological Association.

Betan, E. J. (1997). Toward a hermeneutic model of ethical decision making in clinical practice. *Ethics and Behavior, 7,* 347–365.

Carter, B. (1986). Success in family therapy. *Family Therapy Networker, 10,* 17–22.

Carter, R. T., & Helms, J. E. (1987). The relationship of black value-orientations to racial identity attitudes. *Measurement & Evaluation in Counseling & Development, 19,* 185–195.

Carter, R. T., & Helms, J. E. (1988). The relationship between racial identity attitudes and social class. *Journal of Negro Education, 57,* 22–30.

Christopher, J. C. (1999). Situating psychological well-being: Exploring the cultural roots of its theory and research. *Journal of Counseling & Development, 77,* 141–152.

Clark, D. C. (1995). Epidemiology, assessment, and management of suicide in depressed patients. In E. E. Beckham & W. R. Leber (Eds.), *Handbook of depression* (2nd ed., pp. 526–538). New York: Guilford.

Dana, R. H. (1993). *Multicultural assessment perspectives for professional psychology.* Boston: Allyn and Bacon.

Fabrega, H., Jr. (1995). Hispanic mental health research: A case for cultural psychiatry. In A. M. Padilla (Ed.), *Hispanic psychology: Critical issues in theory and research* (pp. 107–130). Thousand Oaks, CA: Sage Publications.

Gaubatz, M. D. (1997). Subtle ethnocentrisms in the hermeneutic circle. *American Psychologist, 52,* 657–658.

Gonzalez, R. C., Biever, J. L., & Gardner, G. T. (1994). The multicultural perspective in therapy: A social constructionist approach. *Psychotherapy, 31*(3), 515–524.

Hare-Mustin, R. T., & Maracek, J. (1990). *Making a difference: Psychology and the construction of gender.* New Haven: Yale University Press.

Helms, J. E., & Cook, D. A. (1999). *Using race and culture in counseling and psychotherapy: Theory and process.* Boston: Allyn and Bacon.

Herlihy, B., & Corey, G. (1992). *Dual relationships in counseling.* Alexandria, VA: American Association for Counseling and Development.

Katz, J. H. (1985). The sociopolitical nature of counseling. *The Counseling Psychologist, 13*(4), 615–624.

Keller, F., & Wolfersdorf, M. (1993). Hopelessness and the tendency to commit suicide in the course of depressive disorders. *Crisis, 14,* 173–177.

Kubacki, S. R. (1994). Applying Habermas's theory of communicative action to values in psychotherapy. *Psychotherapy: Theory, Research, Practice, Training, 31*(3), 463–477.

Meehan, P. J., Lamb, J. A., Saltzman, L. E., & O'Carroll, P. W. (1992). Attempted suicide among young adults: Progress toward a meaningful estimate of prevalence. *American Journal of Psychiatry, 149,* 41–44.

Peterson, M. R. (1992). *At personal risk: Boundary violations in professional-client relationships.* New York: Norton.

Peterson, N., & Gonzalez, R. C. (2000). *The role of work in people's lives: Applied career counseling and vocational psychology.* Belmont, CA: Wadworth.

Pinderhughes, E. (1989). *Understanding race, ethnicity, and power: The key to efficacy in clinical practice.* New York: Free Press.

Prilleltensky, I. (1997). Values, assumptions, and practices: Assessing the moral implications of psychological discourse and action. *American Psychologist, 52,* 517–535.

Rudd, M. D. (1989). The prevalence of suicidal ideation among college students. *Suicide & Life-Threatening Behavior, 19,* 173–183.

Skogan, W. G. (1990). *Disorder and decline: Crime and the spiral decay in American neighborhoods.* New York: Free Press.

Skogan, W. G. (1994). *Contact between police and public: Findings from the 1992 British Crime Survey.* (Home Office research study number 134). London: HMSO.

Solberg, V. S., Choi, K. H., Ritsma, S., & Jolly, A. (1994). Asian-American college students: It is time to reach out. *Journal of College Student Development, 35,* 296–301.

Speight, S. L., Myers, L. J., Cox, C. I., & Highlen, P. S. (1991). A redefinition of multicultural counseling. *Journal of Counseling & Development, 70,* 29–36.

Sue, D. W. (2001). Multidimensional facets of cultural competence. *Counseling Psychologist Special Issue: Multidimensional facets of cultural competence, 29,* 790–821.

Sue, D. W. & Sue, D. (1977). Barriers to effective cross-cultural counseling. *Journal of Counseling Psychology, 24,* 420–429.

Sue, D. W., & Sue, D. (1999). *Counseling the culturally different: Theory and practice* (3rd ed.). New York: John Wiley & Sons.

Tarasoff v. Board of Regents of the University of California. (1976). 551P. 3d 345.

Tjeltveit, A. C. (1999). *Ethics and values in psychotherapy.* New York: Routledge Press.

Vera, E. M., Speight, S. L., Mildner, C., & Carlson, H. (1999). Clients' perceptions and evaluations of similarities to and differences from their counselors. *Journal of Counseling Psychology, 46,* 277–283.

Vinagradov, S. & Yalom, I. D. (1989). *A concise guide to group psychotherapy.* Washington, DC: American Psychiatric Press.

West-Olatunji, C. A., & Watson, Z. E. (1999). Community-as-client mental health needs assessment: Use of culture-centered theory and research. *Community Psychologist, 32,* 36–38.

Woolfolk, R. L. (1998). *The cure of souls: Science, values, and psychotherapy.* San Francisco: Jossey-Bass.

PART TWO

Major Diagnostic Clusters

3 Childhood and Adolescent Disorders

CHAPTER OVERVIEW

1. Attention Deficit Hyperactivity Disorder (ADHD) is characterized by clinically significant excessive motor activity, poor attention, poor concentration, and distractibility. Differential diagnosis of ADHD must take into consideration the child's developmental norms. Treatment of ADHD is multimodal, including stimulant prescriptions, behavior management, self-management, and parental education.

2. Two common developmental disorders are Mental Retardation and Autistic Disorder. Mental Retardation is characterized by general deficits in adaptive behavior and an IQ below 70 occurring during the developmental period. Autistic Disorder is characterized by qualitative impairments in social interaction, communication, and restrictive and repetitive behaviors. Autism often coexists with mental retardation. Interventions include applied behavior analysis, psychotropic medications, and parental education and support.

3. Learning disorders are characterized by a specific deficit in one area of performance, such as reading or motor skills, in the context of average overall intellectual functioning. Interventions include a variety of forms of remedial education.

4. Separation Anxiety Disorder is characterized by excessive anxiety over separation from the parent or home. Various forms of modified anxiety management and exposure therapy are often used to help children suffering from separation anxiety.

5. Opposition Defiant Disorder is characterized by negativistic, hostile, and defiant behavior. Conduct Disorder is a more serious form of behavior disturbance that violates the rights of others and social norms, which may lead to an adult diagnosis of Antisocial Personality Disorder. Interventions may include applied behavior analysis strategies, psychopharmacology, and, in some cases, legal action.

Attention Deficit Hyperactivity Disorder

Diagnosis

DSM-IV divides ADHD symptoms into two groups: Inattention and Hyperactivity-impulsivity. Symptoms of inattention include failing to pay attention to details, making frequent errors, difficulty in sustaining attention, failing to listen or follow instructions, difficulty in organizing tasks, avoidance of sustained-attention tasks, distraction by external stimuli, and forgetfulness. Symptoms of hyperactivity include fidgeting or squirming, excessive out-of-seat behavior, excessive running or climbing, failing to play quietly, appearing driven or constantly on the go, and excessive talking. Symptoms of impulsivity include blurting out of answers, failure to take turns, and frequent interruptions or butting into conversations. In order to make a diagnosis of ADHD, at least six symptoms of inattention or hyperactivity-impulsivity must be present for a duration of at least six months. These symptoms must begin before the age of 7 years and must result in clinically significant impairment in at least two settings. The following disorders must be ruled out: Pervasive Developmental Disorder, psychotic disorders, mood disorders, anxiety disorders, and personality disorders.

In diagnosing ADHD it is important to ensure that the client's observed behavior is not merely the extreme end of a continuum of normal behavior appropriate to the client's developmental stage. (Because the client's behavior should be compared to behavioral norms for his or her *developmental level* rather than chronological age, special attention must be given in assessing children with developmental delays.) Other factors that should be ruled out include low tolerance or poor skills on the part of parents or teachers and constant exposure to an understimulating environment. In these cases, other interventions, including education of adults, parenting skills training, and environmental restructuring, should be used.

Assessment

Assessment of ADHD includes several elements. First, a clinical interview with several informants is important. At the very least, information is needed from the home and school to determine whether the child exhibits ADHD-related behaviors in at least two settings. This information is also useful in determining whether stressed-out adults or other systemic variables may cause or exacerbate the child's symptoms. Various psychometric instruments used for screening child and adolescent psychopathology also have ADHD scales, including the Child Behavior Checklists (Achenbach & McConaughy, 1985) and the Conners Rating Scale (Conners, 1991).

Direct observation of a child in his or her natural environment, including classroom and home environments, can be an especially good way to assess the situational specificity of the child's symptoms. Direct observation in all these natural settings can be informal (e.g., general impressions of the child's behavior or running narrative notes) or formal (e.g., time sampling of out-of-seat behavior, frequency counts of interruptions or other observable behaviors, antecedent-behavior-consequence diaries). (See Figures 3.1 and 3.2.) Formally documented information can also be useful later to evaluate the effectiveness of behavioral interventions compared to a baseline of pretreatment behaviors. Because such observational measures are often time-consuming, it may be more efficient to

FIGURE 3.1 An example of time-sampling and frequency counts to measure time spent in seat and disruptions. Time-sampling is done here using momentary time-sampling. At the end of each 30-second interval the observer immediately records whether the child is in seat at that instant. Interruptions are scored once for every time the child calls out. The child remained in seat for 40 percent of the time (4/10 intervals). The rate of interruptions was 1.2 per minute (7/5 minutes).

Time	30"	1'	1'30"	2'	2'30"	3'	3'30"	4'	4'30"	5'
In seat	+	+	−	−	−	−	−	−	+	+
Interupts	1	0	0	2	2	0	0	0	1	1

FIGURE 3.2 An example of an ABC diary for child with ADHD.

Time	Location	Antecedent	Behavior	Consequence
9:35	Classroom/ desk	Assigned math task	Left seat	Asked to return to seat
10:10	Classroom/ circle time	Asked to wait	Left seat	Guided back to seat
11:40	Classroom/ desk	Assigned reading	Left seat	Talked to peer

briefly train third parties, such as parents or teachers, to collect important information about the child's behaviors.

The collection of collateral information, including school records or medical consultations, including use of psychotropic medication and general health records, is another important aspect of ADHD assessment. If good school records are not available or if there is no current psychometric information, it may be necessary to conduct additional assessments of the child's intelligence and academic achievement. A simple psychometric battery may help determine whether the child is underperforming for his or her abilities and to assess the impact of the child's symptoms on schoolwork. Assessment also may help rule out a learning disability (LD) or general developmental delay as the cause of the child's symptoms. Table 3.1 breaks commonly used assessments of intellectual functioning and academic achievement into their application to various age groups.

TABLE 3.1   **Some psychometric assessments commonly used in child and adolescent work.**

Domain	Description
Intelligence	The Wechsler tests are the most widely used measures of intelligence. They yield a full-scale, verbal and performance IQ with a mean of 100 and a standard deviation of 15. There are multiple subtests such as arithmetic, vocabulary, picture completion, and digit span with a mean of 10 and a standard deviation of 3. Large verbal and performance differences and wide scatter of subtests may indicate effects of poor education, brain damage, or ADHD.
	WPPSI-III (Psychological Corporation, 2002): Revised in 2002; can be used for children in the age range 4 years through 6 1/2 years.
	WISC-III (Wechsler, 1991): Revised in 1991; can be used to assess children in the age range 6 years through 16 years 11 months.
	WAIS-III (Wechsler, 1997): Measures intelligence in the age range 16 years through 74 years; may be used with older adolescents.
	Leiter International Performance Scale (Roid et al. 1997) is used to assess intelligence using no verbal instructions. May be useful for children for whom English is not their first language and other nonverbal populations.
Adaptive behavior	Vineland Scales of Adaptive Behavior (Sparrow & Cicchetti, 1989) measures adaptive behavior in the domains of social, personal hygiene, language, and maladaptive behaviors. It is available in parent, caregiver, and teacher versions.
Psychiatric symptoms	Child Behavior Checklist (Achenbach & McConaughy, 1985) consists of a series of checklists covering ages 4 years through 18 years. Provides measures of internalizing and externalizing disorders, as well as scales for specific disorders.
	Childhood Autism Rating Scale (CARS; Schopler, Reichler, DeVellis, & Daly, 1980). Rates observable behaviors based on 30 minutes of observation of the child.

Treatment Plan

Treatment of ADHD may include contingency management; teaching academic, social, and self-regulation skills; environmental interventions (e.g., creating a

TABLE 3.2 **Psychotropic medications and their side effects commonly used for ADHD.**

Generic name	Trade name	Negative side effects
Methylphenidate	Ritalin	Common: nausea, vomiting, headache, dry mouth. Occasional: weight loss, appetite loss, diarrhea, constipation. Rare: Tourette's syndrome, blood pressure or pulse changes, toxic psychosis.
Dextroamphetamine	Dexedrine	Common: nausea, vomiting, headache, dry mouth. Occasional: weight loss, appetite loss, diarrhea, constipation. Rare: Tourette's syndrome, blood pressure or pulse changes, toxic psychosis.
Dextroamphetamine and methamphetamine	Adderall	Frequent: nausea, vomiting, headache, dry mouth. Common: weight loss, appetite loss, skin rash, diarrhea, constipation. Rare: Tourette's syndrome, blood pressure or pulse change, toxic psychosis.

dedicated homework desk; minimizing classroom distractions); psychoeducational interventions with parents, siblings, or teachers; and prescribed psychotropic medications. Many clinicians use a multimodal approach that combines several of these elements. Referral to a psychiatrist may be helpful to review the appropriateness of a trial of stimulant medications, which significantly reduce symptoms in 70 percent of children (Cantwell, 1996). Table 3.2 lists some commonly used psychotropic medications for ADHD.

CASE EXAMPLE
Gary

Referral: Gary was an 8-year-old African American boy initially referred for counseling because of increasing behavioral problems in the classroom. Gary's teacher complained that he could not complete his work, that he was easily distractible, and that he frequently interrupted other children. Gary's parents agreed that he played too roughly at home with his younger sister and with boys in his neighborhood and that he was constantly on the go. Gary's parents also reported they frequently had problems getting Gary to go to bed.

(Continued)

CASE EXAMPLE   **Continued**

Immediate concerns: Are there any immediate dangers to the client or other vulnerable persons?

There are no immediate dangers to Gary, his sister, or his peers. Gary's behavior is annoying and he sometimes hurts (or irritates) his peers, but he does not represent a danger to others.

Short-term goals: What goals need to be achieved in the first two to six sessions?

Gary's parents and teacher were given written information about ADHD and behavioral approaches to the management of ADHD symptoms. At a subsequent appointment, Gary's parents and the clinician reviewed how this information applied to Gary. Gary's teacher reported that she would like him to complete assigned tasks during each academic period of the day, a plan to which his parents were agreeable. Gary's parents and teacher created a home/school note to record Gary's satisfactory completion of the work he was assigned each period. Gary was to bring this note home each afternoon.

For the first two weeks, Gary's work assignments were reduced to small amounts of tasks he enjoyed. During weeks 3 to 6 the amount and difficulty of work was gradually increased and a similar contingency management strategy was added to teach Gary to play cooperatively with his sister, tidy up his room, and go to bed without resistance by 8:30 P.M. each night. Gary also was referred to a psychiatrist, who recommended he be placed on Ritalin if no improvements resulted from these interventions.

Long-term goals: What lifestyle changes and other long-term personal, relationship, and career goals need to be achieved?

In addition to maintaining his improved, more controlled behavior, a long-term goal identified by Gary's parents was to help him improve his academic performance. Gary stated also he would like to have more friends in his neighborhood and at school. These goals were achieved by expanding use of the home/school note and by continuing to use the contingent behavioral contract at home. The clinician also worked with Gary's school counselor to educate Gary's new teachers about his efforts and to arrange for his participation in a social skills group. Although the possibility of future psychopharmaceutical treatments was not ruled out, Gary maintained his more controlled behaviors at home and improved his engagement with his schoolwork over the subsequent twelve months. At a one-year follow up, Gary also reported he was enjoying improved friendships both at home and at school.

CASE EXAMPLE

Karen

Referral: Karen was a 14-year-old Anglo-American adolescent with somewhat below-average intelligence and academic performance. She had a long history of academic and behavioral problems that continued from early childhood through early adolescence.

Karen had taken Ritalin and other stimulants for several years with moderate benefit, but she continued to experience problems concentrating in class and avoiding distractions in interpersonal interactions. Karen's mother, with whom she lived alone, reported she was concerned that Karen would not graduate high school.

Immediate concerns: Are there any immediate dangers to the client or other vulnerable persons?

There are no immediate indications of danger to Karen or others. With any adolescent presenting with a wide variety of problems, the clinician should be alert to the possibility of drug abuse, although there are no indications of that here.

Short-term goals: What goals need to be achieved in the first two to six sessions?

A psychometric battery indicated Karen had a full-scale IQ of 86 and that her academic achievement, although generally below average, was in line with her tested intelligence. Combined with the other results of the battery, the clinician was able to rule out learning disabilities and mild mental retardation as explanations for Karen's symptoms. Karen stated she found academic work difficult and could not concentrate on hard work. She reported she did not particularly like school but recognized that she had to graduate. Karen worked with her clinician to set aside times and locations for studying, to learn how to break her assignments into smaller, more manageable chunks, and to redesign her bedroom to remove distractions from schoolwork. Because she also reported she had trouble focusing around other students, Karen made arrangements with her teacher to study privately in quiet parts of the library (contingent on evidence of her continued work). The clinician observed that Karen made several negative self-statements prior to and during academic work, and she was taught to change her cognitions about schoolwork using a simplified form of cognitive therapy.

Long-term goals: What lifestyle changes and other long-term personal, relationship, and career goals need to be achieved?

Karen identified her long-term goals as graduating and getting a satisfying job. Through a referral to her school counselor, she was connected with community resources that encouraged her to maintain her grades and seek out prevocational placement, as well as part-time employment, to build her job skills (and resume) prior to graduation.

Developmental Disorders

Diagnosis

DSM-IV includes a number of developmental disorders, but the two most commonly seen by counselors and psychologists are Mental Retardation and Autistic Disorder. Note that in DSM-IV, mental retardation is recorded on Axis II, whereas autism is recorded on Axis I. Mental retardation is characterized by three criteria: (1) significantly below-average intelligence, which is usually defined as a score of 70 or below on a well-normed intelligence test; (2) significant deficits in adaptive behavior, which typically is assessed by the Vineland Scales of Adaptive Behavior (VSAB); and (3) onset of symptoms before age 18. Mental retardation is classified as mild, moderate, severe, profound, or unspecified on the basis of the client's IQ score (see Table 3.3).

Diagnosis of mental retardation in older children, especially in the moderate through profound range, is relatively straightforward. However, assessment of mild mental retardation is more difficult, especially in younger children, children for whom English is a second language, children with additional disabilities (e.g., cerebral palsy or sensory disabilities), and children suffering the cumulative effects of poverty or other deprivations. It should be noted that the Individuals with Disabilities Education Act (IDEA, 1997), the federal legislation regulating special education in the United States, expressly forbids the diagnosis of mental retardation on the basis of a single test score such as an IQ or adaptive behavior test. Evaluators must also confirm that the person suffers significant adaptive deficits to make an MR diagnosis. Referrals for the evaluation of potentially mentally retarded adults, especially adults in the mental health system who often lack a clear developmental history, should be treated with caution.

Autistic Disorder is defined in DSM-IV by a qualitative impairment in social interaction and communication coupled with restricted, repetitive, and stereotyped patterns of behavior, interest, or activities. The client must also display at least two symptoms of qualitative impairment in social interaction, including impairments in nonverbal communication, such as eye gaze aversion, failure to develop peer relations, lack of spontaneous sharing with others, and lack of social or emotional reciprocity. At least one symptom of qualitative impairment in communication must also be present, such as delay or absence of development of spoken language, impaired ability to sustain interpersonal conversations, idiosyncratic or repetitive speech, and lack of spontaneous make-

---

TABLE 3.3   **Degrees of mental retardation and respective IQ ranges.**

Degree of mental retardation	IQ range
Mild	50–55 to approximately 70
Moderate	35–40 to 50–55
Severe	20–25 to 35–40
Profound	Below 20–25
Unspecified	Mental retardation is strongly suspected, but the person cannot be tested using valid procedures.

Note that when the IQ falls in range of cut-off scores, adaptive behavior and clinical impression are used to decide the degree of mental retardation (Grossman, 1977).

believe or imitative play appropriate to the client's developmental level. Finally, the client must exhibit at least one symptom of restricted, repetitive, or stereotyped behavior, interests, or activities, such as an abnormally intense or focused preoccupation, inflexible adherence to routines or rituals, stereotyped motor movements (e.g., hand-flapping or body-rocking), or persistent preoccupation with parts of objects. These delays must be present prior to the age of 3 years and must not be better accounted for by other developmental diagnoses. Approximately three-fourths of individuals diagnosed with autistic disorder also have mental retardation.

Assessment

Potential developmental disorders are evaluated using psychometric assessments of a client's intelligence and adaptive behavior. Various autism assessments are available, including the widely used Childhood Autism Rating Scale (Schopler, Reichler, DeVellis, & Daly, 1980). Several instruments also have been recently developed to screen, but not to diagnose, children as young as 18 months for autism and related developmental disorders (Baron-Cohen, Allen, & Gillberg, 1992). Both intellectual and adaptive behavior assessments can help a clinician identify the client's areas of strength and weakness, information that can be especially useful in targeting specific skills that might be taught in later interventions.

A good developmental history is an essential component of the diagnosis of Autistic Disorder. Some developmental disorders, such as Down syndrome or multiple physical disabilities, can be readily identified at birth, whereas others, such as Autistic Disorder and Mild Mental Retardation, are only identified gradually over time. Mild Mental Retardation may not be identified until grades 3 to 6, when the child exhibits a clear pattern of general adaptive deficits and persistent failure in the face of increasing academic demands. Direct observation is often essential, both to assess the child's adaptive behaviors and to assess the presence of unusual social, linguistic, and other behaviors.

An interview with family members is important to assess their level of understanding of their child's problems, as well as their to assess own stress and the impact of the child's disorder on siblings and family functioning. A review of collateral information from the child's schools including grades and past test results can also be helpful. A psychologist experienced in behavior analysis may be asked to perform an assessment of concurrent challenging behaviors, and a psychiatric referral may be indicated to review diagnoses, assess the utility of psychotropic medications, or evaluate medication side effects.

Clients with mental retardation are at greater risk for mental health problems, including a wide array of maladaptive behaviors that significantly restrict their daily functioning. Screening for the presence of these problems is good practice. Referral to specialized services is often indicated with MR clients, as this is a relatively specialized area of practice.

Treatment Plan

Effective treatment of clients with mental retardation and/or autism is multimodal. Multiple resources typically are used to address skill deficits; educate and support parents and other caregivers; facilitate client access to remedial, health, and living services; and provide educational and vocational placement. Clinical interventions typically are based on behavioral methods designed to teach specific skills. Problematic or excessive behaviors may be targeted using behavioral techniques coupled with an attempt to understand the client's motivation to engage in the challenging behaviors (e.g., to gain attention or to escape from adult requests). Early intervention for children with autism using 20 to 40 hours of skills training per week has recently become a very active area of practice, and some research suggests it may be very effective for some children with autism (Lovaas, 1987; Smith et al., 2000). Approximately one-third of clients diagnosed with mental retardation and autism receive psychotropic medications to alleviate specific, targeted problems such as aggression, self-injury, and behavioral noncompliance.

CASE EXAMPLE
Lydia

Referral: Lydia was a 4-year-old child referred for evaluation by her parents, who were engaged in a dispute with Lydia's school district about what constituted an appropriate education for their child. Lydia had been placed in a segregated special education classroom one year before the referral. She had been diagnosed with Autistic Disorder, but her school disputed the diagnosis. According to Lydia's parents, she had regressed since her placement in the segregated classroom and had learned very little. Lydia's school principal, however, reported that Lydia was doing as expected and that her parents were merely having a hard time adjusting to her disabilities. Hearing about an intensive early intervention program (consisting of 30 to 40 hours of individual teaching using applied behavior analysis each week), Lydia's parents requested this service from the school. The school refused, indicating that services Lydia currently was receiving met the requirements of IDEA regulations.

Immediate concerns: Are there any immediate dangers to the client or other vulnerable persons?

Although there is no immediate danger to Lydia, her parents felt that she was losing valuable developmental gains every day that she failed to participate in the more intensive program and that Lydia currently was regressing.

Short-term goals: What goals need to be achieved in the first two to six sessions?

The clinician's immediate short-term goals were to determine whether Lydia was receiving an appropriate education and, if appropriate, to assist her parents through their due-process claim with the school district. A review of the school's testing indicated that Lydia's developmental quotients had fallen from the mid-80s at age 3 years to the low 70s at age 4 years. School records suggested Lydia was not meeting any significant educational objectives. Over the previous three months, Lydia's mother obtained a copy of the intensive program and successfully taught Lydia prelanguage and language skills. A review of her test scores indicated that Lydia's development in these domains had increased eight months during that period. As a result of the due-process hearing, during which it was revealed that the school district had committed multiple procedural violations, Lydia's school agreed to provide her with 20 hours of one-on-one in classroom training using the intensive curriculum.

Long-term goals: What lifestyle changes and other long-term personal, relationship, and career goals need to be achieved?

At two-year follow-up Lydia's educational tests indicated she was functioning in the average range of intelligence. Direct observation indicated Lydia had no gross abnormalities in her social or language functioning. She talked a great deal, approached others appropriately, and played with her older brother. Overall, she appeared to be a very active child. Lydia's parents felt that although Lydia would probably continue to experience residual social and academic difficulties, due mostly to her excessive motor activity, she probably was not autistic. Lydia's parents and her school agreed that Lydia would benefit from continued exposure to mainstream classrooms and an afterschool play group. It was recommended that both Lydia's parents and her school staff should continue to monitor her day-to-day behavior and academic progress for any signs of regression.

CASE EXAMPLE
Mr. Montez

Referral: Mr. Montez, a 52-year-old Mexican American man with moderate mental retardation and a severe hearing impairment, was referred to a psychologist who specialized in the use of ABA for severe behavior disorders. Mr. Montez had lived in a group home and worked in a community vocational workshop for the previous ten years without incident, but recently exhibited increasing self-injurious behaviors that have resulted in scalp lacerations and bruises twelve times during the past year. Mr. Montez's group home indicated they hoped to fit him with a helmet designed to prevent further injury, but federal regulations require that a psychological consultation and treatment plan be in place before this intervention could be made.

Immediate concerns: Are there any immediate dangers to the client or other vulnerable persons?

There are significant risks of severe injury to Mr. Montez if his behaviors escalate or remain untreated. Mr. Montez also may present a danger to staff members who attempt to stop his behaviors.

Short-term goals: What goals need to be achieved in the first two to six sessions?

(Continued)

CASE EXAMPLE **Continued**

The clinician established several short-term goals with Mr. Montez, including clarification of his target behaviors and their environmental triggers and identification of alternative communication skills. After observing Mr. Montez in his natural contexts, the clinician recognized that many of his problematic behaviors emerged only in social settings. He often used gestures and noises to ask for snack items, and much of his self-injurious behavior revolved around frustrated requests for snacks and staff attention. An initial treatment plan was developed to teach Mr. Montez to point and use sign language to ask for preferred items. Extra opportunities to interact with staff also were scheduled at Mr. Montez's home. In order to protect him from injury, and because it was a consequence he did not like, staff were taught to apply the helmet immediately after Mr. Montez threatened to injure himself. Within the first month Mr. Montez had learned to communicate his requests for preferred items.

Long-term goals: What lifestyle changes and other long-term personal, relationship, and career goals need to be achieved?

The clinician's main long-term goals in working with Mr. Montez were to ensure his safety, reduce his self-inflicted injuries, and teach adaptive, valued behaviors. A review of Mr. Montez's treatment program was conducted quarterly. At one-year follow-up Mr. Montez had no visits to the emergency rooms for sutures to his head compared to twelve during the previous year. Mr. Montez also continued his communication gains and learned to interact appropriately with staff to receive their positive attention.

Learning Disorders

Diagnosis

Learning Disorders (LDs) are defined as learning difficulties confined to specific areas of academic competence. Learning Disorders typically are diagnosed when standardized tests reveal a discrepancy (e.g., greater than one standard deviation) between a client's scores in a specific area compared to his or her overall intelligence. The DSM-IV recognizes four types of learning disabilities: Reading Disorder, Mathematics Disorder, Disorders of Written Expression, and Learning Disorder Not Otherwise Specified. These impairments must not be due to a sensory deficit.

Assessment

It is critical to LD assessment that the clinician conduct an adequate psychometric evaluation and a systematic application of the DSM-IV diagnostic criteria. Some research suggests LD diagnoses often are used in the place of diagnoses of mild mental retardation (McMillan et al., 1996). A diagnosis of LD should occur only when a systematic evaluation of intelligence and academic performance reveals a *specific* deficit in reading, writing, motor skills, or language. (See Figure 3.3

FIGURE 3.3 Examples of test profiles for assessing learning disabilities. In example A, academic performance is depressed across all subjects areas compared to intelligence. This suggests a more global academic underachievement, rather than a single specific LD. In example C, both intelligence and all measures of academic achievement are depressed, which suggests mild mental retardation, rather than LD. Only example B is an example of a specific LD, because the client's math scores alone are depressed more than 15 points below the client's general intelligence score.

	Intelligence	Reading Comprehension	Reading Expression	Math	Language Comprehension	Language Expression
A. 100		85	89	79	85	92
B. 120		125	120	100	125	130
C. 65		65	68	60	68	65

for examples of LD assessment profiles.) Interviews with the child and his or her parents and teachers may be useful in general terms, but they are not a substitute for psychometric evaluation. A review of collateral school grades and tests of achievement is helpful as well.

Treatment Plan

Clients with learning disabilities typically receive educational modifications intended to accommodate their learning differences and, in some cases, to remediate circumscribed cognitive concerns such as reading or memory problems. LD clients also may learn compensatory behaviors, such as rewriting/distilling course notes, taping lectures, or reading complicated passages aloud, that allow them to address specific deficits they face in their academic lives. Parental support and psychoeducation also may be important, and some clients' families may benefit from clinician's efforts to help them locate and access existing support resources in their communities.

CASE EXAMPLE

Alan

Referral: Alan was a 9-year-old child referred for LD assessment because of poor grades. A psychometric evaluation revealed that Alan possessed a full-scale IQ of 105 but exhibited a reading quotient of 83 with mildly depressed scores in other areas of academic performance. There were no other problems apparent.

(Continued)

CASE EXAMPLE   Continued

Immediate concerns: Are there any immediate dangers to the client or other vulnerable persons?

This problem does not pose any immediate danger to Alan or to others.

Short-term goals: What goals need to be achieved in the first two to six sessions?

Remediation of a specific reading disability cannot be achieved in a few sessions. Instead, Alan's parents were educated about the importance of reading for comprehension (e.g., not just reading aloud). Alan's parents agreed to meet with his teacher once a week to identify outside reading that could be shared between his school and home. Alan's parents agreed to share brief reading sessions with him every evening and to present reading as an enjoyable, rather than anxiety-provoking, activity. In order to promote Alan's sense of mastery over reading, Alan was asked to assist his younger siblings by reading to them from a very easy book from time to time. Alan's parents also enrolled him in reading classes over the semester break and consulted with his school psychologist to develop an individualized education plan for Alan for the academic year.

Long-term goals: What lifestyle changes and other long-term personal, relationship, and career goals need to be achieved?

Alan's reading scores should be monitored on a regular basis, with repeated psychometric assessment of reading if necessary. Alan's reading intervention plan should be continuously evaluated and periodically reformulated.

Separation Anxiety Disorder

Diagnosis

DSM-IV defines Separation Anxiety Disorder as developmentally inappropriate and excessive anxiety relating to a child's separation from home or a parent. At least three anxiety symptoms relating to separation are required, such as school refusal, nightmares, and physical symptoms (e.g., nausea or headaches). These symptoms must be present for at least four weeks, onset before age 15 years, and cause clinically significant distress or impairment to the child. Finally, these problems must not occur exclusively during the course of Pervasive Developmental Disorder, Schizophrenia or another Psychotic Disorder, or Panic Disorder with Agoraphobia.

Assessment

Assessment of separation anxiety can be conducted through clinical interviews with the child and her or his family members and teachers. Some psychometric measures such as the Child Behavior Checklist (Achenbach & McConaughy, 1985) highlight general anxiety symptoms that can be explored during these interviews. Useful information also can be obtained by observing the child with the parents and during attempted separations.

Treatment Plan

As with other anxiety disorders, separation anxiety is often treated effectively with exposure-based therapies that gradually expose the client to the stressor he or she fears. In this case, clients are often exposed, under relaxing conditions, to incrementally longer periods of separation from parental figures. If appropriate, this may be done in their home. Situations in which family members wittingly or unwittingly promote a child's separation anxiety, such as a parent who is affirmed by the child's separation anxiety or a parent who projects his or her own anxieties onto the child, may require more systems-based interventions.

CASE EXAMPLE
Cely

Referral: Cely was a 9-year-old African American girl whose mother described her as "always clingy ever since she was a small child." Cely has suffered a variety of illnesses during her childhood, including bouts of asthma that frequently required medical attention and assistance from her parents throughout the night. Over the past year, Cely has become more withdrawn at school and has often refused to let go of her mother, complaining of chest pains and wheezing, when her mother has dropped her off at school. At times Cely becomes hysterical if separated from her mother and has missed school entirely.

Immediate concerns: Are there any immediate dangers to the client or other vulnerable persons?

There may be an immediate danger to Cely if her asthma is not being managed. The clinician should ensure that she is receiving appropriate medical attention and that her parents are complying with her treatment regime.

Short-term goals: What goals need to be achieved in the first two to six sessions?

The clinician established two short-term goals with Cely and her parents: comfortable separation from her mother and ensuring that Cely's parents do not unwittingly reinforce her sick-role behavior. Graded in-vivo desensitization sessions were conducted during the first six sessions of therapy, including doll play and coloring (two of her favorite activities), to reinforce her ability to relax. Cely's mother was withdrawn for progressively longer periods from Cely's therapy sessions as Cely became more comfortable playing and coloring alone. After the third therapy session, Cely's mother began integrating this protocol into her interactions with Cely at home.

Long-term goals: What lifestyle changes and other long-term personal, relationship, and career goals need to be achieved?

(continued)

The therapist should attend, long-term, to helping Cely grow into an independent, assertive, and self-reliant child. Cely's parents should be educated about the management of her asthma to ensure that they reinforce her independence and, to an appropriate extent, self-management rather than her past solicitous behaviors. Special attention should be given to periods of transition and new stressors with Cely, including future transitions into new classrooms and schools. Giving Cely the chance to see her new classrooms and schools in advance, or to meet her new teacher or classmates before the new school year begins, could be especially helpful.

Oppositional Defiant Disorder and Conduct Disorder

Diagnosis

DSM-IV defines Oppositional Defiant Disorder (ODD) as a pattern of negativistic, hostile, and defiant behavior that has been present for at least six months. At least four of the following symptoms must be present to diagnose a child with ODD: frequently loses temper, argues with adults or defies adult requests, deliberately annoys others or blames others for mistakes, displays anger or resentment, and displays spiteful or vindictive behavior. These symptoms must cause clinically significant impairment in the child's educational or social functioning. Psychotic Disorders and Antisocial Personality Disorder (ASPD) must be ruled out.

DSM-IV defines Conduct Disorder (CD) as a repetitive, persistent pattern of violating others' rights or age-appropriate social norms. Three of the following symptoms must be present for at least twelve months: aggression to people or animals, destruction of property, deceit and theft, and serious violations of rules. These symptoms must cause clinically significant impairment, and, if the client is over 18 years old, must not be part of a pattern of ASPD (see below).

Oppositional Defiant Disorder is generally a less severe disorder than Conduct Disorder. It may develop into CD. CD similarly may be a precursor of ASPD, which is defined by DSM-IV as a pervasive pattern of disregard for, or violation of, the rights of others evidenced at least since the person has reached age 15 years. (Note that ASPD is sometimes referred to as "psychopathy" or "sociopathic personality.")

Assessment

Assessment of ODD and CD begins with a good clinical interview. Because deceit and dishonesty characterize these disorders, it is prudent to include family members or school staff in interviews where appropriate. Establishing rapport may be difficult with these clients, and the information they provide should not be taken only at face value.

It is important to assess for possible substance problems, learning disabilities, and mood disorders when working with clients with ODD or CD. Mood disorders and/or learning disabilities in particular are often masked by an oppositional child's behaviors: Parents and teachers often miss the child's struggles beneath his or her abrasiveness. Collateral information from the client's school is helpful to evaluate school attendance, grade achievement, and school-failure experiences. In some cases, a psychometric battery consisting of an assessment of intelligence and educational achievement coupled with a general screen for behavior disorders can be useful. Such a battery can help identify whether the child's failure is complicated by low intelligence, whether he or she faces particular difficulties with particular classes, and whether he or she has a concurrent learning disability. A psychiatric referral may be helpful to determine whether medications should be prescribed to alleviate any impulse control or concurrent mood disorder symptoms.

Treatment Plan

Any treatment plan for an ODD or CD client should recognize the danger the client might present to self or others. Reckless and dangerous behavior, such as stealing vehicles, substance use, or dangerous sexual behaviors, may present particular difficulties. In some cases, parents or school staff should be alerted to prevent the client from accessing weapons or getting into dangerous situations.

Short-term goals for children and adolescents with ODD or CD should include reestablishing patterns of school attendance and socially appropriate behaviors with peers and adults. Social skills training and anger management efforts may also be helpful for many clients with ODD/CD (Taylor et al., 1999). An important initial step is to establish agreement between the client, the client's parents, and the client's teachers about reasonable standards for behavior at home and in the classroom—standards that permit neither aggression nor defiance, but which also are not rigidly unforgiving (Raser, 1995). Once these standards have been agreed on, contingency contracting and self-monitoring/self-regulation strategies can be designed to promote them. Additional assistance for educational problems may be indicated for some clients, such as additional tutoring or classroom modifications. Clients at risk of alcohol and drug problems should be referred to a specialist if these areas are outside the primary clinician's competence.

Although clients with ODD/CD often present their worst sides to intervening professionals, counselors and psychologists should not overlook ODD/CD clients' strengths, which in many cases include intelligence, interpersonal skills, or sustained interest in particular academic disciplines (e.g., science, history, literature, math).

Establishing long-term goals such as graduation from high school, prevention of teen pregnancy, acquiring vocational skills, and establishing good relationships with family and peers can help ODD/CD clients capitalize on their strengths and buffer against relapse and poor adult adjustment. Timely intervention will help many clients with ODD/CD to be successful within mainstream educational settings. For a significant minority, however, placement in alternative educational settings that provide more informal instruction or participation in programs emphasizing vocational rather than academic achievement may be more appropriate.

CASE EXAMPLE
Simon

Referral: Simon was an 11-year-old Anglo-American adolescent who was shy, miserable, and frequently in trouble at school. He often would report to school but immediately sneak away to hang out with friends on the street. His grades had been average, but were gradually dropping. He stole from peers, shoplifted, committed minor acts of vandalism with his peers, and occasionally would sniff glue or other solvents to get high.

Immediate concerns: Are there any immediate dangers to the client or other vulnerable persons?

The abuse of certain solvents can lead to death by aspiration of vomit or by suffocation from the use of plastic bags over the head or from using substances that coat the user's lungs and prevent the absorption of oxygen. Simon and his parents should immediately be educated about these dangers. His parents also should be made aware of signs of solvent abuse, such as redness around the nose, dizziness, disorientation, and hoarding of solvents in the home or at school.

Short-term goals: What goals need to be achieved in the first two to six sessions?

Simon's parents were most concerned about Simon's truancy and socialization with juvenile delinquents outside school. They also were concerned that Simon's behavioral problems would escalate if he fell further behind in his classes. Simon was clear he did not like school, stating that it was boring and that his teachers picked on him. Simon stated he felt the students at his school "were all geeks" and that he was intellectually inferior to his classmates.

During the second session of therapy, the clinician negotiated a behavioral contract with Simon and his parents in which Simon agreed to consistently attend school and his parents agreed not to nag him or even discuss his grades on the condition that his teacher reported he was making satisfactory progress. Simon's teachers were counseled that emphasis initially should be placed on Simon simply being in school and not on his academic achievement. Simon was expected to make academic progress within four weeks. Simon's parents agreed to buy him one of four favorite video games contingent on each of his first four weeks of consistent school attendance.

Long-term goals: What lifestyle changes and other long-term personal, relationship, and career goals need to be achieved?

After a period of a few weeks, Simon's attendance at school improved to a reasonable, though imperfect, degree. Simon then agreed to work with his counselor on assertiveness and other social skills. He agreed to read some literature on drug abuse that he could discuss with his counselor but did not want to attend a drug education group. Simon and his counselor agreed these strategies may be used in lieu of more intensive interventions based on his continued reengagement with school and absence of substance-using behaviors. Simon improved at school and stopped seeing his counselor after five sessions. A follow-up phone call with his parents confirmed reports from his teachers that he was behaving appropriately and making developmental gains in his academic and social interactions.

Unfortunately, a couple of years later, Simon was involved in a fight at school during which he threw a rock at another boy, blinding him in one eye. Simon was convicted of assault and battery and was placed in a juvenile facility for six months, an experience that scared him considerably. After his release, he returned to school and learned a number of vocational skills in addition to modest performance in his academic courses. As a young adult, Simon was able to maintain employment in skilled manual work and was able to maintain successful relationships with others. He was eventually married and had two children.

Differential Diagnosis Related to School Refusal

Another common reason for child referrals is refusal to attend school. Although no DSM-IV diagnosis exists for "School Refusal Disorder" or "School Phobia," refusing to attend or remain in school can lead to significant problems for children. School refusal behaviors also can reflect a wide range of DSM-IV disorders, including Separation Anxiety Disorder, specific phobia (e.g., travel phobia or fear of student crowds at especially large schools), Agoraphobia with or without Panic Attacks, Social Phobia, Learning Disorder, Conduct Disorder, Oppositional Defiant Disorder, or Antisocial Personality Disorder. It is also possible that a child's school refusal behaviors may be normal reactions to bullying, teasing, or humiliation at school without any underlying psychopathology. It is therefore important to make a careful differential diagnosis when dealing with a child or adolescent whose presenting problem is school refusal. (See Figure 3.4 for guidelines in this area.)

FIGURE 3.4 Guidelines for the differential diagnosis of school refusal.

Observation	Possible diagnoses
Anxiety prominent	Consider SAD, Social Phobia Disorder, specific phobia (such as travel-related phobia), Agoraphobic Disorder, Panic Disorder.
Externalizing behaviors prominent	Consider ODD, CD, ASPD.
Other	Consider LD, normal reaction to bullying or humiliation at school.

Treatment

School refusal problems are handled by treating the diagnosed problems in combination, if necessary, with contingency management/behavior modification interventions specifically targeted to the child's school attendance.

Ethical and Professional Issues in Child and Adolescent Work

Consent and Assent

Parents have legal control of their children until they reach the age of 18 years. As far as the law is concerned, even 17-year-old children are rather like the property of the parents. Children are therefore unable to give informed consent for counseling services. Although this typically is a less salient issue with younger children, parental consent often impedes on therapeutic work with adolescent clients. For example, a parent could consent to treatment of a child without the child's agreement, in which case the clinician faces ethical and legal decisions. In this case, the clinician should attempt to seek a solution and gain the child's *assent* to treatment. The term "assent" is used to indicate the agreement to the treatment where the person cannot legally consent. If the child fails to assent to treatment, it may be possible to find an alternate solution agreeable to both the child and to his or her parents. If no such solution can be negotiated and the child continues to refuse participation in treatment, many clinicians may feel uncomfortable continuing to work with him or her. In such cases the clinician should not abandon the client but instead work with the family to find another treatment referral.

After reaching age 18, the client is a legal adult and may refuse treatment or consent to treatment without the parents' assent unless they obtain guardianship through the courts. Sometimes a young adult may be factually incompetent, but legally competent (e.g., young adults with mental retardation or a psychotic disorder). In these situations it may be necessary to help the client's parents or other family members obtain either full or limited guardianship through the courts. In the meantime, the law assumes a person who has not been declared incompetent is in fact competent. In this situation some form of assent from the client should be documented.

When a parent's legal guardianship has been terminated due to divorce, remarriage, or abuse and neglect, considerable caution should be exercised in the area of consent. Before initiating treatment, copies of the signed divorce papers should be obtained and kept in the child's file. Information should not be released without copies of court papers. Similarly, information should be released to other persons, such as grandparents, stepparents, foster parents, or other relatives only with written consent from the custodial relative. Persons claiming to be custodial parents should be treated with respect and given the information they need to access the child's record or to consent to treatment, but only after the clinician has a copy of the court order.

Release of records to custodial parents should be done carefully. It is possible that a clinician's innocent comments or opinions about other family members could show up as evidence in a court case. It may be necessary to edit and remove all comments from the child's records relating to other family members, with a cover letter explaining why this has been done.

Parents and children aged 18 years and older have full access to all school records, including any records made by a counselor or psychologist. Because the clinician's full records may include raw test scores, parents' rights to this information may present conflicts between APA or ACA ethical standards and the law. APA standards dictate that test scores should only be released to persons competent to interpret them and that test items be kept secure (see discussion in Chapter 1). In these cases it would be both legal and ethical to release test scores to another professional who is competent to interpret them for the child's parents. In certain circumstances, however, such as under a court order, the clinician may be legally forced to release test scores directly to the parents.

When a mental health professional suspects that a child may have experienced physical abuse, sexual abuse, or neglect, she or he is mandated to report these suspicions to the appropriate protective authority (see discussion in Chapter 1). Failing to report suspected abuse or neglect may be both illegal and unethical. Whereas observable marks or direct, credible reports from a child make the clinician's job easy, less credible reports may present a dilemma about whether to report the allegations. As a guideline, the clinician should err on the side of reporting her or his suspicions and letting them be confirmed or disconfirmed by representatives of the appropriate protective agency.

Similar dilemmas can arise when a child or family member confidentially reports abuse that she or he asks the clinician not to report for fear of further violence or other negative consequences. In such cases, state laws still require mental health professional to report the abuse. This aside, however, clinicians should also be cautious about reporting suspicions based on clearly flimsy evidence. False reports of abuse can cause tremendous harm to children and family members alike, as well as provide fuel for lawsuits against clinicians. Suspicions based on the interpretation of repressed memories, play with anatomically correct dolls, therapist-guided drawings, or vague feelings should be very carefully weighed against the well-being of the client and the professional standards of practice.

CASE EXERCISE

Miguel

Miguel is a 15-year-old Mexican American adolescent who is brought to you by his parents. Miguel's parents complain that Miguel respects neither them nor his teachers, reporting that he treats his home "like a motel" (e.g., staying out late at night) and that

(Continued)

CASE EXAMPLE **Continued**

he argues with his family members and has threatened his father with violence. Although Miguel performed within an average range at school until last year, his frequent truancy this year has contributed to dramatic declines in his grades. Miguel's teacher complains that he and his friends talk back, disrupt the class, and often get into fights with other students. The teacher also believes Miguel may be intimidating other students into giving him money. Miguel presents in your office with little eye contact, unsmiling expressions, and arms crossed. He appears to be an angry young man.

Study Questions

1. What are your diagnostic impressions?

2. What is your plan for assessment?

3. What is your treatment plan?

4. If you learn that Miguel's parents immigrated to the United States from Guadalajara, Mexico, thirty years ago, how might this factor into your work with him?

5. Two months into therapy, Miguel asks to see the records you have kept of your work with him, claiming the Freedom of Information Act demands he be permitted to see them. Should you release the records to Miguel?

6. You receive a call from a man who claims to be Miguel's legal parent. Stating that he divorced Miguel's mother ten years ago and reporting he is angry to learn Miguel is "seeing some kind of shrink," he demands to know the details of your work with Miguel. What do you tell the man on the phone—in what exact words? Should you confirm that you are seeing Miguel?

7. Miguel confidentially admits to you that he and his friends occasionally smoke marijuana. Do you report this information to his parents? Do you report this information to the police? Ten months later Miguel is involved in a car wreck under the influence of marijuana in which his passenger is injured. After learning that you knew Miguel had used marijuana in the past, the passenger's parents sue you for malpractice. Are you liable for their son's injury?

REFERENCES

Achenbach, T. M., & McConaughy, S. H. (1985). *Child interview checklist self-report form; Child interview checklist-observation form.* Burlington: University of Vermont.

Baron-Cohen, S., Allen, J., & Gillberg, C. (1992). Can autism be detected at 18 months? The needle, the haystack, and the CHAT. *British Journal of Psychiatry, 161,* 839–843.

Cantwell, D. P. (1996). Attention deficit disorder: A review of the past 10 years. *Journal of the American Academy of Child and Adolescent Psychiatry, 35,* 978–987.

Grossman, H. (1977). *Manual on terminology and classification in mental retardation.* Washington, DC: American Association on Mental Retardation.

Kronenberger, W. G., & Meyer, R. G. (1996). *The child clinician's handbook.* Boston: Allyn and Bacon.

Lovaas, I. O. (1987). Behavioral treatment and normal educational and intellectual functioning in young autistic children. *Journal of Consulting and Clinical Psychology, 55*, 3–9.

McMillan, D. L., Gresham, F. M., Siperstein, G. N., & Bocian, K. M. (1996). The labyrinth of IDEA: School decisions on referred students with subaverage intelligence. *American Journal on Mental Retardation, 101*, 161–174.

The Psychological Corporation. (2002). *Wechsler Preschool and Primary Scaled Intelligence—Third Edition (WPPSI-III)*. San Antonio, TX: The Psychological Corporation

Raser, J. (1995). *Raising children you can live with*. Houston, TX: Bayou Publishing.

Roid, G. H., Miller, H., & Lucy, J. (1997). *Leiter International Performance Scale-Revised*. Wood Dole, IL: Stoeling Company.

Schopler, E., Reichler, R. J., DeVellis, R. F., & Daly, K. (1980). Toward objective classification of childhood autism: Childhood Autism Rating Scale (CARS). *Journal of Autism and Developmental Disorders, 10*, 91–103.

Smith T., Groen, A. D., & Wynn, J. W. (2000). Randomized trial of early intervention for children with pervasive developmental disorder. *American Journal on Mental Retardation, 105*, 269–285.

Sparrow, S. S., & Cicchetti, D. V. (1989). The Vineland Adaptive Behavior Scales. In C. S. Newmark (Ed.), *Major psychological assessment instruments* (vol. 2., pp. 199–231). Boston: Allyn and Bacon.

Taylor, T. K., Eddy, J. M., & Biglan, A. (1999). Interpersonal skills training to reduce aggressive and delinquent behavior: Limited evidence and the need for an evidence-based system of care. *Clinical Child and Family Psychology Review, 2*, 169–182.

Wechsler, D. (1991). *Wechsler Intelligence Scale for Children—Third Edition - WISC-III*. San Antonio, TX: The Psychological Corporation.

Wechsler, D. (1997). *Wechsler Adult Intelligence Scale—Third Edition (WAIS-III)*. San Antonio, TX: The Psychological Corporation.

4 Anxiety Disorders

CHAPTER OVERVIEW

1. Anxiety disorders include Specific Phobias, Social Phobia, Panic Disorder, Agoraphobia with or without Panic Attacks, and Generalized Anxiety Disorder. Anxiety symptoms include physical symptoms such as fear, sweating, palpitations, and dizziness.

2. Clients with anxiety disorders often report fears of fainting, going mad, or some catastrophic event such as fainting or dying.

3. Assessments include clinical interviews and symptom questionnaires. Assessments should rule out medical disorders and medication side effects that can present as anxiety disorders. Assessment should also review co-morbid disorders, such as mood disorders.

4. Interventions can include relaxation training, various forms of exposure therapy, systematic desensitization, and cognitive therapy. Psychotropic medications may also be helpful.

Specific Phobias and Social Phobia

Phobias are the most common of anxiety disorders. One in ten U.S. men and women develop a phobia at some time during their lives, fewer than 35 percent of which abate on their own (Kessler et al., 1994; Reich, Goldenberg, Vasile, & Goisman et al., 1994; Yonkers, Dyck, & Keller, 2001). Although most phobias are more prevalent among women than men, they are experienced by roughly equal numbers of male and female children.

Phobias are marked by fear plus avoidance, an intense, unreasonable anxiety associated with an object or situation that a person unsurprisingly goes out of the way to avoid. For many people, phobic anxiety symptoms become so extreme as to develop into panic attacks (see Panic Disorder and Agoraphobia, beginning on p. 93). The avoidance symptoms associated with phobia prevent many phobic clients from engaging in ordinary patterns of living.

Phobias may be separated into three general categories. *Specific phobias* occur in association with circumscribed objects or situations, such as animals, spiders, or tall buildings. *Social phobias* occur in social situations in which a person becomes unreasonably concerned about her or his scrutiny by others. A third category of phobias, *agoraphobia*, typically is associated with panic disorder and is discussed below.

Many people experience fears associated with specific objects or situations, and many such fears are reasonable. A child who fears jumping from a three-story building, for example, might be said to possess a healthy fear that prevents him from breaking his neck. For some people, however, fears of particular objects or situations become so unreasonable and intense that they interfere significantly with the progress of their lives. In such cases, provided the situation is not social, the diagnosis of specific phobia is assigned.

The essential feature of a specific phobia is a persistent, unreasonable fear of a circumscribed object or situation. According to the DSM-IV, exposure to the feared stimulus nearly always precipitates an immediate flush of anxiety symptoms that the person recognizes to be excessive. He or she also avoids the phobic object or situation, or else endures it with great anxiety or distress, to the degree that his or her occupational, academic, social, or relational functioning is significantly disrupted. When these symptoms are experienced for six months or longer the person meets the criteria for a DSM-IV diagnosis of Specific Phobia. The following disorders should be ruled out when making this diagnosis: Panic Disorder with Agoraphobia, Social Phobia, Obsessive-Compulsive Disorder, Separation Anxiety Disorder, and Post-Traumatic Stress Disorder.

A diagnosis of social phobia should be considered when a person inordinately fears social situations, such as public speaking or conversing at a party, or situations that involve performing a behavior in the presence of others, such as urinating or washing hands in a public bathroom or eating at a restaurant. Social phobias may be specific, that is, involving fears about a particular, circumscribed social situation such as making a speech, or they may be generalized across a variety of social situations. According to the DSM-IV, the diagnosis of Social Phobia is assigned when a person inordinately fears embarrassment in social or performance situations and responds with immediate anxiety or avoidance when exposed to them. Although adults or adolescents with Social Phobia recognize that their fears are excessive, socially phobic children may not. In all cases, however, the anxiety or avoidance significantly interferes with the person's life routines or causes significant distress. Children and adolescents may experience a transient form social anxiety that does not qualify for DSM-IV diagnosis. Symptoms therefore must be present six months or longer among individuals younger than 18 years old to be diagnosed with Social Phobia.

As with specific phobia, diagnoses of Panic Disorder and Separation Anxiety should be ruled out, although these may be assigned in addition to the diagnosis of Social Phobia if warranted. Body Dysmorphic Disorder and Schizoid or Avoidant Personality Disorders also overlap symptoms of Social Phobia and should be ruled out as well. Whereas Body Dysmorphic Disorder invokes fears about one's appearance (usually the appearance of specific body parts), Social Phobia is associated with broader fears about one's scrutiny as a person or conversational participant. Unlike social phobics, individuals with Schizoid Personality Disorder lack interest in interacting with others and typically are not as concerned about how they may be perceived. In many ways, Avoidant Personality Disorder may be the most difficult diagnosis to differentiate from Social Phobia. Individuals with Avoidant Personality Disorder present with many of the same symptoms as Social Phobia, including entrenched patterns of avoiding social interactions for fear of being negatively evaluated. This additional diagnosis, therefore, should be considered when warranted.

Assessment

A thorough history should be taken to assess for other mental conditions, as well as for other phobias, that may co-occur with a phobic client's presenting concerns. Specific and social phobias commonly occur with other psychological disorders, including other anxiety disorders, such as Panic Disorder and Generalized Anxiety Disorder, and substance abuse disorders. As many as 50 percent of patients with Social Phobia may also suffer Major Depression (Ballenger et al., 1998; Lydiard, 2001; Perugi et al., 2001; Van Ameringen et al., 1991; Weiller et al., 1996).

In particular, clients with Social Phobia typically also experience a wide range of other psychosocial difficulties. Research suggests Social Phobia may be associated with a history of limited interactions with relational partners, high divorce rates, and high rates of affiliative coupling with other socially phobic partners. Social Phobia also appears to be associated with family and employment difficulties and in children is associated with academic underachievement and social isolation (Rappaport et al., 2001; Schneier et al., 1994).

When working with children and adolescents, historical information should be gathered not only from parents, but also from schoolteachers (with proper consent), who may be especially helpful in assessing the degree of interference the symptoms may cause in the child's interpersonal and academic functioning. Parents' and teachers' reports also may be helpful in ruling out a diagnosis of Separation Anxiety Disorder.

Treatment

Exposure therapies are based on the view that phobic symptoms emerge when a person associates neutral stimuli with physically threatening or fearful events. Because the avoidance of these previously benign stimuli subsequently reduces the anxiety the phobic individual experiences when in danger of being around them, the person's avoidance behavior (i.e., his or her behavioral symptoms) becomes rewarding in itself. Exposing the phobic individual to the feared stimulus interrupts this reinforcement cycle and increases his or her repertoire of response behaviors.

Exposure to feared stimuli may take place either directly or vicariously. Just as many phobias appear to be learned through observation, vicarious observation of other people's exposure to phobic stimuli often reduces the anxiety many phobic individuals experience when exposed to such stimuli themselves. In-vivo, or live, exposure to feared objects or situations is an extensively evaluated and effective treatment for phobias. In-vivo exposure may be graduated or may involve immediate, massive exposure. In graduated exposure the client and therapist create a hierarchy of fear-evoking situations graded from least to most fear-provoking. The client is then exposed to the lowest item in the hierarchy until it no longer evokes anxiety. Once this level of exposure is mastered, the client progresses to the next step in the hierarchy until she or he is able, eventually, to control his or her reactions to the highest level of exposure. Flooding is the opposite approach to graduated exposure treatments. In flooding, the client is exposed to the most fearful situation he or she can tolerate for as long as possible—as long as 90 to 180 minutes. Although initially the fear the client experiences may be very intense, these fears typically subside as time goes by. Other approaches to treatment of phobias involve imagined, instead of in-vivo, exposure. Again, these exposures may be either graduated or immediate. The latter form is known as implosion. Novice therapists without training should not attempt flooding or implosion techniques.

One of the most influential treatments for phobias, including complex social phobias, is based on Wolpe's (1958) work on reciprocal inhibition. In reciprocal disinhibition, the client learns a response that is incompatible with fear. A series of relaxation exercises typically is employed, although other procedures such as assertiveness or play (e.g., in children) are sometimes used. In Wolpe's approach, an exposure hierarchy is developed and clients are exposed, initially, to the least fearful situation imaginally while maintaining a deep state of relaxation. As each step is mastered without anxiety, the client progressively advances

---

FIGURE 4.1   Four alternate approaches to conducting exposure therapy for Agoraphobia without Panic Attacks.

Nature of fear	Exposure therapy
1. Fear of confusing perceptual situations	Exposure to perceptually confusing situations (e.g. elevators, turns in stairs, open spaces, open stairs)
2. Fear of panic symptoms	Exposure to physical symptoms of anxiety (e.g. deliberately hyperventilating)
3. Fear of embarrassment	Exposure to socially embarrassing situations (e.g., dropping things in front of others)
4. Travel phobia	Expose to traveling independently
5. Fear of criticism	Exposure to criticism by others

FIGURE 4.2 **Example of a hierarchy for a Social Phobia.**

Step (SUDS)	Description
Step 1 (5)	Talking to spouse about day's events.
Step 2 (10)	Talking to spouse about money.
Step 3 (20)	Talking to spouse about upcoming family event.
Step 4 (40)	Going to family event with spouse.
Step 5 (70)	Going to family event with sister.
Step 6 (90)	Going to family event alone.

through the hierarchy until mastering her or his highest level of feared stimuli. See Figure 4.2 for an example of an exposure hierarchy for social phobia.

Generally, psychotropic medications have not been thought to be effective for treating specific phobias (Capafons, 2001; see Benjamin et al., 2000, for contrasting view). However, medications are often used to treat specific anxiety symptoms experienced by individuals with social phobia in the hopes of enabling them to more confidently gain exposure to their feared social situations. Some antidepressants, for instance, appear to reduce social anxiety symptoms and may promote some individuals' abilities to engage in increased social behaviors. In addition, beta-blocker medications may reduce the autonomic physiological symptoms experienced by many individuals with performance anxiety associated with public performances. However, when considering these medications (via a psychiatric referral), it is important to recognize that the side effects of withdrawal from certain anxiolytic medications can mimic the symptoms of anxiety. In addition, some clients may use fast-acting anxiolytics or alcohol as a way to quickly relieve the discomfort of anxiety symptoms.

Cognitive therapies have been effectively used with some phobias. In social phobia, for example, the client's cognitions about his or her interpersonal interactions may play a role in the development and maintenance of phobic symptoms. Research suggests many socially phobic clients overestimate other people's social competence and judgmentalness. In addition, some research suggests clients with social phobia may underestimate their own social competence and may be more sensitive to their commission of routine conversational errors such as word slippage, imperceptible tremors, and nervousness in social situations (Alden & Wallace, 1995; Woody & Rodriguez, 2000). Unfortunately, such distorted appraisals often result in an increased self-consciousness that competes for cognitive attention with the person's management of social interactions, amplifying his or her actual errors and self-fulfilling his or her concerns. Cognitive interventions to challenge and reinforce changes in these patterns should be considered, therefore, as an adjunct to exposure-based behavioral interventions when treating social phobia.

Assertiveness and social skills training also should be considered with socially phobic clients. These interventions especially have been shown to be effective in increasing the resilience of at-risk children and adolescents against the secondary effects of social phobia (cf. Vera & Gaubatz, 2001). Because specific and social phobias often induce secondary gains, such as sympathy and increased attention from others, family therapies may also be indicated to support changes in particularly entrenched phobic behavior patterns. Conversely, because long-term patterns of phobic avoidance may influence other areas of a person's life, occupational, academic, or relational counseling may be indicated to restore healthy functioning in these areas and promote resilience against the development of other psychosocial problems.

CASE EXAMPLE
Mark

Referral: Mark, a 33-year-old information systems engineer, has worked for the past twelve months as a mid-level manager in a small but growing computer services firm, a job that he really enjoys, except for the presentations. Approximately every four to six weeks Mark and his supervisor, the owner of the company, meet with potential corporate clients to describe their services and to finalize consultation contracts. Both before and during these meetings Mark states he experiences sweating, heart palpitations, nervousness, and gastrointestinal symptoms as well as sleeplessness and anxiety that interfere significantly with his ability to concentrate and speak coherently in the meetings. According to Mark, these symptoms begin as early as two weeks before the meetings, when he worries that he will make a fool of himself and be judged negatively by his client and his boss. Mark reports that on two occasions he called in sick to avoid participating in a presentation. He wishes he could do that every time without getting fired. Mark recognizes that his reactions are excessive but reports that he is concerned his symptoms are limiting his ability to perform his job. Because he has experienced these symptoms for more than six months, Mark meets DSM-IV criteria for a diagnosis of social phobia.

Immediate concerns: Are there any immediate dangers to the client or other vulnerable persons?

As with other anxiety disorders (pp. 99–101), the clinician should assess possible comorbid conditions from which Mark may suffer, including, most notably, mood symptoms and substance abuse. Although Mark reported no other psychosocial concerns, a thorough history should be taken to evaluate the chronicity of his symptoms and their effect on other areas of his life, including his relationships with friends, family, and romantic partners.

Mark reports no suicidal ideation and presents with no other apparent symptoms of immediate concern, but it may be important to initiate effective treatment quickly, rather than to treat his concern as a long-term issue in which his reaction to fairly specific social situations might be pathologized. Psychotherapy therefore should be initiated as soon as possible and a referral should be considered for evaluation for psychotropic medication if Mark experiences his symptoms as an immediate stressor.

Short-term goals: What goals need to be achieved in the first two to six sessions?

Cognitive-behavioral psychotherapy was initiated with Mark to increase his comfort with social situations in which he may be subjected to scrutiny, including, as with his presenting concern, situations in which his consulting acumen and speaking skills may be scrutinized. Mark was also enrolled in a six-week social skills workshop in which both microskills (e.g., eye contact, conversational response cues) and macroskills (e.g., reflection skills, public speaking strategies) were addressed. Mark's concerns about his job-related shortcomings were reality-tested in individual psychotherapy and in homework assignments in which he gathered specific feedback about his performance from his supervisor. This feedback contradicted Mark's poor self-assessments. Mark was taught to explore and test alternative cognitive appraisals of the advantages he offered to his company's clients and, through changing appraisals of his increased social skills, of his contributions to the company's client presentations. In particular, Mark learned to avoid catastrophizing his reflections about small and relatively common errors he committed in presentations, such as fumbling for an overhead transparency or mispronouncing a word. Instead, Mark recorded his appraisal of his performance on a graduated 10-point scale and reflected with the clinician about the behaviors and cognitions that were associated with incremental advances in these assessments.

After six social skills sessions and eight individual sessions Mark reported significantly increased self-confidence about both his work-related skills and his public speaking skills. He reported he experienced increased comfort during the days preceding scheduled client meetings and an increased ability to talk and breathe without feeling anxiety symptoms when giving presentations to his company's clients.

Long-term goals: What lifestyle changes and other long-term personal, relationship, and career goals need to be achieved?

Surmounting the relatively circumscribed hurdle of public speaking, Mark reports he is on a career and interpersonal track he greatly enjoys. However, many socially phobic clients experience a chronic history of limited interpersonal relationships that may require longer-term intervention. Psychotherapeutic intervention, possibly coupled with psychoactive medication, should be considered in such cases to manage the client's phobic symptoms and to increase her or his engagement with friends and relational partners. In some cases, occupational or academic counseling may also be indicated. As in Mark's case, the client should be invited to generalize his or her gains in social confidence to other areas of living, and follow-up sessions should be scheduled as necessary to maintain these gains over time.

Panic Disorder and Agoraphobia

Arguably the most terrifying of psychological symptoms, panic attacks are experienced by as many as 15 to 40 percent of Americans at some time during their lives (Eaton et al., 1994; Woodruff-Borden et al., 1997). Brief but frighteningly intense, these acute episodes of anxiety have been described as a "false alarm" activation of the fight-or-flight response, resulting in a cascade of physiological and subjective symptoms that frequently includes marked fears of dying or of losing one's mind (Carter & Barlow, 1995). Unsurprisingly, a significant proportion of individuals experiencing panic attacks fear their return, leading to an interepisodic baseline state of anxiety similar to generalized anxiety disorder (see pp. 99–101). This anticipatory anxiety is the hallmark of the development of full-blown Panic Disorder. In other cases, individuals may come to fear panic attacks to such an extent that they remain in their homes or other safe environments out of concern the attacks may recur in embarrassing situations from which they might be unable to escape. If such concerns become disabling or lead to significant distress (and they often do), the diagnosis of Agoraphobia is assigned.

Interestingly, many more individuals experience panic attacks than go on to develop panic disorder. Whereas up to 15 to 40 percent of U.S. women and men experience a panic attack during their lives, only about 5 percent of women and 2 percent of men go on to develop full-blown panic disorder (Eaton et al., 1994; Reed & Wittchen, 1998; Woodruff-Borden et al., 1997). Of those who do develop panic disorder, approximately one-third also develop agoraphobia, although higher proportions are frequently seen in clinical settings.

Assessment

DSM-IV separates panic attacks from panic disorder, recognizing that panic attacks frequently occur as part of other anxiety disorders (see pp. 99-101). When panic symptoms occur spontaneously, the essential feature of panic disorder—a history of uncued panic attacks coupled with anticipatory anxiety—is recognized.

Most panic attacks come on suddenly and last for only ten to fifteen minutes. The brevity of these events, however, is compensated for by their intensity. According to the DSM-IV, a panic attack consists of four of thirteen listed symptoms, including shortness of breath, heart palpitations or tachycardia, chest pain, dizziness or faintness, sweating, trembling, chills or hot flashes, numbness or tingling, choking, nausea or abdominal distress, derealization or depersonalization, a fear of dying, and a fear of losing control or going crazy. (Derealization means experiencing one's surrounding and things around oneself as if they are not real. Depersonalization means observing oneself as if one were another person.) Panic attacks may be nocturnal, coming abruptly and unexpectedly while the client is asleep.

A DSM-IV diagnosis of panic disorder is met when unexpected, uncued panic attacks are recurrent and the person experiences one or more of the following for at least one month: (1) anxiety about having a panic attack, (2) anxiety about the consequences or implications of panic attacks (e.g., heart attack, loss of control, loss of one's sanity), or (3) significant behavioral changes associated with panic attacks. To meet the criteria for diagnosis, the attacks must not be due to the direct physiological effects of a substance or general medical condition and may not be more accurately attributed to another mental disorder. Specific phobias, obsessive-compulsive disorder, and post-traumatic stress disorder should be ruled out.

DSM-IV criteria for Panic Disorder with Agoraphobia are met when in addition to panic disorder a person experiences significant anxiety about being in situations from which it may be difficult to escape or obtain help when experiencing panic symptoms. According to the DSM-IV, the person also must avoid these situations or else endure them under great stress or only in the company of others. A significantly smaller number of individuals develop agoraphobia without panic disorder.

When assessing a client presenting with panic concerns, the clinician should conduct a thorough psychological interview to review both current problems and history. A medical screening should be conducted to rule out physiological conditions that may account for the client's symptoms, including hyperthyroidism, cardiac arrhythmias, and epileptic seizures. When conducting an assessment the clinician also should take a thorough history to assess the client's past patterns of panic symptoms. The frequency and possible precursors of the client's panic symptoms should be evaluated. Work or school-related stress, surgery, childbirth, family discord, and history of physical or sexual abuse should also be explored. When working with children and adolescents, historical information may be gleaned from parents and schoolteachers, who may be useful informants as to the client's relationships with peers as well as stressors associated with the onset of the client's panic symptoms. With proper consent, collateral records, including school records and medical records, should also be examined.

The following psychological conditions also should be ruled out when diagnosing panic: simple phobia, social phobia, dissociative disorders, drug abuse and/or withdrawal, generalized anxiety disorder, post-traumatic stress disorder, and obsessive-compulsive disorder. If the client's symptoms are better explained by these other conditions, the additional diagnosis of panic disorder is not assigned.

Panic commonly occurs as a co-morbid condition with other psychological disorders, including many anxiety disorders. As many as 50 percent of patients with panic disorder also suffer from social phobia (Starcevic et al., 1993; Stein, Shea, & Uhde, 1989). Thirty to 70 percent of individuals with panic may also be diagnosed with major depression (Cowley, Flick, & Roy-Byrne, 1996; Stein, Tancer, & Uhde, 1990). In such cases, treatment should address both the client's panic symptoms and these coexisting conditions. Recent research has suggested that clients who experience panic disorder, especially clients who experience both panic disorder and major depression, may be more prone to suicide than other individuals (Roy-Byrne, et al., 2000; Woodruff-Borden et al., 1997). A thorough suicidal assessment therefore should be conducted with all clients presenting with panic symptoms. Clients who report active thoughts about suicide should be evaluated for possible immediate intervention prior to addressing their panic symptoms. Finally, a thorough evaluation of a client presenting with panic should also include assessments of his or her patterns of substance use. As many as 28 percent of clients suffering from panic disorder or agoraphobia may self-medicate by abusing alcohol, and another 17 percent may abuse drugs such as marijuana, opiates, benzodiazepines, or stimulants (Regier et al., 1990). For such clients substance abuse treatment may be initiated prior to, or concurrent with, treatment for panic (Marshall, 1997; Myrik & Brady, 2001).

Treatment

Treatments for panic disorder and agoraphobia include two primary areas of intervention: psychotherapies and biological therapies. Treatment of panic disorder generally is prerequisite to treatment of agoraphobia with panic; by treating the panic symptoms to which they are secondary the client's agoraphobic behaviors often subside—if the client is exposed to the specific environments he or she has come to avoid (Maxmen & Ward, 1995; Wickramasekera, 1988).

Cognitive-behavioral psychotherapies may be indicated to reduce the patient's catastrophization of interoceptive (i.e., subjectively experienced) physiological symptoms, and are often effective as a stand-alone treatment for mild to moderate cases of panic disorder (Barlow et al., 2000). Although panic symptoms have been theorized to originate in a fear network of amygdala, thalamus, locus coerelius (i.e., brain stem), or hippocampal activations of the sympathetic nervous system, their cognitive interpretation in the frontal lobe may be more influential in their manifestation as full-blown panic (Gorman et al., 2000; Gorman et al., 1989). If clients are taught to cognitively reinterpret the early signs of these sympathetic nervous system cues and are frequently reassured about the mitigation of future attacks, these symptoms may be prevented from developing into panic attacks and the client may gain a greater sense of control over his or her life. Such cognitive interventions are often coupled with behavioral strategies such as systematic relaxation training, controlled breathing exercises, and exposure-based interventions designed to desensitize the client to both interoceptive and environmental panic stimuli.

Group therapy may also be useful in the treatment of panic disorder. Frequent encouragement from other group members coupled with information from the therapist may assist in the client's increased sense of control over her or his symptoms. As with group interventions for other mental conditions, many clients with panic disorder also benefit from the realization they are not alone in facing their symptoms. Social skills training may also be included as a useful component of more structured group interventions.

Referrals for psychotropic medication evaluation should be considered to alleviate panic symptoms, especially when these are chronic or severe. Three primary classes of medications have been employed for treating panic disorder. Tricyclic antidepressants and serotonin specific reputake inhibitors (SSRIs) (e.g., fluoxetine/Prozac, sertraline/Zoloft) appear to be effective for many clients. However, they also may lead to anticholinergic and other side effects many patients find discouraging. Similar problems are encountered with monoamine oxidase inhibitors (MAOIs), which appear to be effective in reducing panic symptoms for as many as 70 percent of patients. MAOIs have the additional disadvantage of exacting dietary restrictions to which the patient must adhere when taking them. Anxiolytic medications, which become effective more quickly than either antidepressants or psychotherapy, are sometimes used to assuage particular panic episodes, but should be used carefully when treating panic disorder or agoraphobia with panic disorder for significant periods of time. If used at all, these medications are usually withdrawn slowly in systematically tapered dosages to minimize the potential onset of rebound panic symptoms, a not infrequent side effect (Ballenger, 1992; Spiegel, 1999).

For more severe cases of panic marked by retrenched anticipatory anxiety or agoraphobic avoidance behaviors, family therapies may also be indicated. Family members and relational partners are often affected by a client's panic symptoms, especially when these are coupled with agoraphobia. They may be helped by supportive or psychoeducational interventions. Friends and family members furthermore may contribute to the client's treatment by helping to minimize avoidance of anxiety-producing situations, often a key element of rebuilding the client's life and restoring her or his self-confidence.

CASE EXAMPLE
Marcella

Referral: Marcella, a 22-year-old Mexican American hotel maid, experienced her first panic attack when listening to music on headphones at work. Fearing she might be going crazy, Marcella reported she "dug my fingernails into the bed I was making to keep from being pulled into something horrible." Overcome by feelings of derealization and by physiological symptoms she interpreted to be a heart attack, Marcella felt she was "dying and going to hell," and feared the return of the symptoms once they finally subsided. When she experienced a second attack two months later, Marcella admitted herself into a hospital emergency room and was referred to a psychologist, based on her presenting symptoms, for assessment of possible psychosis.

Although a thorough history revealed no psychotic symptoms (after clarifying her report of acute depersonalization and derealization during the panic episodes), a recent history of dysphoria was found to precede Marcella's first attack. Marcella also reported she recently began drinking to assuage her panic-related anticipatory anxiety and that she had begun to withdraw from her friends and extended family members. Marcella reported no history of other psychological symptoms but was found to meet the criteria for a DSM-IV diagnosis of Panic Disorder without Agoraphobia. Although she did not meet the criteria for substance abuse or substance dependence, her recent use of alcohol to assuage her panic-related symptoms was noted.

(continued)

CASE EXAMPLE   Continued

Immediate concerns: Are there any immediate dangers to the client or other vulnerable persons?

Although no suicidal ideation was reported at intake, a clinical interview should assess whether Marcella has experienced suicidal ideation or intent. Marcella reported no agoraphobic behaviors, but her recently diminished engagement with her friends and extended family members points to the need for immediate intervention to reduce her panic symptoms. A referral for benzodiazepines may be necessary to prevent panic episodes while initiating psychotherapy. A medical referral should be made to evaluate preexisting or current physical conditions that may account for her presenting symptoms.

Short-term goals: What goals need to be achieved in the first two to six sessions?

Two main areas were targeted for initial treatment: Marcella's mood/life experiences and her recent interpersonal disengagement, which might develop into agoraphobia. To address her panic attacks, Marcella was taught to recognize her catastrophization of anxiety-based physiological symptoms, including elevated heartbeat and shortened breathing. Whereas Marcella interpreted these symptoms as imminent suffocation during her first two panic attacks, she replaced these cognitions with more reassuring self-statements during exposure to mildly frightening thoughts and images the therapist's office (e.g., "This will be brief and I'm going to get through it"). She was given homework assignments to practice these cognitive reframes and to increase her reengagement with ordinary life activities.

After six sessions, Marcella reported significantly reduced anxiety about the possibility of experiencing an attack and stated she recognized that if she experienced such an attack she "wouldn't be dying and wouldn't be going crazy." She continued to practice self-statements affirming that the attacks would be short-lived and were not indicative of imminent insanity or death. She stated, "I know if I have one that it won't last long and I'll be okay when it's over." Marcella reported she had resumed her previous levels of activities with friends and family and that she had reduced her use of alcohol, since she no longer needed it "to keep myself from worrying all the time."

Long-term goals: What lifestyle changes and other long-term personal, relationship, and career goals need to be achieved?

Long-term management should attend to supporting Marcella's cognitive and affective comfort with possible future attacks and to her engagement with work and family activities. Marcella should also be taught to recognize early signs of anxiety and to reduce stressors associated with increased anxiety in her life such as family demands and conflicts at home or at work. Marcella should recognize that although she may experience another panic attack in the future, such a recurrence would not be a sign of failure. Instead, therapy should consolidate the gains Marcella has made in her struggle with panic disorder and help her utilize these lessons should symptoms arise in the future. A referral should be considered for career counseling and/or assessment if indicated, and follow-up sessions or telephone contacts should be scheduled to assess Marcella's continued progress.

Generalized Anxiety Disorder

The cardinal feature of Generalized Anxiety Disorder is near-constant worry about a variety of things in a person's life. Once viewed as a relatively mild residual diagnosis among the anxiety disorders, research now suggests that individuals suffering from generalized anxiety disorder experience negative affect, overarousal, and disabling anxiety that significantly disrupts the quality of their lives (Kessler et al., 1999; Witchen & Hoyer, 2001).

Assessment

As with most other anxiety disorders, the demarcation between ordinary anxiety and Generalized Anxiety Disorder is a matter of degree. Although most people experience transitory periods of worry during their lives, approximately 7 percent of U.S. women and 4 percent of U.S. men experience worry that is persistent and severe enough to meet the criteria for generalized anxiety disorder (Kessler et al., 1994). According to the DSM-IV, the criteria for generalized anxiety disorder are met when a person experiences excessive worry during most days of her or his life for at least six months. In addition, the person finds the worry difficult to control and experiences at least three of six symptoms—including restlessness, fatigue, impaired concentration, irritability, muscle tension, or disturbed sleep—that cause significant distress or impairment in her or his life.

The following conditions should be ruled out when assessing generalized anxiety disorder: Panic Disorder, Specific or Social Phobia, Hypochondriasis, Separation Anxiety Disorder, Obsessive-Compulsive Disorder, Mood Disorders, and Psychotic Disorders. Clients with panic disorder and phobic disorders often experience anticipatory anxiety. Clients with panic disorder fear the onset of another attack. Clients with a specific phobia worry about encountering a specific social or environmental stimulus. By contrast, the person suffering from GAD worries about a wider range of things in her or his life, most often including family, finances, and work-related issues (Roemer, Molina, & Borkovec, 1997; Wittchen & Hoyer, 2001; Yonkers, Warshaw, Massion, & Keller, 1996). Similarly, hypochondriasis, separation anxiety, and obsessive-compulsive disorder may be differentiated from generalized anxiety by the specificity of the anxieties with which they are associated. Mood disorders and psychotic disorders present more difficult assessment issues, since these clinical presentations often include features of anxiety that are difficult to differentiate from generalized anxiety. If the client's anxiety occurs prior to or outside the course of these disorders, the additional diagnosis of GAD is assigned.

Individuals with GAD often meet the criteria for other coexisting conditions. Many clients with GAD also experience major depression and a significant number abuse substances, such as sleeping pills, alcohol, and tranquilizers. In addition, individuals diagnosed with GAD may also suffer from other anxiety disorders such as panic disorder, specific phobia, and social phobia. A thorough assessment should evaluate symptoms associated with these concerns and additional diagnoses should be assigned where appropriate.

In addition to these psychological concerns, clients presenting with GAD often also experience a variety of somatic symptoms that, in fact, may result in the initiation of their treatment by a physician. Research suggests that the majority of individuals with GAD experience chronic physical symptoms including unsteadiness, tension, an inability to relax, weakness, and sweating hands. Other frequently observed physical symptoms include breathing difficulties, tachycardia, nausea, faintness, diarrhea, and urgency of urination (Ballenger et al., 2001). Clients presenting with such symptoms who are not referred by a physician for therapy should be referred to a physician for a medical evaluation to ensure these symptoms are not caused by a physical condition.

As with the assessment of other anxiety disorders in children and adolescents, information gleaned from parents or, with proper consent, schoolteachers may be helpful in the differential diagnosis of GAD, particularly in differentiating GAD from separation anxiety disorder and mood disorders. Historical information about the client's past social and academic functioning may also be useful in establishing onset and correlates or precursors of the client's symptoms. The chronic free-floating anxiety and autonomic hyperactivity associated with GAD often interferes with child and adolescent clients' academic performance. A review of the client's school records, therefore, may be useful as well.

The impairment observed in child and adolescent clients' school performance often is similarly revealed in adult clients' as well as children's and adolescents' cognitive assessments, because chronic anxiety and tension often are manifested both in diminished WAIS-R performance scores and in diminished digit span and arithmetic verbal scores.

Treatment

Until recently, few treatments were considered to be effective with GAD. Recent research, however, suggests a combination of exposure-based interventions and behavior training, coupled in some cases with limited use of psychotropic medication, may reduce the worry and anxiety associated with GAD to subclinical levels (Roemer, Orsillo, & Barlow, 2002). Where indicated, family, occupational/academic, and other systemic interventions should be coupled with these therapies to enhance the client's overall functioning and promote his or her resilience against future episodes of anxiety.

Among psychotherapeutic approaches, cognitive-behavioral interventions that combine cognitive restructuring strategies with specific training in muscle relaxation appear to be most effective with GAD. Such approaches typically are psychoeducational, inviting clients to consider alternative cognitions about perceived threatening or worrisome events in their life experiences and heightening their perceived control over physical symptoms. Clients also may be asked to maintain diaries of their thoughts and/or worries throughout the day and may rehearse comforting self-statements concurrent with their training in progressive muscle relaxation and other behavioral exercises in the counseling office.

A psychiatric referral should also be considered, especially for clients experiencing more acute anxiety, although it should be recognized that many clients with GAD see family physicians before presenting for psychotherapy and may already have been prescribed medications, most notably benzodiazepines, that may be ineffective. However, busipirone, a recently developed anxiolytic medication, and some antidepressant medications may be useful adjuncts to cognitive-behavioral interventions. Occupational/academic interventions and family therapies also should be considered to address specific areas of stress or dysfunction in the client's life.

CASE EXAMPLE
Roberto

Referral: Roberto, a 26-year-old first-year schoolteacher, has experienced increasing anxiety about his teaching work, his finances, "and everything else in my life." Roberto states he has phoned in sick six times in the past twenty weeks of this, his first, semester. He has experienced headaches, sleeplessness, and stomach pains nearly every other day. According to Roberto, these symptoms began over the summer when he began planning his academic year and have continued since. Roberto reports he has gotten positive feedback from his evaluating principal and from several of his students' parents, but stated, "They don't really know how bad I am—or how badly things are going in the class." Roberto states he has experienced mild anxiety at various times in his life but that in the past six months, "It seems like I've been worrying about everything all the time."

Immediate concerns: Are there any immediate dangers to the client or other vulnerable persons?

Roberto reports no current suicidal ideation or intent to harm others. Despite his occasional frustration in class, he has engaged in no emotional outbursts toward any of his students but rather reports he has "held it all in with everyone else—and then broken down when I get home."

Short-term goals: What goals need to be achieved in the first two to six sessions?

After a history was taken to rule out co-morbid conditions such as depression and substance abuse, psychotherapy was initiated with Roberto to reduce his psychological and physical symptoms of anxiety and to help him realistically deal with his financial and work-related challenges. Cognitive strategies were used to help Roberto gain a balanced view of his teaching performance, including affirmations of his strengths as well as his weaknesses as a teacher. Roberto was taught relaxation strategies to assuage his physical tension and given homework assignments, including journaling, to engage in self-selected recreational/relaxation behaviors at home. In addition, self-management

(continued)

C A S E   E X A M P L E   Continued

strategies were used to help Roberto develop a budget for the remainder of the calendar year, which he discussed as part of consecutive sessions with the clinician and during consultations with a fellow first-year teacher from his graduating college class.

A referral was made to evaluate possible medical causes for Roberto's physiological symptoms. When these were ruled out, biofeedback interventions were developed to help Roberto assuage his headaches and muscle tension. After eleven sessions of psychotherapy, Roberto reported significantly improved confidence at school and increased comfort. Roberto reported he experienced restorative sleep and significantly diminished physiological symptoms and stated that he often found himself looking forward to getting into the classroom and trying something new with his students.

Long-term goals: What lifestyle changes and other long-term personal, relationship, and career goals need to be achieved?

Roberto should be taught strategies by which to monitor his anxieties and continue to realistically appraise his performance in challenging, and especially in new, situations. The clinician should consider encouraging Roberto to develop working relationships with experienced teachers at his school with whom he could reflect on challenges of first-year teaching, as well as to learn specific classroom strategies that would allow him to continue to improve, and gain a sense of agency over, his teaching. Roberto also should be encouraged to continue his self-managed relaxation efforts and should be invited to reinitiate contact with the clinician should his anxiety symptoms resurface in the future.

C A S E   E X E R C I S E

Keith

Keith, a 24-year-old psychology student, reports a history of anxiety about a variety of issues for the past twelve months, including concerns about his courses and his relationship with his partner, Robert. Keith states that he has performed well in school in the past with a GPA of 3.4 on a 4-point scale. However, lately he has become extremely anxious in anticipation of exams and group projects, before which he reports he gets anxious and physically sick to the point where he cannot even study. During a recent exam, Keith felt his face flush and heart race and suffered an episode of depersonalization. During this episode he also experienced overwhelming nausea and a suffocating shortness of breath. Although he states he is positioned to earn Bs in most of his classes this semester, he fears he may earn Ds or Fs in at least two of his six classes. Keith reports that in addition to worries about his classes, he has become increasingly worried about his relationship with Robert, with whom he reports he has had a great relationship for three years. Keith is afraid that Robert is getting bored with him. Keith states that although he has seen no real change in Robert's behavior and Robert has denied any change in his feelings toward Keith, he worries that his problems are adversely affecting their relationship.

Study Questions

1. What are your diagnostic impressions about Keith? What disorders and conditions should be ruled out?

2. What information would you need to verify these impressions? How would you gather this information?

3. Are there any immediate dangers to Keith, or to other vulnerable people?

4. What goals need to be achieved in the first two to six sessions of your work with Keith? What is your treatment plan to achieve these goals, including referrals if indicated?

5. What lifestyle changes and other long-term relationship, personal, and career goals should be achieved in your work with Keith?

6. What cultural issues are raised in Keith's case? How might these issues affect his struggles with anxiety symptoms or behaviors? How might you address sociocultural differences, if any, between you and Keith in therapy?

7. How might your work with Keith be modified if he were a 47-year-old heterosexual businessman studying psychology as part of a planned career change?

8. Six weeks into your work with Keith, he develops symptoms of depression, including sadness, tearfulness, sleeplessness, feelings of overwhelming guilt, diminished concentration, and thoughts of suicide, symptoms he reports he has been suffering for a week. How might you change your approach with Keith to address these additional symptoms?

9. Keith reports he has been abusing ecstasy (MDMH) for the past six weeks. He has kept this information not only from you, but also from Robert, who adamantly opposes drug use. How might your relationship with Keith be affected by this report? How might you address this topic with Keith?

10. Keith reports that he has covertly been giving Robert ecstasy in mixed drinks in advance of several of their recent sexual encounters, in hopes of improving Robert's attraction to him. Are you obligated to report this information to Robert? How would you handle the discovery of this information with Keith?

11. Robert phones you at your office and asks you directly if Keith has been using substances. What do you tell him?

REFERENCES

Alden, L. E., & Wallace, S. T. (1995). Social phobia and social appraisal in successful and unsuccessful social interactions. *Behaviour Research & Therapy, 33*, 497–505.

Ballenger, J. C. (1992). Medication discontinuation in panic disorder. *Journal of Clinical Psychiatry, 53* (suppl. 3), 26–31.

Ballenger, J. C., Davidson, J. R. T., Lecrubier, Y., Nutt, D. M., Bobes, J., Beidel, D. C., Ono, Y., & Westenberg, H. G. M. (1998). Consensus statement on social anxiety disorder from the international consensus group on depression and anxiety. *Journal of Clinical Psychiatry, 59* (suppl. 17), 54–60.

Ballenger, J. C., Davidson, J. R. T., Lecrubier, Y., Nutt, D. M., Borkovec, T. D., Rickels, K., Stein, D. J., & Wittchen, H. U. (2001). Consensus statement on generalized anxiety disorder from the international consensus group on depression and anxiety. *Journal of Clinical Psychiatry, 62* (suppl. 11), 53–58.

Barlow, D. H., Gorman, J. H., Shear, K. M., & Woods, S. W. (2000). Cognitive-behavioral therapy, imipramine, or their combination for panic disorder: A randomized controlled trial. *Journal of the American Medical Association, 283,* 2529–2536.

Benjamin, J., Ben-Zion, I. Z., Karbofsky, E., & Dannon, P. (2000). Double-blind placebo-controlled pilot study of paroxetine for specific phobia. *Psychopharmacology, 149,* 194–196.

Capafons, B. (2001). Tratamientos psicologicos eficaces para las fobias especificas. *Psicothema, 13,* 447–452.

Carter, M. M., & Barlow, D. H. (1995). Learned alarms: The origins of panic. In W. T. O'Donohue & L. Krasner (Eds.), *Theories of behavior therapy: Exploring behavior change* (pp. 209–228). Washington, DC: American Psychological Association.

Cowley, D. S., Flick, S. N., & Roy-Byrne, P. P. (1996). Long-term course and outcome in panic disorder: A naturalistic follow-up study. *Anxiety, 2,* 13–21.

Eaton, W. W., Kessler, R. C., Wittchen, H. U., & Magee, W. J. (1994). Panic and panic disorder in the United States. *American Journal of Psychiatry, 151,* 413–420.

Gorman, J. M., Kent, J. M., Sullivan, G. M., & Coplan, J. M. (2000). Neuroanatomical hypothesis of panic disorder, revised. *American Journal of Psychiatry, 157,* 493–505.

Gorman, J. M., Liebowitz, M. R., Fyer, A. J., & Stein, J. (1989). A neuroanatomical hypothesis for panic disorder. *American Journal of Psychiatry, 146,* 148–161.

Kessler, R. C., Stang, P. E., Wittchen, H., Ustun, T. B., Roy-Burne, P. P., & Walters, E. E. (1998). Lifetime panic-depression comorbidity in the National Comorbidity Survey. *Archives of General Psychiatry, 55,* 801–808.

Kessler, R. C., DuPont, R. I., Berglund, P. & Wittchen, H. U. (1999). Impairment in pure and comorbid generalized anxiety disorder and major depression at 12 months in two national surveys. *American Journal of Psychiatry, 156,* 1915–1923.

Kessler, R. C., McGonagle, K. A, Zhao, S., Nelson C. B., Hughes, M., Eshleman, S., Wittchen, H. U., Kendler, K. S. (1994). Lifetime and 12-month prevalence of DSM-III-R psychiatric disorders in the United States: Results from the National Comorbidity Survey. *Archives of General Psychiatry, 51,* 8–19.

Lydiard, B. R. (2001). Social anxiety disorder: Comorbidity and its implications. *Journal of Clinical Psychiatry Special Issue: Advances and emerging treatments in social phobia, 62* (suppl. 1), 17–24.

Marshall, J. R. (1997). Alcohol and substance abuse in panic disorder. *Journal of Clinical Psychiatry, 58* (suppl. 2), 46–49.

Maxmen, J. S., & Ward, N. G. (1995). *Essential psychopathology and its treatment* (2nd ed.). New York: W. W. Norton & Co.

Myrik, H., & Brady, K. (2001). Management of comorbid anxiety and substance use disorders. *Psychiatric Annals Special Issue, 31,* 265–271.

Perugi, G., Frare, F., Toni, C., Mata, B., & Akiskal, H. S. (2001). Bipolar II and unipolar comorbidity in 153 outpatients with social phobia. *Comprehensive Psychiatry, 42,* 375–381.

Rappaport, M. D., Denney, C. B., Chung, K. M., & Hustace, K. (2001). Internalizing behavior problems and scholastic achievement in children: Cognitive and behavioral pathways as mediators of outcome. *Journal of Clinical Child Psychology, 30,* 536–551.

Reed, V. & Wittchen, H. U. (1998). DSM-IV panic attacks and panic disorder in a community sample of adolescents and young adults: How specific are panic attacks? *Journal of Psychiatric Research, 32,* 335–345.

Regier, D. A., Farmer, M. E., Rae, D. S., Locke, B. Z., Keith, S. J., Judd, L. L., & Goodwin, F. K. (1990). Comorbidity of mental disorders with alcohol and other drug abuse. *Journal of the American Medical Association, 264,* 2511–2518.

Reich, J., Goldenberg, I., Vasile, R., Goisman, R., et al. (1994). A prospective follow-up study of the course of social phobia. *Psychiatry Research, 54*(3), 249–258.

Roemer, L., Molina, S., & Borkovec, T. D., (1997). An investigation of worry content among generally anxious individuals. *Journal of Nervous Mental Disorders, 185,* 314–319.

Roemer, L., Orsillo, S. M., & Barlow, D. H. (2002). Generalized anxiety disorder. In D. H. Barlow (Ed.), *Anxiety and its disorders: The nature and treatment of anxiety and panic* (2nd ed.). New York: Guilford Press.

Roy-Byrne, P. P., Stang, P., Wittchen, H. U., Ustun, B., Walters, E. E., & Kessler, R. C. (2000). Lifetime panic-depression comorbidity in the National Comorbidity Survey: Association with symptoms, impairment, course and help-seeking. *British Journal of Psychiatry, 176,* 229–235.

Schneier, F. R., Heckelman, L. R., Garfinkel, R., Campeas, R., et al. (1994). Functional impairment in social phobia. *Journal of Clinical Psychiatry, 55*(8), 322–331.

Spiegel, D. A. (1999). Psychological strategies for discontinuing benzodiazepine treatment. *Journal of Clinical Psychopharmacology, 19* (6, suppl. 2), 17S–22S.

Starcevic, V., Uhlenhuth, E. H., Kellner, R., et al. (1993). Comorbidity in panic disorder, II: Chronology of appearance and pathogenic comorbidity. *Psychiatric Research, 46,* 285–293.

Stein, M. B., Shea, C. A., & Uhde, T. W. (1989). Social phobic symptoms in patients with panic disorder: Practical and theoretical implications. *American Journal of Psychiatry, 146,* 7–16.

Stein, M. B., Tancer, M. E., & Uhde, T. W. (1990). Major depression in patients with panic disorder: Factors associated with course and recurrence. *Journal of Affective Disorders, 19,* 287–296.

Van Ameringen, M., Mancini, C., Styan, G., & Donison, D. (1991). Relationship of social phobia with other psychiatric illnesses. *Journal of Affective Disorders, 21,* 93–99.

Vera, E. M., & Gaubatz, M. D. (2001). Promoting social competencies in school-age children. In C. L. Juntunen & D. R. Atkinson (Eds.), *Counseling across the lifespan: Prevention and treatment* (pp. 57–70). Thousand Oaks, CA: Sage Publication.

Weiller, E., Bisserbe, J. C., Boyer, P., Lepine, J. P., & Lecrubier, Y. (1996). Social phobia in general health care: An unrecognized undertreated disabling disorder. *British Journal of Psychiatry, 168,* 169–174.

Wickramasekera, I. E. (1988). *Clinical behavioral medicine: Some concepts and procedures.* New York: Plenum Press.

Wittchen, H. U., & Hoyer, J. (2001). Generalized anxiety disorder: Nature and course. *Journal of Clinical Psychiatry Special Issue, 62* (suppl. 11), 15–19.

Wolpe, J. (1958). *Psychotherapy by reciprocal inhibition.* Stanford, CA: Stanford University Press.

Woodruff-Borden, J., Stanley, M. A., Lister, S. C., & Tabacchi, M. R. (1997). Nonclinical panic and suicidality: Prevalence and psychopathology. *Behaviour Research & Therapy, 35,* 109–116.

Woody, S. R., & Rodriguez, B. F. (2000). Self-focused attention and social anxiety in social phobics and normal controls. *Cognitive Therapy & Research, 24,* 473–488.

Yonkers, K. A., Warshaw, M. G., Massion, A. O., & Keller, M. B. (1996). Phenomenology and course of generalized anxiety disorder. *British Journal of Psychiatry, 168,* 308–313.

Yonkers, K. A., Dyck, I. R., & Keller, M. B. (2001). An eight-year longitudinal comparison of clinical course and characteristics of social phobia among men and women. *Psychiatric Services, 52*(5), 637–643.

5

Eating Disorders

CHAPTER OVERVIEW

1. DSM-IV distinguishes Anorexia Nervosa from Bulimia Nervosa and Eating Disorders Not Otherwise Specified. A number of other eating disorders are associated with childhood and adolescence or developmental disability, such as Pica and Rumination Disorders.

2. Anorexia is characterized by abnormally low weight, fear of becoming overweight, abnormal body perception, and, in menarchal women, missing periods. Bulimia is characterized by binge eating, vomiting, and purging or excessive exercise to control weight.

3. Comorbid anxiety and mood disorders are common in both disorders. Substance abuse, impulse and personality disorders are also associated with bulimia.

4. Standardized assessment interviews and questionnaires, such as the Eating Disorders Inventory, may be used to assess eating disorders.

5. Treatment of anorexia, which is associated with a poor prognosis, may require long-term counseling and support. Treatment of bulimia usually leads to relatively positive outcomes, especially when cognitive-behavioral techniques and psychotropic medications are used to address symptoms of anxiety, mood, and impulsivity.

6. Pica refers to the consumption of non-nutritive substances. Although culturally appropriate under certain circumstances, pica can be a serious and life-threatening problem. Pica may be treated by mineral and other dietary supplements, or by applied behavior analysis.

7. Rumination Disorder is a rare disorder characterized by repeated regurgitation of consumed food. Exclusion of medical causes is an important part of assessment. Treatments may include behavioral therapy strategies and medical interventions. Feeding Disorder of Infancy or Early Childhood is a relatively common disorder in which the infant refuses food or is highly selective about the food being offered. Exclusion of medical causes is an important component of assessment.

8. Treatment of rumination and feeding disorders is multidisciplinary and may include simple interventions, such as changes in food texture, more intrusive medical interventions such as medications and surgery, and interventions based on applied behavior analysis.

This chapter reviews two kinds of eating disorders. The first part of the chapter reviews anorexia nervosa and bulimia nervosa, which, although often beginning in adolescence, are broken into a separate DSM-IV chapter on eating disorders.

The latter part of the chapter reviews pica, rumination, and feeding disorder of infancy or early childhood, which DSM-IV (American Psychiatric Association, 1994) includes in its chapter "Disorders Usually First Diagnosed in Infancy, Childhood or Adolescence."

Diagnosis

Anorexia Nervosa

According to the DSM-IV, Anorexia Nervosa is characterized by four cardinal symptoms. First, a client with anorexia refuses to maintain normal body weight, defined by the DSM-IV as at least 85 percent of the weight expected for one's height, age, and body frame. For adolescents, the client refuses to gain normal body weight. Second, anorexia is characterized by an intense fear of becoming fat, even though the person is underweight. Third, anorexia is characterized by an abnormal perception of one's body. For example, people with anorexia may worry they have enormous hips when this is obviously not true, or deny they are underweight when, in fact, they are suffering serious physical consequences from being underweight. Finally, for menarchal women with anorexia, there is an absence of at least three consecutive menstrual cycles.

It is important, but often difficult, to distinguish anorexia from overzealous dieting, unusual eating patterns, and excessive but nonpathological concerns with eating and weight. Dieting is very common in both adolescents and adults, and a large proportion of the normal population may report being on a diet at any one time. Concerns over body image, appearance, and social evaluation by others are also very common parts of both adolescence and adulthood. Anorexia and bulimia may be distinguished from normal behavior by the absence of social, personal, or occupational impairment and by the presence of accurate perception of body image.

DSM-IV divides Anorexia Nervosa into two types: Restricting, and Binge-eating/Purging Types. Bingeing/purging anorexics often eat either normally or excessively, then self-induce vomiting or abuse laxatives, diuretics, or enemas to prevent caloric absorption. Restrictive anorexics maintain low body weight by restricting their food intake. It is important to note that bingeing and purging do not immediately point to a diagnosis of bulimia. Clients who are anorexic, like clients with bulimia, may binge and purge instead of restricting their food intake. The key characteristic that distinguishes these diagnoses is abnormally low weight.

Anorexia clients are predominantly, but not exclusively, female, although research suggests an increasing minority of anorexics are male (Mussell et al., 2001). Clients with anorexia often exhibit perfectionist traits and a high need for control (Slade et al., 1991). Mood disorders, such as major depression and dysphoric disorder, are common among clients with anorexia, as are social and other anxiety disorders. In a minority of clients, disturbances in body image may also shade into dysmorphophobia, which is a strongly held belief of almost delusional intensity (Sturmey & Slade, 1986). As a result of these problems, social functioning may be quite impaired. Clients with anorexia may be socially isolated and have few sources of support. Others may have entangled and enmeshed relationships with family members (Calam et al., 1990) and/or spouses. In addition, anorexia often leads to multiple medical complications, including gastrointestinal disorders, dental deterioration, and bone demineralization. Medical problems typical of starvation also may appear, including emaciation, brittle hair, lethargy, hypotension, anemia, dry skin, and vulnerability to infections.

People in certain occupations and lifestyles where appearance, weight, and fitness are a key component of that occupation—such as dancers and athletes—may be at a greater risk for anorexia than others (Byrne & McLean, 2001).

Bulimia Nervosa

People with bulimia have normal weight, but abnormal patterns of eating. DSM-IV defines bulimia with five diagnostic criteria. First, the person engages in recurrent episodes of binge eating, characterized by the consumption of an amount of food much larger than most people would eat within a two-hour period of time coupled with a loss of control over eating during the binge episode. Second, the person with bulimia engages in recurrent and inappropriate use of vomiting, laxatives, diuretics, enemas, other medications, fasting, or exercise to prevent weight gain after eating. Third, the person's bingeing and purging behaviors must occur at least twice per week for three or more months. Fourth, the person's self-evaluations are unduly influenced by his or her body weight and shape. Finally, the person's disturbance does not occur exclusively during episodes of anorexia nervosa (i.e., when the person weighs less than 85 percent of her or his normal body weight).

Like anorexia, bulimia nervosa is often accompanied by other psychiatric problems. Mood and anxiety disorders are common, as are substance abuse and addiction problems. Sometimes, borderline or other personality disorders may also be present. Additionally, social relationships are often made difficult by problems associated with impulsivity and emotionality. Thus, assessment of intervention of bulimia nervosa may have to address multiple, co-occurring problems.

Eating Disorder Not Otherwise Specified (NOS)

Eating Disorder NOS is diagnosed in clients who do not meet the exact criteria for anorexia nervosa or bulimia nervosa, but who clearly have a psychiatric disorder related to eating. This can include women who met all diagnostic criteria for anorexia except amenorrhea; clients who meet all criteria for anorexia except low body weight; clients who meet the criteria for bulimia except the required frequency of bingeing and/or purging; or other abnormal patterns of eating. For all of these examples, it is important to remember that they must be distinguished from normal patterns of eating and the criteria of clinically significant distress or limitations in functioning must be met.

Differential Diagnosis of Eating Disorders

Eating disorders should be distinguished from one another and from a variety of physical and mental disorders than can account for similar behaviors. Many physical disorders can present with weight loss; however, these are not likely to be associated with distorted body image. Social phobia, obsessive-compulsive disorder (OCD), and body dysmorphic disorder also share a number of features with anorexia nervosa. Nonetheless, whereas people with social phobia may be reluctant to eat in public out of fear of embarrassment or criticism, they are not likely to present with the drastically low weight and body image concerns associated with anorexia. Similarly, whereas clients with OCD might restrict their calorie intake out of food contamination fears, they do not share the body weight and body image problems and distortions exhibited by people with anorexia. Although clients with body dysmorphic disorder may present with preoccupation with body image, they typically do not have abnormal patterns of eating.

Bulimia nervosa may sometimes be confused with unusual eating patterns associated with rare physical disorders, mood disorders, or borderline personality disorder, but it can be distinguished by the bulimic person's excessive eating, consistent use of compensatory (i.e., purging) behaviors, and excessive body image concerns. Binge eating sometimes occurs in clients with borderline personality disorders, however, and it is possible to diagnose bulimia nervosa and borderline personality disorder together.

Assessment

Clinical interviews can be very reliable in the diagnosis of eating disorders. Several authors have reported good psychometric results using DSM-IV-based structured interviews for the purpose of diagnosis. Fichter, Herpertz, Quadflieg, and Herpertz-Dahlmann (1998), for instance, developed a semistructured interview using DSM-IV and ICD-10 criteria that reliably identified current and past eating disorder symptoms in a group of several hundred patients and community controls. It is also important, through clinical interview, self-report instruments, or other assessment measures, to assess for common comorbid conditions, such as mood disorders, anxiety disorders, personality disorders, addictions and substance abuse, and social and interpersonal functioning.

A wide range of psychometric instruments are also available to assist in diagnosis of eating disorders and associated psychopathology, personality characteristics, behavioral patterns, and dysfunctional thoughts. Several versions of these instruments have been developed for younger populations and for clients who speak a primary language other than English. The Eating Disorders Inventory (Garner, Olmsted, Polivy, & Garfinkel, 1984) is among the most popular, because it has robust reliability and validity and is relatively quick to administer (Lee, Lee, Leung, & Yu, 1997). A variety of questionnaires also are available to assess eating disordered clients' cognitive patterns (Mizes & Christiano, 1995) and personality traits, such as perfectionism and impulsivity (Newton, Freeman, & Munro, 1993), that may be helpful in developing cognitive-behavioral interventions. Assessment of body image can be done through interview and/or various methods of rating photographs and line drawings. Assessment of body image can assess both the accuracy of estimating body size and the social-emotional evaluation aspects of body image (Skrzypek, Wehmeier, & Remschmidt, 2001).

A variety of self-recording strategies, such as structured diaries and ABC charts, can also help identify points of intervention and yield diagnostic information with clients with eating disorders. Self-assessments of the antecedents and consequences of clients' bingeing behaviors, for example, have been shown to reveal patterns to which cognitive-behavioral interventions might be targeted. Stickney, Miltenberger, & Wolff (1999) found that clients with whom this strategy was used experienced negative emotions, such as depressed mood or anger, immediately before their bingeing behaviors, and that these emotions were significantly reduced when they binged. Based on these findings, cognitive-behavioral treatments were used to help clients manage their negative mood or anger symptoms before engaging in bingeing behaviors. (See the case examples beginning on page 113.) Self-recording and use of ABC records can be useful for pinpointing times where specific coping strategies, such as scheduling alternate activities, engaging in activities that raise mood, relaxation training, eating preferred-low calorie snacks instead of bingeing, or rehearsing appropriate cognitions need to be developed.

Assessment should include a physical workup to ensure the client has no untreated medical disorders contributing to the presenting problems. Thus, a referral to a general physician for a regular checkup may be indicated for a review of a wide range of potential medical problems, including gynecological problems, dental problems, osteoporosis, electrolyte imbalance, and so on.

Interviews with families of adolescents and young adults living at home may be useful in gaining insight into family dynamics and coping mechanisms. Interviews with spouses, partners, and children may also be helpful for clients who live with partners and/or who have children living with them. In addition, a psychiatric consultation might be indicated to evaluate the appropriateness of psychotropic medications for the client. Finally, a comprehensive assessment should include evaluation of the client's sexual functioning. This should include their adaption to adolescence or adult sexuality and their attitudes to upcoming or present adult roles.

Outcome

In a longitudinal study of a cohort of 103 patients with anorexia, Fichter and Quadflieg (1999) found substantial improvement during therapy and slow but continuous progress during the ensuing six years for many of the clients. At six-years follow-up, 56 percent no longer met DSM-IV criteria for an eating disorder; in total, over 75 percent had good or intermediate outcomes. Nonetheless, 23 percent of the patients continued to experience amenorrhea after six years, over 20 percent continued to exhibit poor adjustment, and six patients had died. Although, in treating anorexia, one can expect symptom reduction for many clients within the first two to six months, a minority may need continued support for more extended periods of time. Thus, in this cohort, the primary referral problem—anorexia—improved slowly. Many clients continued to have significant residual problems and a minority functioned poorly.

Treatment Plans for Anorexia Nervosa

Overall, regardless of treatment approach, anorexia appears to be a more difficult clinical problem to treat than bulimia. Strong evidence of the long-term impact of behavior therapy, cognitive therapy, pharmacotherapy, or psychotherapy on anorexia is scarce (Wilson, Vitousek, & Loeb, 2000); however, some research suggests that behavioral family-oriented therapy may help many anorexia clients (e.g., Robin et al., 1999). It may be possible that some clients with more mild problems of recent onset can be successfully treated on an outpatient basis using primarily education methods, especially if there are no additional complicating factors.

Clients with anorexia may require longer-term support and refeeding during a period of hospitalization to ensure their health and safety (Bowers & Andersen, 1994). A minority may require inpatient treatment, perhaps even on an involuntary admission to ensure their safety. Russell (2001) argued that involuntary admission maybe required for clients who are a significant risk to themselves because of the risk of self-harm, multiple failed admissions, and readmissions, and those with very low weight who are at risk for significant illness or death. Russell (2001) also recommended that careful supervision of access to the bathroom to prevent purging and vomiting, restriction of access to opportunities for exercise, and sedation of extremely anxious clients might be needed for some clients. Obviously, such approaches raise considerable ethical questions. Effective treatment, in some cases saving lives through restrictive methods, must be balanced against client dignity, due process, and consent. When the client is a legal minor, as may be the case for many clients with anorexia, the clinician must gain written informed consent from the parent or guardian for treatment. At the same time, the clinician faces the challenge of maintaining a good working alliance with a client who may oppose treatment for the problem.

No simple and effective interventions currently exist to reliably treat clients with anorexia. Instead, long-term support and counseling may be necessary to continue to guide them through slow, and always supervised, recovery. Incremental goals to gradually improve social functioning and deal with manageable problems one at a time may be more realistic for clients with more severe problems.

Treatment Plans for Bulimia Nervosa

In contrast to treatment studies of anorexia, several studies have found positive outcomes for cognitive behavior therapy (CBT), antidepressant medication, and combinations of both in the treatment of bulimia (Bulik et al., 1998; Hay & Bacaltchuk, 2001; Walsh et al., 1997; Wilson et al., 2000). A recent meta-analysis of several published studies concluded that CBT might be an effective treatment in reducing purging and, perhaps, binge eating. Various kinds of antidepressants may also be effective in the treatment of bulimia. There is no evidence that one kind of antidepressant is more effective than another for this problem; however, antidepressants are associated with greater client dropouts than CBT. Client dropout is also greater in combined CBT and antidepressants than in CBT treatments alone (Bacaltchuk, Hay, & Trefiglio, 2001). Some studies have evaluated the effects of exposure therapy for bulimia, in which clients are exposed to foods they typically either avoid or whose consumption is followed by self-induced vomiting. In these treatments, the client eats a trigger food, after which he or she typically feels anxious and uncomfortable, but is prevented from purging or vomiting. The client is repeatedly exposed to the trigger food item and waits out his or her anxiety until it subsides. Although there is some evidence that this approach may be effective, its effect may be modest above and beyond simpler procedures, such as CBT.

Limited support exists for the effectiveness of other psychotherapies or antidepressants for bulimia (Bacaltchuk et al., 2000). Nevertheless, various adjunctive therapies, including individual and group psychotherapy, inpatient treatment protocols, and various kinds of family therapy, may play important roles in clients' recovery.

CASE EXAMPLE
Jean

Referral: Jean was a 19-year-old Anglo-American student referred by her family physician to a university clinic specializing in the treatment of eating disorders. She reported a three-year history of anorexic behaviors, including severe restriction of her eating during the day. Early in the day she would eat little or nothing, perhaps consuming only water and diluted fruit juice. Jean typically consumed only water and crackers for lunch. She might begin to eat late in the afternoon, but would eat many snacks throughout the evening. If she felt depressed, bloated, or guilty, she might make herself

(*continued*)

C A S E   E X A M P L E   **Continued**

vomit. Although she felt proud to show this much self-control, she said that she also felt depressed and disgusted that she had to make herself vomit in secret. Jean also exercised excessively, especially when she felt overweight (which was often) and when she had eaten normal or high-calorie foods. Jean had experienced irregular periods for the last two years. She had experienced extreme guilt over her eating problems and regarded herself as a weak person. She also experienced depressed mood and other symptoms of major depressive disorder and dysthymic disorder for the last three years.

Jean had responded well to an antidepressant prescribed by her physician, which she continued to take when she began psychotherapy. Although the medication alleviated her depressed mood, it had not resulted in any significant improvement in her weight or pattern of eating. She had changes from one antidepressant to another and had various medication doses. Although her mood continued to improve, no significant change in her core eating disorder had occurred.

Jean reported she did not have any close interpersonal relationships outside her family. She had a few friends in the past, but rarely heard from them any more and did not initiate contact with them. She described herself as lonely, anxious, and painfully shy, but unable to do anything about it. She reported that her parents, who lived two to three miles away from her, were loving but overbearing and continued to treat her like a child. She periodically went over to their home, usually at weekends. On these occasions, they would try to coerce her into eating as much as possible in a fairly unsubtle way. When they did succeed in making her eat more that she could tolerate, she would go home and make herself vomit. Although Jean's parents were sympathetic to Jean's struggles, they became frustrated with her and arguments often ensued over meals and family occasions, such as birthdays and holidays. She loved her parents and knew that they were concerned for her, but did not know how to stand up to them as an adult.

Immediate concerns: Are there any immediate dangers to the client or other vulnerable persons?

An evaluation by Jean's physician indicated she was in moderately good health, although she had a history of frequent colds and minor infections associated with periods of low mood. During the initial clinical interview Jean denied any suicidal thoughts, drug use, or laxative use to control her weight. She therefore appeared to pose no *immediate* harm to herself or to others. Long-term harm from anorexia could be significant.

Short-term goals: What goals need to be achieved in the first two to six sessions?

Jean kept a two-week diary of her eating and exercise, which revealed a pattern of almost no eating between awaking in the morning and the late afternoon. Jean often began eating during the afternoon, but then typically became very anxious about gaining weight and exercised vigorously to compensate for her meal. When negotiating goals for change, Jean refused to consider any interventions that would increase her weight. She had insight into her problem and agreed that it would probably cause health problems in the future, but her fear of becoming obese was so intense that she would not consider the possibility of change in this domain.

Jean expressed interest in becoming more comfortable with other people and stated she hoped to have friends and a boyfriend at some point in the future. She agreed to

CASE EXAMPLE   **Continued**

learn relaxation techniques, which she picked up quickly and immediately applied in familiar stressful settings. Jean also agreed to join an exercise club in which she could restrict her exercise to times other than after eating and in which she could meet other people. Jean benefited from a referral to a brief social skills workshop that addressed conversation initiation skills and empathy/listening skills. She also worked with the therapist to identify and increase pleasurable activities associated with improvements in her mood. Although after the first two months of therapy she had made no progress on her weight, she felt more relaxed with others, had made a couple of friends, and agreed that her life was better than it had been before counseling.

Long-term goals: What lifestyle changes and other long-term personal, relationship, and career goals need to be achieved?

Although the main treatment concern was not immediately addressed it was hoped that progress in other areas of Jean's life could lead to later progress in her eating behaviors. Indeed, after the first two months of treatment, Jean was agreeable in principle to changing her eating patterns. She agreed that at some point she should learn to eat three meals a day without feeling bad and that she should gain at least six pounds over the next six months. She agreed to begin experimenting with her eating pattern, gradually broadening the range of foods she ate until moving toward a more typical pattern of eating. She was not willing to consider eating large meals out in public at this time.

Jean stated her parents were pleased to hear about her progress, but that she continued to struggle with them over a variety of other issues when she was in their home. Future sessions were scheduled to explore Jean's relationship with her family, and it was agreed that Jean would invite her parents to a consultation session with the therapist. A family therapy referral also was considered to maintain Jean's progress toward both her primary (eating behaviors) and secondary (lifestyle gains) goals.

CASE EXAMPLE

Doreen

Referral: Doreen was a 25-year-old Anglo-American woman who referred herself to a local psychologist for treatment for bulimia nervosa. At her initial interview, Doreen admitted to bingeing on large quantities of high-calorie food several times a week, after which she would force herself to vomit by drinking large quantities of water and placing her fingers down her throat. Although she was only slightly above normal weight ranges for her age and body frame, Doreen viewed herself as being disgustingly fat and out of control. She was visibly tense and nervous during the interview, asking if she could smoke to calm her nerves. She sat on the edge of the chair, wringing her hands, her legs tightly

(*continued*)

CASE EXAMPLE   Continued

crossed and her brow furrowed. She described her lifestyle as crazy. She admitted that she often stayed out until 4:00 A.M., got drunk, smoked marijuana, and occasionally used cocaine. She also hinted at casual sex with multiple partners during these events.

Doreen reported that she experienced periods of depressed mood. She reported that she could not go to work on some days and stayed at home miserable and unable to get out of bed. When she did get to work, she described these periods as "a living hell, forcing herself to talk or move as if she might be normal." She also described what she called panic attacks when she became overwhelmed with anxiety and panic.

She lived alone in an apartment and saw little of her family, by her own choice. With the exception of recent dental cavities, Doreen's health was generally good, but she was concerned that in the long run her eating disorder and lifestyle were going to catch up with her somehow.

Immediate concerns: Are there any immediate dangers to the client or other vulnerable persons?

Doreen engages in behaviors that are a danger to herself, although there are no immediate, imminent threats to her own health or the health of others. She is in danger of unwanted pregnancy or possible HIV infection or other sexually transmitted disease. She could also be the easy victim of abuse or crime. Since there was no imminent danger to her at the first appointment these issues were not discussed at that time.

Short-term goals: What goals need to be achieved in the first two to six sessions?

Doreen agreed that the main reason she had come for therapy was to stop bingeing and vomiting. She kept a good diary of her food consumption, vomiting, and overall mood for a week. It was clear that vomiting was associated with eating high-calorie foods. Feelings of loneliness and isolation typically preceded her episodes of vomiting, and she often binged after solo shopping excursions.

The therapist selected exposure therapy to the cues associated with vomiting as an initial treatment. Once a week for several weeks, Jean was asked to bring in a pastry or trigger food of her choice, eat the item, and rate her subsequent anxiety over the next 90 minutes. Doreen agreed to the intervention on one condition: She would not eat the food in front of her therapist because she found it too embarrassing. Her therapist reluctantly agreed. Over the next few weeks Doreen reported she had been able to eat trigger food items without vomiting and without gaining weight. She seemed genuinely pleased at her progress.

On her last session, Doreen's therapist confronted her with the unpleasant fact that a pile of decomposing pastries had been found outside his office window a few days previously. Doreen laughed nervously, then asked if she could leave to go to the bathroom. She never came back or made any future appointments, even though they were offered to her by mail and phone message. After receiving no reply to his messages, the psychologist contacted Doreen's primary physician, who had been instrumental in making the referral, and offered appointments if Doreen was willing to come. His offer was never taken up.

Long-term goals: What lifestyle changes and other long-term personal, relationship, and career goals need to be achieved?

It was not possible to undertake any long-term goals with this client.

Pica

Besides anorexia and bulimia, DSM-IV describes eating disorders that typically are characteristic of infancy and/or developmental disorders. Pica is characterized by eating non-nutritive substances, such as grass or cigarette butts. It is often, but not always associated, with mental retardation or autism. Some infants and children may also exhibit pica. For example, Ivascu et al. (2001) and Roberts-Harewood and Davies (2001) reported that children with sickle-cell anemia were at high risk for pica. Pica also should be differentiated from culturally appropriate behaviors. In some cultures, eating specific kinds of dirt or clay may be normal, possibly because of the minerals contained in some types of soils. During pregnancy, some women also eat unusual substances, such as coal. In this section, the kind of pica that will be discussed relates to behavior that is clinically significant because of the danger it poses to the person. Such types of pica, in fact, may be life-threatening (Jancar & Speller, 1994). For example, clients may choke on ingested nonfood items. A small minority of clients may damage or irritate their digestive tracts or require surgery to remove items blocking their digestive tracts. Sometimes these very dangerous forms of pica are treated by restrictive procedures, such as restraints and fence masks to prevent the person from engaging in pica under any circumstances. Nevertheless, even these restrictive procedures may not prevent all occurrences of pica.

Sometimes a medical assessment of mineral and dietary deficiencies may also be done to identify possible dietary deficiencies that might be easily treatable through dietary supplements. For example, Lofts, Schroeder, and Maier (1990) reported that people with mental retardation with pica were much more likely to have zinc deficiency than those that did not display pica. Further, when they evaluated the effects of zinc supplementation on pica they found that it led to a reduction in pica for many people. Therefore, they concluded that zinc supplementation could be an important adjunctive treatment for pica. Pace and Toya (2000) were able to demonstrate that a common multiple vitamin was effective in reducing pica in a child with severe mental retardation. Thus, various mineral supplements might be relatively cheap and easy forms of intervention for pica.

Assessment and treatment of pica is primarily done through behavior analysis. As with any behavioral treatment, intervention is based on an analysis of the environmental variables that might influence the behavior (Sturmey, 2001). For example, Mace and Knight (1986) conducted a functional analysis of pica behavior in a 19-year-old man with mental retardation. His pica behavior was so severe that it was prevented by use of a helmet. In their analysis, they systematically compared periods of no, limited, and high rates of staff interaction. They found that in periods of high rates of interaction, pica was 66 percent lower than when there was no interaction. In a second, preintervention analysis, they found that removing the helmet strangely led to a reduction in pica. Therefore, the intervention they developed included removing the helmet accompanied by high rates of interaction from staff members. They reported that this was an effective intervention for this client.

Pica is sometimes a relatively difficult and intractable problem to treat. Interventions based on medical treatments such as mineral, vitamin, and dietary supplementation involve the least effort and carry minimal risk. Treatment of pica based on applied behavior analysis requires greater expertise in both assessment and treatment than what many practitioners typically have. Further, these interventions depend upon staff and parents carrying out interventions. Thus, mineral and dietary interventions generally should be considered as first-line treatments. If they are ineffective and the problem remains stigmatizing and/or dangerous, then referral to a professional with expertise in applied behavior analysis should be considered.

Rumination and Feeding Disorder of Infancy or Early Childhood

Diagnosis

Rumination Disorder is characterized by repeated regurgitation of food, which is then chewed or expelled from the mouth. DSM-IV specifies that this is not related to gastrointestinal problems, such as esophageal reflux or other general medical causes. Further, the problem must continue for at least one month. Additionally, DSM-IV specifies that the behavior does not occur exclusively during the course of anorexia or bulimia. If rumination occurs in someone with mental retardation or a pervasive developmental disorder, then the problem must be sufficiently severe to require separate clinical attention. It may appear that this problem must be a relatively easy one to recognize. However, some authors have noted that it may be underdiagnosed in some situations (Fredericks, Carr, & Williams, 1998).

Rumination can be very problematic. It may place the client at risk for medical problems, such as malnutrition, dental problems associated with the effects of stomach acid on the teeth and esophagus, respiratory problems, failure to thrive, as well as other medical problems. The social consequences are also important. For example, other people, including parents, may avoid the client because of the unattractive nature of the problem. Rumination in infants can be associated with fussiness, colic, food refusal, crying, sleeplessness, and other behaviors indicating distress. Rumination is often associated with developmental delay. In some cases, the infant may not receive sufficient stimulation to promote normal development, because caretakers avoid the infant. In rare cases, rumination may also be fatal (Shepherd et al., 1987).

Rumination is classified as a disorder of infancy or childhood. Shepherd et al. (1987) reported a median age of onset of 2.5 months for infants and young children referred for medical treatment. Rumination may also be seen in adolescents and rarely in adults, including older adults. In adults, it may be referred to as "psychogenic vomiting." People with mental retardation and autism are at risk for this disorder, especially those with severe and profound mental retardation in institutional settings (Fredericks et al., 1998; Gravestock, 2000). Kuhn, Matson, Mayville, and Matson (2001) reported that adults with mental retardation who ruminate were more likely to have poor social skills that those who did not ruminate. In rare cases, abuse and neglect of an infant may also be a relevant factor (Shepherd et al., 1987).

Feeding Disorder of Infancy or Early Childhood is characterized by at least one month of failing to eat sufficiently, associated with weight loss or failure to gain weight appropriately. As with rumination disorder, feeding disorder behaviors must not be due to gastrointestinal or other medical difficulties. Other DSM-IV diagnoses that could better account for these behaviors should be excluded. DSM-IV specifies that the age of onset must be before 6 years.

One of the main problems in diagnosing these disorders is differentiating them from normal variations in infant behavior. Armstrong, Previtera, and McCallum's (2000) evaluation of a residential program for mothers of infants treated for irritability, including feeding disorders, illustrates this point and illuminates potential treatment strategies. All infants in the program were receiving a variety of medical treatments and had been previously seen by multiple practitioners. At the beginning of the program, the infants received a medical workup and their mothers were assessed on a depression scale. Under medical supervision, all infants were taken off medications for irritability, after which their mothers received education about normal infant behavior and development and were taught to establish feeding and bedtime routines. Family issues were also explored. At three months' follow up, twenty-two of the forty-eight infants who entered the program were determined to have behavioral problems, twenty were determined to have feeding problems, and only nine were determined to have an identified organic problem causing their irritability. In addition, participating mothers' moods improved significantly from the beginning of the program. The authors concluded that many infants with normal irritability were receiving inappropriate medical treatments.

Assessment and Treatment

Assessment of rumination involves tricky questions of differential diagnosis of general medical causes versus psychiatric and psychological causes of the problem. There are a wide variety of general medical causes of rumination, which must be first evaluated, excluded, and if appropriate, treated physically. Therefore, in order to ensure access to appropriate medical intervention and potentially effective treatment, clients with rumination disorder should be referred to a specialist clinic for pediatric gastroenterology. A challenging clinical problem is when a referral is made for psychological treatment and evaluation from a medical center, but it is unclear if there are still undiagnosed general medical causes of rumination. Because of the specialized nature of the problem, assessment and treatment should take place within the context of specialized services that include medical, psychiatric, and psychological services.

Once medical causes have been eliminated, assessment should include the evaluation of other environmental factors. Olden (2001) has speculated that rumination is caused by the disruption of infant-mother bonding. At this time, there are no systematic evaluations of assessment or treatments based on this hypothesis. Interventions based on applied behavior analysis have shown promise in the treatment of rumination. Therefore, an analysis of the antecedents and consequences around rumination as well as the possible effects of diet texture and food type can be helpful in designing interventions.

Medical interventions for rumination often utilize relatively simple, low-risk procedures. Thickening foods and fluids is sometimes used as well, as is keeping an infant in an upright position after feeding to reduce the likelihood of regurgitation. Antacids or medical treatment of underlying acid reflux disease and other medical problems, such as gastric or esophageal ulcers, have been used successfully by some clinicians (Shepherd et al., 1987; Zimmermann et al., 2001). In a minority of cases, surgery may be performed to tighten the sphincter around the stomach to make regurgitation more difficult (Shepherd et al., 1987). Nevertheless, several authors have expressed concerns that surgery carries considerable risks for clients who are physically compromised by weight loss (Lockwood, Maenpaa, & Williams, 1997). Rantaanen, Salo, and Sipponen (1999), for example, reported that approximately 1 percent of clients died and an additional approximate 1 percent suffered life-threatening complications from anti-reflux surgery. Obviously, these risks and benefits should be explained thoroughly to family members during the process of gaining consent for medical interventions.

Behavioral treatment of rumination is based on the hypothesis that attention from favored people, avoidance of other people, or continued access to food or chewing might reinforce rumination (Winston & Singh, 1983). Relatively few positive behavioral interventions have emerged for chronic, severe rumination, although Weakley, Petti, and Karwisch (1997) successfully treated rumination in an adolescent girl using chewing gum after meals as an alternate behavior (and reinforcement). Positive behavioral treatments for rumination in children with mental retardation and autism have included increasing social stimulation before, during, and after meals, by holding the child (Whitehead et al., 1985). Other treatments that may be effective include increasing access to starchy foods, such as bread, so the person can eat as much as he or she wants (Thibadeau et al., 1999), and increasing the number of choices of food and reinforcements (Lockwood et al., 1997).

CASE EXERCISE

A community mental health team refers Ms. Ghezzi and her 15-week-old infant to you. Ms. Ghezzi, a 24-year-old Anglo-American single mother, has been a member of a women's group for several years because of anorexia and dysthymic disorder. Her social worker was concerned because she has complained her child does not eat enough and is underweight. According to the social worker, Ms. Ghezzi is concerned that her daughter is going to develop an eating disorder, like herself. Ms. Ghezzi says that when she bottle-feeds her daughter, the infant gags on the food and refuses to cooperate. She thinks her daughter does this to get back at her when she is busy. She is also concerned that she is a bad mother and causing these problems. This is Ms. Ghezzi's first child and she feels overwhelmed by the problem.

Study Questions

1. What assessments would you recommend for Ms. Ghezzi's daughter?
2. List your possible diagnoses, if any, for the child.
3. What assessments would you recommend for Ms. Ghezzi?

A few months later Ms. Ghezzi reports that her daughter, now aged 9 months, refuses to be weaned from the bottle. The child will take certain foods, but often spits them out and turns away when they are offered.

Study Questions

4. Describe the assessments you might make at this point.
5. Describe your possible interventions.

Two months later, the child is significantly underweight, has repeated colds and infections, and periodically regurgitates her food. Ms. Ghezzi appears more depressed than usual and states she cannot cope with her thoughts about what might happen to her daughter. The social worker calls and asks you to teach Ms. Ghezzi how to reinforce appropriate eating in her daughter.

Study Questions

6. What actions should you take?
7. What ethical and legal issues are present in this case?

REFERENCES

American Psychiatric Association. (1994). *Diagnostic and statistical manual of mental disorders* (4th ed.) *(DSM-IV)*. Washington, DC: Author.

Armstrong, K., Previtera, N., & McCallum, R. (2000). Medicalizing normality? Management of irritability in babies. *Journal of Pediatric Child Health, 36*, 301–305.

Bacaltchuk, J., Hay, P., & Trefiglio, R. (2001). Antidepressant versus psychological treatments and their combination for bulimia nervosa (Cochrane review). *Cochrane Database Systematic Review*, CD 003385.

Bacaltchuk, J., Trefiglio, R. P., Oliveira, I. R., Hay, P., Lima, M. S., & Mari, J. J. (2000). Combination of antidepressants and psychological treatments for bulimia nervosa: A systematic review. *Acta Psychiatrica Scandanavica, 101*, 256–264.

Bowers, W. A., & Andersen A. E. (1994). Inpatient treatment of Anorexia Nervosa: Review and recommendations. *Harvard Review of Psychiatry, 2*, 193–203.

Bulik, C. M., Sullivan, P. F., Carter, F. A., McIntosh, V. V., & Joyce, P. R. (1998). The role of exposure with response prevention in the cognitive-behavioural therapy for bulimia nervosa. *Psychological Medicine, 28*, 611–623.

Byrne, S., & McLean, N. (2001). Eating disorders in athletes: A review of the literature. *Journal of Science and Medicine in Sports, 4*, 145–159.

Calam, R., Waller, G., Slade, P. D., & Newton, T. (1990). Eating problems and perceived relationships with parents. *International Journal of Eating Disorders, 9*, 479–485.

Fichter, M. M., Herpertz, S., Quadflieg, N., & Herpertz-Dahlmann, B. (1998). Structured interview for anorexic and bulimic disorders for DSM-IV and ICD-10: Updated (third) revision. *International Journal of Eating Disorders, 24*, 227–249.

Fichter, M. M., & Quadflieg, N. (1999). Six-year course and outcome of anorexia nervosa. *International Journal of Eating Disorders, 26*, 359–385.

Fredericks, D. W., Carr, J. E., & Williams, W. L. (1998). Overview of the treatment of rumination disorder for adults in a residential setting. *Journal of Behavior Therapy and Experimental Psychiatry, 29*, 31–40.

Garner, D. M., Olmsted, M. P., Polivy, J., & Garfinkel, P. E. (1984). Comparison between weight-preoccupied women and anorexia nervosa. *Psychosomatic Medicine, 46*, 255–266.

Gravestock, S. (2000). Eating disorders in adults with intellectual disability. *Journal of Intellectual Disabilities Research, 44*, 625–637.

Hay, P. J., & Bacaltchuk, J. (2001). Psychotherapy for bulimia nervosa and bingeing (Cochrane review). *Cochrane Database Systematic Review, 3*, CD000562.

Ivascu, N. S., Sarnaik, S., McCrae, J., Whitten-Shurney, W., Thomas, R., & Bond, S. (2001). Characterization of pica prevalence among patients with sickle cell disease. *Archives of Pediatric and Adolescent Medicine, 155*, 1243–1247.

Jancar, J., & Speller, C. J. (1994). Fatal intestinal obstruction in the mentally handicapped. *Journal of Intellectual Disabilities Research, 38*, 413–422.

Kuhn, D. E., Matson, J. L., Mayville, E. A., & Matson, M. L. (2001). The relationship of social skills as measured by the MESSIER to rumination in persons with profound mental retardation. *Research in Developmental Disabilities, 22*, 503–510.

Lee, S., Lee, A. M., Leung, T., & Yu, H. (1997). Psychometric properties of the Eating Disorders Inventory (EDI-1) in a nonclinical Chinese population in Hong Kong. *International Journal of Eating Disorders, 21*, 187–194.

Lockwood, K., Maenpaa, M., & Williams, D. E. (1997). Long-term maintenance of a behavioral alternative to surgery for severe vomiting and weight loss. *Journal of Behavior Therapy and Experimental Psychiatry, 28*, 105–112.

Lofts, R. H., Schroeder, S. R., & Maier, R. H. (1990). Effects of serum zinc supplementation on pica behavior of persons with mental retardation. *American Journal on Mental Retardation, 95*, 103–109.

Mace, F. C., & Knight, D. (1986). Functional analysis and treatment of severe pica. *Journal of Applied Behavior Analysis, 19*, 411–416.

Mizes, J. S., & Christiano, B. A. (1995). Assessment of cognitive variable relevant to cognitive behavioral perspectives on anorexia nervosa and bulimia nervosa. *Behaviour Research and Therapy, 33*, 95–105.

Newton, J. R., Freeman, C. P., & Munro, J. (1993). Impulsively and dyscontrol in bulimia nervosa: Is impulsively an independent phenomenon or a marker of severity? *Acta Psychiatrica Scandanavica, 87,* 389–404.

Olden, K. W. (2001). Rumination. *Current Treatment Options in Gastroenterology, 4,* 351–358.

Pace, G. M., & Toya, E. A. (2000). The effects of a vitamin supplement on the pica of a child with severe mental retardation. *Journal of Applied Behavior Analysis, 33,* 619–622.

Rantaanen, T. K., Salo, J. A., & Sipponen, J. T. (1999) Fatal and life-threatening complications in anti-reflux surgery: Analysis of 5,502 operations. *British Journal of Surgery, 87,* 1573–1577.

Roberts-Harewood M., & Davies, S. C. (2001). Pica in sickle cell disease: "She ate the headboard." *Archives of Diseases of Childhood, 85,* 510.

Robin, A. L., Siegel, P. T., Moje, A. W., Gilroy, M., Dennsi, A. B., & Silkand, A. (1999). A controlled comparison of family therapy versus individual therapy for adolescents with anorexia nervosa. *Journal of the Academy of Child and Adolescent Psychiatry, 38,* 1482–1489.

Russell, G. F. (2001). Involuntary treatment in anorexia nervosa. *Psychiatric Clinics of North America, 24,* 337–349.

Shepherd, R. W., Wren, J., Evans, S., Lander, M., & Ong, T. H. (1987). Gastroesophogeal reflux in children. Clinical profile, course and outcome with active therapy in 126 cases. *Clinical Pediatrics, 26,* 55–60.

Skrzypek, S., Wehmeier, P. M., & Remschmidt, H. (2001). Body image assessment using body size estimation in recent studies on anorexia nervosa. A brief review. *European Child Adolescent Psychiatry, 10,* 215–221.

Slade, P. D., Newton, T., Butler, N. M., & Murphy, P. (1991). An experimental analysis of "perfectionism and dissatisfaction." *British Journal of Clinical Psychology, 30,* 169–176.

Stickney, M. I., Miltenberger, R. G., & Wolff, G. (1999). A descriptive analysis of factors contributing to binge eating. *Journal of Behavior Therapy and Experimental Psychiatry, 30,* 177–189.

Sturmey, P. (2001). Pica and developmental disability. *Journal of the American Board of Family Practitioners, 14,* 80–81.

Sturmey, P., & Slade, P. D. (1986). Anorexia nervosa and dysmorphophobia: A case study. *British Journal of Psychiatry, 149,* 780–782.

Thibadeau, S., Blew, P., Reedy, P. & Luiselli, J. K. (1999). Access to white bread as an intervention for chronic ruminative vomiting. *Journal of Behavior Therapy and Experimental Psychiatry, 30,* 137–144.

Walsh, B. T., Wilson, G. T., Loeb, K. L., Devlin, M. J., Pike, K. M., Roose, S. P., Fleiss, J., & Waterneaux, X. (1997). Medication and psychotherapy in the treatment of bulimia nervosa. *American Journal of Psychiatry, 154,* 523–531.

Weakley, M. M., Petti, T. A., & Karwisch, G. (1997). Case study. Chewing gum treatment of rumination in an adolescent with an eating disorder. *Journal of the American Academy of Child and Adolescent Psychiatry, 36,* 1124–1127.

Whitehead, W. E., Drescher, V. M., Morrill-Corbin, E., & Cataldo, M. F. (1985). Rumination syndrome in children treated by increased holding. *Journal of Pediatric Gastroenterology and Nutrition, 4,* 550–556.

Wilson, G. T., Vitousek, K. M., & Loeb, K. L. (2000). Stepped care treatment for eating disorders. *Journal of Clinical and Consulting Psychology, 86,* 564–572.

Winton, A. S. & Singh, N. N. (1983). Rumination in pediatric populations: A behavioral analysis. *Journal of the Academy of Child Psychiatry, 22,* 269–275.

Zimmermann, A. E., Walters, J. K., Katona, B. G., Souney, P. E., & Levine, D. (2001). A review of omeprazole use in the treatment of acid-related disorders in children. *Clinical Therapy, 23,* 660–679.

6 Substance-Related Disorders

CHAPTER OVERVIEW

1. DSM-IV differentiates Substance Use Disorders from Substance-Induced Disorders. Included under Substance Use Disorders are Substance Abuse and Substance Addiction Disorders. A wide range of substances can be abused.

2. Tolerance and withdrawal are key concepts in diagnosing Substance Use Disorders.

3. Co-morbid mental health problems, such as depression and anxiety disorders, are common.

4. Treatment of substance-related disorders is controversial. Many accepted forms of treatment, such as Alcoholics Anonymous, have a weak scientific basis. Other treatment strategies have stronger empirical support but are not widely used.

5. Treatment of substance-related disorders raises numerous ethical challenges related to confidentiality, illegal behavior, and potential dangers to the client and to others. Clinicians should directly address these issues early in therapy.

Diagnosis

DSM-IV divides Substance-Related Disorders into two groups: Substance Use Disorders (which are subdivided into Substance Dependence and Substance Abuse Disorders) and Substance-Induced Disorders. Substance-Related Disorders involve up to eleven types of substances, as specified by the DSM (see Table 6.1). The specific name, rather than type, of the substance a client uses should be specified when recording her or his diagnosis. For example, "*Diazepam* Withdrawal" should be recorded rather than simply "*Anxiolytic* Withdrawal."

Substance Dependence and Abuse Disorders

DSM -IV differentiates abuse from addiction (or dependency) disorders. In general terms, abuse disorders are less severe diagnoses, whereas dependency disorders reflect more insidious, widespread substance use patterns. Although not stated explicitly, the DSM-IV also intimates a view that, unlike abuse disorders, dependence disorders have a biological basis as "real physiological" addictions.

TABLE 6.1   General characteristics of the eleven groups of substances associated with Substance-Related Disorders.

Substance	Comments
Alcohol	Widely known in many cultures.
Amphetamines, etc.	Amphetamine, dextroamphetamine, methamphetamine, and amphetamine-like substances are included in some commercially available diet pills. Pure methamphetamine can be smoked as "crack-cocaine." Khat is a naturally occurring plant derivative that includes amphetamine-like compounds. Legal drugs, such as those used for ADHD (e.g., Ritalin) or weight loss.
Caffeine	Present in coffee, tea, over-the-counter medications, and some chocolate and cocoa products, but at small doses.
Cannabis	Various derivatives of the cannabis plant. May be smoked, added to food, or used as an oil. Synthetic versions are used to treat nausea and other medical problems.
Cocaine	Derived from the coca plant as leaves, paste, and other derivatives. Paste may be smoked. Powder may be either "snorted," injected as a "speedball," or smoked as "rocks" of "crack-cocaine."
Hallucinogens	Examples include LSD, mescaline, psilocybin, "ecstasy," and various naturally occurring substances.
Inhalants	A wide range of substances including gasoline, glue, thinners, paints, cleaners, and correction fluid. These are often inhaled using rags, plastic bags, or directly from aerosols.
Nicotine	Available as cigarettes, cigars, chewing tobacco, snuff, and nicotine gum and patches.
Opioids	Includes naturally occurring morphine, semi-synthetics (e.g., heroin), and synthetics (e.g., codeine, methadone).
Sedatives, Hypnotics, and Anxiolytics	Prescribed medications for anxiety disorders, sleep disorders, and anticonvulsants, such as benzodiazepines, carbamates (e.g., meprobamate), barbiturates, and barbiturate-like drugs. These may be obtained legally or illegally.

This distinction is by no means pure, however, and both substance use patterns actually lie on a continuum of impairment.

According to the DSM-IV, substance dependence is characterized by "a pattern of repeated self-administration [of a substance] that usually results in tolerance, withdrawal and compulsive drug-taking" (APA, 1994, p. 176). Many persons with substance dependence experience craving for their substance of choice.

To receive a diagnosis of substance dependence a client must experience at least three of seven symptoms over a twelve-month period. The first of these, *tolerance*, is shown either by a need for taking increased amounts of a substance to achieve the same desired effects or by reduced potency when the same amount of a substance is taken over a prolonged period or time. *Withdrawal*, closely related to tolerance, is exhibited by a specific set of symptoms associated with abstinence from a substance or by the need to ingest the substance to avoid these symptoms. Other symptoms of substance dependence include taking substances in larger amounts or over longer periods than intended; engaging in unsuccessful efforts to cut down or rein in the use of a substance; spending significant amounts of time obtaining, using or recovering from the effects of a substance; social, occupational or other life impairment due to substance use; and continued substance use despite awareness of the problems it brings to one's life (APA, 1994, p.181).

DSM-IV adds two specifiers to substance dependence diagnoses. The specifiers "With Physiological Dependence" or "Without Physiological Dependence" are used to indicate the presence or absence of withdrawal symptoms. Course specifiers are used to indicate patterns of remission during which a client fails to meet criteria for dependence or abuse. If a client who has been symptom-free for one month experiences the periodic reappearance of dependence symptoms over the subsequent twelve months, for example, the specifier "Sustained partial remission" may be added to her or his diagnosis to indicate this pattern.

A diagnosis of substance abuse is assigned when a client exhibits at least one of four symptoms, including failure to meet major role obligations due to her or his recurrent substance use (e.g., expulsions from school, neglect of children); recurrent substance use in dangerous situations (e.g., driving or operating machinery); recurrent legal problems related to substance use; or continued use of a substance despite persistent associated social or interpersonal problems. As with most other diagnoses, she or he also must experience impairment or distress to receive the diagnosis. Finally, the client must not meet the diagnostic criteria for substance dependency for the substance in question, although she or he might meet dependency criteria for another substance.

Substance-Induced Disorders

DSM-IV includes two substance-induced disorders, "Substance Intoxication" and "Substance Withdrawal," both of which are defined generically. These diagnoses may be used in association with any substance related to dependency or abuse.

A DSM-IV diagnosis of substance intoxication is assigned when three criteria are met. First, there is "a reversible substance-specific syndrome due to the recent ingestion of (or exposure to) a substance" (APA, 1994, p. 184). Intoxication typically produces diverse changes in overt behavior, thinking, and perception that are specific to the substance used. For example, alcohol intoxication often produces observable changes in speech, coordination, and coordination, coupled with general behavioral disinhibition (e.g., marked gregariousness, aggression, or inappropriate sexual behavior) and changes in perception and thinking (e.g., impairment of memory and attention) (see Table 6.2). Intoxication with sedatives, hypnotics, or anxiolytics similarly produces slurred speech, poor coordination, unsteady gait, impaired attention and memory, and, in extreme cases, stupor or coma. By contrast, cannabis intoxication usually produces impaired motor coordination, euphoria, increased appetite, and a markedly slowed perception of time. Intoxication with other substances vary with equal diversity.

The second DSM-IV criterion for substance intoxication is "clinically significant maladaptive behavioral or psychological changes that are due to the effect of that substance on the central nervous system" (p. 184). Thus, DSM-IV emphasizes that only substances that affect behavior via the brain are considered under substance-related disorders. In addition, the person must experience changes in her or his behavior that are both "significant" and "maladaptive," assessments that involve considerable judgment. Whereas some clinicians would consider returning to a job after a couple of beers "significant " and "maladaptive," others might consider such behavior culturally appropriate and not worthy of mention. The third criterion is that other general medical conditions or mental disorders cannot better account for the client's symptoms.

Substance withdrawal is recognized for only the following substances: alcohol; amphetamines; cocaine; nicotine; opioids; and sedatives, hypnotics, or

---

TABLE 6.2 **Signs and symptoms of intoxication and withdrawal for each of the eleven classes of substances in DSM-IV.**

Substance	Comments
Anabolic steroids	May produce an initial sense of well-being or euphoria. Long-term use may lead to dysphoric symptoms, depressive symptoms, or liver damage.
Nitrite inhalants ("poppers")	Produces intoxication including a full feeling in the head, mild euphoria, relaxation of smooth muscle, and enhanced sexual feelings. May cause impaired immune functioning, irritation of respiratory system, and toxicity.
Nitrous oxide ("laughing gas")	Rapid onset of a floating sensation and light-headedness. May cause confusion. Effects rapidly subside.
Catnip	Results in a cannabis-like high and LSD-like perceptions.
Betel nut	A chewed nut that produces a mild euphoria and a floating sensation. Commonly used in many cultures.
Kava	A derivative of the pepper plant. Causes sedation and incoordination.
Over-the-counter and prescription drugs	Cortisol, anti-Parkinsonian agents, and antihistamines may be abused.

anxiolytics. Unsurprisingly, substance withdrawal is often accompanied by a strong craving for the substance. Withdrawal signs and symptoms tend to be opposite to those observed in intoxication for a given substance.

A diagnosis of substance withdrawal is assigned when three criteria are met. First, after heavy and prolonged use of the substance, the client experiences a substance-specific syndrome due to her or his cessation or reduction of use of the substance. Second, this syndrome causes clinically significant distress or impairment in the client's social, occupational, or other important areas of functioning; and third, these symptoms are not due to another general medical or mental disorder.

Like intoxication, withdrawal patterns vary with the specific substances a client uses. Whereas alcohol withdrawal produces such symptoms as autonomic hyperactivity, motor tremor, nausea, hallucinations, agitation, and seizures, for example, nicotine withdrawal produces dysphoric mood, insomnia, frustration, anger, anxiety, restlessness, and impaired concentration. Cannabis withdrawal, by contrast, produces no recognized pattern of symptoms at all.

Each of the eleven substance groups described by DSM-IV is associated with a variety of specific disorders. For example, disorders related to cocaine include Cocaine-Induced Psychotic Disorder, Cocaine-Induced Mood Disorder, Cocaine-Induced Anxiety Disorder, Cocaine-Induced Sexual Disorder, Cocaine-Induced Sleep Disorder and Cocaine-Related Disorder NOS. DSM-IV also includes a diagnosis of Polysubstance-Related Disorders, which is used for persons repeatedly using at least three substances (excluding caffeine and nicotine). In addition, the diagnosis "Other (or Unknown) Substance-Related Disorders" may be assigned to clients experiencing significant problems with substances other than those noted, such as anabolic steroids, nitrite inhalants, nitrous oxide, anti-Parkinsonian agents, and antihistamines. (See Table 6.3 for a summary of these substances.)

TABLE 6.3 Substances included under Other (or Unknown) Substance-Related Disorders.

Substance	Intoxication	Withdrawal
Alcohol	Inappropriate sexual or aggressive behavior, mood lability, impaired judgment, or impaired social or occupational functioning. Signs include slurred speech, incoordination, unsteady gait, nystagmus, impairment in attention or memory, stupor, or coma (APA, 1994, p. 197).	Signs include sweating or fast pulse; increased hand tremor; insomnia; nausea or vomiting; transient visual, tactile, or auditory hallucinations or illusions; agitation; anxiety; or grand mal seizures (APA, 1994, pp. 198–199).

(continued)

TABLE 6.3   continued

Substance	Intoxication	Withdrawal
Amphetamines, etc.	Ingestion of amphetamine or amphetamine-like substances may produce euphoria or blunting affect, changes in sociability, hypervigilence, stereotyped behaviors, etc. Signs include fast or slowed heart rate, dilated pupils, elevated or lowered blood pressure, perspiration or chills, weight loss, motor agitation or retardation, weakness, respiratory depression, confusion, or seizures (APA, 1994, p. 208).	Signs include fatigue, vivid dreams, sleep disturbance, increased appetite, motor agitation or retardation (APA, 1994, p. 209).
Caffeine	Consumption of more than 2–3 cups of brewed coffee. Signs include restlessness, nervousness, excitement, insomnia, or flushed face.	No syndrome associated with caffeine withdrawal is described in APA, 1994.
Cannabis	Impaired motor coordination, euphoria, anxiety, sensation of slowed time. Signs include conjunctival injection, increased appetite, dry mouth, and fast heartbeat (APA, 1994, p. 218).	No syndrome associated with cannabis withdrawal is described in APA, 1994.
Cocaine	Euphoria, changes in sociability, hypervigilence. Signs include fast or slow heart beat; dilated pupils; increased or lowered blood pressure; perspiration or chills; nausea or vomiting; weight loss; motor agitation or retardation; muscular problems; confusion; or coma (APA, 1994 pp. 224–225).	Signs include fatigue; vivid, unpleasant dreams; sleep disturbance; increased appetite; motor retardation or agitation. (APA, 1994, pp. 225–226).

TABLE 6.3 **Continued**

Substance	Intoxication	Withdrawal
Hallucinogens	Symptoms of anxiety, depression, or paranoia. Perceptual changes, such as wakefulness and alertness. Signs include dilated pupils, heart racing, sweating, palpitations, blurred vision, tremors, and incoordination (APA, 1994, pp. 232–233). Flashbacks may occur months or years after use.	No syndrome associated with hallucination withdrawal is described in APA, 1994.
Inhalants	Behaviors include belligerence, apathy, impaired judgment. Signs include dizziness, nystagmus, incoordination, slurred speech, lethargy (APA, 1994, p. 239).	No syndrome associated with inhalant withdrawal is described in APA, 1994.
Nicotine	Nicotine intoxication is rare.	Signs include dysphoric or depressed mood, insomnia, irritability, anxiety, poor concentration, restlessness. (APA, 1994, pp. 244–245).
Opioids	Intoxication is characterized by initial euphoria followed by dysphoria and apathy. Signs include drowsiness or coma, slurred speech, and attention or memory impairments (APA, 1994, p. 250).	Signs include dysphoric mood, nausea and vomiting, muscle aches, runny eyes and nose, dilated pupils, diarrhea, fever, and insomnia.
Sedatives, Hypnotics, and Anxiolytics	Behavior such as inappropriate sexual or aggressive behavior, or mood lability. Signs include slurred speech, incoordination, unsteady gait, nystagmus, impaired memory or attention, and stupor or coma (APA, 1994, p. 264).	Signs such as sweating, rapid pulse, increased hand tremor, insomnia, nausea or vomiting, transient hallucinations or illusions, agitation, anxiety, and grand mal seizures (APA, 1994, p. 266).

Differential Diagnosis

It is sometimes difficult to distinguish substance-related disorders from substance use that does not rise to the level of abuse or dependence or from the legitimate use of medical substances. Like all DSM-IV diagnoses, substance-related disorders must result in clinically significant distress, clinically significant impairment in a person's ability to meet occupational or personal roles, or significant danger to the person. (See Chapter 1 for discussion of DSM-IV's definition of a mental illness.) In principle, then, substance-related disorders can be distinguished from social drinking, recreational use of illegal drugs, and drugs that are medically prescribed and legitimately used. This can be done because substance-related disorders result in tolerance, withdrawal, compulsive use, and substance-related problems (e.g., disrupted social roles, distress, medical problems related to the substance use, and legal and financial problems). In some instances, confusion may also arise in distinguishing withdrawal from intoxication. It can also be difficult to distinguish substance-related disorders from other mental or medical disorders, such as mania, psychoses, temporal lobe epilepsy, and some neurological disorders.

Dual Diagnosis

Recent research suggests that persons with substance-related disorders are at significant risk of experiencing additional psychiatric disorders (e.g., Grant, 1995). Substance dependency and co-morbid depression is particularly common, as are co-morbid diagnoses of anxiety disorders (e.g., Pozzi, Bacigalupi, & Tempests, 1997; Scott, Gilvarry, & Farrell, 1998).

Scott et al. (1998) provide a useful review of treatment of anxiety and mood disorders in persons with dual diagnosis, suggesting that antidepressant and anxiolytic medications may be appropriate in some of these cases. However, they noted that the use of such medications may be limited by their risks, not only of increased side effects but also of abuse. They recommended manualized, cognitive therapies as a useful approach to treat dually diagnosed clients.

Treatment Plan

Literature Review

Perhaps more than any other area of clinical literatures, substance use treatment research is plagued by disagreement at every juncture. Researchers and clinicians disagree, for instance, about the nature of substance-related disorders. Some clinicians are convinced that substance-related disorders are physical illnesses that require medical treatment, a model that sometimes portrays the client as an innocent victim of an illness society misunderstands. Others argue that clients with substance-related disorders are criminals who knowingly engage in illegal behaviors dangerous not only to themselves but often to others. Some clinicians see substance-related disorders as merely one more example of inappropriate and maladaptive behaviors that arise from learning, behaviors that can be unlearned and replaced with more adaptive ways of coping.

Practitioners and researchers also disagree about the appropriate goals of substance-use treatment. Some treatment programs (e.g., Alcoholics Anonymous) assert that the only permissible goal of treatment is abstinence; although clients may achieve remission, these models argue, they are never cured of their underlying illness and risk total remission if they resume even moderate drinking. Other clinicians, relying on research that suggests up to 15 percent of substance use clients may successfully resume moderate drinking patterns, recommend controlled drinking as an appropriate, and often more realistic, treatment goal (e.g., Kahler, 1995; Sobell & Sobell, 1973, 1976, 1995).

Finally, there is considerable disagreement over the appropriate methods of intervention with substance-using clients. Whereas organizations like Alcoholics Anonymous believe that a kind of religious process can be used to transform the person's life, including his or her history of substance-related disorder, other programs suggest not only that appropriate drinking can be taught but that other skills, such as problem solving, social skills, anxiety management, anger management, and so on can be taught to replace the possible functions of alcohol abuse. In addition, a variety of programs have emerged to intervene early with school-age adolescents to inculcate socially reinforcing views of appropriate drinking behaviors, before (in theory) chronic drinking problems emerge. Recent research suggests these approaches may be particularly useful with minority adolescents (Botvin et al., 2001a, 2001b).

Alcoholics Anonymous (AA) and Narcotics Anonymous (NA).

AA and NA use a twelve-step treatment program. These steps include acceptance of one's alcoholism (or addiction to narcotics), acceptance that alcoholism is a disease, breaking down denial, and development of a healthy dependency (Marron, 1993). Twelve-step programs often involve a spiritual, if not frankly Christian, commitment. These programs are immensely popular and widespread to the point of becoming, in some ways, twentieth- and twenty-first-century cultural icons of substance dependency treatment.

Unfortunately, outcome research supporting the AA/NA approach has been relatively meager in quality and quantity. For example, a longitudinal study of 157 adolescents in AA/NA programs for chemical dependency reported that whereas participants completing treatment were more likely to be abstinent at the end of treatment, their abstinence dropped off sharply at two-year follow-up (Alford, Koehler, & Leonard, 1991). Meta-analyses of the outcome literature generally support the robustness of these findings, suggesting, in some cases, that attending AA meetings may actually lead to worse outcomes than no treatment or alternate treatments (Kownacki & Shadish,1999). Perhaps most troublingly, Kownacki and Shadish's (1999) review of twenty-one studies found that those conducted most rigorously revealed the worst outcomes for AA-based treatments. In addition, although surveys suggest such elements of the twelve-step treatment program as using recovering alcoholics as therapists, creating an atmosphere of social support and receiving fellowship from former addicts seem important to participants, other putatively key elements of the twelve-step program (e.g., spirituality) have received considerably less empirical support (e.g., Nealon-Woods, Ferrari, & Jason, 1995).

In summary, although AA and NA programs are widespread, there is relatively little empirical support for their effectiveness. Dropout before and during the program and relapse after the program are major problems that may limit the effectiveness of this approach. In addition, some participants may suffer from the "self-fulfilling prophecy" effect of the dichotomous equation of even mild drinking with abstinence violation. However, participants in AA/NA-style programs may benefit from the social support they receive in these programs, particularly the support of fellow members and therapists who themselves are recovering from substance dependence.

Psychotherapy.   There is little research support for the effectiveness of traditional psychotherapy with substance-related disorders. There currently appears to be no strong indication for the use of traditional therapies as the sole interventions for these diagnoses.

Some evidence suggests that solution-focused therapies (SFT), which help clients enhance incremental or envisioned improvements in their cognitive, behavioral, and family systems patterns, may be effective with chronic substance dependent clients with few supportive resources (e.g., Juhnke & Coker, 1997). Further research may validate this model as a useful element of a comprehensive substance treatment approach (Mason, Chandler, & Grasso, 1995; Osborn, 1997).

Counseling.   Adjunctive counseling is an important element of the management of substance-related disorders. A meta-analysis of fifteen studies evaluating nursing and health visitors' brief interventions for smoking with at least six-month follow-up, for example, found that brief psychoeducational interventions were associated with reduced smoking rates (Rice & Stead, 2000). Fleming et al. (1999) similarly found that counseling in a primary care setting led to reduction in alcohol use, binges, and excessive drinking, including a remarkable 74 percent reduction in binge drinking. Wilk, Jensen, and Havighurst (1997) reported similarly optimistic results in a meta-analysis of twelve randomized trials of brief (less than one hour) motivational interventions to reduce alcohol intake in heavy drinkers, an arguably economical approach to a fairly common problem. It is important to note, however, that the goal of many such interventions is reduction in consumption, rather than total abstinence (Wilk et al., 1997).

Investigations of adjunct counseling with clients with more severe abuse patterns suggests it may be modestly helpful. A recent meta-analysis of interventions for drinking/driving offenders, for example, found that in studies that used adequate methodological designs, counseling led to an 8 to 9 percent reduction in clients' recidivism rates (Wells-Parker et al., 1995). Multimodal interventions that included education, psychotherapy/counseling, follow-up contact, and probation appeared to be most effective in reducing clients' recidivism behaviors. In addition, simple educational counseling that transmits information and increases clients' motivation may have a significant impact on some substance-related disorders, at least those associated with more moderate, uncomplicated problems.

Medical Treatments.   Although beyond the scope of this brief review, an extensive range of medical treatments are available for use with persons with substance abuse disorders. This review highlights some common applications of psychotropic medications with substance-use clients, such as controlled nicotine delivery systems and antabuse with alcohol-dependent clients.

Nicotine patches and gum have been popular medical interventions to assist clients in stopping smoking. Evidence suggests these methods are both safe and effective. A meta-analysis of nicotine gum treatment studies, for example, found that the use of nicotine gum at specialist clinics led to a 27 percent cessation rate at six months follow-up, compared to an 18 percent cessation rate for placebo treatments (Lam et al., 1987). These interventions were far less effective when used in general practice, however, producing no differences from placebo treatments. A meta-analysis by Fiore et al. (1994) similarly found cessation rates of 27 percent and 13 percent for patch and placebo, respectively, at end of treatment and 22 percent and 9 percent for patch and placebo, respectively, at six months follow-up. Intensive behavioral counseling was also associated with a modest increase in cessation rates.

The most common medical intervention used with alcohol-dependent clients has been the prescription of antabuse to induce nausea upon consumption of alcohol. Authors disagree over the effectiveness of this treatment. Although several double-blind placebo trials have suggested antabuse is superior to placebos in reducing alcohol intake (e.g, Fuller et al. 1986; Peachey et al., 1983; Wilson et al., 1978), other studies have failed to replicate these findings (e.g., Johnsen & Moreland, 1991; Ling et al., 1983). Other important clinical questions related to antabuse are treatment compliance issues (which impact its real-world effectiveness; cf. Fuller et al., 1986), side-effects complications, and ascertainment of effective dosing (Kranzler, 2000). Other medications currently being evaluated with substance use clients, such as naltrexone (an opioid antagonist) and buspirone, are beyond the scope of this chapter, although it should be noted that benzodiazepines are often used effectively (albeit carefully) as an adjunct to acute alcohol withdrawal treatments (e.g., Holbrook et al., 1999). In any case, medical treatments are best supplemented with psychosocial interventions (e.g., Griffiths et al., 2000).

Drying out and Cold Turkey.   Abrupt cessation of long-term substance abuse is often referred to as going "cold turkey." This method has been used for the abuse and dependency of alcohol, nicotine, and a variety of other substances. Depending upon the substance at hand, going cold turkey may be dangerous and is best done only under supervision or in an inpatient setting. Although immediate cessation of the use of a substance might be indicated because of imminent medical dangers, the outcome literature indicates that going cold turkey is not by itself an effective strategy. Cinciripini et al. (1995), for example, compared three schedules of gradual reduction in cigarette intake three weeks prior to quitting smoking. Abstinence rates at one-year follow-up were 44 percent for the group who progressively increased the interval between cigarettes; by contrast, the abstinence rates for nonspecific instructions to reduce smoking gradually and for no reduction prior to quitting were only 18 percent and 22 percent, respectively.

An alternative approach to gradual reduction in smoking is known as "brand fading" (i.e., switching incrementally from high to low tar brands of cigarettes prior to quitting smoking). Comparing brand fading with self-monitoring of nicotine and tar intake and a modified American Cancer Society program, Foxx and Brown (1979) found that abstinence at eighteen-month follow-up was 40 percent for the brand-fading group, whose intake of nicotine and tar were well below baseline for those participants that did not quit. Participants in other groups had lower rates of quitting and higher intakes of tar and nicotine. Another permutation of this method is the gradual reduction of nicotine doses through nicotine patch or gum programs. In summary, alternatives to cold turkey may be not only safer but more effective than going cold turkey, at least in terms of clients' reduction in their use of nicotine.

Controlled Drinking.   Considerable controversy arose in the mid-1970s over the possibility of teaching controlled drinking as an alternate to sobriety. (In some ways this debate parallels the contemporary debate over abstinence and safe sex and contraception for HIV and teen pregnancy prevention.)

Sobell and Sobell (1973, 1976) reported data from a trial of controlled drinking. The clients were hospitalized alcoholics. (Thus, they were not clients with mild drinking problems.) Both data from the initial trial and subsequently reported follow-up data at one year demonstrated that controlled drinking was superior to abstinence. In response, Pendry, Maltzman, and West (1982) challenged these findings. After reviewing records, interviewing participants, and a ten year follow-up, they concluded that the participants did not achieve controlled drinking. Six had become abstinent, eight drank excessively, four were dead from alcohol-related causes, and one was missing. Pendry et al. accused the Sobells of fraud. After extensive investigation, the Sobells were cleared of any scientific misconduct. To date, no study has shown that abstinence produces superior outcomes to controlled drinking.

The debate over the effectiveness of controlled drinking remains in the research literature and services. Some authors continue to see controlled drinking as immoral and dangerous; others see it as a scientifically validated approach to treatment (Peele, 1992).

Behavior Therapy.   Behavior therapy has been used to address a variety of substance-related disorders. Azrin et al. (1994) reported a well-designed study comparing behavior therapy versus supportive counseling for treatment of illegal drug use, including cocaine, marijuana, and hard drugs. Behavior therapy consisted of stimulus control procedures, urge control, contracting and family support, competing response procedures and contingencies based on the results of urinalysis.

After nineteen sessions of therapy, the proportion of participants who were drug-free increased from 37 percent at two months to 65 percent at twelve months of therapy, compared to an approximately constant 20 percent of those receiving only supportive counseling. Behavior therapy was also consistently superior to supportive counseling on measures of employment and a rage of other broad mental health and social functioning measures. A follow-up investigation approximately nine months after termination indicated these differences were maintained on measures of drug use and psychosocial functioning (Azrin et al., 1996).

Behavior therapy also has been used as elements of relapse prevention (RP) packages of cognitive-behavioral interventions that address relapse in a variety of substance-related disorders. A meta-analysis of twenty-six studies involving nearly 10,000 participants found that RP was generally effective, especially for alcohol- and polysubstance-related disorders (Irvin et al., 1999). Thus, behavior therapy, either singly or combined with other treatment modalities, can be an important and effective method of intervention. It can be used to help substance-using clients immediately reduce their substance intake, to teach clients alternative, adaptive ways of living and coping with stress, or to help clients identify and circumvent relapse behaviors.

CASE EXAMPLE

Ms. Gardner

Referral: Ms. Gardner, an Anglo woman in her mid-fifties, had lost her husband several years previously. Ms. Gardner was a co-owner of a large and usually profitable family business. She was articulate and of above-average intelligence. She had experienced progressively more frequent bouts of drinking over the past few years. Ms. Gardner had always been a social drinker, but following the death of her husband she assumed additional responsibilities in the family business and found the increasing responsibilities, the loss of her husband, and her subsequent financial instability to be tremendously stressful.

Ms. Gardner's drinking pattern was fairly characteristic. She could remain sober for weeks or months at a time, then have an occasional drink with no loss of control. However, she stated she had always been very anxious and at times became severely anxious at social occasions. Ms. Gardner repeatedly relapsed when she had large social gatherings at her house, which became an intense source of embarrassment to her and her family. On several occasions, she made all the arrangements for a gathering at her home, then lost control as the gathering approached and drank excessively, after which her guests arrived to find her drunk and stuporous. Ms. Gardner appeared highly motivated for change but at a loss to know what to do. She had taken a variety of anxiolytics and antidepressants over the last two years. She reported that they had helped reduce her overall level of anxiety but had not impacted her specific problem situations of drinking.

Immediate concerns: Are there any immediate dangers to the client or other vulnerable persons?

(*continued*)

C A S E   E X A M P L E   Continued

There are no immediate concerns for Mrs. Gardner's safety or the safety of others. She does not have a history of violence, IV-drug usage, unsafe sexual practices, or risk-taking behavior. Ms. Gardner owns an automobile, but she typically takes the subway to her place of employment and reports she does not drive after drinking.

Short-term goals: What goals need to be achieved in the first two to six sessions?

Ms. Gardner agreed to six goals for her first two months of therapy. First, she wanted to learn to relax, especially in anticipation of major social situations. Second, she agreed to keep a log a daily stress to attempt to identify triggers for anxiety. Third, she agreed that she would temporarily reduce the number of social events she had to cater at home. Fourth, she agreed to review her workload and to draw up a realistic set of priorities at work and to reassign or drop certain assignments altogether. Fifth, she agreed to get a review of her medication from her consulting psychiatrist. Finally, she agreed she would draw up a list of activities that were pleasant for her but which did not involve any demands from others. Ms. Gardner was knowledgeable about alcohol, including the health complications associated with bouts of excessive drinking.

During the first month of therapy, Ms. Gardner learned relaxation exercises, which she was quickly able to apply in real-life situations. Ms. Gardner resolved several of her work problems and reduced her workweek to four days a week. She used her additional time for activities she enjoyed alone, without friends and family, whom she often found to be more a source of stress than help. She went to a hair salon every week and signed up for an aerobics class in the afternoon, followed by a leisurely hot tub and sauna. She contacted her financial advisor and received some reassurance about her personal financial situation. She also had her psychotropic medication reviewed, and modified, by her psychiatrist.

Long-term goals: What lifestyle changes and other long-term personal, relationship, and career goals need to be achieved?

After three months of treatment, all appeared to be going well. On occasion, Ms. Gardner had one or two social drinks, but no episodes of excessive drinking or drunkenness. After a phone conversation with a friend, she felt confident to schedule one of her usual large-scale parties. Everything went well until the day of the party, when she suddenly felt panicky and overwhelmed. She made it through to evening, laying the table and preparing the food, but the thought of all of her friends arriving was more than she could stand. By the time her first guest arrived 30 minutes later, she had consumed a half of a bottle of brandy and could barely speak.

At her next appointment, Ms. Gardner was intensely embarrassed and guilty at her disappointment. She agreed that she had gone for nearly three months without an episode of drunkenness and that was the longest she had been sober for over three years. She reviewed the elements of her treatment plan and agreed that it was a good plan. However, she agreed that she had probably tried to tackle a situation too early that was too difficult for her.

Ms. Gardner and her clinician agreed her treatment plan needed revision. Ms. Gardner agreed to complete additional Antecedent-Behavior-Consequence diaries related to social demands that were milder than her large parties. She also agreed to learn more about relapse prevention and took a long-term view of recovery, acknowledging that she might not fully know if she was going to recover from her Alcohol Dependency and

CASE EXAMPLE   Continued

anxiety problems for even a couple of years. Finally, Ms. Gardner agreed to work to resolve other broader, existential issues in her life related to her possible upcoming retirement and to the change in her life role from a married, successful businesswoman to a woman still mourning the loss of her husband.

Ethical and Professional Challenges

Confidentiality and Illegal Behavior

Some clients with substance-related disorders engage in illegal behaviors. Some take, buy, and sell illegal substances. Others steal to support their habit or engage in illegal and dangerous behaviors, such as drunk driving or operating machinery while intoxicated. Still others engage in prostitution or other illegal or dangerous behaviors to support their habits. Their therapists routinely become aware of these illegal acts. What is the responsibility of these therapists? What limits to confidentiality, if any, exist in these situations?

Two ethical principles apply here: confidentiality and beneficence. Since client-therapist communications are generally confidential, this information can not be divulged to others without the client's consent, except under limited circumstances. For example, under certain circumstances a court may compel a therapist to release notes or testify without the client's consent. But generally, information about illegal activities remains confidential. Although Tarasoff might apply to some situations (e.g., cases involving an identified potential victim), common recklessness, such as drunk driving or working while intoxicated, may not present dangers specific enough to invoke Tarasoff principles. However, this does not absolve a therapist from making a reasonable effort to ensure the safety of people other than the client. It would be prudent to make a reasonable effort to insure the well-being of both the client and of others.

Cultural Issues

Finn (1994) has observed that many drug treatment programs experience problems in recruiting, retaining, and treating minority clients. Others have argued that this is part of a broader challenge that mental health professions such as psychology face in response to an ever more diverse population (e.g., Hall, 1997). There are apparently simple solutions to some but not all of these issues. Some language barriers, for example, can be overcome in recruiting clients by advertising services in the languages of client population. Considerable controversy exists, however, as to how culturally sensitive and effective services should be developed. Recognizing the different cultural norms for drug use between ethnic and other subcultures also may be difficult. If a therapist comes from a culture where the recreational use of marijuana is the norm, for example, how should she or he work with the child of a committed Southern Baptist family who regards the use of even one marijuana joint as a sin offensive to God?

Professional ethical guidelines (e.g., ACA, 1995; APA, 1992) are clear about a clinician's responsibilities in these situations: Her or his first duty is to the well-being of the client. The laws relating to negligence are also clear: Therapists have a duty of care to their clients. The clinician's behavior therefore must be comparable to the same standards offered by a reasonable person, or in this case, another reasonable therapist. In addition, professional ethical standards relating to competence may also apply to such a case. The notion of cultural competence—one's skills, knowledge, attitudes, and training in working with people from diverse cultural backgrounds—could be viewed as a training issue for the therapist.

Both professional ethical standards and the law, then, push clinicians in the direction of ensuring their clients' well-being first. In culturally diverse situations between a therapist and client, the therapist has a responsibility to learn about the client's culture through reading or by seeking a consultation from another therapist who is of similar cultural background to the client. If the therapist recognizes that she or he is harming the client because of a lack of thorough competence in working with clients of a given background, the therapist has an obligation to find the client alternative help. She or he must do so in a way that results in the least harm to the client (see Case Exercise).

CASE EXERCISE

A beginning clinician worked with a 19-year-old upper-class Los Angeles woman for three sessions, when she insouciantly reported she snorted cocaine at weekend parties and frequently engaged in promiscuous and reckless sexual behavior. When she further reported she often drove dangerously when high, her therapist, who lost his partner to an intoxicated driver eight years previously, became exasperated to the extent that he felt he could no longer help the woman. The actions he subsequently took outline an appropriate response to an ethical dilemma. First, when he recognized he could not effectively help the client, he consulted with a trusted colleague, without disclosing the client's identity. After reviewing the situation, the therapist and his colleague identified a more experienced drug counselor who worked successfully with similar clients. Once the counselor's services were affirmed to be available, the therapist met with the client, openly and honestly discussed his dilemma, and offered her the alternative services. The therapist then offered to work with the new clinician to smooth the client's transition and arranged a signed release (with her informed consent) to do so. He then followed up with the client to ensure she was able to initiate the services, which she did.

The therapist's actions here were both ethical and legal. He put his client's interests first and did not continue to receive fees for what easily might constitute inappropriate services. He also ensured the client was safe and continued to receive services.

Most therapists would agree that his actions were not only reasonable but were good services in the circumstances.

Study Questions

1. What client attitudes or behaviors involving substance use would you find troubling?

2. Under what circumstances would you consider referring a client with whom you felt you were mismatched?

3. Identify three resources in your geographical area to which you would consider referring a client with whom you could not conscionably work.

4. Identify two mental health professionals with whom you could consult if you were in a situation similar to that of the therapist described in this case.

CASE EXERCISE

A client with whom you have been working in a substance-dependence setting reports during your third session together that he has been giving rohyponol to his cat "to see what happens." He states that several of his friends have observed him doing this and that "it's the most hilarious thing you'll ever see—watching a cat get so stoned he can't walk across the room without vomiting or blacking out." The client further reports that one of his friends has been giving rohyponol to women he has met at parties and that "he says his sex life has been going through the roof."

Study Questions

1. What ethical issues are raised by the client's disclosure of his behaviors with his cat? What personal issues are raised for you by this report? What concerns might you have that he could administer rohyponol to other unwitting victims?

2. How would you deal with this situation? Are you obligated to protect the confidentiality of the client's disclosure of his behaviors? Are you obligated to continue working with him? If you felt you could not work with this client, how might you arrange alternate help for him?

3. What are your ethical obligations involving the client's report about his friend's behaviors? What actions should you take upon hearing this information?

4. With whom might you consult if you were working with this client? Would you inform the client if you chose to do so?

Drug Use by Mental Health Professionals

Illegal drug use among professionals, a not altogether uncommon problem, appears to be related to the presence of concurrent mental health problems, work-related stress and access to illicit substances (e.g., Brooke, Edwards, & Andrews, 1993; McGovern, Angres, & Leon, 2000; Trinkoff & Storr, 1994). Mental health professionals who use illegal drugs face several ethical challenges. First, professional guidelines clearly state that competence is an important professional standard (e.g., ACA, 1995; APA, 1992). Practicing while impaired because of the misuse of alcohol, cannabis, or even legal drugs violates professional ethical guidelines, is probably illegal, and raises liability issues for the practitioner. As in other liability issues, the standard against which practitioners are held may be quite stringent. Errors made while under the influence of illegal substances that result in harm to a client are likely to be viewed very dimly by professional bodies and courts. In some cases, insurance companies may exclude coverage of professionals engaged in these behaviors, leaving them personally liable for damages.

It also may be difficult for a mental health professional to recommend abstinence from an illicit substance when he or she is using the same substance on a recreational basis. Some health professionals come from cultural or subcultural backgrounds that normalize the use of certain illicit drugs (e.g., Baldwin et al., 1991). Professionals who use illicit substances, however, may face significant conflicts between their own behaviors and the legal and professional standards of their host cultures. Whereas the use of cannabis to alleviate the nausea among AIDS patients is accepted among some subcultures, for example, it is explicitly illegal in many states. When a psychologist or counselor becomes aware of a client's illegal use of cannabis for this purpose, what should she or he do? Since the information is revealed within the context of a confidential relationship and there is no imminent harm to a specific person, should she or he condone or condemn the client's behavior? Similarly, if a clinician comes from a conservative cultural background that proscribes the use of all illicit substances, should she or he impose their own values on clients? Professional ethical guidelines are clear that if a value conflict between a practitioner and a client may result in harm to the client, the practitioner's first obligation is to the client's well-being. In some cases, the clinician should excuse him- or herself from working with the client, help the client find an alternative therapist, and ensure that she or he experiences as little harm as possible from the interruption (and transition) of services.

Adolescents and Confidentiality

Another common ethical dilemma arises when therapists become aware of the use of illegal substances by adolescent clients. These circumstances can present a number of difficult ethical conflicts to a therapist, including issues related to confidentiality and identifying who the client is—the adolescent or the parent or legal guardian. Additional challenges can come from the potential conflict between establishing rapport with an adolescent client and permitting his or her parents to have full access to any information about their minor child they may wish to have. Some clinicians, recognizing this issue up front, raise it early on with both the adolescent and parents and establish agreements about the limits of confidentiality, if any, during treatment.

HIV Risk

Clients who use IV drugs or engage in risky sexual behavior while drunk or high are at risk for HIV infection and other sexually transmitted diseases. In some cases, clients are at risk of infecting others with HIV or other sexually transmitted diseases. One of the principal ethical challenges a clinician faces in working with such clients is that of confidentiality when there is the potential harm to the client or others. The potential for harm to the client is relatively easy to deal with: The therapist should educate the client as to the risks he or she may be experiencing. The therapist also should exercise a duty of care to the client. However, in this situation there might be considerable variability in professional practice. Should the clinician tell the client that he or she must not engage in any sexual behavior, or only in "safe" sexual practices? Or should the clinician recognize variations exist in standards of sexual conduct and let it go at that? At what point, if ever, should the therapist breach confidentiality to prevent the possible HIV infection of an identifiable other person? These issues are discussed in Chapter 2, but the bottom line is that clinicians should be familiar not only with their ethical codes and standards but also with the laws of the states and communities in which they practice.

Homelessness

Research suggests that people who are homeless experience high rates of substance use. Homeless persons also may experience other health-related problems, including mental health problems. Although they have great need they have poor access to services. In the United States homeless persons are unlikely to have health insurance. Additionally, even in situations in which they have insurance, they may have considerable difficulty in accessing services. Further problems include the poor quality and lack of continuity in services that they receive.

Applying the principle of beneficence to these situations requires that the clinician attend to all of his or her clients' needs. Therapy may not be the most effective way to address someone's depression if he or she is cold, miserable, and hungry.

References

American Counseling Association (ACA). (1995). *Code of ethics and standards of practice*. Alexandria, VA: Author.

American Psychiatric Association. (1994). *Diagnostic and statistical manual of mental disorders* (4th ed.) *(DSM-IV)*. Washington, DC: Author.

American Psychological Association. (1992). *Ethical principles for psychologists and code of conduct.* Washington, DC: Author.

Alford, G. S., Koehler, R. A., & Leonard, J (1991). Alcoholics Anonymous-Narcotics Anonymous model inpatient treatment of chemically dependent adolescents: A 2-year outcome study. *Journal for the Study of Alcohol, 52,* 118–126.

Azrin, N. H., Acierno, R., Kogan, E. S., Donohue, D. Besalel, V. A., & McMahon, P. T. (1996). Follow-up results in supportive versus behavioral therapy for illicit drug use. *Behaviour, Research and Therapy, 34,* 41–46.

Azrin, N. H., McMahon, P. T., Donohue, B., Besalel, V. A., Lapinski, K. J., Kogan, E. S., Acierno, R. E., & Galloways, E. (1994). Behavioral therapy for drug abuse: A controlled treatment outcome study. *Behaviour, Research and Therapy, 32,* 8875–8866.

Baldwin, D. C., Hughes, P. H., Conard, S. E. Storr, C. L., & Sheehan, D. V. (1991). Substance use among senior medical students. A survey of 23 medical schools. *Journal of the American Medical Association, 265,* 2074–2078.

Botvin, G. J., Griffin, K. W., Diaz, T., & Ifill-Williams, M. (2001a). Preventing binge drinking during early adolescence: One- and two- year follow-up of a school-based preventive intervention. *Psychology of Addictive Behaviors, 15*(4), 360–365.

Botvin, G. J., Griffin, K. W., Diaz, T., & Ifill-Williams, M. (2001b). Drug abuse prevention among minority adolescents: Posttest and one-year follow-up of a school-based preventive intervention. *Prevention Science, 2*(1), 1–13.

Brooke, D. Edwards, G. & Andrews, T. (1993). Doctors and substance misuse: Types of doctors, types of problems. *Addiction, 88,* 655–663.

Chick, J., Anton, R., Checinski, K., Croop, R., Drummond, D. C., Farmer, R., Labriola, D., Marshall, Moncrief, J., Morgan, M. Y. Peters, T., & Ritson, B. (2000). A multi-centered, randomized, double-blind, placebo-controlled trial of naltrexone in the treatment of alcohol dependence or abuse. *Alcohol and Alcoholism, 35,* 587–593.

Cinciripini, P. M., Lapintsky, L., Seay, S., Wallfisch, A., Kitchens, K., & Van Vunakis, H. (1995). The effects of smoking schedules on cessation outcome: Can we improve on common sense methods of gradual and abrupt nicotine withdrawal. *Journal of Clinical and Consulting Psychology, 63,* 388–399.

Finn, P. (1994). Addressing the needs of cultural minorities in drug treatment. *Journal of Substance Abuse Treatment, 11,* 325–337.

Fiore, M. C., Smith, S. S., Jorenby, D. E., & Baker, T. B. (1994). The effectiveness of the nicotine patch for smoking cessation. A meta-analysis. *Journal of the American Medical Association, 271,* 22–29.

Fleming, M. F., Manwell, L. B., Adams, W., & Stauffacher, E. A. (1999). Brief physician advice for alcohol problems in older adults: A randomized community based trial. *Journal of Family Practice, 48,* 378–384.

Foxx, R. M., & Brown, R. A. (1979). Nicotine fading and self-monitoring for cigarette abstinence or controlled smoking. *Journal of Applied Behavior Analysis, 12,* 111–125.

Fuller, R. K., Branchey, L., Brightwell, D. R., Derman, R. M., Emrick, C. D., Iber, F. L., James, K. E., Lee, K. K., Lowenstam, I., et al. (1986). Disulfiram treatment of alcoholism. A Veterans Administration cooperative study. *Journal of the American Medical Association, 256,* 1449–1455.

Grant, B. R. (1995). Comorbidity between DSM-IV drug use disorders and major depression: Results of a national survey of adults. *Journal of Substance Abuse, 7,* 481–497.

Greenfland, S., Satterfield, M. H., & Lanes, S. F. (1998). A meta-analysis to assess the incidence of adverse effects associated with the transdermal nicotine patch. *Drug Safety, 18,* 297–308.

Griffiths, J. D., Rowan-Szal G. A., Roark, R. R., & Simpson, D. D. (2000). Contingency management in outpatient methadone treatment: A meta-analysis. *Drug and Alcohol Dependency, 1,* 55–66.

Hall, C. C. (1997). Cultural malpractice. The growing obsolescence of psychology with the changing U.S. population. *American Psychologist, 52,* 642–651.

Holbrook, A. M., Crowther, R., Lotter, A. Cheng, C. & King, D. (1999). Meta-analysis of Benzodiazepines use in the treatment of acute alcohol withdrawal. *CMAJ* *, *160*, 649–655.

Irvin, J. E., Bowers, C. A., Dunn, M. E., & Wang, M. C. (1999). Efficacy of relapse prevention: A meta-analytic review. *Journal of Clinical and Consulting Psychology, 67*, 563–570.

Johnsen, J., & Morland, J. (1991). Disulfiram implant: A double-blind placebo controlled follow-up study. *Alcohol Clinical Experimental Research, 15*, 532–536.

Juhnke, G. A., & Coker, J. K. (1997). A solution-focused intervention with recovering, alcohol-dependent, single parent mothers and their children. *Journal of Addictions & Offender Counseling, 17*(2), 77-87.

Kahler, C. W. (1995). Current challenges and an old debate. *Addiction, 90*(9), 1169-1171.

Kownacki, R. J., & Shadish, W. R. (1999). Does Alcoholics Anonymous work? The results from a meta-analysis of controlled experiments. *Substance Use and Misuse, 34*, 1879–1916.

Kranzler, H. R. (2000). Pharmacotherapy of alcoholism: Gaps in knowledge and opportunities for research. *Alcohol and Alcoholism, 35*, 537–547.

Lam, W., Sze, P. C., Sacks, H. S., & Chalmers, T. C. (1987). Meta-analysis of randomized controlled trials of nicotine chewing gum. *Lancet, July 4 (8549)*, 27–30.

Ling, W., Weiss, D. G., Charuvastura, V. C., & O'Brien, C. P. (1983). Use of disulfiram for alcoholics in methadone maintenance programs. A Veterans Administration Cooperative Study. *Archives of General Psychiatry, 40*, 851–854.

Malek, T. S., Malek, E. A., & Dongier, M. (1996). Efficacy of buspirone in alcohol dependence: A review. *Alcohol Clinical and Experimental Research, 20*, 853–858.

Marron, J. T. (1993) The twelve steps. A pathway to recovery. *Primary Care, 20*, 107–119.

Mason, W. H., Chandler, M. C., & Grasso, B. C. (1995). Solution-based techniques applied to addictions: A clinic's experience in shifting paradigms. *Alcoholism Treatment Quarterly, 13*(4), 39-49.

McGovern, M. P., Angres, D. H., & Leon, S. (2000). Characteristics of physicians presenting for assessment at a behavioral health center. *Journal of Addictive Disorders, 19*, 759–763.

Nealon-Woods, M. A. Ferrari, J. R., & Jason, L. A. (1995). Twelve-step use among Oxford House residents: Spirituality of social support in sobriety. *Journal of Substance Abuse, 7*, 311–318.

Osborn, C. J. (1997). Does disease matter? Incorporating solution-focused brief therapy in alcoholism treatment. *Journal of Alcohol & Drug Education, 43*(1), 18-30.

Peachey, J. E., Zilm, D. H., Robinson, G. M., Jacob, M., & Cappell, H. (1983). A placebo-controlled double-blind comparative clinical study of the disulfiram- and calcium carbide-acetaldehyde mediated ethanol reactions in social drinkers. *Alcohol Clinical and Experimental Research, 7*, 180–187.

Peele, S. (1992). Alcoholism, politics, and the bureaucracy: The consensus against controlled-drinking therapy in America. *Addictive Behaviors, 17* (1), 49–62.

Pendry, M. L., Maltzman, I. M., & West, L. J. (1982, July 9). Controlled drinking by alcoholics? New findings and a reevaluation of a major affirmative study. *Science, 4555*, 169–175.

Pozzi, G., Bacigalupi, M., & Tempests, E. (1997). Comorbidity of drug dependence and other mental disorders: A two-phase study of prevalence at outpatient treatment centers in Italy. *Drug and Alcohol Dependence, 6*, 46–77.

Rice V. H., & Stead, L. F. (2000). Nursing interventions for smoking cessation. *Cochrane Database Systematic Reviews*, CD001188.

Scott, J., Gilvarry, E., & Farrell, M. (1998). Managing anxiety and depression in alcohol and drug dependence. *Addictive Behaviors, 23*, 919–931.

Sobell, M. B., & Sobell, L. C. (1973). Alcoholics treated by individualized behavior therapy: One year treatment outcome. *Behaviour Research and Therapy, 11*, 599–618.

Sobell, M. B., & Sobell, L. C. (1976). Second year treatment outcome of alcoholics treated by individualized behavior therapy: Results. *Behaviour Research and Therapy, 14*, 195–215.

Sobell, M. B., & Sobell, L. C. (1995). Controlled drinking after 25 years: How important was the great debate? *Addiction, 90*(9), 1149-1153.

Trinkoff, A. M., & Storr, C. L. (1994). Relationship of specialty and access to substance use among registered nurses: An exploratory analysis. *Drug and Alcohol Dependence, 36,* 215–219.

Wells-Parker, E. Bangert-Drowns, R., McMillan, R., & Williams, M. (1995). Final results from a meta-analysis of remedial interventions with drink / drive offenders. *Addiction, 90,* 907–926.

Wilk, A. I., Jensen, N. M., & Havighurst, T. C. (1997). Meta-analysis of randomized control trials addressing brief interventions in heavy alcohol drinkers. *Journal of General Internal Medicine, 12,* 274–283.

Wilson, A., Davidson, W. J., Blanchard R., & White, J. (1978). Disulfiram implantation. A placebo-controlled trial with two-year follow-up. *Journal of Studies of Alcohol, 39,* 809–819.

CHAPTER

7 Mood Disorders

CHAPTER OVERVIEW

1. Mood symptoms include symptoms of unusually depressed and unusually elevated mood. Depressive symptoms include depressed mood, loss of appetite, lack of motivation, and vegetative disturbances, such as changes in eating and sleeping. Symptoms of elevated mood include excitation, excessive energy and drive, risk-taking, and hypersexuality.

2. Mood disorders include Major Depressive Disorder, Dysthymia, Manic Disorder, and Cyclothymic Disorder. Diagnosis of mood disorders involves first recognizing mood episodes and then applying other diagnostic criteria. Mood episodes include Depressed Episode, Manic Episode, and Mixed Episode.

3. Assessments can include psychometric assessments of mood and related functioning and clinical interviews. Attention should be paid to assessing the risk of suicide related to mood disorders.

4. Interventions may include psychotropic medication, cognitive therapy, and behavior therapy. Admission to a long-term facility may be indicated in a small proportion of cases.

DSM-IV distinguishes mood disorders from the acute mood episodes they are most often associated with, such as depressed or manic/excited moods (APA, 2000b). Additionally, clients who experience mood symptoms that are not extreme enough to meet DSM-IV criteria for full-blown depressive or manic episodes may still experience distress or interference with the conduct of their lives. DSM-IV recognizes this possibility with various categories of more moderate yet distressful mood experiences: Hypomanic Mood Episode, Dysthymia, and Cyclothymia (APA, 2000b).

Depressed mood symptoms reflect a generally dampened physical and mental state, including negative affect, diminished cognition, and vegetative physical symptoms, such as insomnia, hypersomnia, and change in appetite. Conversely, manic mood symptoms reflect a state of agitation or excitement. They are often coupled with cognitive symptoms that may include confusion, expansiveness, and a dizzying flight of ideas.

Major Depressive Disorder and Dysthymic Disorder

Diagnosis

DSM-IV recognizes two groups of depressive disorders (APA, 2000b). Major Depressive Disorders are associated with circumscribed but intense dysphoric mood episodes that last at least two weeks (but which often last much longer). Dysthymia, by contrast, is associated with sustained, but often more moderate, dysphoric episodes lasting two years or more. In children and adolescents the latter criteria is relaxed to one year. To qualify for a major depressive disorder, a client must present a history or current episode of major depressive episode(s). During a major depressive episode a person experiences at least five depressive symptoms during the same two-week period, including either depressed mood or anhedonia (i.e., loss of interest in pleasurable activities) plus four or more other depressive symptoms, such as weight loss or gain, insomnia or hypersomnia, physical agitation or retardation, fatigue or energy loss, diminished concentration, feelings of worthlessness or guilt, and recurrent thoughts of death or suicide. It should be noted, however, that children and adolescents commonly present with irritability, rather than explicitly depressed moods or anhedonia, as their primary symptoms. These symptoms, most of which are experienced nearly every day of the two-week period, also must cause the person clinically significant distress or impairment and must not be due to the direct effects of a substance, medical condition, or uncomplicated bereavement.

In diagnosing major depressive episode, it is important to confirm that the symptoms represent a change from the client's previous levels of functioning. To meet DSM-IV criteria, symptoms must either be recently emerged or clearly exacerbated from the client's pre-episode status. It is also important to assess whether the client's symptoms might be better described by a diagnosis of mixed episode. If the client has experienced symptoms satisfying criteria for *both* a major depressive episode and a manic episode during a one week period, the diagnosis of mixed episode is assigned (see below).

The assignment of a major depressive episode often, but not always, leads directly to the diagnosis of major depressive disorder. If the client has never experienced a manic, hypomanic, or mixed episode, and, if the major depressive episode cannot be explained more appropriately by a diagnosis of schizoaffective or other psychotic disorder, then the diagnosis of major depressive disorder is assigned. If the presenting symptoms represent the client's first depressive episode, the qualifier "single episode" is indicated. If the client reports a history of past depressive episodes, then the qualifier "recurrent episode" is assigned.

In contrast with the acute symptomology of major depression, some individuals may experience more sustained periods of depressed mood during which they may or may not meet all the criteria for a depressive episode. The DSM-IV accommodates these experiences with the diagnosis of Dysthymic Disorder

(APA, 2000b). This category is paralleled by the Cyclothymic Disorder diagnosis described below. The root word shared by both of these terms is the same as for the plant commonly employed as a spice: Both terms derive from the ritualistic burning of *fumos* (or *thymos*, thyme) during the fifth century B.C. During this ritual the fumes from the burning plant came to symbolize the rising spirits of departed family members. To be dysthymic, then, etymologically, is to be dispirited, which is a rough description of the DSM-IV diagnosis of dysthymia.

To qualify for a diagnosis of dysthymia, an individual must experience a chronically depressed mood more days than not for at least two years. Again, this criterion is relaxed to one year for children and adolescents. This mood is characterized by at least two symptoms described by the DSM-IV (APA, 2000b). These symptoms include poor or inflated appetite, disturbed sleep, low energy or fatigue, low self-esteem, poor concentration or decision making, and feelings of hopelessness. These symptoms must be present consistently during the two-year period and absent for no more than two consecutive months during that time. Major Depression, Chronic (when the onset of depressive symptoms are severe and continuing), Adjustment Disorder with Depressed Mood, Psychotic Disorders, Mood Disorder Due to a General Medical Condition, and Substance-Induced Mood Disorder should be ruled out as alternate diagnoses.

Assessment

A very large number of psychometric instruments are available to assess mood disorders. Some of the more common ones for both adults and children and adolescents are summarized in Table 7.1. Diagnosis with many of these instruments suffers from high false-positive reports; that is, clients score over the cut-off, but do not meet DSM-IV criteria for a mood disorder. Therefore, these instruments should be used as indicants, but not stand-alone assays, of depression or dysthymia. Clients who score over the cut-off on these instruments should be evaluated more carefully to evaluate if they meet DSM-IV criteria for depression. In older adults, distinguishing mood disorders from Alzheimer's disease or other dementias and from the effects of physical illnesses is an important issue. (See Chapter 9 for a more detailed discussion of this issue.)

TABLE 7.1   **Some psychometric assessments commonly used in mood disorder cases.**

Adults (self-report)

Minnesota Multiphase Personality Inventory-2

Center for Epidemiological Studies—Depression Scale (CES-D)

Zung Self-Rating Depression Scale (ZSRDS)

(*continued*)

TABLE 7.1 Continued

Adults (self-report)
Beck Depression Inventory (BDI)
Inventory for Diagnosing Depression (IDD)
Inventory of Depressive Symptomatology—Self-Report (IDS-SR).

Adults (clinician ratings)
Hamilton Rating Scale for Depression (HRS-D)
Bech-Rafaelsen Depression Scale (BRDS)
Montgomery-Asberg Depression Rating Scale

Children and Adolescents (self-report)
MMPI-A (which may be administered to adolescents)
Children's Depression Rating Scale (CDRS)
Bellevue Index of Depression (BID)
Children's Depression Inventory (CDI, based on the BDI)
Children's Depression Scale (CDS)
Center for Epidemiological Studies-Depression Scale for Children (CES-DC).

Self-report instruments are useful for initially screening individuals thought to be at risk for depression or dysthymia. Short self-report measures have also been used to survey the general population to identify those who are at risk for depression or who have undiagnosed depression. Those who report significant depressive symptoms should be further evaluated by a clinician using a clinical interview to investigate the duration and intensity of depressive symptoms, including vegetative symptoms, and family, medical, and occupational/academic history. Referral to a psychiatrist may be indicated to clarify diagnostic issues and to review the appropriateness of pharmacotherapy treatments.

When working with children or adolescents, information from parents and other parties with whom the client interacts in natural contexts may be especially useful. Schoolteachers, in particular, may provide information about the client's relationships with peers, attention patterns, and vegetative symptoms experienced throughout the day. With proper consent, the clinician also may wish to observe the child directly in his or her school classroom or home settings. The collection of collateral records, including school records and medical/health records, should also be considered.

Because between 50 percent and 70 percent of depressed clients also report anxiety symptoms (Gotlib & Nolan, 2000; Rapaport, 2001), clinical assessment also should assess for comorbid anxiety disorders. If present, treatment for anxiety symptoms should proceed concurrently with mood interventions.

A thorough suicidal assessment also should be conducted with all clients presenting with depressive symptoms, including clients presenting with dysthymic symptoms (Klein et al., 2000). Whereas the risk of suicide among the general population in the United States is about 1.5 percent (Clark & Fawcett, 1992; Fawcett, 1992), the risk of suicide for individuals suffering from mood disorders may be as high as 15 percent (Clark, 1995). As discussed in Chapter 2, clients recovering from depressive episodes, as well as clients transitioning from depressive to manic episodes, may be at particular risk of self-harm.

Assessment of suicidal ideation should begin with questions about possible passive ideation, such as the client's thoughts of being better off dead or not caring if he or she accidentally died in the near future. If appropriate, questions should then move to assessments of the client's active suicidal ideation. Clients who report active thoughts about suicide should be asked the reasons they have not actually committed suicide. Those reporting ego-dystonia (i.e., because suicide conflicts with the client's basic beliefs), religious reasons, and family support are generally considered at lower risk of taking their lives than those who report insufficient energy or access to lethal means. If indicated, the client should be explicitly asked if she or he has had or currently has a specific plan for methods, time, and/or location of a suicide attempt.

A thorough evaluation of a client presenting with depressive or dysthymic symptoms should also include patterns of substance use. Clients suffering from mood disorders often self-medicate, most frequently by abusing alcohol, but also by using other substances such as cocaine, amphetamines, and, less commonly, opiates or marijuana. As many as 30 percent of depressed clients may develop substance dependency (Regier et al., 1990; cf. Frank & Thase, 1999).

Treatment Plans

Both biological and a wide range of psychological treatments are available for depression and dysthymia. Many of them have been extensively evaluated and considerable controversies exist as to the relative merits of different treatments. However, depression and dysthymia often respond well to a variety of different forms of intervention. Treatments for depression and dysthymia commonly include four modes of intervention: psychotherapies, biological therapies, family therapies, and suicide intervention.

Cognitive Therapies.   Cognitive therapies are based on the premise that many mental health conditions grow from maladaptive patterns of thought and perception. A variety of cognitive therapies have been used to treat depression and dysthymia, including Beck's (1976; Beck, Rush, Shaw, & Emery, 1987) cognitive model, which has received wide empirical support.

Beck has argued that depressed individuals often hold overly negative views of themselves, the world, and the future, which he has collectively termed the "cognitive triad." According to Beck, people commonly use several thinking patterns to maintain these views, including dichotomous thinking, arbitrary inference, and overgeneralization, among others. A client who employs dichotomous thinking evaluates the outcome of events in his or her life through absolute lenses; such a person would be inclined to see her or his small errors (e.g., in a professional presentation or interview) as catastrophic examples of global incompetence. A client who employs arbitrary inference jumps to negative conclusions on the basis of minimal or ambiguous evidence, inferring, for instance, that a friend who is late in returning a phone call no longer likes him or her or holds a grudge for a long-forgotten slight. Similarly, a client who overgeneralizes draws broad conclusions from specific examples, concluding he or she is unattractive on the basis of a single unflattering wedding photograph, for example, or that he or she is unfit for college on the basis of a single poor test grade.

Beck's model of therapy is built on helping clients identify and change their core dysfunctional beliefs and assumptions (Beck, 1976). Core beliefs can be identified through clinical interviews and assigned "thought" diaries. For example, a divorced middle-aged woman with dysthymia might learn to recognize her underlying beliefs that she is stupid because her daughter dropped out of college or unattractive because she has not been in a relationship since divorcing three years ago. Once such beliefs are identified, reality checking and hypothesis testing may be used to test their accuracy and validity. For example, the woman might be asked to pay careful attention to whether men at social events respond differently to her than to other women or to whether other parents assume blame for the academic struggles of their sons or daughters. Beck initially uses a fairly neutral form of questioning to solicit information from clients and would likely avoid directly confronting them with their maladaptive beliefs. Later, he may use homework or role-play activities to increase clients' engagement in everyday activities and pleasurable hobbies. For example, a client might be helped to develop a plan to clean one part of his or her house every day or to speak with at least one friend every afternoon. (Note the overlap of this component of cognitive therapy with the behavioral therapies described below.)

Cognitive therapy has been used with a wide range of depressed clients, including adolescents, elderly individuals, and clients who fail to respond to antidepressant medications. Widely accepted since its introduction in the 1970s, cognitive therapy subsequently has been the target of extensive empirical investigation (Clark et al., 1999; Strunk & DeRubeis, 2001). A meta-analysis of twenty-eight studies conducted by Dobson (1989), for instance, found that cognitive therapy led to greater improvement among depressed clients than behavior therapy, pharmacotherapy, and no-treatment conditions (cf. Strunk & DeRubeis, 2001). Elkin et al.'s (1989) NIMH study offered similar support for cognitive treatments for depressed clients, although its efficacy relative to recent pharmacotherapy protocols remains an area of active debate (e.g., DeRubeis et al., 1999; Persons et al., 1996; Taylor, 2000). On the whole, cognitive therapy can be safely concluded to be an effective model of treatment for many depressed clients.

Rational Emotive Behavior Therapy. A closely related treatment model that also includes both cognitive and behavioral interventions is Rational Emotive Behavior Therapy (REBT; Ellis, 1984; Ellis & Dryden, 1997). REBT is based on the premise that people often respond irrationally to stressors. If clients' irrational thoughts can be replaced by more rational ways of thinking, therefore, they would be less likely to be depressed. Many such thoughts are built on underlying catastrophizations. After a hassle-filled day at work, for instance, a client might misperceive his or her job as an intolerable disaster, a pattern of thinking that in fact might render the job even less tolerable. Other irrational thoughts are built around self-blame, such as that of a man who sees himself as a "bad father" when he arrives late for his daughter's soccer game after being caught in traffic.

In REBT these maladaptive thinking patterns are directly challenged by the therapist. A catastrophizing client, for instance, may be asked to consider the possibility of much worse outcomes than those she or he is facing, including outcomes many people throughout history have faced with positive spirits. Similarly, a self-blaming client may be challenged to consider whether he or she should be perfect (or perfectly on time) in everything he or she tries. REBT therapists also may teach clients to practice more rational appraisals of stressful situations, directly confronting them (unlike Beck) with the irrationality or inappropriateness of their current beliefs. In addition, REBT therapists often use behavioral assignments, such as shame-attacking exercises or logs of competent performances, to overcome clients' interpersonal anxieties and ingrained patterns of self-blame.

Behavior Therapy. Depression and dysthymia are characterized by important observable behaviors, including behavioral excesses, such as crying and complaining, and behavioral deficits, such as motoric slowing, laconic speech, and long response latencies to conversational questions. Many clients also exhibit social skills deficits and failures to engage in interactions that others typically find rewarding (Segrin, 2000). In addition, depression is often associated with a restrictive range of reinforcers and with histories of both recent punishment and punishment during early development periods. Behavior therapy targets both clients' depressive behaviors and the patterns of reinforcement from which they often derive.

Behavior therapy for depression can include a number of intervention methods. One important approach begins by identifying potential sources of reinforcement in the client's life, gradually reinstating preferred activities and contact with preferred people to increase the client's enjoyment of daily living. Another approach directly addresses clients' behavioral deficits through skills training, such as group or individual social skills interventions (e.g., Bellack, Herson, & Himmelhoch, 1981). In order to address depressed clients' lack of activity, goals may be established for other behavioral tasks such as preparing meals, sorting through emails, or exercising (e.g., Lawlor & Hopkins, 2001; Norris et al., 1992). Other behavioral interventions include developing reinforcers for non-depressive behaviors and mapping plans to extinguish behavioral excesses (e.g., Brannon & Nelson, 1987).

Evaluation of behavior therapy as a stand-alone treatment for depression has been limited on a number of counts. First, many studies of behavioral interventions have evaluated treatments, such as Beck's cognitive therapy, that include both behavioral and cognitive interventions. Second, many researchers and practitioners, assuming that depression is a primarily cognitive-emotional or biological disorder, have regarded behavior therapy as an inappropriate treatment and consequently failed to include it in outcome assessments. Finally, many empirical assessments of behavioral interventions have not been tailored to individual clients, but rather have used a standard package of behavioral techniques, such as social skills training or exercise programs. Thus, individualized treatment, a hallmark of behavior therapy, has been missing from this literature.

Interpersonal Psychotherapy.   Interpersonal Psychotherapy (IPT) is a time-limited form of psychotherapy that focuses on interpersonal relations as the source-points of mental illness. As a treatment for depressed clients, IPT is based on the premise that depression can be caused by, and may reciprocally impair, clients' relationships with significant people in their lives. The underlying strategy of IPT is therefore to reduce clients' depression by helping them deal more effectively with other people. IPT is time-limited, focusing more on current relationships than past historical experiences and usually requiring only fifteen to twenty weeks of treatment. It has received significant research support as an effective intervention with mild-to-moderate depressed clients (e.g., Elkin et al., 1989).

Family Therapies and Adjunctive Interventions.   In addition to individual therapy and pharmacotherapy, family interventions have been shown to be helpful for some clients with mood disorders. Marital/relational therapies may be especially helpful for clients experiencing both depression and relational discord (Persons, Thase, & Crits-Christoph, 1996; Jacobson et al., 1991). Family therapies ranging from supportive psychoeducation to brief or ongoing systems therapies should be considered for all depressed or dysthymic clients. Occupational or academic counseling interventions also should be considered where indicated.

Suicide Intervention Plans.   As noted above, suicide risk should be assessed with every client presenting with depression or dysthymia. Passive suicidal ideation is common, if fleeting, among many healthy people. If a client presents with active suicidal ideation, however, the clinician will need to assess the particularity of the client's thoughts and intervene accordingly. Suicide interventions may include no-suicide contracts (short-term, ongoing agreements not to commit suicide; these are most effective when frequently reassessed or updated) or hospitalization if the client's suicidal ideation is linked to specific plans or disamenable to change.

Several approaches have been developed to manage suicidality. Some researchers have focused on compliance with treatment. This approach assumes that if clients continue with antidepressant medication and other therapy, they will be less likely to repeat a suicide attempt. Others have focused on crisis management and inpatient admission to ensure client safety. Some researchers and practitioners have extended cognitive-behavioral models to specifically address suicidal thoughts and behavior (e.g., Rudd, 2000). Under this model, suicidal behavior is seen as a maladaptive behavior response to cognitive dysfunctions. Like other forms of cognitive therapy, cognitive therapy to prevent suicide includes steps to identify and modify maladaptive cognitions.

A review of suicide interventions by Van der Sande et al. (1997) found that despite their extensive use and evaluation, little empirical evidence has supported the effectiveness of crisis management and inpatient care in preventing repeat suicide attempts. Cognitive-behavioral therapy, on the other hand, appears promising.

Psychotropic Medications. Three primary classes of medications have been employed for depression: selective serotonin reuptake inhibitors (SSRIs), tricyclic antidepressants, and monoamine oxidase inhibitors (MAOIs). All three medications have been theorized to influence monoamine neurotransmission. Whereas tricyclic antidepressants appear to affect norepinephrine and serotonin pathways, SSRIs (e.g., fluoxetine/Prozac, sertraline/Zoloft) appear to affect serotonin pathways only and therefore may result in fewer side effects. MAOIs have more significant negative side effects, including potentially lethal cross reactions with a litany of commonplace foods. Therefore, MAOIs are usually used as a third-line treatment or for cases of atypical depression (e.g., symptoms of hypersomnia, depression with panic attacks, worsening mood throughout the day). An overview of commonly prescribed antidepressants is shown in Table 7.2.

TABLE 7.2   Antidepressant medications and some common side effects.

Trade name	Generic name	Potential side effects
Adapin	doxepin	Constipation, blurred vision, drowsiness, dry mouth, or low blood pressure.
Amfebutamone	bupropion	Agitation, change in appetite, constipation, diarrhea, dizziness, dry mouth, headache, increased perspiration, insomnia, nausea, or vomiting.
Amitril, Dohme, PMS-Levazine, Sharpe, SK-Amitriptyline	amitriptyline	Blurred vision, constipation, drowsiness, dry mouth, increased sensitivity to sun, low blood pressure, increase in sweating, or sleepiness.

(continued)

TABLE 7.2   Continued

Trade name	Generic name	Potential side effects
Anafranil	clomipramine	Blurred vision, constipation, drowsiness, dry mouth, low blood pressure, nausea, or vomiting.
Asendin	amoxapine	Blurred vision, constipation, drowsiness, dry mouth, impaired urination, or low blood pressure.
Aurorix	moclobemide (not yet available in the U.S.)	Orthostatic hypotension (a sudden drop in blood pressure upon standing), drowsiness or insomnia, dizziness. May also cause birth defects and should not be taken by pregnant women. Very dangerous side effects can occur from interactions with other antidepressants, including SSRIs.
Aventil	nortriptyline	Blurred vision, constipation, cramps, disorientation, drowsiness, dry mouth, headache, low blood pressure, or sensitivity to bright lights.
Bolvidon	mianserin	Dry mouth, constipation, blurred vision, sexual dysfunction, weight gain, difficulty in urinating, drowsiness, dizziness, or blood pressure may drop suddenly when sitting up or standing. Also, increased risk of idiopathic pulmonary fibrosis (IPF), which can cause lung inflammation and scarring.
Celexa	citalopram	Somnolence, insomnia, dry mouth, nausea, or increased sweating.
Desyrel	trazodone	Dizziness, drowsiness, or light-headedness.
Dohme	amitriptyline	Blurred vision, constipation, drowsiness, dry mouth, increased sensitivity to sun, low blood pressure, increase in sweating, or sleepiness.
Effexor, Effexor XR	venlafaxine	Anxiety, constipation, delayed orgasm, depression, difficulty breathing, dizziness, dry mouth, itching, loss of appetite, loss of strength, nausea, nervousness, difficulty in urinating, sedation, skin rash, sleepiness/sleeplessness, sweating, tingling hands/feet, tremors, vomiting, unusual dreams, weight loss, or weakness.
Elavil, Emitrip, Endep,	amitriptyline	Blurred vision, constipation, drowsiness, dry mouth, increased sensitivity to sun, low blood pressure, increase in sweating,

TABLE 7.2 Continued

Trade name	Generic name	Potential side effects
Enovil, Etrafon, Etrafon-A, Etrafon-Forte		sleepiness, or weight gain.
Janimine, Norfranil, Tofranil	imipramine	Dry mouth, constipation, blurred vision, sexual dysfunction, weight gain, difficulty in urinating, drowsiness, dizziness, or blood pressure may drop suddenly when sitting up or standing. Also, increased risk of idiopathic pulmonary fibrosis (IPF), which can cause lung inflammation and scarring.
Ludiomil	maprotiline	Dry mouth, constipation, blurred vision, sexual dysfunction, weight gain, difficulty in urinating, drowsiness, dizziness, or blood pressure may drop suddenly when sitting up or standing.
Luvox	fluvoxamine maleate	Anorexia, constipation, dry mouth, headache, nausea, nervousness, skin rash, sleep problems, or somnolence.
Manerix	moclobemide (not yet available in the U.S.)	Orthostatic hypotension (a sudden drop in blood pressure upon standing), drowsiness or insomnia, dizziness. May also cause birth defects and should not be taken by pregnant women. Dangerous side effects can occur from interactions with other antidepressants, including SSRIs.
Marplan	isocarboxazid	Orthostatic hypotension (a sudden drop in blood pressure upon standing), drowsiness or insomnia, dizziness, or sexual dysfunction. May also cause birth defects and should not be taken by pregnant women. Dangerous side effects can occur from interactions with other antidepressants, including SSRIs.
Nardil	phenelzine	Orthostatic hypotension (a sudden drop in blood pressure upon standing), drowsiness or insomnia, dizziness, or sexual dysfunction. May also cause birth defects and should not be taken by pregnant women. Dangerous side effects can occur from interactions with various foods as well as with other antidepressants, including SSRIs.

(*continued*)

TABLE 7.2   Continued

Trade name	Generic name	Potential side effects
Norfranil	imipramine	Dry mouth, constipation, blurred vision, sexual dysfunction, weight gain, difficulty in urinating, drowsiness, dizziness, or blood pressure may drop suddenly when sitting up or standing. Also, increased risk of idiopathic pulmonary fibrosis (IPF), which can cause lung inflammation.
Norpramine	desipramine	Blurred vision, constipation, drowsiness, dry mouth, or low blood pressure.
Pamelor	nortriptyline	Blurred vision, constipation, cramps, disorientation, drowsiness, dry mouth, headache, low blood pressure, or sensitivity to bright lights.
Parnate	tranylcypromine	Orthostatic hypotension (a sudden drop in blood pressure upon standing), drowsiness or insomnia, dizziness, or sexual dysfunction. May also cause birth defects and should not be taken by pregnant women. Dangerous side effects can occur from interactions with various foods as well as with other antidepressants, including SSRIs.
Paxil	paroxetine	Blurred vision, chills, constipation, diarrhea, dizziness, headache, insomnia, itching, loss of appetite, nausea, nervousness, palpitations, sedation, skin rash, sweating, taste disorders, tingling in hands, upset stomach, or weakness.
PMS-Levazine	amitriptyline	Blurred vision, constipation, drowsiness, dry mouth, increased sensitivity to sun, low blood pressure, increase in sweating, or sleepiness.
Prothiaden	dothiepin	Dry mouth, constipation, blurred vision, sexual dysfunction, weight gain, difficulty in urinating, drowsiness, dizziness, or blood pressure may drop suddenly when sitting up or standing. Also, increased risk of idiopathic pulmonary fibrosis (IPF), which can cause lung inflammation and scarring.
Prozac	fluoxetine	Anxiety or nervousness.

TABLE 7.2 Continued

Trade name	Generic name	Potential side effects
Remeron	mirtazapine	Can cause drowsiness, which may make it a useful drug for depressed patients who suffer from insomnia. It also causes increased appetite, dry mouth, or constipation. The drug has been associated with weight gain, although in one study it was not significant. It does not appear to have the adverse acute effects on the heart that other newer antidepressants have, although it may elevate cholesterol and triglyceride levels slightly.
Serzone	nefazodone	Orthostatic hypotension (a sudden drop in blood pressure upon standing). May also cause headaches, somnolence, dizziness, asthenia, insomnia, light-headedness, confusion, dry mouth, nausea, or constipation.
Sharpe	amitriptyline	Blurred vision, constipation, drowsiness, dry mouth, increased sensitivity to sun, low blood pressure, increase in sweating, or sleepiness.
Sinequan	doxepin	Constipation, blurred vision, drowsiness, dry mouth, or low blood pressure.
SK-Amitriptyline	amitriptyline	Blurred vision, constipation, drowsiness, dry mouth, increased sensitivity to sun, low blood pressure, increase in sweating, sleepiness, or skin rashes/allergies.
St. John's wort	hypericum perforatum	Nausea, dry mouth, allergic reactions, or fatigue, although, in general, side effects are quite uncommon. Avoid sunlight or cover up when going outdoors. There is evidence to suggest that St. John's wort interacts with other drugs to cause toxic reactions. Note: This herbal substance is not regulated and there is no guarantee of quality in any brands currently available.
Surmontil	trimipramine	Dry mouth, constipation, blurred vision, sexual dysfunction, weight gain, difficulty in urinating, drowsiness, dizziness, or blood pressure may drop suddenly when sitting up or standing.

(continued)

TABLE 7.2 Continued

Trade name	Generic name	Potential side effects
Tipramine, Tofranil	imipramine	Dry mouth, constipation, blurred vision, sexual dysfunction, weight gain, difficulty in urinating, drowsiness, dizziness, or blood pressure may drop suddenly when sitting up or standing. Also, increased risk of idiopathic pulmonary fibrosis (IPF), which can cause lung inflammation.
Trazon, Trialodine	trazodone	Dizziness, drowsiness, light-headedness, pain, nausea, nervousness, shortness of breath, skin rash, or vomiting.
Vivactil	protriptylin	Dry mouth, constipation, blurred vision, sexual dysfunction, weight gain, difficulty in urinating, drowsiness, dizziness, or blood pressure may drop suddenly when sitting up or standing.
Wellbutrin, Wellbutrin SR	bupropion	Agitation, change in appetite, constipation, diarrhea, dizziness, dry mouth, headache, increased perspiration, insomnia, nausea, or vomiting.
Zoloft	sertraline	Diarrhea, dizziness, drowsiness, dry month, headache, indigestion, fatigue, insomnia, nausea, nervousness, tingling, or vomiting.
Zonalon	doxepin	Constipation, blurred vision, drowsiness, dry mouth, or low blood pressure.

Source: Drug Facts and Comparisons (1996); Franklin, (2001); *PSYweb* (2002); Simon (2002) .

Many antidepressants have been extensively evaluated by randomized controlled trials. Indeed, this literature is now so extensive that meta-analyses have been published addressing the differential effectiveness of specific types of antidepressants, as well as the effectiveness of antidepressants with specific populations, such as adolescents and elderly clients. The simple question of whether antidepressants are more effective than placebos in treating depression has appeared to be answered (Anderson, 2000; Lima & Moncrieff, 2000). Although there appear to be minimal differences between the effectiveness of different classes of antidepressants in treating the main symptoms of depression, SSRIs may be better tolerated by many clients. Because they often lead to fewer side effects, SSRIs also may be associated with fewer dropouts and fewer lifestyle restrictions than other antidepressant medications.

Despite their effectiveness for many clients and their widespread acceptance as a treatment for depression, clinicians should be aware of the limitations to the use of antidepressants. A significant proportion of clients fail to respond to medications and a considerable number of those who do find their side effects to be intolerable. Further, although these medications may be effective in restoring clients' mood and other depressive symptoms, they often do not impact other important aspects of clients' lives, such as their ability to find meaningful jobs, enjoy rewarding lifestyles, and build positive, healthy relationships with friends and family members.

Electro-Convulsive Therapy. Electro-convulsive therapy (ECT) is a controversial treatment for depression. Often portrayed in the media as a sadistic historical artifact, legitimate concerns have also been raised among psychiatric professionals about its long-term effects on memory and other cognitive functions.

ECT involves passing an electric current through a depressed patient's brain in order to induce an epileptic seizure. In its modern form, this seizing is not visibly apparent, as the patient is given a muscle relaxant to prevent her or his muscles from contracting violently (although brain activity that is typical of a seizure does occur).

Professional opinion about the use of ECT for depression varies widely. Some authorities hold that it should be reserved for refractory and severe depression that does not respond to other interventions. For such clients, ECT may result in faster improvements than other forms of therapy. For example, Folkerts et al. (1997) found that refractory depressed clients (who had on average failed five trials of different antidepressants) experienced 59 percent reductions in their scores on Hamilton ratings of depression compared to 29 percent reductions among clients receiving paroxitine. However, other authors have expressed concern that clients given ECT may relapse after initially effective responses (e.g., Devanand, Sackeim, & Prudic, 1991). In addition, ECT raises obvious ethical dilemmas when used with clients who may be involuntary or incompetent to consent to treatment. It is beyond the scope of this section to discuss this complicated matter in detail.

CASE EXAMPLE
David

Referral: David was a 26-year-old college student complaining of a quiet but constant dysphoric mood. David reported at intake that he could not remember ever feeling really happy. He rarely socialized with any of his friends. A subsequent interview revealed

(*continued*)

CASE EXAMPLE   Continued

David had no history of previous or current severe mood or vegetative symptoms. David reported he often was tired, easily became fatigued during his classes, and had a hard time focusing on his academic work at home. Given the chronicity of his symptoms, he met the criteria for a DSM-IV diagnosis of Dysthymic Disorder.

Immediate concerns: Are there any immediate dangers to the client or other vulnerable persons?

Clinical interview should assess whether David has any suicidal ideation and, if so, to what extent he has operationalized his suicidal thoughts. If David has significant suicidal ideation or a history of past suicidal attempts, a no-suicide contract coupled with removal of lethal items/medications from his home should be considered. With appropriate consent, the clinician may consider involving David's family or friends in the no-suicide plan. If David reports active suicidal intent or an active suicidal plan, or refuses no-suicide interventions, he may need to be referred to inpatient treatment until he is no longer a danger to himself.

Short-term goals: What goals need to be achieved in the first two to six sessions?

A thorough assessment/history was taken to rule out medical concerns often associated with depressive symptoms (e.g., hypothyroidism). Because David had not recently seen a physician, a referral was made for a physical examination, as a result of which physical concerns were tentatively ruled out. Co-morbid disorders common to depression/dysthymia, including substance abuse and anxiety disorders, were also evaluated during clinical interviews. David reported that he experienced no psychological symptoms other than those associated with the dysthymia.

Two main areas were targeted for initial treatment: David's mood/life experiences and his academic disengagement. To address his dysphoric mood, David was initially taught to explore and challenge underlying cognitions associated with his dysthymic symptoms, including what he came to view as his frequent overgeneralization of negative experiences and his dichotomized self-perceptions (e.g., view of self as an academic "failure"). David was asked to note small, incremental upward changes in his mood between sessions and to report back activities and thoughts associated with these experiences. Whereas these experiences initially were associated with therapeutic homework tasks (e.g., assignment to observe the activities of birds on campus), they gradually emerged more often from David's ordinary life routines. Similar strategies directed toward increasing David's academic engagement were associated with his increased use of planning/time management and self-management strategies and an overall improvement in his course grades.

After six sessions, David reported increased socialization with friends, engagement in numerous spontaneous activities, including his resumption of guitar songwriting, and increased academic success. David reported his baseline mood was significantly improved and that he felt confident about his academic life and his future plans.

Long-term goals: What lifestyle changes and other long-term personal, relationship, and career goals need to be achieved?

Long-term management should attend to helping David explore career and/or future academic plans and to increase his use of self-management strategies to maintain his focus on academic work in the classroom and at home. A referral should be considered

CASE EXAMPLE   Continued

for career counseling and/or assessment if indicated. To prevent relapse of dysthymic symptoms, David should be taught to recognize cognitive and behavioral patterns associated with his negative mood experiences. Solution-focused interventions may be used to help David build on incremental social and academic successes by using effective strategies more consistently in these areas of his life. A follow-up meeting to assess David's continued progress should be considered, although David should be invited to resume treatment at any time should his dysthymic symptoms reoccur.

CASE EXAMPLE
Thomas

Referral: Thomas, 21-year-old Anglo-American college sophomore, presents with depression that began after he experienced hazing in the fraternity he was hoping to join this semester. A clinical interview reveals Thomas has suffered two major depressive episodes since his senior year of high school, when he was worried about getting into the school of his choice. He has not consulted a psychologist or other mental health professional before.

Immediate concerns: Are there any immediate dangers to the client or other vulnerable persons?

During the clinical interview, Thomas denies any suicidal ideation, past or present, and states that he has no plans to harm anyone else, although he reports he is disappointed and irritated with the members of the fraternity he had planned to join. He appears to be under no danger of harm from members of the fraternity, although he reports he now feels intimidated by them and hopes to avoid them when on campus. At this time, there are no apparent dangers to Thomas or other vulnerable persons with which the clinician should be concerned.

Short-term goals: What goals need to be achieved in the first two to six sessions?

The extent of Thomas's history of mood disorders, including the potential triggering role played by external stressors, was assessed in a clinical interview, and other psychological conditions, including possible co-morbid anxiety disorders, were ruled out. Initial goals for Thomas's treatment included reengagement with his academic work, identification of potential interpersonal relationships/friendships outside the fraternity in which he had spent most of his time during the academic year, restoration of consistent eating and sleeping patterns, and increased ability to focus at work.

Thomas was asked to keep a diary of his cognitions and activities, including sleeping and eating patterns that were associated with both depressed and positive mood experiences. After introduction to cognitive behavioral treatment strategies, Thomas observed that much of his negative mood experiences were associated with automatic negative thoughts about himself, including ruminations that his failure to join the fraternity implied he was a failure at the university overall. As Thomas began associating

(continued)

CASE EXAMPLE   Continued

with other friends at work and in his classes, he noticed he worried less about academic and other stressors. Thomas was helped to reorganize his approach to his academic work and engaged in a self-management plan that included the use of pleasurable activities (e.g., tossing a football with friends, an afternoon at the museum, a pizza delivery) as reinforcers for completion of prioritized tasks. Thomas observed that he thought more positively about himself as he regained a global sense of agency and control over his life.

Long-term goals: What lifestyle changes and other long-term personal, relationship, and career goals should be achieved?

Although an initial psychiatric referral indicated Thomas might initially benefit from psychotherapy more than from antidepressant medications, long-term management of Thomas's mood symptoms should include continued psychiatric consultation and referral as indicated. Although Thomas initially reported he was adverse to taking prescribed medications, these may play an important role in the long-term management of his symptoms.

A referral for legal consultation, through university resources, should be considered if Thomas feels under threat of harm by members of the fraternity, and a referral for family intervention should be considered if family issues are revealed to play a significant role in the development or maintenance of Thomas's symptoms.

To prevent relapse of depression, Thomas should be taught to recognize cognitive and behavioral patterns associated with negative mood experiences, especially including early cues of depressive episodes. Solution-focused interventions may also be considered to build on successful cognitive-behavioral strategies. Given Thomas's history of recurrent depressive episodes, follow-up sessions and/or phone consultations should be scheduled to assess his continued progress after the termination of initial treatment.

Bipolar Disorders and Cyclothymia

Diagnosis

The diagnosis of Bipolar Disorders and Cyclothymia is based on the presence of a Manic, Hypomanic, or Mixed Episode. In this way, the diagnosis of these disorders is similar to the diagnosis of Major Depression.

During a manic episode a person experiences an abnormally expansive, elevated, or irritable mood. Additionally, he or she experiences at least three additional symptoms (four, if the mood is irritability) during the same one-week period. These symptoms include inflated self-esteem, decreased need for sleep, talkativeness (usually loud, nonstop, and rapid), racing ideas, high distractibility, markedly increased goal-directed activity or physical agitation, and excessive involvement in sexual or other risk-related pleasurable activities. These symptoms must cause clinically significant impairment or be severe enough to warrant hospitalization. They must not be due to the direct effects of a substance or a general medical condition.

Individuals experiencing manic episodes are often described by friends and family members as exhausting to be around. With sudden turns, a person experiencing a manic episode may comment on a variety of personal or peripheral topics. He or she may change subjects and mood rapidly, without any room for interruption. The initial presentation to people with whom he or she is unfamiliar may be one of engagingly energetic, if overly dramatic, interpersonal competence. However, the change in behaviors and interaction patterns is obvious to those who know the person. Persons experiencing manic episodes often regret or are ashamed of their manic behaviors after returning to baseline mood levels. During their manic episodes they may engage in extravagant sexual behaviors, excessive and reckless spending, and grandiose or dangerous social behaviors.

Hypomanic episodes parallel manic episodes but are shorter in duration. Whereas the DSM-IV specifies that three or more manic symptoms must be sustained for a period of one week to meet the criteria for a Manic Episode, these symptoms must be experienced for only four days to satisfy a diagnosis of Hypomanic Episode.

As their name suggests, Mixed Episodes combine elements of both manic and depressive episodes. According to the DSM-IV, a person experiencing a Mixed Episode must display symptoms sufficient to satisfy a diagnosis of both Manic and Major Depressive episodes nearly every day for at least a one-week period (APA, 2000b). Symptoms exhibited for less than two weeks are excluded from the depressive episode duration criteria.

Individuals who experience a manic, hypomanic, or mixed episode may be diagnosed with Bipolar I Disorder or Bipolar II Disorder, depending on present symptoms and history. A past or present manic episode leads directly to a diagnosis of Bipolar I Disorder, regardless of past history of depressive episodes. In absence of past manic or mixed episodes, a person currently experiencing a hypomanic episode will be diagnosed with Bipolar II Disorder, if he or she has ever experienced a major depressive episode. If the person has experienced depressive symptoms insufficient to satisfy the criteria for major depressive episode, he or she may be diagnosed with Cyclothymia.

DSM-IV allows for the assessment of chronic but milder cyclical mood variations under the diagnosis of Cyclothymia (APA, 2000b). Just as Dysthymia may be described as a sustained period of dispirited mood, cyclothymia may be described as a sustained period of vacillation between spirited and dispirited moods. An individual experiencing cyclothymia experiences numerous periods of hypomania, but not full-blown manic episodes, and numerous periods of subclinical depression. This continues for two years or more, during which the person's symptoms may be absent for no more than two consecutive months. Substance-Induced Mood Disorder, Mood Disorder Due to a General Medical Condition, Bipolar I or Bipolar II Disorder, Rapid Cycling, which may resemble

Cyclothymic patterns, and Borderline Personality Disorder should be ruled out. Note that Cyclothymia may be diagnosed co-morbidly with Borderline Personality Disorder. Approximately 15 percent to 50 percent of clients diagnosed with cyclothymia may later be diagnosed with Bipolar I or Bipolar II (APA, 2000a).

Assessment

Clinical interviews with a client exhibiting manic symptoms should attend to both current, presenting problems and longitudinal issues. It is particularly important to assess the patterns of the client's symptoms, including timing of past episodes, the client's experiences between manic or depressive episodes, precipitating stressors, and the psychosocial consequences of the client's behaviors. For the last of these especially, it may be useful to gain the views of other people in the client's life. With appropriate consent, family members, friends, and, in the case of children and adolescents, teachers may offer insights into the client's behaviors that he or she may not be capable of reporting accurately. Additionally, whereas clients currently experiencing manic symptoms may underreport past episodes of depression or even suicidality, friends and family members may prove more helpful in gaining longitudinal perspective into the cyclical nature of the client's mood patterns.

Clients experiencing manic, hypomanic, or mixed episodes may present characteristic response patterns on the MMPI-2, WAIS-R, and other measures (Meyer & Deitsch, 1996). However, these are largely secondary effects of directly observable phenomena. Manic episodes themselves may be more obviously observed directly. A labile, expansive, overly excited or irritable presentation bordering on and sometimes overlapping with rapidly changing psychotic features may cue the clinician toward the appropriate diagnosis.

Self-report measures may be equally superfluous for diagnosing current manic episodes, in part because manic clients may provide flippant responses to stimulus items (Solovay, Shenton, & Holzman, 1987, cited in Meyer & Deitsch, 1996). The clinical interview, therefore, including information elicited from friends and relatives may be the best diagnostic instrument for assessing both the client's history and current presentation of manic episodes.

Although bipolar disorders appear to be less prevalent among children and adolescents than adults, recent clinical evidence indicates as many as 15 percent of bipolar patients may experience childhood or adolescent onset of their symptoms (Giedd, 2000; Weller, Weller, & Fristad, 1995). Children who experience a depressive or bipolar disorder may be more likely to develop more severe bipolar symptoms (Birmaher, Brent, & American Academy of Child & Adolescent Psychiatry [AACAP], 1998; Birmaher et al., 1996; Johnson, Cohen, & Brooks, 2000).

As with adult clients, it is important to gain the perspective of others when assessing a child or adolescent's current problems and their history. Parents' reports of cyclically exuberant behavior, which formerly may have been attributed to other causes, may be particularly diagnostic of manic or hypomanic patterns. Collateral records, including school records and medical records, may be useful in identifying interepisodic functioning, as well as cyclical variations in the child's symptoms. In addition, the child's teachers may provide important information about fluctuations in his or her responsiveness to others, academic engagement, irritability or mood changes, and playground interactions. As with assessments of childhood or adolescent depression, the clinician also may wish to directly observe the child in these natural contexts.

It may be difficult to differentiate bipolar patterns from ADHD or conduct disorder at times. However, research suggests strongly cyclical variations in mood or psychotic symptoms, such as associated with grandiosity, coupled with such classic manic symptoms as pressured speech, flight of ideas, and grossly inflated self-esteem may mark bipolar disorder in children and adolescents. This may be especially so if these behaviors represent changes from previous patterns (Spencer et al., 2001). Although the clinician should be cautious in diagnosing bipolar disorder in children, he or she also should not overlook the possibility that the client may be displaying developmentally excessive signs of the disorder. Pediatric bipolar disorder may be as prevalent as 1 percent of the U.S. population (Lewinsohn, Klein, & Seeley, 1995; Silva et al., 2000).

Suicidal Assessment.   Clients with bipolar disorder are at particular risk of suicide, especially during the depressive phases of their disorders. Research has suggested rapid cycling clients, as well as clients with early ages of onset of manic symptoms, may present a higher suicide risk (Sharma & Markar, 1994; see Wu & Dunner, 1993 for contrasting view). A thorough assessment of the client's present and past suicidal ideation should be made, keeping in mind that during the manic or hypomanic phases of the disorder the client may deny or may not even remember past suicidal ideation.

As with depression, bipolar disorder is highly co-morbid with substance abuse and dependency. The clinician should recognize that a client currently experiencing a manic or hypomanic episode may underreport his or her substance use. With proper consent, family reports may be useful in this regard as well.

Treatment Plans

Treatment for bipolar disorder begins with an assessment of appropriate placement for the client's care. Clients presenting in the active phase of acute mania, who may be at risk of harm to self or others, may require placement in inpatient settings. Consideration should be given to the client's ability to care for himself or herself, and level of cognitive functioning and risk-taking behaviors. Active manic symptoms may also necessitate immediate psychotropic intervention. A referral to a psychiatrist should be made for clients actively experiencing manic, mixed, or hypomanic episodes.

Psychotropic Medications.   Psychotropic medications for mania include lithium, valproate, and divalproex, and combinations of lithium with tricyclic or SSRI antidepressants. Psychotherapies appear less effective for the manic phases of bipolar disorders than for depression or dysthymia. Treatment therefore should begin with a referral for appropriate psychiatric assessment. Psychotropic medications shown to be effective for the management of bipolar disorder include lithium, which has been shown to be effective in modulating both affective "highs" and "lows" for up to 78 percent of bipolar clients (APA, 2000a). Additionally, benzodiazepines or neuroleptics are sometimes given to manage the acute phases of mania while waiting for mood-stabilizing medications to become effective. Reviews of randomized control trials have been quite supportive of lithium, valproate, and divalproex in the treatment of mania (Burgess et al., 2001; Macritchie et al., 2001)

Communication with all members of the treatment team as well as members of the clients' family and/or school system is essential. Because the titration of psychotropic medications varies substantially across clients, the clinician and other members of the treatment team may provide important information about changes in the client's behavior and possible side effect experiences. The clinician additionally should work with other members of the treatment team to educate the client and family about the need to consistently take, and to monitor the side effects of, the prescribed medications. It is important to note that lithium has a narrow therapeutic window; that is, the blood-plasma levels associated with its therapeutic effectiveness are comparatively close to those associated with toxicity. Negative side effects of lithium are especially unpleasant and potentially dangerous, including cognitive problems, weight gain, lethargy, hair loss and hypothyroidism, the last of which may in turn exacerbate depressive symptoms. Women of childbearing age should be advised to speak with the consulting psychiatrist about the pregnancy risks associated with medications, especially during the first trimester of pregnancy. All three medications commonly prescribed to manage manic symptoms, including lithium, are associated with increased risks of birth defects (Cohen et al., 1994).

Despite these side effects, psychological treatment should promote the client's ongoing compliance with all aspects of treatment, including medication compliance. Many clients may be discouraged by the unpleasant side effects of the medications commonly prescribed for bipolar symptoms. They may also be vulnerable, especially during acute manic phases of their disorders and after psychotropic medication has been effective, to denial of their need for continued treatment. Continuation of treatment may be especially important in light of research that suggests that electrophysiological kindling—the repeated overstimulation of brain areas associated with manic symptoms—may contribute to the exacerbation of bipolar patterns (Ghaemi, Boiman, & Goodwin, 1999; Post & Weiss, 1989; Wolpert, Berman, & Bornstein, 1999; see Hlastala et al., 2000, for contrasting view). Maintenance treatment, including continued prophylactic pharmacotherapy, may play an important role in diminishing this effect.

Other Therapies.   Family and psychosocial intervention is an important part of treatment for many bipolar clients. Clients with a history of florid manic or hypomanic episodes may suffer significant psychosocial consequences in work and academic settings as well as in their family systems. Obviously, these consequences may compromise many clients' recovery. For children and adolescent clients, the clinician should communicate with the school to plan appropriate behavioral interventions as well as to monitor the appearance of possible ADHD, conduct, or oppositional behaviors exhibited at school or home. Because repeated episodes of mood lability may interfere with the child's normal academic and interpersonal development, the clinician also should also conduct a thorough learning/academic assessment.

Although no research supports the effectiveness of psychotherapy with mania or hypomania, psychotherapy has been shown to be effective for depression phases of bipolar disorder. Commonly employed psychotherapies include cognitive, interpersonal, and behavioral therapies, although family systems interventions may be effective as well. (See discussion under depressive disorders above.)

Recently, Beck has extended his own CBT to treat mania and cyclothymia (Newman et al., 2002). Several case studies and trials now suggest that CBT might be a useful adjunct to psychotropic medications for the treatment of mania (Garland & Moorhead, 2001; Satterfield, 1999).

Treatment of co-morbid substance abuse, if present, should proceed concurrently with management and treatment of bipolar disorder if at all possible. Just as negative changes in each of these syndromes may amplify the other, therapeutic changes in the client's mood functioning may reciprocally promote positive changes in substance use patterns (APA, 2000a; Frank & Thase, 1999).

CASE EXAMPLE
Henrietta

Referral: Henrietta, an 18-year-old African American woman with a recent history of peripheral gang involvement, was caught stealing after dropping out of high school last year. Referred for counseling by her probation officer, Henrietta reports she has recently experienced sustained moods of sadness alternating with briefer periods of irritability and expansiveness that she describes as "a big view of the world—with me at the center above everybody else." During these episodes, which typically last for three or four days, Henrietta reports she requires little sleep and often stays out all night partying with men and women she has not met before.

Henrietta admits to a recent history of suicidal ideation. She states she bought a knife four months ago and cut herself with it, but denies any current suicidal thoughts or intent. According to Henrietta, she experienced her first depressive episode approximately one year ago when her mother's boyfriend moved into their home and Henrietta,

(*continued*)

CASE EXAMPLE   **Continued**

learning that she was pregnant, dropped out of school. When Henrietta decided to have an abortion, Henrietta reported her mother became upset to the point that she would not speak with her for a number of days. Henrietta subsequently moved into an apartment on the opposite side of the city and reports that although she and her mother now speak occasionally, they do not have the kind of relationship they used to have. Henrietta reports that she never knew her father, who now lives in a distant city. She also states she has never gotten along with her 10-year-old stepsister who lives in her mother's home.

Immediate concerns: Are there any immediate dangers to the client or other vulnerable persons?

Henrietta denies current suicidal ideation, but her recent suicidal gesture underscores the need to monitor her thoughts of self-harm and intervene as necessary. In particular, Henrietta may be vulnerable to suicidal ideation during periods of mania or hypomania as well as during the more extended periods of sadness. The clinician should be alert to the additional possibility that Henrietta may abuse substances during her periods of elevated and irritable mood and that, if present, her use of substances during these episodes may amplify her risk of self-harm.

Short-term goals: What goals need to be achieved in the first two to six sessions?

Psychotherapy was initiated with Henrietta with the immediate goal of addressing her suicidal thoughts and establishing behavioral plans to deal more appropriately with her periods of irritable/expansive mood. A clinical assessment revealed she met the criteria for a DSM-IV diagnosis of Bipolar II Disorder, Most Recent Episode Hypomanic. Cognitive interventions were used to modify negatively distorted self-evaluations that predominated during Henrietta's depressive episodes, and consistent sleeping and eating patterns were established using behavioral and self-management strategies. Henrietta made a plan to enroll in daytime classes to earn her GED and, with her consent, the clinician consulted with her academic counselor to develop strategies to help Henrietta succeed in her academic efforts. These included breaking assignments into smaller, more manageable tasks, and self-monitoring work to prevent becoming overwhelmed. Psychotherapy sessions also explored strategies by which to help Henrietta return to previous levels of interpersonal engagement with her family, highschool, and neighborhood friends.

As a result of a psychiatric referral, Henrietta was prescribed a mood-stabilizing medication and Henrietta's psychiatrist collaborated with her psychologist to promote her medications compliance. A referral to a social worker was also made to connect Henrietta to social and community resources, including occupational services affiliated with the community college at which she attended her GED course work. It was hoped these activities also would improve Henrietta's involvement in her community and reinforce her termination from gang-related activities. With Henrietta's consent, she and her mother participated in three family sessions with her social worker in which her mother gained an understanding of her cyclical symptoms and in which relational ground rules were established that were intended to improve their interactions.

Long-term goals: What lifestyle changes and other long-term personal, relationship, and career goals should be achieved?

CASE EXAMPLE   Continued

Long-term goals with Henrietta include continued work toward completion of her GED and assessment-based counseling to explore her subsequent occupational and academic plans. Therapeutic interventions should solidify her improved cognitive self-appraisals and psychosocial interventions should be continued to enhance Henrietta's sense of control over her social and academic life. A referral for more extensive family interventions should be considered to improve Henrietta's relationship with her mother, her mother's boyfriend, and her stepsister, as well as with other extended family members who may be important in her life. The clinician should work with Henrietta to establish a self-management plan to promote her continued consultation with her psychiatrist as well as her medications compliance. Henrietta should also learn to monitor changes in her mood and suicidal ideation and learn to identify periods of stress—and strategies to manage such periods—associated with the onset of her bipolar symptoms. After termination of therapy, Henrietta should be invited to contact and, if indicated, resume her work with the clinician if these issues become a concern.

CASE EXERCISE

Sheila, a 24-year-old Anglo-American secretary, has been married for three years to a 27-year-old African American engineer. She reports a history of depressive episodes beginning her freshman year of college. During these periods of depression, Sheila reports she sometimes spends money on clothes and restaurant meals to lift her spirits. Sheila also occasionally experiences manic episodes that she describes as "periods of titillating happiness." During these episodes, she reports that she gets giddy and laughs for days. During the most recent of these expansive episodes, Sheila reports she charged approximately $7,000 to credit cards she shares with her husband. Most of the money was spent on drinks, food, and gifts for people she did not even know. When she returned home the next evening, her husband reacted angrily and left their apartment to stay with a friend. Sheila stated she subsequently went to a dance club with one of her girlfriends, became intoxicated, and ingested ecstasy (MDMH) for the first time. She reported she had never used drugs before. She stated she met a man on the dance floor and returned with him to his apartment when the club closed. Once at his apartment, she backed out of a clearly sexual situation and called for a taxi from her cellular phone.

She reports she made the decision to seek psychotherapy when she woke up in her own home the subsequent morning and was still intoxicated. She stated that she apologized to her husband for her spending spree but has not told him about the club incident, although she thinks he may have noticed the taxicab phone number in her cell phone menu screen. Sheila states that her husband no longer trusts her.

C A S E   E X E R C I S E   **Continued**

Study Questions

1. What are your diagnostic impressions about Sheila? What disorders and conditions should be ruled out?

2. What information would you need to verify these impressions? How would you gather this information?

3. Are there any immediate dangers Sheila or other vulnerable people face?

4. What goals need to be achieved in the first two to six sessions of your work with Sheila?

5. What is your treatment plan to achieve these goals (including referrals if indicated)?

6. What lifestyle changes and other long-term personal, relationship, and career goals should be achieved in your work with Sheila?

7. What cultural issues are raised in Sheila's case, including her relationship with her husband? How might these issues affect her struggles with her mood-related symptoms or behaviors?

8. How might your work with Sheila be modified if she were a 24-year-old African American woman? How might your work be modified if she were a 36-year-old African American woman?

9. Sheila reports she misled you during your initial assessment and that she had sex with the man from the dance club before calling for a taxi. She now fears she may have contracted HIV from the man, although she has no evidence to support this fear. What are your ethical and legal obligations to her, her husband, and any other sexual partners? What are your ethical and legal obligations if she tests positive for HIV?

10. After three weeks of individual therapy, you agree with Sheila that her husband should be invited to two or three sessions in which relational issues between them will be discussed, an invitation he accepts. Prior to the first of these meetings, Sheila reveals to you that she is pregnant with the child of the man she met at the club. She now plans to have an abortion. Do you reveal this information to her husband? What do you do if he asks you directly about this possibility during one of the sessions?

R E F E R E N C E S

American Psychiatric Association. (2000a). *American Psychiatric Association practice guideline for the treatment of patients with major depressive disorder* (2nd ed.). Washington, DC: Author.

American Psychiatric Association. (2000b). *Diagnostic and statistical manual of mental disorders* (4th ed., text revision) *(DSM-IV-TR)*. Washington, DC: Author.

Anderson, I. M. (2000). Selective serotonin reuptake inhibitors versus tricyclic antidepressants: A meta analysis of efficacy and tolerability. *Journal of Affective Disorders, 58,* 19–36.

Beck, A. T. (1976). *Cognitive therapy and the emotional disorders.* New York: International Universities Press.

Beck, A. T., Rush, A. J., Shaw, B. F., & Emery, G. (1987). *Cognitive therapy for depression.* London: Guilford Press.

Bellack, A. S., Hersen, M., & Himmelhoch, J. (1981). Social skills training compared with pharmacotherapy and psychotherapy in the treatment of unipolar depression. *American Journal of Psychiatry, 138,* 1562–1567.

Birmaher, B., Brent, D., & American Academy of Child & Adolescent Psychiatry Work Group on Quality Issues. (1998). Practice parameters for the assessment and treatment of children and adolescents with depressive disorders. *Journal of the American Academy of Child & Adolescent Psychiatry, 37*(10, suppl.), 63S–83S.

Birmaher, B., Ryan, N. D., Williamson, D. E., Brent, D. A., et al. (1996). Childhood and adolescent depression: A review of the past 10 years, Part I. *Journal of the American Academy of Child & Adolescent Psychiatry, 35,* 1427–1439.

Brannon, S. E., & Nelson, R. O. (1987). Contingency management treatment of outpatient unipolar depression: A comparison of reinforcement and extinction. *Journal of Consulting and Clinical Psychology, 55,* 117–119.

Burgess, S., Geddes, J., Hawton, K., Townsend, E., Jamison, K., & Goodwin, G. (2001). Lithium for maintenance treatment of mood disorders. *Cochrane Database Systematic Review,* CD003013.

Clark, D. A., Beck, A. T., & Alford, B. A. (1999). *Scientific foundations for cognitive theory and therapy of depression.* Chichester, UK: Wiley.

Clark, D. C. (1995). Epidemiology, assessment, and management of suicide in depressed patients. In E. E. Beckham & W. R. Leber (Eds.), *Handbook of depression* (2nd ed.; pp. 526–538). New York: Guilford.

Clark, D. C., & Fawcett, J. (1992). Review of empirical risk factors for evaluation of the suicidal patient. In B. Bongar (Ed.), *Suicide: Guidelines for assessment, management, and treatment.* New York: Oxford University Press.

Cohen, L. S., Friedman, J. M., Jefferson, J. W., Johnson, E. M., & Weiner, M. L. (1994). A reevaluation of risk of in utero exposure to lithium. *Journal of the American Medical Association, 271,* 146–150.

Devanand, D. P., Sackeim, H. A., & Prudic, J. (1991). Electroconvulsive therapy in the treatment-resistant patient. *Psychiatric Clinics of North America, 14*(4), 905–923.

DeRubeis, R. J., Gelfand, L. A., Tang, T. Z., & Simons, A. D. (1999). Medications versus cognitive behavior therapy for severely depressed outpatients: Meta-analysis of four randomized comparisons. *American Journal of Psychiatry, 156*(7), 1007–1013.

Dobson, K. S. (1989). A meta-analysis of the efficacy of cognitive therapy for depression. *Journal of Consulting and Clinical Psychology, 57,* 414–419.

Drug Facts and Comparisons. (1996). St. Louis: Wolters Kluwer.

Elkin, I., Shea, M. T., Watkins, J. T., Imber, S. D., Sotsky, S. M., Collins, J. F., Glass, D. R., Pilkonis, P. A., Leber, W. R., Docherty, J. P., Fiester, S. J., & Parloff, M. B. (1989). National Institute of Mental Health Treatment of Depression Collaborative Research Program: General effectiveness of treatments. *Archives of General Psychiatry, 46,* 971–982.

Elkin, I., Gibbons, R. D., Shea, M. T., Sotsky, S. M., Watkins, J. T., Pilkonis, P. A., & Hedeker, D. (1995). Initial severity and differential treatment outcome in the National Institute of Mental Health Treatment of Depression Collaborative Research Program. *Journal of Consulting & Clinical Psychology, 63,* 841–847.

Ellis, A. (1984). *Rational emotive therapy and cognitive behavior therapy.* New York: Springer.

Ellis, A. & Dryden, W. (1997). *The practice of rational emotive behavior therapy* (2nd ed.). New York: Springer.

Fawcett, J. (1992). Suicide risk factors in depressive disorders and in panic disorder. *Journal of Clinical Psychiatry, 53*(3, suppl.), 9–13.

Folkerts, H. W., Michael, N., Tolle, R., Schonauer, K., Mucke, S., & Schulze-Monking, H. (1997). Electroconvulsive therapy vs. paroxetine in treatment-resistant depression: A randomized study. *Acta Psychiatrica Scandanavica, 96,* 334–342.

Frank, E., & Thase, M. E. (1999). Natural history and preventative treatment of recurrent mood disorders. *Annual Review of Medicine, 50,* 453–468.

Franklin, D. J. (2001). *Psychology Information Online. Medication for depression.* Retrieved January 29, 2002, from 2001PatientCommunity.com.

Garland, S. J. & Moorhead, S. (2001). A pilot study of cognitive therapy in bipolar disorders. *Psychological Medicine, 31,* 459–467.

Ghaemi, S. N., Boiman, E. E., & Goodwin, F. K. (1999). Kindling and second messengers: An approach to the neurobiology of recurrence in bipolar disorder. *Biological Psychiatry, 45,* 137–144.

Giedd, J. N. (2000). Bipolar disorder and attention-deficit/hyperactivity disorder in children and adolescents. *Journal of Clinical Psychiatry, 61*(suppl. 9), 31–34.

Gotlib, I. H., & Nolan, S. A. (2000). Depressive disorders. In M. Hersen & A. S. Bellack (Eds.), *Psychopathology in adulthood* (2nd ed.; pp. 252–277). Boston: Allyn and Bacon.

Hlastala, S. A., Frank, E., Kowalski, J., Sherrill, J. T., Tu, X. M., Anderson, B., & Kupfer, D. J. (2000). Stressful life events, bipolar disorder, and the "kindling model." *Journal of Abnormal Psychology, 109,* 777–786.

Jacobson, N. S., Dobson, K., Fruzetti, A. E., Schmaling, K. B., & Salusky, S. (1991). Marital therapy as a treatment for depression. *Journal of Consulting and Clinical Psychology, 59,* 547–557.

Johnson, J. G., Cohen, P., & Brook, J. S. (2000). Associations between bipolar disorder and other psychiatric disorders during adolescence and early adulthood: A community-based longitudinal investigation. *American Journal of Psychiatry, 157,* 1679–1681.

Klein, D. N., Schwartz, J. E., Rose, S., & Leader, J. B. (2000). Five-year course and outcome of dysthymic disorder: A prospective, naturalistic follow-up study. *American Journal of Psychiatry, 157,* 931–939.

Lawlor, D. A., & Hopkins, S. W. (2001). The effectiveness of exercise as an intervention in the treatment of depression: Systematic review and meta-regression analysis of randomized controlled trials. *British Medical Journal, 322,* 763–767.

Lewinsohn, P. M., Klein, D. N, & Seeley, J. R. (1995). Bipolar disorders in a community sample of older adolescents: Prevalence, phenomenology, comorbidity, and course. *Journal of the American Academy of Child and Adolescent Psychiatry, 34,* 454–463.

Lima, M. S. & Moncrieff, J. (2000). Drugs versus placebo for dysthymia. *Cochrane Database Systematic Review,* CD001130.

Macritchie, K. A., Geddes, J. R., Scott, J., Haslam, D. R., & Goodwin, G. M. (2001). Valproic acid, valproate and divalproex in the maintenance treatment of bipolar disorder. *Cochrane Database Systematic Review,* CD003196.

Meyer, R. G., & Deitsch, S. E. (1996). *The clinician's handbook: Integrated diagnostics, assessment, and intervention in adult and adolescent psychopathology.* Boston: Allyn and Bacon.

Newman, C. F., Leahy, R. L., Beck, A. T., Reilly-Harrington, N. A., & Gyulai, L. (2002). *Bipolar disorder: A cognitive therapy approach.* Washington, DC: American Psychological Association.

Norris, R., Carroll, D., & Cochrane, R. (1992). The effects of physical activity and exercise training on psychological stress and well-being in an adolescent population. *Journal of Psychosomatic Research, 36,* 55–65.

Nursing 2001 Drug Handbook. (2001). 21st ed. Springhouse, PA: Springhouse Corporation.

Patient Community.com. Retrieved January 29, 2002, from http://ibd.patientcommunity.com/features/treatments.cfm?link_id=2155.

Persons, J., Thase, M. E., & Crits-Christoph, P. (1996). The role of psychotherapy in the treatment of depression: Review of two practice guidelines. *Archives of General Psychiatry, 53,* 283–290.

Post, R. M., & Weiss, S. R. B. (1989). Kindling and manic-depressive illness. In T. G. Bolwig & M. R. Trimble (Eds.), *The clinical relevance of kindling* (pp. 209–230). New York: John Wiley & Sons.

PSYweb. Antidepressants. Retrieved January 29, 2002, from http://www.psyweb.com/drughtm/antidp.html.

Rapaport, M. H. (2001). Prevalence, recognition, and treatment of comorbid depression and anxiety. *Journal of Clinical Psychiatry, 62* (suppl. 24), 6–10.

Reed, M. K. (1994). Social skills training to reduce depression in adolescents. *Adolescence, 29,* 293–302.

Regier, D. A., Farmer, M. E., Rae, D. R., Locke, B. Z., Keith, S. J., Judd, L. L., & Goodwin, F. K. (1990). Comorbidity of mental disorders with alcohol and other drug abuse. *Journal of the American Medical Association, 264,* 2511–2518.

Rudd, M. D. (2000). The suicidal mode: a cognitive-behavioral model of suicidality. *Suicide and Life Threatening Behavior, 30,* 18–33.

Satterfield, J. M. (1999). Adjunctive cognitive-behavioral therapy for rapid cycling bipolar disorder: An empirical case study. *Psychiatry, 62,* 357–359.

Segrin, C. (2000). Social skills deficits associated with depression. *Clinical Psychology Review, 20,* 379–403.

Sharma, R., & Markar, H. R. (1994). Mortality in affective disorder. *Journal of Affective Disorders, 31,* 91–96.

Silva, R. R., Matzner, F., Diaz, J., Singh, S., & Dummit, E. S., III. (2000). Bipolar disorder in children and adolescents: A guide to diagnosis and treatment. In K. J. Palmer (Ed.), *Topics in pediatric psychiatry* (pp. 29–43). Kwai Chung, Hong Kong: Adis International Publications.

Silver, R. J., Isaacs, K., & Mansky, P. (1981). MMPI correlates of affective disorders. *Journal of Clinical Psychology, 37,* 836–839.

Simon, H. (Editor-in-Chief). *WebMD. Health What are the drugs used for depression?* Retrieved January 29, 2002, from http://my.webmd.com/content/article/1680.51006.

Solovay, M., Shenton, M., & Holzman, P. (1987). Comparative studies of thought disorders: 1. Mania: 2. Schizoaffective disorder. *Archives of General Psychiatry, 44,* 13–30.

Spencer, T. J., Biederman, J., Wozniak, J., Faraone, S. V., Wilens, T. E., & Mick, E. (2001). Parsing pediatric bipolar disorder from its associated comorbidity with the disruptive behavior disorders. *Biological Psychiatry, 49,* 1062–1070.

Strunk, D. R., & DeRubeis, R. J. (2001). Cognitive therapy for depression: A review of its efficacy. *Journal of Cognitive Psychotherapy Special Issue: Review of cognitive behavioral therapy, 5*(4), 289–297.

Taylor, M. A. (2000). Medication treatment versus cognitive behavior therapy. *American Journal of Psychiatry, 157*(6), 1025.

Van der Sande, R., Buskens, E., Allart, E., van der Graaf, Y., & van Engeland, H. (1997). Psychosocial intervention following suicide attempt: A systematic review of treatment interventions. *Acta Psychiatrica Scandanavica, 96,* 43–50.

Weller, E. B., Weller, R. A., & Fristad, M. A. (1995). Bipolar disorder in children: Misdiagnosis, underdiagnosis, and future directions. *Journal of the American Academy of Child and Adolescent Psychiatry, 34,* 709–714.

Wolpert, E. A., Berman, V., & Bornstein, M. (1999). Efficacy of electroconvulsive therapy in continuous rapid cycling bipolar disorder. *Psychiatric Annals, 29,* 679–683.

Wu, L. H., & Dunner, D. L. (1993). Suicide attempts in rapid cycling bipolar disorder patients. *Journal of Affective Disorders, 29*(1), 57–61.

Schizophrenia and Other Psychotic Disorders

CHAPTER OVERVIEW

1. Psychotic symptoms include hallucinations, delusions, and illusions, in addition to negative symptoms such as restricted emotion and disrupted motivation.

2. DSM-IV distinguishes nine psychotic disorders. Schizophrenia, Schizophreniform Disorder, and Schizoaffective Disorder are reviewed most extensively in this chapter.

3. Schizophrenia is characterized by two or more characteristic symptoms, such as hallucinations and flat affect, for at least one month, with evidence of disturbance for at least six months, and impaired social or occupational functioning. Subtypes include Paranoid, Disorganized, Undifferentiated, and Residual Schizophrenia.

4. Schizophreniform Disorder is characterized by a shorter period of psychotic disturbance. This diagnosis is used either during the prodromal period prior to the completion of six months of disturbance or for briefer, discrete episodes of psychosis that resolve within six months.

5. Schizoaffective Disorder is characterized by features of Schizophrenia coupled with at least one Depressive, Manic, or Mixed Episode.

6. Psychotropic medications include neuroleptic medications and newer atypical antipsychotic medications. Neuroleptic medications are associated with several side effects, including extra-pyramidal symptoms and tardive dyskinesia. Both classes of medications are effective for treating positive symptoms of psychoses. There is debate over whether atypical antipsychotics are superior for the treatment of negative symptoms, or whether their advantage reflects only the effects of high doses of neuroleptic medications, which often leave the client with significant residual symptoms. Medication compliance may be a problem, and social adaptation following active episodes of psychosis is often poor.

7. Psychosocial rehabilitation includes management of expressed emotions, cognitive therapy, patient education, relapse prevention, cognitive-behavior therapy, assertive community treatment, and case management. Common ethical problems involved in the treatment of schizophrenia include involuntary commitment, possible overrepresentation of minority clients in hospital settings, and the use of seclusion and restraint.

Psychotic Disorders

DSM-IV notes that the term *psychosis* has been used with varying degrees of breadth over time (APA, 2000). In its narrowest sense, psychosis refers only to delusions and hallucinations. In a broader sense, the term is sometimes used to refer to a range of symptomology, including hallucinations with insight, disorganized speech, and disorganized or catatonic behavior. Psychosis may also be used to refer to a single but firmly held delusion, with little other impairment in daily functioning. Table 8.1 lists other terms commonly used in the diagnosis of psychotic disorders.

TABLE 8.1   Common terms in the diagnosis of psychotic disorders.

Term	Definition
Alogia	It is inferred from observed speech that thinking is impaired. This is observed through poverty of speech (i.e., brief, concrete replies and reduced quantity of speech). It is also inferred from poverty of content, as shown by overly concrete, uninformative speech.
Avolition	The person is unmotivated to initiate or complete any goal-directed action.
Catalepsy	The person maintains a posture for extended periods of time, but can be moved (so called "waxy flexibility"), or maintains rigid body posture over extended periods of time.
Catatonic behavior	Immobility shown through catalepsy or stupor, excessive motor activity, extreme negativism, mutism, posturing stereotyped movements, echolalia, or echopraxia.
Command hallucinations	An auditory hallucination that tells the person to perform a specific action.
Disorganized speech	Speech that is clearly disrupted, sometimes taking the form of nonsensical rhyming or "word salads" of jumbled grammatical construction (e.g., "grocery men, man, find-out beauty cuts against northerns").
Echolalia	Repetition of a word or phrase that has just been spoken.
Echopraxia	An apparently automatic, involuntary repetition of another person's actions.
Flat affect	No or few signs of affect (e.g., happiness or sadness or anger).
Grossly disorganized behavior	A variety of behaviors including silliness, agitation, failure to maintain appropriate hygiene, lack of goal-directed behavior, unusual dress, or inappropriate sexual behavior, such as public masturbation.

(continued)

TABLE 8.1 Continued

Term	Definition
Inappropriate affect	Affect and content of speech and thought do not match. For example, crying when being told neutral information.
Mutism	Not speaking when the person is physically capable of doing so.
Negative symptoms	Withdrawal, lack of motivation, and flat affect are examples of negative symptoms.
Positive symptoms	Hallucinations and delusions are examples of positive symptoms.
Prodromal symptoms	The early signs or symptoms of a disorder. For example, a person with schizophrenia may become progressively more withdrawn and strange prior to full-blown onset of an episode of positive symptoms.
Residual symptoms	Symptoms that remain after the florid or full-blown syndrome remits. For example, a person may not have hallucinations or delusions, but may still be apathetic, unmotivated, and socially withdrawn.
Stupor	Unresponsiveness and lack of arousal while conscious.
Thought broadcast	A delusion that others can hear or perceive your own thoughts because they are being broadcast.
Thought insertion	A delusion that someone else's thoughts have been inserted into one's mind.

Delusions and Hallucinations

The terms *delusion* and *hallucination* are commonly used when diagnosing psychoses. DSM-IV defines a delusion as "a false belief based on incorrect inferences about external reality that is firmly sustained despite what almost everyone else believes and what constitutes incontrovertible and obvious proof or evidence to the contrary" (APA, 2000, p. 821). This definition excludes culturally appropriate beliefs, such as religious or spiritual convictions and false beliefs based on value judgments. It also excludes overvalued ideas, which although false and unreasonable, are not as firmly held as delusions. For example, a client who continued to believe his or her teeth had been implanted with alien devices even when shown X-ray evidence to the contrary (e.g., by asserting that the dentist fabricated the negatives) might be suspected to suffer from schizophrenia. In contrast, a client who accepted the X-rays as compelling (and relieving!) evidence might not.

DSM-IV defines a hallucination as "a sensory perception that has the compelling sense of reality of a true perception but that occurs without external stimulation of the relevant sensory organ" (APA, 2000, p. 823). A person who claimed to hear the voices of space aliens commanding him to follow various behaviors, for instance, would be said to suffer hallucinations. Hallucinations may be contrasted with illusions, which are misperceptions of actual stimuli. Although illusions may reflect psychological motivations, they are not at all uncommon and do not reflect psychosis. Many dormitory residents, for example, have misperceived an innocent, overheard conversation as the makings of an interpersonal conspiracy. Such misperceptions are illusions (presuming they were false) not hallucinations. Hallucinations involve hearing conversations, or perceiving other stimuli, that are not actually being spoken. In their most common, auditory, form, hallucinations often involve running critical commentaries directed against the listener. Hallucinations also may be visual, tactile, somatic, olfactory, or even gustatory.

Diagnosis

DSM-IV distinguishes nine forms of psychotic disorders: Schizophrenia, Schizophreniform Disorder, Schizoaffective Disorder, Delusional Disorder, Brief Psychotic Disorder, Shared Psychotic Disorder (Folie à Deux), Psychotic Disorder Due to a General Medical Condition, Substance-Induced Psychotic Disorder, and Psychotic Disorder NOS. This section will focus on the first three disorders and review the other psychotic disorders only briefly.

Schizophrenia

Among the psychotic disorders, Schizophrenia is the one with which counselors and psychologists are most likely to work. DSM-IV defines schizophrenia as the sustained presence for at least one month of two or more of the following symptoms: delusions, hallucinations, disorganized speech, grossly disorganized or catatonic behavior, and negative symptoms such as flat affect, alogia (absence of the use of words by someone capable of speaking), or avolition (absence of motivated action). These symptoms must cause significant social or occupational dysfunction and must not be better accounted for by another DSM-IV disorder, such as Schizoaffective Disorder, Mood Disorders, Substance Abuse, or a general medical conditions. The person's disturbance must be evident for at least six months. (See Table 8.1 for definitions of terms used in this paragraph.)

Paranoid Schizophrenia. DSM-IV recognizes several subtypes of schizophrenia. *Paranoid Schizophrenia* is defined by preoccupation with one or more delusions or frequent auditory hallucinations and little disorganized speech, disorganized or catatonic behavior, or flat or inappropriate affect (APA, 1994,

p. 287). Although the content of client's delusions typically are persecutory, it also may be grandiose, jealous, religious, or somatosized. The onset for schizophrenia, paranoid type, is typically marked and discrete. Despite their distorted beliefs, people with paranoid schizophrenia often continue to exhibit relatively normal cognitive and affective functioning. Ironically, their mental functioning may be kept organized by the unvarying content of their delusions. They may also be anxious, angry, aloof, argumentative, patronizing, or very intense.

Disorganized Schizophrenia. Disorganized schizophrenia is defined by the presence of disorganized speech, disorganized behavior, and flat or inappropriate affect beyond the criteria for catatonic type (discussed below). Disorganized clients arguably experience the worst form of schizophrenia. Without the coherent delusions or hallucinations of the paranoid type to organize their disrupted perceptions, clients with disorganized schizophrenia often display inappropriate, odd behaviors and suffer significant disruptions in their daily lives. In contrast with paranoid type, the onset of disorganized schizophrenia is usually insidious and slow: The person may evidence prodromal symptoms, such as clumsiness and interpersonal isolation (Walker, Grimes, Davis, & Smith, 1993; Walker, Savoie, & Davis, 1994) for years before losing the capacity to make sense of his or her sensory and psychological experiences. Unsurprisingly, the prognosis for disorganized schizophrenic clients is poor.

Catatonic Schizophrenia. The client with *Catatonic Schizophrenia* is predominantly recognized by motor symptoms that include stuporous immobility or waxy flexibility, purposeless and excessive motor movement, mutism or resistance to external suggestions (e.g., maintenance of rigidity in spite of attempts to be moved), bizarre posturing, stereotyped movements or prominent grimacing, and echolalia (mimicking speech), or echopraxia (mimicking behaviors) (APA, 1994, p. 289).

In addition to these three subtypes, DSM-IV offers two diagnoses to be used in special cases. *Undifferentiated Schizophrenia* is diagnosed when a person meets two of five of the characteristic symptoms of a schizophrenia diagnosis but does not meet the full criteria for any one specific subtype. *Residual Schizophrenia* is used when a person continues to experience negative schizophrenic symptoms or mild forms of two or more positive symptoms, but no longer suffers the delusions, hallucinations, or disorganized speech of full-blown schizophrenia.

Schizophreniform Disorder

Schizophreniform Disorder is an intermediate diagnosis between Schizophrenia and Brief Psychotic Disorder. This diagnosis is used for a period of one to six months during which a client otherwise meets the criteria for schizophrenia and in which mood disorders, substance-related disorders, and general medical conditions are ruled out. If the client's symptoms continue for more than six months, the diagnosis is changed to schizophrenia. Impaired occupational or social functioning is not required to diagnose schizophreniform disorder.

Schizoaffective Disorder

As its name implies, Schizoaffective Disorder features symptoms of both schizophrenia and affective disorders that coexist within the same episode of an illness. To diagnose Schizoaffective Disorder, four criteria must be met. First, the person must meet the criteria of a Major Depressive Episode, Manic Episode, or Mixed Episode (see Chapter 7). Second, he or she must experience hallucinations or delusions for at least two weeks in the absence of affective symptoms. The client's mood symptoms also must be present for a substantial part of the entire episode of the illness and must not be better accounted for by a substance-related disorder or general medical condition.

Clients experiencing severe major depressive episodes sometimes experience delusions and/or hallucinations that are not associated with psychotic disorders, including Schizoaffective Disorder. These distortions usually may be differentiated from psychotic episodes by their mood-congruent content. A depressed client may believe that the insides of his or her body are rotting away, for example, or that susceptibility to gravity has amplified, weighing down his or her movements. Such explanations typically are consistent with the perceived data of the client's depressive symptoms.

Other Psychotic Disorders

The remaining psychotic disorders are grouped together here because counselors and psychologists are less likely to work with clients suffering from them. The reader should refer to DSM-IV for further discussion of their diagnostic criteria.

Delusional Disorder.   This disorder is diagnosed when a person who does not otherwise meet the criteria for a schizophrenia diagnosis experiences nonbizarre delusions. That is, delusions involving real people and situations. For example, a person might believe that the president is in love with him or her (an erotomanic delusion), that he or she has a special relationship with the pope (a grandiose delusion), that a partner is being unfaithful to him or her (a jealous delusion, if not true), or that he or she has a physical defect but does not (a somatic delusion).

Brief Psychotic Disorder.   Brief Psychotic Disorder is used to diagnose psychotic symptoms that last between one day and one month. A client suffering this disorder displays one of the following four characteristic symptoms of schizophrenia: delusions, hallucinations, disorganized speech, or grossly disorganized or catatonic behavior (APA, 1994, p. 304). Brief Psychotic Disorder is often associated with a marked stressor, such as pregnancy or the death of a family member, and with personality disorders.

*Shared Psychotic Disorder (*Folie à Deux*).* This is a very rare disorder in which a second person comes to share delusions similar to those experienced by an inducer who already has a psychiatric disorder. Symptoms of *folie à deux* must not be better accounted for by other psychiatric or general medical conditions.

Psychotic Disorder Due to a General Medical Condition. This diagnosis is used when clients present with prominent hallucinations or delusions that are caused by a general medical condition. A wide range of medical conditions can cause hallucinations and delusions, including neurological conditions such as brain tumors, brain damage resulting from strokes, temporal lobe epilepsy, thyroid disorders, and metabolic or electrolyte disorders. Note that hallucinations or delusions associated with the *medication* taken to alleviate medical conditions, rather than the conditions themselves, should be diagnosed as Substance-Induced Psychotic Disorder, which may also be associated with the use of illicit substances, such as intoxication or withdrawal from cocaine, amphetamines, or hallucinogens. (See Chapter 6 for discussion of substance-related disorders, intoxication, and withdrawal.)

Psychotic Disorder Not Otherwise Specified (NOS). Finally, Psychotic Disorder NOS is diagnosed when a client presents with the characteristics of schizophrenia, but presents insufficient or contradictory information to make a specific psychotic diagnosis.

Differential Diagnosis

The differential diagnosis of psychosis involves several unique problems. First, the range of psychotic behavior observed in the general population is surprisingly broad: Many people report hearing voices from time to time both during normal experiences (Young et al., 1987) and during bereavement (Grimby, 1993). Nonsymptomatic people also hold a range of strange beliefs, some of which may be subculturally appropriate, such as denials of the age or approximate spherical shape of the Earth by some anti-Enlightenment conspiracy theorists. Although such beliefs may not interfere with daily occupational or social functioning for some people, others find themselves in a gray area where strange beliefs shade into delusions.

A second area of concern is judgments related to cultural beliefs. For example, strongly held religious convictions may lead to putatively abnormal behaviors within particular subcultures, such as speaking in tongues or taking up serpents among some fundamentalist Christian groups. Other religious or quasi-religious subgroups, which may be proliferating with the expansion of the World Wide Web, hold strange beliefs about the imminent arrival of aliens from outer space or elite conspiracies to internationalize U.S. citizens. Furthermore, chronic experiences of abuse or discrimination can give rise in minority cultures to what others might regard as paranoid beliefs or behavior that may be difficult to distinguish from abnormality (e.g., government conspiracies to spread HIV viruses among minority populations).

The differentiation of schizophrenia and other psychotic disorders from general medical conditions and substance-related disorders also may be difficult, in part because there are so many general medical conditions, many of which can be difficult to diagnose, that can cause hallucinations and delusions. This may be especially true for people who are medically compromised, for example, through malnutrition, dehydration, or exhaustion. In older clients a wide range of relatively minor general medical conditions can also cause psychotic-like symptoms if allowed to continue without appropriate treatment. It is also important to recall that severe mood disorders can be associated with hallucinations and delusions and that some OCD clients may hold beliefs so intensely that they take on a delusional quality.

Substance-related disorders and substance-induced psychotic disorders may also be confused with other psychotic disorders. In ruling out such diagnoses, clinicians should be aware that clients often do not disclose information about the illegal substances they take and that many clients find it difficult to accurately recount their prescribed medications and dosages. As with general medical conditions, seniors and clients who are medically compromised may be especially vulnerable to substance-induced psychoses. A simple reevaluation of the medications a client takes for colds or allergies (e.g., by a family physician), for example, can sometimes lead to the resolution of psychotic symptoms.

Intervention

This section focuses on the treatment of schizophrenia, for which a wide range of interventions has proven effective. As discussed below, psychotropic medications are important for alleviating acute disturbances and significantly reducing positive symptoms for many schizophrenic clients. The recent introduction of atypical antipsychotics, which have fewer side effects than traditional neuroleptics, has also given promise for the treatment of negative symptoms (e.g., flat affect, poor communication). The treatment of psychosis, however, does not end with pharmacotherapy. Many clients who receive psychotropic medications continue to experience significant problems in daily living, even when their positive and negative symptoms are effectively treated. Other clients are medication-resistant, experiencing no reduction in their symptoms at all. Even those for whom medication has proven effective remain at risk for relapse. Enhanced psychosocial programming, such as cognitive therapy and caregiver interventions, can lead to enhanced social functioning and further symptom reduction even in clients with additional substance abuse problems (Barrowclough et al., 2001).

Psychosocial interventions such as symptom monitoring, modifying patterns of family interaction, and enhancement of life skills are also important aspects of treatment. Simply ensuring the client's compliance with psychotropic interventions, especially for those medications with multiple, unpleasant side effects, can also enhance treatment. For some clients the course of psychotic disorders is one of repeated psychotic episodes with interim periods of recovery, often with residual symptoms in the interim. For others, it involves a progressive deterioration of functioning and severe interference with occupational and social functioning throughout their lives. Clients who suffer psychotic symptoms should not be merely medicated and sent on their way. The goals shared by other therapy clients, such as job satisfaction, engagement in living, and participation in family and community affairs, apply equally to clients suffering from psychotic disorders.

The treatment of psychoses, then, involves many different professionals and agencies. Helping the client and the family coordinate these services can be one of the clinician's most difficult, but important, tasks.

Psychotropic Medications

Traditional Neuroleptic Medications. It is impossible to underestimate the impact that psychotropic medications have had on the treatment of schizophrenia. Prior to their development in the 1950s, psychiatrists had few treatment options other than bromides, electroconvulsive therapy, insulin shock treatment (inducing a coma from which the client hoped to emerge with reduced symptoms), cold wraps, hot and cold baths, and psychotherapy for a few wealthy clients. Tens of thousands of people with schizophrenia and other psychotic disorders languished in underfunded, understaffed, and overcrowded state hospitals.

The development of Haldol in the 1950s changed the treatment of schizophrenia dramatically. Within the five years following its introduction, the population of state hospitals across the United States and Europe dropped from 339 per 100,000 people to 20 per 100,000 (Lamb, 1998), a reduction of over 90 percent. Tens of thousands of previously untreatable clients were released to the community, many of whom became productive and happy citizens. The continued development of antipsychotic medications, coupled with improved community mental health services and fiscally conservative ideological changes, has led to further diminution of the number of schizophrenic clients treated in institutional settings over the past twenty-five years (Witkin, Atay, & Manderscheid, 1996).

Having taken the treatment of schizophrenia out of the dark ages, neuroleptics have only recently been gradually displaced by newer, atypical antipsychotics (see Table 8.2). Traditional and new antipsychotics are usually taken orally. In Europe, long-lasting intramuscular versions are occasionally prescribed to overcome medication compliance issues associated with oral medications. These intramuscular medications also provide a useful means of tracking and evaluating clients at least once a month when clients come in for monthly shots.

Since their introduction in the 1950s, antipsychotics have been subject to numerous double-blind studies (Sultana, Reilly, & Fenton, 2000). Although the

---

TABLE 8.2   Commonly used antipsychotic medications.

Generic name	Proprietary name

Some traditional neuroleptics

chlorpromazine	Thorazine
haloperidol	Haldol
fluphenazine	Permitil, Prolixin
mezoridazine	Serentil
perphenazine	Trilafon
prochlorperazine	Compazine
thioridazine	Mellaril

Some atypical antipsychotic medications

clozapine	Clorazil
olanzapine	Zyprexa
quietapine	Seroquel
risperidone	Risperdal
sertindole	Serlect

---

primary question of their effectiveness in treating the positive symptoms of schizophrenia seems to be answered, concerns remain about their side effects, dosages, promotion of compliance, and overall impact on clients' quality of life. Atypical neuroleptics may prove to answer some of these concerns, but long-term evaluation remains ongoing.

First evaluated with clients who were refractory to typical antipsychotics, atypical neuroleptics were shown immediately to reduce their positive symptoms and appeared poised to become an important secondary treatment option for meds-resistant clients. Later studies, however, found that atypical neuroleptics addressed a prominent gap in traditional neuroleptic treatment: clients' negative symptoms. Additionally, recent research has shown that atypical neuroleptics are less likely to cause extra-pyramidal side effects, such as tardive dyskinesia (an intractable disorder involving involuntary movement of the mouth, lips, upper body, and face), which can be extremely stigmatizing and cause major impairments in clients' daily functioning (Slovenko, 2000). Although atypical antipsychotics are more expensive than traditional neuroleptics, they may reduce the overall costs of clients' treatment by reducing their stay in hospitals (Gheami et al., 1998). Together, these findings point to their increased use over the next five to ten years, a trend likely to be amplified by political efforts by clinicians and mental health advocates pressuring insurance companies and state agencies to pay for them.

A recent meta-analysis comparing clients taking atypical and traditional neuroleptics seems to support these political efforts (Geddes et al., 2000). With the exception of quetapine, proportions of clients who were worse off in terms of both positive and negative symptoms when taking traditional neuroleptics ranged from 59 percent for those taking olanzapine to 75 percent for those taking clozapine. Dosage levels, however, significantly moderated these effects. Recognizing that antipsychotic medications are frequently used at much higher dosages than recommended, Geddes et al. (2000) dichotomized existing studies into those that used low and those that used high doses of traditional neuroleptics and found that atypical antipsychotics did *not* outperform tradition neuroleptics when the latter were used at lower doses. These findings suggest atypical antipsychotics may not be the panacea for schizophrenia that many have thought, but rather that their most appropriate use may be when clients fail to respond to, or suffer significant side effects from, traditional medications (Geddes et al., 2000).

Psychosocial Rehabilitation

Family Interventions and Expressed Emotions. Expressed Emotion (EE) refers to family members' display of high levels of criticism, hostility, or overinvolvement toward a fellow family member with schizophrenia. Expressed emotion has been shown repeatedly to predict relapse in clients recovering from schizophrenic episodes (Bebbington & Kuipers, 1995; Butzlaff & Hooley, 1998). Its effects on clients appear to be independent of medication and medication compliance (Bebbington & Kuipers, 1995).

On the basis of these findings, several interventions have been developed to reduce EE, including family psychoeducational interventions (e.g., educating clients and family members about the relationship between EE and relapse) and cognitive behavioral interventions to reduce criticism and hostility in the home (Mari & Streiner, 1994). Family members also may be taught to schedule time apart from each other to take emotional holidays from the stress of living daily with a schizophrenic client, or conversely, with a parent or other family member who exacerbates the stress a schizophrenic client faces. Outcomes of EE interventions have been modestly positive. A meta-analysis by Pharoah, Mari, and Steiner (2000), for example, found a modest impact on relapse rates after one year of EE interventions. Family interventions also appeared to reduce hospitalization and medication noncompliance issues, although treatment dropout rates did not appear to be similarly affected by EE interventions (cf. Mari & Streiner, 2000).

Cognitive Therapies. Because psychoses are characterized by irrational and bizarre thinking, it seems reasonable to use cognitive therapy to ameliorate their symptoms. Several recent trials of cognitive therapy with long follow-up have now been reported. Drury, Birchwood, Cochrane, and MacMillan (1996a,

1996b), for example, found that 56 percent of a control group, but only 5 percent of members of a cognitive therapy treatment group, reported moderate or severe residual symptoms after receiving psychopharmaceutic treatment. The authors also found that cognitive therapy appeared to reduce clients' recovery times by 25 percent to 50 percent, as assessed by various measures. Five-year follow-ups by Drury, Birchwood, and Cochrane (2000; Kuipers et al., 1997, 1998) of clients receiving similar treatments found that cognitive therapy clients also were more likely to report greater perceived control over their illness and more likely to report reduced psychotic symptoms.

Patient Education.   Patient education involves providing clients with information about the symptoms, medication, prognosis, signs of relapse, and other aspects of their illness. These interventions appear to be effective for at least two reasons: First, psychoeducation addresses the lack of insight by which many psychotic disorders are characterized. Second, psychoeducation directly addresses important treatment compliance issues, including medication compliance, appointment follow-through, and help-seeking before relapse, that are important factors in reducing relapse.

   Although the economic advantage of conducting family psychoeducation in large-group formats may seem attractive, however, a recent review found little evidence that this technique improved clients' medication compliance rates, and no evidence that it improved clients' insight, attitudes toward their medications, or overall life satisfaction (Pekkala & Merinder, 2000). However, large-group format (psychoeducational) interventions were associated with reduced readmission rates at nine and eighteen months compared to standard psychiatric care and with improved client well-being on a range of measures.

Relapse Prevention and Management.   Several studies have suggested that identification of the signs of relapse coupled with relapse prevention interventions may be critical facets of the treatment of schizophrenia. The Early Signs and Scale (ESS; Birchwood et al., 1989), for example, has been shown to detect early signs of relapse and may correctly predict relapse in 80 percent of cases (Jorgensen, 1998). Once identified, early interventions may be used to thwart actual relapse episodes, using such techniques as psychoeducation, monitoring of prodromal syndromes, and weekly therapy groups for clients and family members (Birchwood, 2000; Birchwood, Fowler, & Jackson, 2000; Hertz et al., 2000).

The Token Economy.   Token economies are often used with psychotic clients to teach daily living skills, reestablish client motivation, reduce levels of aggression and restraint, and promote clients' placement in community settings. Early evidence of the effectiveness of token economies in managing positive symptoms and reducing relapse rates (Glynn, 1990) have been replicated by numerous subsequent studies (Fullerton, Cayner, & McLaughlin-Reidel, 1978). A recent investigation by Li and Wang (1994), for example, found that hospital inpatients in a token economy group had fewer negative symptoms and higher levels of community integration (e.g., 91 of 125 token economy participants were employed at three year follow-ups) than controls.

Cognitive-Behavior Therapy. Skills-training interventions based on cognitive-behavioral models have been applied extensively with clients with schizophrenia and other psychotic disorders. Cognitive-behavioral approaches have been used successfully to teach clients with schizophrenia and other psychotic disorders a variety of self-help skills, life skills, and problem-solving skills (Heinssen, Lieberman, & Kopelowicz, 2000).

Assertive Community Treatment and Case Management. Assertive Community Treatment (ACT; Phillips et al., 2001) is a team-based approach to maintain contact between clients and service providers, reduce hospital admissions, and improve clients' social functioning and quality of life. ACT was developed in response to the dramatic downsizing of state hospitals in the 1970s and 1980s, which led to debilitating cycles of readmission, discharge, medication lapses, and symptom relapses for many schizophrenic clients. As Marshall and Lockwood (2000) reported, ACT clients are more likely to remain in contact with service providers, remain in their communities, and spend less time in hospitals than clients receiving only traditional psychiatric care. Compared to more typical community care arrangements, clients receiving ACT also are more likely to live independently, to be employed, and to be satisfied with their services than even clients receiving brokered care (Wolff et al., 1997).

Although other reviews (e.g., Marshall et al., 2000) have found that traditional case management alone may significantly increase client's contact with services, case management may not always improve compliance with treatment, mental status, social functioning, vocational functioning, substance abuse, or quality of life (Mueser et al., 1998). Research in this area, however, is admittedly incomplete. Since it appears that different forms of case management may lead to different client outcomes, it is important that future investigators identify the most effective forms of case management for people living with severe mental illness in community settings.

Ethical Issues

Consent for Treatment and Medication

In certain circumstances state laws permit involuntary medication of actively psychotic clients. These laws may often apply to persons with schizophrenia and other psychotic disorders because of the danger they may present to themselves or others and because they may lack insight about their psychological status. However, such laws may be tenuous against the current impulse of civil liberty affirmation in the United States. For example, shortly after New York State enacted a law permitting involuntary admission and medication of persons who were homeless and gravely disabled, Joyce Brown, the first homeless person to whom the law was applied, successfully won a case defending her right not to be forcibly medicated "based on her capacity to understand the proposed treatment and to express a partially rational opinion about [involuntary medication]" (Cournos, 1989). At about the same time, the California Supreme Court confirmed a lower court's decision that antipsychotic drugs cannot be administered without a *legal*, rather than clinical, determination of client incompetency (Binder & McNiel, 1991). Despite these rulings, informed consent is still not often sought in clinical practice. Schachter, Kleinman, and Williams (1999), for example, found that less than half of primary physicians disclosed the risk of tardive dyskinesia to their patients before prescribing antipsychotic medications, even though approximately 25 percent might be expected to experience this side effect.

Involuntary Commitment

Involuntary commitment of a person into a state hospital or other locked facility is one of the most restrictive procedures in clinical practice today. Approximately 5 to 10 percent of psychiatric hospitals admissions are involuntary (Malla, Norman, & Helmes, 1987; Isohanni et al., 1991; Reicher et al., 1991; Munk-Jorgensen & Machon, 1991). Clients with schizophrenia and mania are more likely than clients with any other diagnoses to be involuntarily admitted to treatment (Jaworowski & Zabow, 1995; Malla, Norman, & Helmes, 1987; Reicher et al. 1991; Sanguineti et al., 1996). They are also at greater risk for repeated involuntary admission (Sanguineti et al., 1996).

Local state laws, policies, and procedures significantly affect the use of involuntary admission. The introduction of a North Carolina law revising outpatient commitment policies, for instance, led to a subsequent reduction in the number of involuntary admissions in North Carolina and significantly reduced clients' average length of stay (Fernandez & Nygard, 1990). Involuntary admission usually is done because of imminent danger of harm to the client or to others, such as credible threats of suicide or threatening harm to others. ACA and APA guidelines, as well as the legal duty of care to the client, are clear that imminent danger of self-harm is sufficient reason for a therapist to take restrictive actions to ensure the client's safety. Although clients should be persuaded to self-admit when possible, therapists often are forced to break confidentiality and request client admission when clients present a significant danger to themselves. This is often done by phoning someone physically near the client to ensure his or her immediate safety, by phoning the police, or by asking a psychiatrist or physician to arrange for involuntary admission.

The issue of breaking client confidentiality when a client poses a danger to others is less clear. *Tarasoff* found that the regents of the University of California were negligent when one of their employees, a psychiatrist, failed to inform a third party of imminent danger from one of his patients. (See discussion in Chapter 2.) However, equivalents of the *Tarasoff* law do not exist in every state. Whereas some states require therapists to break confidentiality by disclosing the risk to the third party, others only *permit* it.

Overrepresentation of Minorities in State Hospitals

Extensive debate has taken place in the United States, Britain, and other Western countries over the apparent overrepresentation of minority clients admitted to state hospitals with diagnoses of schizophrenia (Thompson et al., 1995). Birchwood et al. (1992), for example, found that relapse rates after admission to a state hospital for a first episode of schizophrenia in white, Afro-Caribbean, and Asian patients varied significantly (where "Asian" was used to refer predominantly to people originating from India, Pakistan, and Bangladesh). Whereas readmission rates one year after discharge ranged from 16 percent to 30 percent for Asian and white patients (respectively), they reached 49 percent for Afro-Caribbean patients. Afro-Caribbean patients also appear to experience increased rates of misdiagnosis and readmission, longer hospitalizations, and more involuntary admissions than white patients (Callan, 1996; Hickling et al., 1999; Takei et al., 1998; see McGovern et al., 1994 for a contrasting view). Such discrepancies may indicate either that Afro-Caribbeans experience systematic discrimination or that they are given less access than white and Asian clients to preventive care. Similar concerns have been raised in Western Australia (Bruxner et al., 1997) and, in much more widespread research, in the United States (Thompson et al., 1995).

Participation in Research

Significant concerns have been expressed about the participation of people with schizophrenia in research. Ethical dilemmas can arise when experimental procedures induce psychotic symptoms or fail to provide effective treatments, as in drug trials involving placebos. These concerns are further heightened when participants are of questionable factual or legal competence or when researchers have a conflict of interest between the benefits to participants and their own desire to conduct (or publish) research (Lehrman & Sharav, 1997; Shore, 1996; Zipursky, 1999). The National Institute of Health has issued specific guidelines in this area that should be accessed by every researcher contemplating research with schizophrenic clients (Shore, 1996).

Suicide Risk

Schizophrenia is an important risk factor for suicide (Martin, 2000). The same principles described in Chapter 7 relating to suicide assessment and mood disorders apply here. (See Chapter 7 for discussion.)

Seclusion and Restraint

Seclusion and restraint are two highly restrictive procedures that are commonly used in public and private psychiatric hospitals, educational settings, correctional facilities, and youth treatment facilities. Seclusion refers to locking a person in a room designed for that purpose. Restraint refers to personal take-downs and physical holds. Some authorities also include emergency psychotropic medications among restrictive procedures (which may fall under the guise of "as needed" or "PRN" medications). Restraint has also been included in treatment plans for violent and aggressive behavior, self-injury, and other forms of maladaptive behaviors as part of behavior modification procedures. A 1983 sample of clients in an inpatient psychiatric unit found that 51 percent of these persons had experienced seclusion or restraint at least once, a surprisingly high figure (Phillips & Nasr, 1983). More recent research by Reinish and Ciccone (1995) found that 34 percent of police referrals to a psychiatric emergency department had experienced restraint and that 58 percent of other involuntarily admitted patients had experienced restraint or seclusion. People with psychotic disorders may be especially at risk for experiencing seclusion (Brown & Tooke, 1992).

Despite the widespread use of seclusion and restraint, several legal and ethical objections have been raised against both practices. As some writers have observed (e.g., Brown & Tooke, 1992), there is no relationship between the duration of seclusion and the reasons for its use; the use of seclusion also varies enormously between geographical areas, hospitals, and units. Similarly, the U.S. General Accounting Office (GAO, 1999) has pointed out that restraint is poorly regulated by individual states and that restraint-related deaths may be far more common than previously realized. Extensive research recently has emerged to limit its use (Busch & Shore, 2000; Donat, 1998).

The use of seclusion and restraint, including chemical restraint, raises many ethical and legal issues. First, the issue of consent is especially muddied. Who should consent to the procedure in the case of a court-ordered client? Who should consent if the client is factually incompetent, but not legally declared to be so? A second issue is client safety and the need to balance the risks and benefits of restrictive procedures, which rarely but all too commonly result in death (death is a good proxy for morbidity: For every client who dies from restraint there is likely a much larger number who suffer undisclosed harm and injury). Facilities that use restraint have an ethical obligation to ensure their clients' safety through frequent staff training, oversight procedures, and intervention monitoring. Treatment teams also should ensure that the benefits of restraint (e.g., reduction of harm to self, staff or others) outweigh its risks.

Smoking

The issue of schizophrenic clients' smoking rights surfaces in two clinical contexts. First, some token economy procedures employ cigarettes as a reinforcer, to which physicians and other team members sometimes object because of the obvious health risks associated with smoking. When conflicts over these concerns emerge, they should be resolved through the client, the client's team treatment members, and the local Human Rights Committee on an individual, rather on a blanket policy, basis. Based on an assessment of the client's skills, symptoms, and target behaviors (and the danger of the latter), the decision to use cigarettes should be based on a balanced view of the overall costs and benefits to the client, just as more restrictive procedures might be justified for changing self-injury or aggression as compared to programmatic noncompliance. Teams also should consider the relative risks and benefits associated with the client's cigarette use. A procedure using two cigarettes a day, for example, might pose a less significant risk than one using forty cigarettes a day.

Another ethical issue surrounding the use of cigarettes is the interaction of nicotine with psychotropic medications (Dursun & Kutchner, 1999). Several authors have noted that 70 to 80 percent of people with schizophrenia smoke cigarettes, which is an unusually high figure (McEvoy, Freudenreich, & Wilson, 1999). Some investigators have hypothesized that smoking is actually an attempt to self-medicate with nicotine, which binds to receptors in the brain and may actually reduce the negative symptoms of schizophrenia (Dalack, Healy, & Meador-Woodruff, 1998). Nicotine also may improve clients' processing of auditory information by reducing sensory overload (Lyon, 1999). According to these views, poorly timed (or capriciously imposed) reductions in cigarette smoking may lead to increases in clients' psychotic symptoms, although this effect has not yet been verified in controlled studies (Addington et al., 1998). On the other hand, however, smoking has been argued by some authors to accelerate the metabolism of psychotropic medications, thereby potentially *reducing* their effectiveness (Apud, Egan, & Wyatt, 2000; Lyon, 1999). These issues currently remain unresolved.

CASE EXAMPLE

Mr. Gutierrez

Referral: Mr. Gutierrez was a 20-year-old Hispanic student at a state university. As far as anyone could remember, Mr. Gutierrez seemed normal until he was 17 years old, when he became withdrawn and behaved a bit unusually. Mr. Gutierrez entered college at age 18, but failed to make any friends and was ostracized for his strange behavior. By the middle of the first semester, he had become provocative and bizarre, hanging a Nazi flag outside his dorm window and stalking two students whom he thought had thrown food at his flag. A few days later, Mr. Gutierrez became violent. After significantly damaging his dorm room, he was involuntarily admitted to a psychiatric hospital, where he remained for approximately three months. He received a diagnosis of schizophrenia, paranoid type. His positive symptoms largely responded to mellaril and he was discharged back to his family home, but he did not receive any

(continued)

CASE EXAMPLE   Continued

significant aftercare other than quarterly reviews by a local psychiatrist. During eight months with his family Mr. Gutierrez did not go to school or work, partly because his parents felt he should not be put under additional stress. When Mr. Gutierrez returned to college a year later, he suffered his second psychotic break within three weeks. After another admission to a psychiatric hospital, he was returned to his family home again.

Immediate concerns: Are there any immediate dangers to the client or other vulnerable persons?

Mr. Gutierrez has a history of potentially violent behavior, including a history of stalking others when paranoid. So far, he has no reported history of suicidal ideation and he appears to be no immediate threat to himself or to others, but the clinician should carefully review these risks at frequent intervals.

Short-term goals: What goals need to be achieved in the first two to six sessions?

Following his previous episode of schizophrenia, Mr. Gutierrez received little aftercare other than quarterly reviews by his psychiatrist. He and his family were not informed about the symptoms of schizophrenia, its prognosis, or the psychosocial interventions from which he might benefit. With his current therapist, Mr. Gutierrez agreed to several joint sessions with parents to learn more about schizophrenia and various psychosocial treatment options (e.g., the signs and symptoms of schizophrenia, his medications, the need to continue taking his antipsychotic medications per his psychiatrist's recommendations, and side effects to which the psychiatrist should be alerted). Mr. Gutierrez and his family were intelligent, well-educated, and supportive, and they requested additional printed information about schizophrenia, medications, and local support groups.

After three weekly sessions, Mr. Gutierrez expressed an interested in monitoring signs and symptoms of possible relapse. He worked with his therapist to develop a weekly checklist to use with his family, therapist, and psychiatrist. After session four, Mr. Gutierrez and his therapist identified another short-term goal, to find employment that did not involve the considerable stress he experienced at college. Mr. Gutierrez had previously identified several possible job options, but made no progress in obtaining one. After discussion with a counselor at the university, he was referred to ancillary services targeting career interest exploration and the development of job-seeking skills, such as looking for jobs in the paper, building a resume, completing job application forms, and interviewing.

Long-term goals: What lifestyle changes and other long-term personal, relationship, and career goals need to be achieved?

An important concern for both Mr. Gutierrez and his family is whether he can go back to school and, if not, what kind of occupation he might be able to have. Mr. Gutierrez also identifies an important goal as leaving home, getting married, and having children while maintaining positive relationships with his family of origin. Mr. Gutierrez's therapist will continue to meet with Mr. Gutierrez weekly to monitor progress toward these goals and monitor for any signs of relapse while continuing to reinforce Mr. Gutierrez's continued engagement with psychiatric services.

CASE EXERCISE

Mrs. Michelle is a 49-year-old married Asian American clerk in a large chemical plant. After twenty years of working at the plant, Mrs. Michelle began to believe that her management was deliberately exposing her to a new chemical, the name of which could not be released even to members of the factory for commercial reasons. Mrs. Michelle believed this chemical would poison her and that she could identify members of the conspiracy by a special kind of light in their eyes. She believed that this chemical was going to make her and other workers millionaires once it hit the market. One day she became frantic at work and was unable to sit, concentrate, or work. She became convinced that members of the Russian Economic Unit had ruined the company's plans to develop the new chemical by sabotaging its production. She called the police and pulled the safety whistle at the plant, causing evacuation and temporary shutdown of the plant.

Study Questions

1. What are the possible diagnoses in this case? Select the most appropriate diagnosis and provide a justification for your choice.

2. What ethnic or cultural factors may impact your work in this case? How might your treatment approach change if Mrs. Michelle were an African American or Anglo-American woman?

Mrs. Michelle was admitted to a state hospital and was stabilized with antipsychotic medication and lithium. Her delusions resolved within two weeks, although she still had significant residual symptoms. She was discharged to her family and referred to a community psychiatrist who saw her three days after discharge. According to her history, she had been admitted to a state hospital on two occasions for similar brief admissions when she was 23 and 30 years old. The psychiatrist has referred her to you for psychosocial rehabilitation.

Study Question

3. What assessment information would you collect to decide what form of intervention you should use? How would you collect the information?

Mrs. Michelle and her husband have participated in weekly sessions of education about schizophrenia, medication, relapse prevention, and expressed emotion. They are both happy with the information they have received. Mrs. Michelle returned to work two weeks ago. She has done well, but she and her husband missed their last appointment. One afternoon Mr. Michelle calls to tell you his wife has been acting strangely during the last two weeks and is getting worse. He thinks she may no longer be taking her medications and asks you to arrange her immediate readmission to the hospital for her safety.

(continued)

C A S E   E X E R C I S E   Continued

Study Question

4.   What action should you take at this point in time?

Mr. Michelle calls you again two hours later to inform you that Mrs. Michelle has taken the car and is heading for work. During the past hour she has become more psychotic and apparently plans to prevent new members of the Russian Economic Unit from taking over the plant. She took a kitchen knife with her.

Study Question

5.   What action should you take at this point in time?

Suppose you decided not phone anyone in order to protect Mrs. Michelle's confidentiality. Suppose then that Mrs. Michelle then drove to work and attacked and injured her supervisor.

Study Question

6.   If you were an expert witness at a trial in which you were asked to comment on this case, what would your testimony be? What would your defense be, as a clinician, if you were sued for malpractice?

R E F E R E N C E S

Addington, J., el-Guebaly, N., Campbell, W., Hodgins, D. C., & Addington, D. (1998). Smoking cassation treatment for patients with schizophrenia. *American Journal of Psychiatry, 155,* 974–976.

American Psychiatric Association. (2000). *Diagnostic and statistical manual of mental disorders* (4th ed., text revision) *(DSM-IV-TR).* Washington, DC: Author.

Apud, J. A., Egan, M. F., & Wyatt, R. J. (2000). Effects of smoking during antipsychotic withdrawal in patients with chronic schizophrenia. *Schizophrenia Research, 15,* 119–127.

Barrowclough, C., Haddock, C., Tarrier, N., Lewis, S. W., Moring, J., O'Brien, R., Schonfield, N., & McGovern, J. (2001). Randomized controlled trial of motivational interviewing, cognitive therapy and family intervention for patients with comorbid schizophrenia and substance use. *American Journal of Psychiatry, 158,* 1706–1713.

Bebbington, P., & Kuipers, L. (1995). The predictive utility of expressed emotion in schizophrenia: An aggregate analysis. *Psychological Medicine, 24,* 707–718.

Binder, R. L., & McNiel, D. E. (1991). Involuntary patient's rights to refuse medication: Impact of the Reise decision on a California inpatient unit. *Bulletin of the American Academy of Psychiatry and Law, 19,* 531–537.

Birchwood, M. (2000). Early intervention and sustaining the management of vulnerability. *Australia and New Zealand Journal of Psychiatry, 34* (suppl.) S, 181–184.

Birchwood, M., Cochrane, R., MacMillan, F., Copestake, S., Kucharska, J., & Carriss, M. (1992). The influence of ethnicity and family structure on relapse in first-episode schizophrenia. A comparison of Asian, Afro-Caribbean and white patients. *British Journal of Psychiatry, 161,* 783–790.

Birchwood, M., Fowler, D. R., & Jackson, C. (2000). *Early intervention in psychosis: A guide to concepts, evidence and interventions.* Chichester, UK: Wiley.

Birchwood, M., Smith, J., MacMillan, F., Hogg, B., Prasad, R., Harvey, C., & Bering, S. (1989). Predicting relapse in schizophrenia: The developmental and implementation of an early signs monitoring system using patients and families as observers, a preliminary investigation. *Psychological Medicine, 19,* 649–659.

Brown, J. S., & Tooke, S. K. (1992). On the seclusion of psychiatric patients. *Social Science and Medicine, 35,* 711–721.

Bruxner, G., Burvill, P., Fazio, S., & Febbo, S. (1997). Aspects of psychiatric admissions of migrant hospitals in Perth, Western Australia. *Australia and New Zealand Journal of Psychiatry, 31,* 532–542.

Busch, A. B., & Shore, M. F. (2000). Seclusion and restraint: A review of recent literature. *Harvard Review of Psychiatry, 8,* 261–270.

Butzlaff, R. L., & Hooley, J. M. (1998). Expressed emotion and psychiatric relapse: A meta-analysis. *Archives of General Psychiatry, 55,* 547–552.

Callan, A. F. (1996). Schizophrenia in Afro-Caribbean immigrants. *Journal of the Royal Society of Medicine, 89,* 253–256.

Cournos, F. (1989). Involuntary medication and the case of Joyce Brown. *Hospital and Community Psychiatry, 40,* 726–740.

Dalack, G. W., Healy, D. J., & Meador-Woodruff, J. H. (1998). Nicotine dependence in schizophrenia: Clinical phenomena and laboratory findings. *American Journal of Psychiatry, 155,* 1490–1501.

Daniel, D. G., & Copeland, L. F. (2000). Ziprasidone: Comprehensive overview and clinical use of a novel antipsychotic. *Expert Opinions in Investigative Drugs, 9,* 819–828.

Donat, D. C. (1998). Impact of mandatory behavioral consultation on seclusion/restraint utilization in a psychiatric hospital. *Journal of Behavior Therapy and Experimental Psychiatry, 29,* 13–19.

Drury, V., Birchwood, M., & Cochrane, R. (2000). Cognitive therapy and recovery from acute psychosis: A controlled trial. 3. Five-year follow-up. *British Journal of Psychiatry, 177,* 8–14.

Drury, V., Birchwood, M., Cochrane, R., & MacMillan, F. (1996a). Cognitive therapy and recovery from acute psychosis: A controlled trial. I. Impact on psychotic symptoms. *British Journal of Psychiatry, 169,* 593–601.

Drury, V., Birchwood, M. Cochrane, R., & MacMillan, F. (1996b). Cognitive therapy and recovery from acute psychosis: A controlled trial. II. Impact on recovery time. *British Journal of Psychiatry, 169,* 602–607.

Dursun, S. M., & Kutchner, S. (1999). Smoking, nicotine and psychiatric disorders: Evidence for therapeutic role, controversies and implications for future research. *Medical Hypotheses, 52,* 101–109.

Fernandez, G. A., & Nygard, S. (1990). Impact of involuntary outpatient commitment on the revolving door syndrome in North Carolina. *Hospital and Community Psychiatry, 41,* 1001–1004.

Fullerton, D. T., Cayner, J. J., & McLaughlin-Reidel, T. (1978). Results of a token economy. *Archives of General Psychiatry, 35,* 1451–1453.

Geddes, J., Freemantle, N., Harrison, P., & Bebbington, P. (2000). Atypical antipsychotics in the treatment of schizophrenia: Systematic overview and meta-regression analysis. *British Medical Journal, 321,* 1371–1376.

General Accounting Office. (1999). *Improper restraint or seclusion use places people at risk.* Washington, DC: General Accounting Office.

Ghaemi, S. N., Zielger, D. M., Peachey, T. J., & Goodwin, F. K. (1998). Cost-effectiveness of clozapine therapy for severe psychosis. *Psychiatric Services, 49,* 829–831.

Glynn, S. M. (1990). Token economy approaches for psychiatric patients. Progress and pitfalls over 25 years. *Behavior Modification, 14,* 383–407.

Grimby, A. (1993). Bereavement among elderly people: Grief reactions, post-bereavement hallucinations and quality of life. *Acta Psychiactrica Scandanavica, 87,* 72–80.

Hertz, M. I., Lamberti, J. S., Mintz, J., Scott, R., O'Dell, S. P., McCarten, L., & Nix, G. (2000). A program for relapse prevention in schizophrenia: A controlled study. *Archives of General Psychiatry, 57,* 277–283.

Heinssen, R. K., Lieberman, R. P., & Kopelowicz, A. (2000). Psychosocial skills training for schizophrenia: Lessons from the laboratory. *Schizophrenia Bulletin, 26,* 21–46.

Hickling, F. W., McKenzie, K. Mullen, R., & Murray, R. (1999). A Jamaican psychiatrist evaluates diagnoses at a London psychiatric hospital. *British Journal of Psychiatry, 175,* 283–285.

Isohanni, M., Nieminen, P., Moring, J., Pylkkanen, K., & Spalding, M. (1991). The dilemma of civil rights versus the right to treatment: Questionable involuntary admissions to a mental hospital. *Acta Psychiatrica Scandanavica, 83,* 256–261.

Jaworowski, S., & Zabow, A. (1995). Involuntary psychiatric hospitalization of minors. *Medicine and Law, 14,* 635-640.

Jorgensen, P. (1998). Early signs of psychotic relapse in schizophrenia. *British Journal of Psychiatry, 172,* 327–330.

Kuipers, E., Garety, P., Fowler, D., Dunn, G., Bebbington, P., Freeman, D., & Hadley, C. (1997). London-East Anglia randomized controlled trial of cognitive-behavioural therapy for psychosis. I: Effects of the treatment phase. *British Journal of Psychiatry, 171,* 319–327.

Kuipers, E., Fowler, D., Garety, P., Chisholm, D., Freeman, D., Bebbington, P., & Hadley, C. (1998). London-East Anglia randomized controlled trial of cognitive-behavioural therapy for psychosis. III: Follow-up and economic evaluation at 18 months. *British Journal of Psychiatry, 173,* 61–68.

Lamb, H. R. (1998). Deinstitutionalization at the beginning of the new millennium. *Harvard Review of Psychiatry, 6,* 1–10.

Lehrman, N. S., & Sharav, V. H. (1997). Ethical problems in psychiatric research. *Journal of Health Administration, 24,* 227–250.

Li, F., & Wang, M. (1994). A behavioural training programme for chronic schizophrenic patients. A three month randomized controlled trial in Beijing. *British Journal of Psychiatry (Suppl. August 24),* 32–37.

Lyon, E. R. (1999). A review of the effects of nicotine on schizophrenia and antipsychotic medications. *Psychiatric Services, 509,* 1346–1350.

Malla, A., Norman, R. M., & Helmes, E. (1987). Factors associated with involuntary admission to psychiatric facilities in Newfoundland. *Canadian Medical Association Journal, 136,* 1166–1171.

Mari, J. J., & Streiner, D. L. (1994). An overview of family interventions and relapse on schizophrenia: Meta-analysis of research findings. *Psychological Medicine, 24,* 565–578.

Marshall, M., Gray, A., Lockwood, A., & Green, R. (2000). Case management for people with severe mental disorders. *Cochrane Database Systematic Review,* CD000050.

Marshall, M., & Lockwood, A. (2000). Assertive community treatment for people with severe mental disorders. *Cochrane Database Systematic Reviews,* CD 001089.

Martin, B. A. (2000). The Clark Institute experience with completed suicide: 1996 to 1997. *Canadian Journal of Psychiatry, 45,* 630–638.

McEvoy, J. P., Freudenreich, O., & Wilson, W. H. (1999). Smoking and therapeutic response to clozapine in patients with schizophrenia. *Biological Psychiatry, 46,* 125–159.

McGovern, D., Hemmings, P., Cope, R., & Lowerson, A. (1994). Long-term follow-up of young Afro-Caribbean Britons and white Britons with a first admission diagnosis of schizophrenia. *Social Psychiatry and Psychiatric Epidemiology, 29,* 8–19.

Mueser, K. T., Bond, G. R., Drake, R. E., & Resink, S. G. (1998). Models of community care for persons with severe mental illness: a review of research on case management. *Schizophrenia Bulletin, 24,* 37–74.

Munk-Jorgensen, P. B., & Machon, R. A. (1991). Hospitalization patterns in schizophrenia. A 13-year follow-up. *Schizophrenia Research, 4,* 1–9.

Pekkala, E., & Merinder, L. (2000). Psychoeducation for schizophrenia (Cochrane Review). *Cochrane Database Systematic Review,* CD 002831.

Pharoah, F. M., Mari, J. J., & Streiner, D. (2000). Family intervention for schizophrenia. *Cochrane Database Systematic Review,* CD000088.

Phillips, S. D., Burns, B. J., Edgar, E. R., Mueser, K. T., Linkins, K. W., Rosenheck, R. A., Drake, R. E., & McDonel-Herr, E. C. (2001). Moving assertive community treatment into standard practice. *Psychiatric Services Special Issue, 52,* 771-779.

Phillips, P., & Nasr, S. J. (1983). Seclusion and restraint. *American Journal of Psychiatry, 140,* 229–232.

Reicher, A., Rossler, W., Loffler, W., & Fatenheuer, B. (1991). Factors influencing compulsory admission of psychiatric patients. *Psychological Medicine, 21,* 197–208.

Reinish, L. W., & Ciccone, J. R. (1995). Involuntary hospitalization and police referrals to a psychiatric emergency department. *Bulletin of the American Academy of Psychiatry and Law, 23,* 289–298.

Sanguineti, V. R., Samuel, S. E., Schwartz, S. L., & Robeson, M. R. (1996). Retrospective study of 2,200 involuntary psychiatric admissions. *American Journal of Psychiatry, 153,* 392–396.

Schachter, D., Kleinman, I., & Williams, J. I. (1999). Informed consent for antipsychotic medication. *Canadian Family Physician, 45,* 1502–1508.

Shore, D. (1996). Ethical Principles and informed consent: An NIMH perspective. *Psychopharmacology Bulletin, 32,* 7–10.

Slovenko, R. (2000). Update on legal issues associated with tardive dyskinesia. *Journal of Clinical Psychiatry, 51 (Suppl. 4),* 45–57.

Sultana, A., Reilly, J., & Fenton, M. (2000). Thioridazine for schizophrenia. *Cochrane Database Systematic Reviews,* CD001944.

Takei, N., Persaud, R. Woodruff, P., Brockington, I., & Murray, R. M. (1998). First episode of psychosis in Afro-Caribbean and white people. An 18-year follow-up population-based study. *British Journal of Psychiatry, 172,* 147-153.

Thompson, J. W., Belcher, J. R., DeForge, B. R., Myers, C. P., & Henderson, M. J. (1995). Trends in the inpatient care of persons with schizophrenia. *Schizophrenia Bulletin, 21,* 75–85.

Walker, E. F., Grimes, K. E., Davis, D. M., & Smith, A. J. (1993). Childhood precursors of schizophrenia: Facial expressions of emotion. *American Journal of Psychiatry, 150,* 1654–1660.

Walker, E. F., Savoie, T., & Davis, D. (1994). Neuromotor precursors of schizophrenia. *Schizophrenia Bulletin, 20,* 441–451.

Witkin, M. J., Atay, J., & Manderscheid, R. W. (1996). Trends in state and country mental hospitals in the U.S. from 1970 to 1992. *Psychiatric Services, 47,* 1079–1081.

Wolff, N., Helminiak, T. W., Morse, G. A., Calsyn, R. J., Klinkberg, W. D., & Trusty, M. L. (1997). Cost-effectiveness evaluation of three approaches to case management for homeless mentally ill clients. *American Journal of Psychiatry, 154,* 341–348.

Young, H. F., Bentall, R. P., Slade, P. D., & Dewey, M. E. (1987). The role of brief instructions and suggestibility in the elicitation of auditory and visual hallucinations in normal and psychiatric subjects. *Journal of Nervous and Mental Diseases, 175,* 41–48.

Zipursky, R. B. (1999). Ethical issues in schizophrenia research. *Current Psychiatric Reports, Oct 1,* 13–19.

CHAPTER

9 Delirium and Dementias

CHAPTER OVERVIEW

1. This chapter reviews three diagnoses that are commonly, but not exclusively, seen later in life. The first of these, Delirium, is characterized by changes in consciousness, memory, and cognition. Onset is relatively rapid; the course is fluctuating and relatively brief. Delirium is treated by identification and resolution of the general medical conditions that caused it.

2. Dementia refers to loss of memory functioning and other broad declines in cognitive functioning. The two most common forms of dementia are Alzheimer's disease and vascular dementia. Alzheimer's disease is characterized by an insidious onset and broad cognitive decline. Vascular dementia is characterized by focal neurological signs, a stair-step pattern of function loss, and partial recovery. Differential diagnosis of dementia versus normal aging, depression, and delirium are important assessment tasks.

3. Interventions for dementia eventually may include psychotropic medications to slow clients' cognitive declines. Some of these medications appear to have a modest effect on cognition and memory in the early stages of Alzheimer's disease. Psychosocial interventions include family support, psychoeducation, and environmental design.

4. Amnestic Disorders are disorders of memory. These can be associated with alcoholism, as in Korsakoff's syndrome, and other causes of brain damage.

5. Rehabilitation of memory function involves assessment of residual memory and compensatory strategies, such as memory aids and supports.

Delirium

Delirium is a disorder characterized by changes in consciousness and cognition that develop over a short period of time. A broad range of cognitive changes can occur in association with delirium, including attention problems, rambling, pressured or incoherent speech, disorientation, and language problems. Perceptual disturbances, such as illusions, hallucinations, and delusions, also may occur. The severity of a client's delirium symptoms may increase or decrease over the course of a day. Deliriums are typically due to a general medical condition, although they also may be substance-induced or occur for other, sometimes multiple, reasons. Approximately 10 percent of people over 65 years of age develop delirium when hospitalized for a general medical condition. (Readers should refer to DSM-IV for diagnostic criteria.)

Interventions for deliriums involve identifying and resolving the general medical condition causing the delirium, although it can sometimes be difficult to identify the medical cause of delirium. Even a relatively minor medical problem, such as athletes' foot, can sometimes produce an infection leading to delirium symptoms.

It is important for counselors and psychologists to be aware of delirium as a rule-out condition for clients presenting with possible dementias. This differentiation may be difficult, and a delirium can even occur in a person who already has a dementia. Clients presenting with possible dementias should receive a medical referral to rule out medical problems as the source of their symptoms.

Dementias

Diagnosis

Dementia of the Alzheimer's Type (DAT).   DAT is characterized by multiple cognitive deficits, including memory impairments and at least one other impairment. Memory impairments associated with DAT can manifest as difficulties either in recalling old material or in learning new material. Other DAT-related impairments include aphasia (language impairment), apraxia (impairments in carrying out motor tasks, despite unimpaired motor function), agnosia (impairment in recognizing objects, despite unimpaired sensory function), and disturbances in executive functioning (e.g., difficulties in planning, organizing, sequencing, or abstracting). To receive a diagnosis of DAT, a client's symptoms must cause significant problems in occupational or social functioning and must represent a decline in functioning. Other physical causes and psychiatric disorders, including delirium, should be ruled out (APA, 2000).

Vascular Dementia.   Vascular dementia is diagnosed when a client shows the cognitive, social, and occupation impairments and decline in functioning described above *and* presents evidence of focal neurological signed and symptoms. Focal neurological signs and symptoms include abnormal reflexes and laboratory tests showing evidence of cerebrovascular disease (APA, 2000). Focal neurological signs can include transient neurological symptoms, such as transient word-finding problems, transient aphasia, or transient apraxia.

Other Forms of Dementia.   The term *dementia* refers simply to any global loss of cognitive functioning. Dementias may occur in a wide variety of contexts, although Alzheimer's disease and cerebrovascular disease are by far the most common causes of dementia. Among other causes of dementia, DSM-IV lists the following: Dementia Due to HIV Disease, Dementia Due to Head Trauma, Dementia Due to Parkinson's Disease, Dementia Due to Huntington's Disease, Dementia Due to Pick's Disease, Dementia Due to Creuzfeldt-Jacob Disease, Dementia Due to Other General Medical Conditions, Substance-Induced Persisting Dementia, Dementia Due to Multiple Etiologies, and Dementia Not Otherwise Specified (NOS).

Dementia Due to HIV can be characterized by memory and concentration problems as well as behavioral manifestations, such as apathy and withdrawal, motor impairments (e.g., tremor), and so on. Children with HIV infection can also manifest dementia through developmental delay. Dementia due to head trauma may be seen after a single insult to the brain, such as a car wreck, or after repeated insults associated with recurrent injuries, as in boxing, martial arts, or possibly soccer-heading. It also may be associated with repeated periods of anoxia, such as when diving, or multiple incidents of unconsciousness that may occur in some sports or occupations.

A variety of progressive neurological disorders may be associated with dementia. Parkinson's disease, characterized initially by motor problems such as tremor, rigidity, and poor control over voluntary movements, is associated with dementia in its later stages, as is Huntington's chorea, a genetically caused disorder that typically does not express until middle age. Note that because children of clients with Huntington's chorea have a 50 percent chance of acquiring it themselves, family members should receive genetic counseling from a qualified physician when a client is diagnosed with the disease. (See DSM-IV for a more detailed description of these and other forms of dementia.)

Differential Diagnosis

Dementia versus Normal Aging. As people get older, their cognitive processes often decline. These declines may be observed under testing conditions in some people in their forties. Prior to the onset of Alzheimer's disease, a period of mild cognitive impairment may be observed (Shah, Tangalos, & Petersen, 2000). Making a differential diagnosis between this mild cognitive impairment and normal aging is difficult. Further, most cases of early dementias come to the attention of primary care professionals, such as family doctors, rather than specialists in geriatric psychiatry. Many primary care providers may not have specialist skills in the diagnosis of dementia and other psychiatric disorders in older adults.

Dementia versus Major Depressive Disorder. Major depressive disorder may present atypically in older adults. Mood symptoms may not predominate, or may be minor or altogether absent. In older adults, confusion, complaints of cognitive impairment, concentration, agitation, or irritability may instead predominate, all of which may impair their performance on simple cognitive tests.

Older adults with a major depressive disorder or other mood disorder, then, may easily be misdiagnosed as suffering from dementia. This misdiagnosis, sometimes referred to as *pseudodementia*, is unfortunately quite common. The differentiation of dementia and pseudodementia has serious treatment implications. For example, a client misdiagnosed as suffering from a dementia who actually suffers from major depressive disorder may suffer unnecessarily from what are relatively treatable symptoms.

Differential diagnosis between these illnesses may be made on the basis of both clinical and psychometric assessment. In principle, a differential diagnosis can be made clinically on three grounds. First, whereas mood disorders tend to fluctuate during the onset of the disorder, the course of dementia is insidious and gradual. Thus, if the client's symptoms are characterized by periods of relative impairment followed by periods of relative recovery, a diagnosis of mood disorder is more likely. Second, mood symptoms, unlike dementia, often fluctuate during the course of a day. If a client is more oriented in the afternoon than in the morning, then, for example, he or she may be suffering from a mood disorder rather than a dementia. Finally, a family history of mood disorder increases the likelihood the client may suffer from this illness and may add weight to a diagnostic decision in favor of a mood disorder rather than a dementia.

Dementia versus Delirium.   Although delirium and dementia both involve cognitive disturbances, they may be differentiated by their patterns of fluctuation, history, and cause. Whereas the onset of delirium is quick, within a day or two or even a few hours, the onset of dementia is slow and insidious. In addition, the course of delirium is variable during a relatively short span of time. A person with delirium might be quite impaired in the morning, improved in the afternoon, and again impaired by evening. As mentioned above, the course of dementia is, by contrast, relatively unvarying. Over the course of months and years, people with dementia experience progressive declines in their cognitive functioning. Memory disorders that persist for months are better classified as either dementias or amnestic disorders, rather than deliriums. Finally, whereas a general medical condition or substance-related disorder may directly lead to a delirium, this is not true for dementias. (Dementias caused by conditions such as HIV or Pick's disease are obvious exceptions.)

Alzheimer's versus Vascular Dementia.   Two clinical characteristics differentiate the course of Alzheimer's disease from vascular dementia. First, in Alzheimer's disease, the course is one of constant decline without any recoveries, whereas in vascular dementia the person may suffer a transient ischemic attack (TIA) leading to transient, and sometimes residual, impairment. Second, whereas people with vascular dementia often show focal neurological signs (e.g., aphasia, apraxia), the cognitive impairments of Alzheimer's disease tend to be more global. In addition to these clinical differentiations, medical tests sometimes may be used to detect physiological changes associated with TIAs (but not, yet, with Alzheimer's disease).

Depression Secondary to Dementia. The cognitive declines and memory losses associated with dementia are among many people's most dreaded fears. Unsurprisingly, many clients suffering dementia also experience depression, especially in the early stages of their illness, in which they retain awareness of their condition (Meyers, 1998). It is important, therefore, to look for mood disorder symptoms not only as a cause of clients' cognitive and memory losses (see pseudo-dementia discussion above), but as a secondary effect of the underlying changes associated with the onset of their illness. As discussed below, psychotherapy or antidepressant medications, especially those with limited cognitive side effects, may be helpful for some clients suffering from dementia.

Psychometric Assessment

The psychometric assessment of people with dementias is a fast-growing field of research and practice. Many instruments and procedures have been developed for a wide variety of purposes related to the assessment of dementias. This section highlights some of the commonly used procedures in this area.

Psychometric assessment of people with dementias may be performed for several purposes. First, assessment may provide information useful in diagnostic questions, such as whether a client is experiencing cognitive declines unusual for his or her age and, if so, whether those changes are due to Alzheimer's disease, vascular dementia, mood disorder, or some other cause. Second, information about the client's ability to function in tasks of daily living (e.g., ability to dress, feed, ambulate) and areas in which assistance or training is needed may be useful for treatment planning. Assessments of changes in clients' symptoms, such as cognitive declines during dementia or changes in response to medications, can also provide important "formative" treatment-planning information.

One instrument commonly used to assess clients' cognitive states is the Mini-Mental State Examination (MMSE; Folstein, Folstein, & McHugh, 1975). Requiring just over ten minutes to administer, the MMSE can be used at the client's bedside or in a private office (cf. Fillenbaum et al., 1987). Several important refinements have been offered to the original MMSE that have improved its reliability and application to more severely impaired populations (e.g., Harrell et al., 2000; Molloy & Standish, 1997). Despite these modifications, however, important linguistic/cultural biases and sensitivity issues should be addressed when it is selected as a primary assessment instrument (Clark et al., 1999; Hohl et al., 1999).

A second area that has received attention has been the development of assessments instruments to plan intervention (e.g., Brooker et al., 1993). A review by Sturmey concluded these instruments could be organized around four dimensions: (1) activities of daily living; (2) cognition; (3) extra-personal maladaptive behaviors, such as aggression; and (4) intrapersonal maladaptive behaviors, such as depression and withdrawal.

A final area that has received attention has been assessment to measure change. This has been especially important in the evaluation of change in response to drugs that might improve cognitive functioning. Demers et al. (2000b) reviewed a variety of scales used in drug trials for Alzheimer's disease, including scales to assess function (e.g., activities of daily living), quality of life (Demers et al., 2000a), behavior and mood (Perrault et al., 2000), and global scales of functioning (Oremus, Perrault, & Wolfson, 2000). Demers et al. identified three widespread problems in instruments used to assess each of these areas: poor assessment of reliability and validity, poor assessment of the sensitivity of the instruments to change over time, and the evaluation of many of them on only small samples.

Intervention

Medical Interventions.

Cognitive Enhancers. Some researchers have investigated the possibility of slowing the progress or remediating the cognitive deficits of Alzheimer's disease. Although an obviously intriguing possibility with enormous potential implications, however, few breakthroughs have occurred so far (Patterson et al., 1999).

Although vitamin B (thiamine) has been proposed as a putative agent, for instance, little evidence has supported its effectiveness (Rodriguez-Martin, Lopez-Arrieta, & Qizilbash, 2000). Considerably greater optimism surrounds the use of anticholinergic drugs, based in part on the observation that people with Alzheimer's disease lose cholinergic cells (Gottwald & Rozanski, 1999; Nordberg & Svenson, 1998). To date, three cholinesterase inhibitors—tacrine, donezepil, and rivastigamine—have been actively investigated, and others, including galantamine and metrifonate, are in development (Qizilbash et al., 2000; Raskind et al., 1999; Scott & Goa, 2000). Some reason for optimism does exist. For example, a review of seven trials of rivastigamine with over 3,300 participants found it appeared to slow cognitive deterioration among patients with mild to moderate impairment (Birks, Melzer, & Beppu, 2000). In addition, a recent review of eight double-blind trials of donezipil (Birks, Melzer, & Beppu, 2000) found modest improvements in patients' cognitive and mental states. Although more research is needed to validate these hopes, and although many clinically important questions (e.g., dosage levels and timing, side effects, restricted application among patients with more severe symptoms) have yet to be answered, the appearance of even possible solutions to the ravaging losses of Alzheimer's disease represents a tidal wave of optimism in an area of practice that previously has had little to offer.

Medical management of vascular dementia can be important in preventing progression of a broad range of underlying medical conditions causing dementia. Hypertension and diabetes are two common risk factors for vascular dementias. Others have considered smoking, peripheral arterial disease, and some cardiovascular disorders to be important manageable risk factors for vascular dementia (Skoog et al., 1999). Active medical management of these conditions by primary physicians or geriatricians can prevent progression of vascular dementias has included interventions such as aspirin. Although commonly used, Williams, Rands, Orrel, and Spectator (2000) found little evidence to support this practice.

A range of psychotropic mediations that have shown some promise are being developed as cognitive enhancers for vascular and mixed dementias (Kittner, Rossner, & Rother, 1997). As of the time of publication, these drugs were still under development and were not available for clinical use. Emre and Hanagasi (2000) concluded that, as of the late 1990s, the only psychotropic medications that are well supported by evidence are acetylcholinesterase inhibitors.

The Role of Antidepressants in Dementia.   As noted earlier, the differential diagnosis of dementia from pseudodementia is not always easy. Further, mood disorders are relatively common in seniors (Katona, 2000) and may occur secondarily to dementia, stroke, or Parkinson's disease, as well as other conditions related to dementias (Boland, 2000). Some evaluations of antidepressants, in fact, have included patients with dementias as well as patients with mood disorders (Karlson et al., 2000). Although concerns often have been expressed that older, tricyclic antidepressants are more likely to lead to negative side effects compared to SSRIs, not all drug trials have found this (Karlson et al.). Some clinicians have used a trial of antidepressants as a diagnostic aid and empirical therapy when the differential diagnosis of mood disorder or dementia is unclear.

Psychosocial Interventions.
Family Education and Respite.   Most people with dementias live at home and are often cared for by their daughters or mothers. Caregivers are often under tremendous psychological stress and social isolation as they struggle with the losses and, in some cases, behavioral problems of their loved ones. Caregivers also must deal with considerable physical demands, include lifting, bathing, feeding, and interrupted sleep, all of which may place their own health at risk.

In light of these risks, several interventions have been designed to address caregivers' needs and adjustments to the changes in their extended family lives. Empirical evidence suggests these interventions may be effective if well designed (cf. Thompson & Briggs, 2000). A three-year evaluation of an interdisciplinary psychosocial intervention for caregivers of people with dementia, for instance, including psychoeducation, family support, and skills training, found it reduced caregivers' subjective feelings of burden and negative reactions to their relatives' disruptive behaviors (Ostwald et al., 1999).

One important, if obvious, form of intervention for caregivers is respite. Respite can include in-home support or temporary admission of the family member to a specialized unit or nursing home that allows the caregiver to leave the home. Respite may be planned and used intermittently (e.g., as a brief vacation) or on an emergency basis, for example, when the caregiver is ill and temporarily cannot care for the family member (Grasel, 1997).

Interventions with Staff and Environmental Design.   Environmental design for people with dementia encompasses a wide range of variables, from macro/geographic factors (e.g., facility size, location, institutional features) to the design of plates and cups. Safety features including lighting, design of handrails, toilets, and kitchens have also been evaluated (Day, Carreon, & Stump, 2000). In addition, psychologists have focused on "molecular"-level variables, such as patterns of staff interaction and recreational materials.

Many people with dementias who live in congregate care spend hours inactively sitting with few recreational materials and little staff or peer interaction. Although some psychologists have suggested this "disengagement" is an adaptation to aging and imminent death, others argue it is a sign of learned helplessness or depression that may be blamed, in part, on unstimulating, institutional environments in which many seniors find themselves. Jenkins, Felce, Lint, and Powell (1977), for instance, successfully increased nursing home patients' levels of engagement by simply providing recreational materials and prompting and reinforcing their use. Similar results have been achieved by providing indoor gardening opportunities (Powell et al., 1979) or sensory activities for residents who were very impaired (e.g., Cash, Sturmey, & Bush, 1995). Redesigning the physical and social environments in which seniors live can increase their levels of activity, even among those with severe dementia.

Amnestic Disorders

Diagnosis

Amnestic disorders are disorders of memory due to the direct effects of a known physiological or general medical condition. DSM-IV subdivides Amnestic Disorders into those due to a General Medical Condition, Substance-Induced Persisting Amnestic Disorder, and Amnestic Disorder Not Otherwise Specified (NOS). All amnestic disorders are characterized by impairments in learning new information and in recalling previously learned information. In all cases, the symptoms must result in impaired social or occupational functioning and must represent a decline from previous levels of functioning.

Assessment

A wide range of psychometric instruments may be used to assess memory function. A simple comparison of a client's scores on the Wechsler intelligence tests (Wechsler, 1981) with scores on the Wechsler Memory Scales (Wechsler & Stone, 1974), for instance, can yield significant information about relative impairment in memory. The WMS provides a "Memory Quotient" (MQ) that is analogous to IQ scores. Large differences between this index and a client's IQ scores can indicate the presence or absence of a memory deficit.

Treatment

Korsakoff's Syndrome and Vitamin B.   Korsakoff's syndrome is a memory disorder seen in people with prolonged alcohol use. Korsakoff's memory losses appear to be due to vitamin B (thiamine) deficiency that results from a person's dependence on alcohol as a primary source of calories, obviating his or her opportunity to ingest vitamin B (among other vitamins and minerals). In addition, some evidence suggests that alcohol may interfere with the absorption of vitamin B at the cellular level. Characteristics of Korsakoff's syndrome include failure to retain new information and frequent confabulation that results from the person's attempts to explain information he or she doesn't remember. For example, a patient asked to identify a family member may reply that the person was a frequently visiting friend or physician. Although some authors suggest Korsakoff's syndrome may be treatable with vitamin B supplements, this treatment is underutilized (Cook & Thompson, 1997; see Lishman, 1990, for contrasting view).

Rehabilitation of Memory Disorders.   Clinical interventions based on analyses of the specific nature of clients' memory deficits have been evaluated. Prosthetic devices also have been used to remediate specific memory deficits, including cue cards and other prosthetic memory aids. Other approaches have included training family members and staffs to use strategies to enhance the use of residual memory functioning in clients with Alzheimer's. For example, caregivers can be trained to make memory cues salient to facilitate encoding, repeat information, or use spaced presentation of materials and present clear cues for recall.

One example of memory rehabilitation comes from a study (Van den Broek et al., 2000) that evaluated an electronic memory aide called a "voice organizer," which was designed as a prosthetic device to reduce prospective memory errors. Five clients with acquired memory problems participated. The clients were given tasks analogous to everyday memory tasks. The tasks were passing on a message after nine hours and recalling the household chores of the day. Van den Broek found significant improvements in their ability to recall messages after a nine-hour delay in all subjects and four of five participants significantly improved on measures of recalling domestic tasks.

CASE EXAMPLE
Mr. Tomlinson

Referral: Mr. Tomlinson, a 61-year-old Anglo-American man, was referred to psychological services for assessment for a differential diagnosis of dementia versus normal aging. Mr. Tomlinson was referred by his family physician after his wife complained that he was "losing his mind." After working for years as a laboratory technician in a photography company, Mr. Tomlinson recently took early retirement. He had previously

(continued)

C A S E   E X A M P L E   Continued

completed two years of college education and appeared to be in good physical health. He admitted to having some problems remembering things, but stated that everything else in his life was fine. He used a book to take notes and to write himself brief reminders throughout the day. During the initial interview, Mr. Tomlinson seemed bright and alert. He was somewhat distressed, but denied any major problems in his life or relationship with his wife. He ascribed most of his current situation to his wife "fussing too much."

Immediate concerns: Are there any immediate dangers to the client or other vulnerable persons?

There were no immediate concerns for Mr. Tomlinson's safety or the safety of others around him. Mr. Tomlinson's mood was normal. There was no hint of depression or suicide.

Short-term goals: What goals need to be achieved in the first two to six sessions?

The most important short-term goal with Mr. Tomlinson was to complete a psychometric assessment for possible dementia. Because he did not present with any symptoms of depression, there was no need to rule out this possibility with formal psychometric testing.

Mr. Tomlinson was administered a measure of intelligence and memory function.

His full-scale IQ was 94; his verbal IQ was 99; and his performance IQ was 89. His memory quotient was 73, a significant impairment in memory function for his IQ (a difference of 21 points). Mr. Tomlinson's IQ was somewhat below what might be expected for someone with two years of college education, results that were consonant with some decline in function. In addition, his higher verbal IQ score suggested possible preservation of verbal skills and knowledge (as opposed to apparent loss of performance IQ functions).

Evidence revealed in an interview suggested that Mr. Tomlinson had experienced a recent decline in function. Mrs. Tomlinson stated she felt he had been "different from his former self" for the previous eighteen months and that he began using the notebook when she discussed his memory issues with him about nine months ago. Mr. Tomlinson exhibited no evidence of focal neurological signs and no evidence of a pattern of loss of function and partial recovery. He also exhibited no evidence of mood or attentional losses. After a telephone conversation with Mr. Tomlinson's family physician (after informed consent) revealed he had no medical issues, a diagnosis of Alzheimer's disease was made.

Psychometric testing gave rise to two additional goals. The first of these, disclosure of the diagnosis to Mr. Tomlinson, led to the second goal, support of Mr. Tomlinson and his family members, especially his wife, through the initial stages of adjustment to the diagnosis.

Disclosure of the diagnosis was done privately and directly. Mr. Tomlinson asked for his wife to accompany him to the appointment. After the initial diagnosis, both were given some time together. They initially greeted the news with mild disbelief and asked if something medical had not been investigated. A follow-up appointment was made for both Mr. and Mrs. Tomlinson to see the clinician one week later, at which additional information about Alzheimer's disease was given to them orally and in the form of a brief, written brochure. Information on the local Alzheimer's society was also given. A further appointment one month later was also offered, although Mrs.

CASE EXAMPLE   Continued

Tomlinson called prior to that appointment to cancel it, stating that they both were doing significantly better at that time. They were offered the opportunity to contact the clinician any time they wished to facilitate additional help or support, and a follow-up phone conversation was scheduled two months in the future.

Long-term goals: What lifestyle changes and other long-term personal, relational, and career goals need to be achieved?

No long-term goals were formulated at present, since Mr. Tomlinson and his family felt they did not need help on an ongoing basis at this time. However, the clinician will maintain contact with Mr. and Mrs. Tomlinson (with their consent) and any reinitiation of services would lead to additional treatment goals, including provision of supportive services, continued retirement and financial planning, residential and care planning for the long-term future, and caregiver support opportunities for Mr. Tomlinson's family members.

CASE EXERCISE

Mrs. Lee is an 85-year-old Chinese American woman who has lived in a nursing home for the past three months. Prior to entering the home, Mrs. Lee's daughter, age 63, had looked after her. Mrs. Lee had an extensive family in her state of residence, but most family members lived over an hour's drive away. She had been placed in the nursing home when her daughter could no longer look after her. Over time, the physical demands of caring for Mrs. Lee had become significantly greater and her daughter was no longer able to meet her needs, especially when Mrs. Lee was no longer able to walk around her apartment.

Mrs. Lee was referred to you by the nursing home social worker, because she has become confused and agitated over the last two weeks. She is losing weight and now eats very slowly, if at all. Often, she does not eat her meals, even with assistance. The nursing home care staff and Mrs. Lee's daughter are very concerned about her recent deterioration and want to know if Mrs. Lee has become depressed.

Study Questions

1. What are the possible alternate diagnoses in this case? What information would allow you to rule out these diagnoses?

2. Describe how you will conduct an assessment with Mrs. Lee and with what possible instruments (or referrals). How would you obtain relevant cultural information about the background of Mrs. Lee and her family and how might it affect your work with her?

3. Assume that Mrs. Lee has a diagnosis of pseudodementia. Should you work with her yourself? If so, what treatment plan might you develop with her?

4. Assume that Mrs. Lee and her daughter arrived in the United States from China two years ago. How might this alter your formulation of her case? What if, instead, she was born and raised in the United States?

(continued)

C A S E   E X E R C I S E   **Continued**

5. Mrs. Lee's daughter phones you at your office and asks to see her mother's psychological records. She states that she has seen the family lawyer and that she is now her mother's legal guardian. What ethical and legal issues does this raise? What actions should you take, and why?

6. Mrs. Lee's family physician prescribed a tricyclic antidepressant for her, but after a few weeks she notifies you that she has secretly refused to take it, saying that she does not want to take mind-altering drugs. What professional issues are raised by this disclosure? What actions should you take?

REFERENCES

American Psychiatric Association. (2000). *Diagnostic and statistical manual of mental disorders* (4th ed., text revision) (DSM-IV-TR). Washington, DC: Author.

Birks, J., Grimley-Evans, J., Iakovidou, V., & Tsolaki, M. (2000). Rivastigamine for Alzheimer's disease. *Cochrane Database Systematic Reviews*, CD001191.

Birks, J., Melzer, D., & Beppu, H. (2000). Donezepil for mild and moderate Alzheimer's disease (Cochrane review). *Cochrane Database Systematic Reviews*, CD001190.

Boland, R. J. (2000). Depression in Alzheimer's disease and other dementias. *Current Psychiatric Reports, 2*, 427–433.

Brooker, D. J., Sturmey, P., Gatherer, A. J., & Summerbell, C. (1993). The Behavioural Assessment Scale of Later Life (BASOLL): A description, factor analysis, scale development, validity and reliability data for a new scale for older adults. *International Journal of Geriatric Psychiatry, 8*, 747–754.

Cash, J., Sturmey, P., & Bush, D. (1995). The effects of room management and small-group procedures on the behavior of older adults who have Alzheimer's disease. *Behavioral Interventions, 10*, 181–195.

Clark, C. M., Sheppard, L., Fillenbaum, G. G., Galasko, D., Morris, J. C., Koss, E., Mohrs, R., & Heyman, A. (1999). Variability in annual mini-mental state examination score in patients with probably Alzheimer disease: A clinical perspective of data from the consortium to establish a register for Alzheimer's Disease. *Archives of Neurology, 56*, 857–862.

Cook, C. C., & Thompson, A. D. (1997). B-complex vitamins in the prophylaxis and treatment of Wernicke-Korsakoff syndrome. *British Journal of Hospital Medicine, 57*, 461–465.

Day, K., Carreon, D., & Stump, C. (2000). The therapeutic design of environments for people with dementia: A review of the research. *Gerontologist, 40*, 397–416.

Demers, L., Oremus, M., Perrault, A., Champoux, N., & Wolfson, C. (2000a). Review of outcome measurement instruments in Alzheimer's disease trials: Psychometric properties of functional and quality of life scales. *Journal of Geriatric Psychiatry and Neurology, 13*, 170–180.

Demers, L., Oremus, M., Perrault, A., & Wolfson, C. (2000b). Review of outcome measurement instruments in Alzheimer's disease trials: Introduction. *Journal of Geriatric Psychiatry and Neurology, 13*, 161–169.

Emre, M., & Hanagasi, H. A. (2000). Evidence-based pharmacological treatment of dementia. *European Journal of Neuropsychology, 7*, 247–253.

Fillenbaum, G. G., Heyman, A., Wilkinson, W. E., & Haynes, C. S. (1987). Comparison of two screening tests in Alzheimer's disease. The correlation and reliability of the mini-mental state examination and the modified Blessed test. *Archives of Neurology, 44*, 924–927.

Folstein, M .F., Folstein, S. E., & McHugh, P. R. (1975). "Mini-Mental State." A practical method for grading the cognitive state of patients for the clinician. *Journal of Psychiatric Research, 12*, 189–198.

Gottwald, M. D., & Rozanski, R. I. (1999). Rivastigamine, a brain-region selective acetyl-cholinesterase inhibitor for treating Alzheimer's disease: Review and current status. *Expert Opinion Investigative Drugs, 10*, 1673–1682.

Grasel, E. (1997). Temporary institutional respite in dementia cases: Who utilizes this form of respite care and what effect does it have? *International Psychogeriatrics, 9*, 437–448.

Harrell, L. E., Marson, D., Chatterjee, A., & Parrish, J. A. (2000). The severe mini-mental state examination: A new neuropsychologic instrument for the bedside assessment of severely impaired patients with Alzheimer disease. *Alzheimer Disease & Associated Disorders, 14*, 168–175.

Hohl, U., Grundman, M., Salmon, D. P., Thomas, G. P., & Thal, L. J. (1999). Mini-mental state examination and Mattis dementia rating scale performance differs in Hispanic and non-Hispanic Alzheimer's disease patients. *Journal of International Neuropsychology Society, 5*, 301–307.

Jenkins, J., Felce, D., Lint, B., & Powell, L. (1977). Increasing engagement in activity of residents in old people's homes by providing recreational materials. *Behaviour Research and Therapy, 15*, 429–439.

Karlson, I., Godderis, J., De Mendonca Lima, C. A., Nygaard, H., Simanyi, M., Taal, M., & Eglin, M. (2000). A randomised, double-blind comparison of the efficacy and safety of citalopram compared to mianserin in elderly, depressed patients with or without mild to moderate dementia. *International Journal of Geriatric Psychiatry, 15*, 295–305.

Katona, C. (2000). Managing depression and anxiety in the elderly patient. *European Journal of Neuropsychopharmacology, 10*, S427–S432.

Kittner, B., Rossner, M., & Rother, M. (1997). Clinical trials in dementia with propentofylline. *Annals of the New York Academy of Science, 826*, 307–316.

Lishman, W. A. (1990). Alcohol and the brain. *British Journal of Psychiatry, 156*, 635–644.

Meyers, B. S. (1998). Depression and dementia: Comorbidities, identification and treatment. *Journal of Geriatric Psychiatry, 11*, 201–205.

Molloy, D. W., & Standish, T. I. (1997). A guide to the standardized mini-mental state examination. *International Psychogeriatrics, 9*, S199–S194.

Nordberg, A., & Svensson, A. L. (1998). Cholinesterase inhibitors in the treatment of Alzheimer's disease: A comparison of tolerability and pharmacology. *Drug Safety, 19*, 465–480.

Oremus, M., Perrault, L., & Wolfson, C. (2000). Review of outcomes measurement instruments in Alzheimer's disease drug trials: Psychometric properties of global scales. *Journal of Geriatric Psychiatry and Neurology, 13*, 197–205.

Ostwald, S. J., Hepburn, K. W., Caron, W., Burns, T., & Mantell, R. (1999). Reducing caregiver burden: A randomized psychoeducational intervention for caregivers of persons with dementia. *Gerontologist, 39*, 299–309.

Patterson, C. J., Gauthier, S., Bergman, H., Cohen, C. A., Feightner, J. W., Fledman, H., & Hogan, D. B. (1999). The recognition, assessment and management of dementing disorders: Conclusions from the Canadian Consensus Conference on Dementia. *Canadian Medical Association Journal, 160*, S1–S15.

Perrault, L., Oremus, M., Demers, L., Vida, S., & Wolfson, C. (2000). Review of outcomes measurement instruments in Alzheimer's disease drug trials: Psychometric properties of behavior and mood scales. *Journal of Geriatric Psychiatry and Neurology, 13*, 181–196.

Powell, L., Felce, D., Jenkins, J., & Lunt, B. (1979). Increasing engagement in a home for the elderly by providing an indoor gardening activity. *Behaviour Research and Therapy, 17*, 127–135.

Qizilbash, N., Birks, J., Lopez-Arrieta, J., Lewington, S., & Szeto, S. (2000). Tacrine for Alzheimer's disease. *Cochrane Database Systematic Reviews*, CD000202.

Raskind, M. A., Cyrus, P. A., Ruzicka, B. B., & Gulanski, B. I. (1999). The effects of metrifonate on the cognitive, behavioral, and functional performance of Alzheimer's disease patients. Metifonate Study Group. *Journal of Clinical Psychiatry, 60*, 318–325.

Rodriguez-Martin, J. L., Lopez-Arrieta, J. M., & Qizilbash, N. (2000). Thiamine for Alzheimer's disease. *Cochrane Database Systematic Reviews*, CD001498.

Scott, L. J., & Goa, K. L. (2000). Galantamine: A review of its use in Alzheimer's disease. *Drugs, 60*, 1095–1122.

Shah, S., Tangalos, E. G., & Petersen, R. C. (2000). Mild cognitive impairment. When is it a precursor to Alzheimer's disease? *Geriatrics, 62*, 65–68.

Skoog, I, Kalaria, R. N., & Breteler, M. M. (1999). Vascular factors in Alzheimer disease. *Alzheimer Disease Association Discord, 13*, S106–114.

Thompson, C., & Briggs, M. (2000). Support for carers of people with Alzheimer's type dementia. *Cochrane Database Systematic Reviews*, CD000454.

Van den Broek, M. D., Downes, J., Johnson, Z., Dayus, B., & Hilton, N. (2000). Evaluation of an electronic memory aid in the neuropsychiatric rehabilitation of prospective memory deficits. *Brain Injury, 14*, 455–462.

Wechsler, D. (1981). *Wechsler Adult Intelligence Scale-Revised*. New York: Psychological Corp.

Wechsler, D., & Stone, C. P. (1974). *Wechsler Memory Scale*. New York: Psychological Corp.

Williams, P. S., Rands, G., Orrel, M., & Spectator, A. (2000). Aspirin for vascular dementia (Cochrane review). *Cochrane Database Systematic Review*, CD001296.

CHAPTER

10 Post-Traumatic and Acute Stress Disorders

CHAPTER OVERVIEW

1. Post-Traumatic Stress Disorder (PTSD) and Acute Stress Disorder (ASD) are disorders in response to external stressors. PTSD is characterized by lasting over one month and more severe psychopathology, whereas ASD lasts less than one month.

2. PTSD is characterized by recurrent and intrusive, distressing recollections, numbed responsiveness to stimuli related to the traumatic event, and dissociative symptoms. ASD is characterized by at least three dissociative symptoms.

3. Assessment can be conducted by clinical interviews and psychometric assessments. Clinicians should be aware of the possibility of secondary gains from PTSD and ASD and concomitant inaccurate self-reports.

4. Although there is an extensive outcome literature on psychological debriefing, there is evidence that it may actually be harmful. Interventions using flooding, other exposure-type behavioral treatments, and antidepressants may also be effective.

5. Ethical dilemmas raised by PTSD and ASD include selection and identification of effective treatments.

Diagnosis

Post-Traumatic Stress Disorder (PTSD) and Acute Stress Disorder (ASD) are considered together in this section because they share many common features and because it is important to differentiate between both of these diagnoses and a normal reaction to a stressful event when formulating a case. PTSD and ASD can arise in reaction to a wide range of life-threatening or other traumatic situations, including direct or vicarious experiences with war, torture, life-threatening accidents, burns, physical assault, rape, or sexual victimization. To be diagnosed with PTSD or ASD, a person must respond to these events with fear, horror, helplessness (or disorganized behavior in children), and clinically significant impairment, a criterion not included in previous editions of the DSM. (Comparisons of DSM-III-R and DSM-IV prevalence data may be affected by the inclusion of this more stringent criterion. See Wang et al., 2000.)

PTSD and ASD are differentiated by the severity and duration of the person's symptoms. First, PTSD is characterized by recurrent, intrusive, distressing

215

recollections that may take the form of dreams, illusions, hallucinations, flash-backs, or intense distress in response to external cues. Second, PTSD clients exhibit a numbed responsiveness to, or direct avoidance of, thoughts, people, and places related to the traumatic event. PTSD clients also may exhibit an inability to recall details, loss of interest and detachment from others, restrictive range of affect, and a foreshortened view of the future. Two of the following symptoms also are evident: sleep disturbance, irritability or anger, poor concentration, hypervigilence, and excessive startle response. These symptoms must endure for at least one month and may not necessarily onset at the time of the trauma (e.g., they may begin on an anniversary date or coincidentally with some other event).

In ASD, at least three *dissociative* (not merely anxiety-related) symptoms must be present, such as numbing, reduced awareness of surroundings, depersonalization, derealization, and dissociative amnesia. As in PTSD, the person must also reexperience the traumatic event in some form (e.g., flashbacks, dreams, hallucinations) and must exhibit some form of avoidance or increased anxiety and arousal. ASD can last from two days to four weeks. Drugs, medical causes, psychosis, and other psychological disorders, including Brief Psychotic Disorder, must be ruled out as alternate explanations for these symptoms.

Clients commonly experience PTSD or ASD after near-death experiences, such as wars, automobile wrecks, natural disasters (e.g., floods, earthquakes), traumatic imprisonment, kidnapping, rape, or torture. It is important that the client's symptoms be in response to events of this magnitude, and not merely a situation that is intensely embarrassing, humiliating, or anxiety provoking. PTSD may endure for more than forty years for some people (Schreuder, Kleijn, & Rooijmans, 2000) and is often associated with other psychiatric disorders, such as anxiety disorders, mood disorders, and substance abuse. Unsurprisingly, it is often observed among war veterans, refugees, law enforcement officers, and health care workers.

Assessment

A wide range of psychometric instruments are available for assessing PTSD and ASD symptoms. Some of these are listed in Table 10.1. Some studies suggest that psychometric instruments, such as the Clinician-Administered PTSD Scale, have similar psychometric properties to structured clinical interviews but are much quicker to administer (Foa & Tolin, 2000). A variety of scales derived from the MMPI (e.g., Mann, 1995) and the Symptom Checklist-90 (Rosen et al., 2000), as well as several scales developed specifically for ASD (Bryant et al., 2000), may be helpful during initial diagnostic screening.

The use of assessment interviews to determine treatment goals and strategies has received less attention than diagnostic assessment. Diagnostic interviews based on DSM criteria, however, appear effective for diagnosing PTSD, including the ability to distinguish veterans with and without PTSD. Bremner, Stein-

TABLE 10.1   Examples of psychometric Instruments Used to assess PTSD.

Measure	Brief description
The Clinician-Administered PTSD Scale (CAPS)	An extensively researched measure of adult PTSD (Weathers, Keane, & Davidson, 2001)
Screen for Posttraumatic Stress Symptoms	A brief self-administered screen for PTSD (Carlson, 2001)
Child PTSD Symptom Scale	A measure for children (Foa et al., 2001)

berg, Southwirck, Johnson, and Charney (1993) found that the symptoms that may best distinguish PTSD from non-PTSD in some clients (e.g., veterans) are amnesia and, to a lesser extent, depersonalization, derealization, identity confusion, and identity alteration. (Recall from above that general anxiety symptoms, even intense ones, are not specifically associated with PTSD and may reflect a wide range of other disorders.)

During assessment, clinicians should be aware that many clients intentionally report inaccurate information. Several studies have found that putative PTSD clients tend to fake by reporting high levels of diffuse psychopathology (Frueh, Hamner, Cahill, Gold, & Hamlin, 2000). In some cases the potential secondary gains from a PTSD diagnosis may be an important consideration. These can include both material benefits, such as worker's compensation or lawsuit awards, and psychological gains associated with the acquisition of special status as a trauma survivor.

Treatment Plan

Prevention

An increasing number of psychologists and counselors have become interested in preventing PTSD following natural and man-made disasters. Several studies have identified predisposing factors that could be targeted for preventive intervention. It appears, for example, that childhood burn victims who receive higher doses of morphine for pain management are less likely to experience PTSD symptoms later (Saxe et al., 2001), and periods of unemployment following an assault victimization are correlated with symptoms of PTSD and impairment in activities of daily living (Feehan et al., 2001). Other studies have found that such early onset symptoms of PTSD as sleep disturbance, fear and anxiety, and physical symptoms are highly predictive of subsequent PTSD diagnoses (Weisaeth,

2001). Thus, it may be relatively easy to identify those clients who are susceptible to later PTSD diagnoses and to intervene early, and arguably more effectively, with them immediately following their trauma.

On the basis of this kind of research, various types of counseling and post-traumatic debriefing procedures have been developed for both individuals and groups. These procedures have been widely adopted in the armed forces and as part of operational procedures for fire departments, ambulance staff, and medical staff, who may commonly be exposed to trauma during their work. Unfortunately, however, there is little evidence to suggest that psychological debriefing is effective; in fact some evidence suggests that it is harmful. In a randomized control trial of psychological debriefing for adult burn victims, for example, Bisson, Jenkins, Alexander, and Bannister (1997) found that psychological debriefing led to *higher* rates of PTSD. A treatment evaluation of auto accident victims by Mayou, Ehlers, and Hobbs (2000) found similar results. In a meta-analysis of eleven randomized control trials, Suzanna, Jonathan, and Simon (2001) concluded that clients participating in psychological debriefing were no better off three to five months later than clients who received no intervention, and at one-year follow-up suffered *higher* rates of PTSD. Future research in this area should attend to identifying new and different forms of intervention that may be more effective than current practices.

These studies raise an interesting provocation. The assumption that psychological and counseling treatments are necessarily effective or benign is not always confirmed by controlled research data. Indeed, unfolding (but preliminary) evidence suggests current psychological debriefing practices may actually harm clients. Despite this, psychological debriefing remains palatable to many therapists and is viewed by many as a sensitive approach to the victims of trauma.

Treatment

Psychological treatments based on counseling and support are not likely to be effective on their own. There is good evidence that intervention based on exposure therapies and pharmacology may be necessary adjuncts to treatment. Indeed, clinical trials directly comparing counseling and support versus exposure therapy strongly favor the latter.

Behavior Therapy.   Exposure therapy for PTSD is based on a respondent extinction model of therapy, one of the few areas in which respondent conditioning has proven to be more effective than operant conditioning (see Figure 10.1). The respondent conditioning model assumes that PTSD symptoms have been established by respondent (or classical) conditioning in which neutral, unconditioned stimuli, such as the sights, sounds, and smells of a physical location, are paired with an unconditioned response, such as terror in response to a near-death experience. If sufficient numbers of pairings occur, or if a single pairing is extremely traumatic, classical conditioning of PTSD symptoms takes place.

FIGURE 10.1   A classical conditioning model for Post-Traumatic Stress Disorder and its treatment by classical extinction.

Step 1: Prior to classical conditioning

Unconditioned Stimulus   →   Unconditioned Response

Near death experience   →   *Extreme terror and physiological arousal*

Step 2: Pairings

Multiple pairings of US with CS or single very traumatic pairing of US with very powerful UR

Step 3: After conditioning

Conditioned Stimulus   →   Conditioned Response

Landscape where trauma occurred   →   *Extreme terror and physiological arousal*

Step 4: Treatment by classical extinction

Conditioned Stimulus repeatedly presented   →   No terror or physiological arousal

Prolonged exposure to fearful stimuli   →   *No terror or physiological arousal*

The second component of a learning model of PTSD involves operant conditioning. Because the person's avoidance of fear-eliciting stimuli is negatively reinforcing (i.e., the avoidance behaviors lead to reductions in anxiety), PTSD symptoms like amnesia, emotional numbing, and avoiding the physical location of the trauma become long-standing and intractable. Generalization of these responses occurs when stimuli similar to the unconditioned stimuli, which vary along some dimension from them, also elicit PTSD responses. Over time, then, locations similar to those where a traumatic event occurred come to elicit similar emotional responses. Such generalization also occurs along other dimensions, such as axes of distance from locations where the trauma took place.

If the classical conditioning model is correct, then, the appropriate learning procedure is classical extinction. Classical extinction means presenting the conditioned stimulus repeatedly many times, or for prolonged periods of time, until it no longer elicits the conditioned responses of physiological arousal, horror, and fear.

In practice, classical treatment means prolonged exposure to the things that the PTSD client fears the most. This can be a distressful experience, but it also can be a powerful and effective treatment. For example, a person with PTSD symptoms related to the death of a loved one might be assigned to visit the person's graveside (which he or she previously may have been unable to visit) to say his or her final goodbyes. This procedure may be repeated (or gradually introduced) until the client no longer experiences any physiological arousal when thinking of, or actually visiting, the loved person's grave. Similarly, a person with recurrent traumatic nightmares might be asked to vividly imagine, verbally describe, or draw these nightmares several times, a procedure that would be repeated until he or she can describe them with no traumatic emotion. In some cases, the endings of the nightmare scenarios might be rewritten from traumatic endings to benign or successful endings in which the client triumphs over adversity (Marks, 1988).

An assessment of PTSD clients treated under these models found that whereas 56 percent of clients who received only supportive counseling met diagnostic criteria for PTSD six months later, only 14 percent of clients who received prolonged exposure and 20 percent of clients who received exposure plus anxiety management did so (Bryant et al., 1999). Participants in supportive counseling conditions also showed greater avoidance of traumatic situations than did participants in the exposure groups, suggesting that supportive counseling alone may be ineffective for these symptoms. Similar assessments of the effectiveness of imagery rehearsal for PTSD clients who had experienced rape or other sexual assault found that exposure therapy clients reported less severe nightmares, improved sleep, and fewer PTSD symptoms compared to waiting list controls (Krakow et al., 2001).

EMDR.   A treatment similar in many ways to classical therapies is Eye Movement Desensitization and Reprocessing (EMDR; Shapiro, 1989, 2001). Developed in the early 1990s to address trauma symptoms, EMDR couples cognitive rehearsal and other cognitive behavioral strategies with physiological stimulation such as eye movement or hand taps (Shapiro, 2001, 2002). Recent evaluations have suggested EMDR may be effective for PTSD symptoms and may apply equally well to anxiety disorder clients (De Jongh, Ten Broeke, & Renssen, 1999; Goldstein & Feske, 1994), although this conclusion has been contested by some.

Psychotropic Medication.   A number of well-controlled drug trials have supported the effectiveness of tricyclic antidepressants for PTSD (Frank et al., 1988; Reist et al., 1989). However, many, but not all, of these studies reported only the drugs' effects on clients' mood symptoms, not on their core PTSD symptoms. Nevertheless, several recent evaluations of sertraline have found positive results for PTSD symptoms (Davidson et al., 2001), although it should be noted that this medication frequently produces negative side effects such as insomnia and diarrhea. Trials of fluoxetine, although ongoing, initially have reported mixed results (Connor et al., 1999; Hertzberg et al., 2000). PTSD clients who see family physicians or psychiatrists are likely to receive psychotropic medications, both for core PTSD symptoms and for co-morbid mood, anxiety, and sleep disorders. Preliminary evidence suggests some SSRIs may be effective with both core symptoms of PTSD and associated mood and anxiety symptoms (Lydiard, Brawman-Mintzer, & Ballenger, 1996).

Ethical and Professional Issues

Clinicians may encounter a host of ethical and professional issues when working with clients with PTSD or ASD. Some of these are illustrated in the case presentation and case exercises below. The following section discusses one key ethical question related to treatment PTSD: the selection of effective treatments. Although a review of APA and ACA ethical principles (see Chapter 2) reveals that many address this issue, APA Principle E, Concern for Other's Welfare, is most relevant. This principle states that therapists contribute to their clients' welfare and do not exploit or mislead others. The prototypical application of Principle E is determining the appropriate actions to take when a client fails to benefit from therapy.

The previous section of this chapter outlined the possibility that psychological debriefing is not merely ineffective for PTSD clients, but may actually harm them. If this possibility gains additional support over the next several years, the question is raised whether therapists should refrain from conducting any psychological debriefing at all. A narrower course of action might be to refrain from using just the forms of psychological debriefing used in the trials in which they proved ineffective, an action that arguably invites the possibility that unevaluated debriefing methods might also harm clients.

One alternative is for therapists to rigorously monitor the effectiveness of their interventions to demonstrate to themselves and others that their therapy did no harm. Few therapists, however, systematically track their clients' responses to treatment other than through global impressions of their progress. It would be relatively easy to include Likert ratings of clients' global progress or to ask clients to complete a brief symptom checklist each month, actions that might ensure that at least one's *current* clients are benefiting from ongoing treatment. Failing this, a therapist may at least monitor clients' progress and terminate ineffective interventions with clients whom they suspect are not progressing. By contrast, assessing clients' responses to treatment would be difficult when using psychological debriefing with large audiences of possible victims. How could a therapist ensure that harm was not done to someone in a large group that received psychological debriefing?

Another principle that may be relevant to this situation is APA Ethical Principle B, Integrity, which requires honesty, fairness, and respect. Given the research results discussed above, should therapists tell clients of the potential harm of psychological debriefing prior to treatment so clients may make an informed choice about the potential risks and benefits of therapy? Would it be acceptable for therapists who become aware of this information (including the reader) to knowingly withhold it? (See Figure 10.2 on page 222 for more consideration of these questions.)

FIGURE 10.2   Malpractice and debriefing: Some questions.

Could a therapist be sued for malpractice if his or her psychological debriefing harmed a client? Recall the four elements of malpractice: a professional relationship, a demonstrable standard of care, harm or injury to the client, and breach of duty that legally and proximately causes injury to a client (Bennett et al., 1990). The first and third elements might be incontrovertible; clients could readily demonstrate they paid their therapist's bills and saw them on a regular basis. They also could easily prove harm, for example, by demonstrating they have been unable to work or have suffered psychological suffering. But what is the demonstrable standard of care in the psychological debriefing situation? Could a therapist argue that psychological debriefing was the demonstrable standard of care? If it was the demonstrable standard of care in the past, is it still the demonstrable standard of care after the publication of recent treatment trials questioning its effectiveness? How might a clinician argue that the client's symptoms were not due to his or her interventions?

CASE EXAMPLE

Mr. Strickland

Referral: Mr. Strickland, a 42-year-old African American client was referred by his primary physician to a psychologist because of an abnormal grieving reaction following his son's death, complicated by long-standing depressed mood and anxiety. Mr. Strickland was a construction worker who had been unemployed for a number of months when his 25-year-old son died in an automobile accident. Mr. Strickland stated his son had been involved in excessive drinking and violence routinely throughout his teenage years and that their relationship had always been difficult because of his long-standing disagreements over his son's lifestyle (including concerns over his safety). The accident occurred when his son left the house drunk on a weekend night and wanted to drive. Mr. Strickland asked him to call a friend for a ride, and they argued stridently before his son left the house and drove away. Shortly afterward, Mr. Strickland's son was killed in a wreck near their home. When Mr. Strickland received the news by phone, he ran to the site of the wreck and saw EMS technicians moving his son's heavily lacerated body into an ambulance. He was horrified at this scene and felt extremely guilty that he did not prevent his son from leaving the house.

Mr. Strickland stated that his life fell apart after this event. He became very depressed, began drinking excessively, and became increasingly isolated from his wife and extended family members. He was divorced within two years and left his family home to live in a single-room apartment.

Two years after his son's death, Mr. Strickland was still unable to visit his grave and stated he had never yet "said goodbye to him." He still visited his wife, but insisted that she not touch anything in their son's bedroom and that it be left alone. He stated

CASE EXAMPLE   Continued

he was unable to look at his son's own child and would often burst into tears if he saw his grandson, especially when his grandson sat near him or asked him for a hug.

Immediate concerns: Are there any immediate dangers to the client or other vulnerable persons?

There are several potential immediate dangers to Mr. Strickland and other vulnerable persons that should be evaluated. These include the possibility of suicide and dangerous behaviors. Assessment of suicidality can be undertaken from a combination of direct interviews and actuarial predictors. Mr. Strickland was asked directly if he currently had specific suicidal thoughts, a plan to kill himself, or a sense of hopelessness about the future. He was also asked whether he had any personal goals such as hope of recovery from his current problems, a desire to reestablish a relationship with his wife or his grandchild, or hopes to return to work. He was also asked about his history over the last two years, including direct questions about whether he had ever attempted suicide or ever had any plans for suicide.

The interview revealed that Mr. Strickland had experienced periods of intense hopelessness at various times in the past. He also had occasional thoughts about suicide, but had never attempted suicide or formulated a specific plan. He expressed hope that he could reestablish a relationship with his wife and stated that he wanted his grandchild to "have a man in his life," stating that this was his duty as his grandfather and that he owed his son this debt. Mr. Strickland was counseled that if he ever did become suicidal he should call immediately for an additional appointment and that some form of help could be found for him. It therefore appeared there was a relatively modest risk of immediate harm to Mr. Strickland.

Although Mr. Strickland reported considerable emotional lability in the past, especially related to drinking episodes, he reported that he had never actually engaged in any violent behavior toward others. There was no documentation of any history of violence by Mr. Strickland and the risk of him harming others appeared to be low.

Short-term goals: What goals need to be achieved in the first two to six sessions?

In the first two sessions Mr. Strickland and the therapist clarified several short-term goals. These included (1) being able to say goodbye to his son, (2) being able to help with his grandson without becoming tearful, (3) improving his mood, and (4) communicating to his former wife that he wanted to maintain and improve their relationship. Using an evidence-based approach to selecting an appropriate intervention with Mr. Strickland, the therapist identified the need to use prolonged exposure techniques to desensitize Mr. Strickland to the cues for his traumatic grief. These included, incrementally: (1) interacting with his grandson, (2) going into his son's room and deciding what to do with his son's belongings, and (3) going to his son's grave and saying goodbye to him.

Mr. Strickland's therapist explained that facing up to the triggers for his grief was an important step to surmounting his problems and that avoidance of trauma cues had contributed to the continuation of his problems. The therapist suggested going to the grave as a first step, but Mr. Strickland was unwilling to do that. He agreed to bring in some of his son's photographs and personal processions to look at in one session.

(*continued*)

CASE EXAMPLE   Continued

At the next appointment he brought in the items. Initially, he was unable to do more than hand over the photographs to his therapist. During the first twenty minutes, however, he was encouraged to hold and eventually look at the photographs. After more encouragement, he was able to describe and talk about the photographs. Eventually, with his therapist's encouragement, Mr. Strickland was able to tell his son that he loved him and that he missed him. At the end of a ninety-minute appointment Mr. Strickland stated he felt greatly relieved and modestly optimistic that he could face up to similar situations. Over the next two months, he had similar in-vivo exposure experiences in his son's bedroom, playing with his grandson, and visiting his son's graveside.

These sessions were accompanied by a general improvement in Mr. Strickland's mood, as well as reduced drinking. Mr. Strickland stated he was gratified at being able to enjoy increased contact and playful interaction with his grandson. He was encouraged to plan activities with his grandson that they both would enjoy.

Long-term goals: What lifestyle changes and other long-term personal, relationship, and career goals need to be achieved?

Over the next two months Mr. Strickland agreed he should begin to look for a job and work toward reestablishing a positive relationship with his wife. After a while, he went to a government-sponsored program to retrain people who had been out of work for more than six months.

His wife was unwilling to consider that they should live together again. However, he was able to accept that they could have a more amicable relationship, especially built around their grandson.

At six-month follow-up Mr. Strickland reported his mood was greatly improved and that he rarely drank to excess. He had maintained good relationships with his wife and grandchild, was continuing to attend job retraining, and believed that he was going to get a job in the near future. Although he had experienced a depressed mood during several anniversary dates, such as major holidays and his son's birthday, he had made a good recovery from these occasions and reported that he felt able to manage them in the future.

CASE EXERCISE

Mr. Bobby Singh, a 33-year-old man of Indian (continental) descent, is referred to you for help. Three years ago he was working as a commercial diver in a port city. His typical work involved underwater repair work, some tourist diving, and conducting occasional diving classes. He also agreed to receive training for police recovery diving, which involved searching for and recovering bodies lost in the local estuaries. After receiving his training, Mr. Singh performed recovery work for several months without a problem. As time went on, however, he reported becoming increasingly bothered by

CASE EXERCISE Continued

it. The diving was cold, sometimes dangerous, and frequently involved the possibility of periods of oxygen deprivation. More significantly, the recovery of the bodies was horrible. If a body was recovered within a week it might be bloated and partly decomposed; if it was recovered weeks later it might be partly preserved on one side (typically the side that lay in mud) and eaten to the skeleton by fish on the other.

Three years ago Mr. Singh participated in a dive in which he recovered the body of an adolescent girl. At one point during the dive he got lost and disoriented in weeds and feared briefly that he would not find the surface. When he came across the girl's decomposing body, he was startled and disturbed. When he arrived on shore, he experienced a prolonged period of horror, finally removed his diving gear and leaving it at the side of the river. When he arrived home, he was in a state of terror, but could not explain the situation to his family. He grabbed a bottle of whiskey and drank himself into a stupor alone in the basement.

Since this incident Mr. Singh has quit all of his diving activities and has studiously avoided large bodies of water. He has worked periodically in several low-paid, unskilled jobs, most of which he quit after getting into interpersonal disputes with his supervisors. His family life also has soured; he stated he now avoids his family when he can and no longer has sexual relations with his wife. He also reports that his children, with whom he once had a positive relationship, now just frustrate and anger him. He says he feels guilty and sorry for his family because he knows he is "a bad father and husband." His sleep is often disturbed by nightmares, and he is often tense and angry. Because he has been unable to work, his family has suffered financial distress, and his wife has been forced to take up a part-time job. This has been a considerable source of friction between them.

Study Questions

1. List the emotional and behavioral symptoms Mr. Singh exhibits. Which symptoms are specific to ASD and PTSD and which are not? Does Mr. Singh meet the criteria for ASD or PTSD?

2. What additional assessment information would you like to collect? What culturally relevant information would be helpful in working with Mr. Singh? How would you go about collecting this information?

3. What are your immediate concerns with this case?

4. Sketch a brief treatment plan for Mr. Singh and his family, including three short-term goals for therapy.

5. What are three long-term goals you might have for Mr. Singh and his family?

6. As therapy proceeds, Mr. Singh admits there are times he feels so angry he fears he might harm his wife or two young children. Should you report this to the police or other protective agency?

7. Mr. Singh later admits to you that he and his wife have florid fights and that he has given her a black eye more than once in the past. How should you respond to this information?

8. Your cultural assessment reveals that Mr. Singh is a third-generation immigrant whose family originally came from India. He has never been to India and only

(continued)

CASE EXERCISE   Continued

vaguely remembers his grandparents. He is a Sikh and attends temple every week. How does this affect your case formulation?

9. Assume that you have never known or worked with anyone who is a Sikh from India and you know nothing about Mr. Singh's culture or background. Describe what actions you should take.

10. If Mr. Singh were a recently arrived immigrant who had lived in this country for only five years, how might your case formulation be changed?

REFERENCES

Bennett, B. E., Bryant, B. K., VandenBos, G. R., & Greenwood, A. (1990). *Professional liability and risk management*. Washington, DC: American Psychological Association.

Bisson, J. I., Jenkins, P. L., Alexander, J., & Bannister, C. (1997). Randomized controlled trial of psychological debriefing for victims of acute burn trauma. *British Journal of Psychiatry, 171,* 78–81.

Bremner, J. D., Steinberg, M., Southwirck, S. M., Johnson, D. R., & Charney, D. S. (1993). Use of the structured clinical interview for DSM-IV dissociative disorders for systematic assessment of dissociative symptoms in post-traumatic stress disorder. *American Journal of Psychiatry, 150,* 1011–1014.

Bryant, R. A., Moulds, M. L., & Gutherie, R. M. (2000). Acute Stress Disorder Scale: A self-report measure of acute stress disorder. *Psychological Assessment, 12,* 61–68.

Bryant, R. A., Sackville, T., Dang, S. T., Moulds, M., & Gutherie, R. (1999). Treating acute stress disorder: An evaluation of cognitive behavior therapy and supportive counseling techniques. *American Journal of Psychiatry, 156,* 1780–1786.

Carlson, E. B. (2001). Psychometric study of a brief screen for PTSD: Assessing the impact of multiple traumatic events. *Assessment, 8,* 431–441.

Connor, K. M., Suterland, S. M., Tupler, L. A., Malik, M. L., & Davidson, J. R. (1999). Fluoxetine in post-traumatic stress disorder. Randomized, double-blind study. *British Journal of Psychiatry, 175,* 17–22.

Davidson, J. R., Rothbaum, B. O., van der Kilk, B. A., Sikes, C. R., & Farfel, G. M. (2001). Multicenter, double-blind comparison of sertraline and placebo in the treatment of posttraumatic stress disorder. *Archives of General Psychiatry, 58,* 485–492.

De Jongh, A., Ten Broeke, E., & Renssen, M. R. (1999). Treatment of specific phobias with eye movement desensitization and reprocessing (EMDR): Protocol, empirical status, and conceptual issues. *Journal of Anxiety Disorders, 13,* 69–85.

Feehan, M., Nada-Raja, S. Martin, J. A., & Langley, J. D. (2001). The prevalence and correlates of psychological distress following physical and sexual assault in a young adult cohort. *Violence and Victims, 16,* 49–63.

Foa, E. B., Johnson, K. M., Feeny, N. C., Treadwell, K. R. (2001). The child PTSD Symptom Scale: a preliminary examination of its psychometric properties. *Journal of Clinical and Child Psychology, 30,* 376–384.

Foa, E. B., & Tolin, D. F. (2000). Comparison of PTSD symptom scale interview version and the clinician-administered PTSD scale. *Journal of Trauma and Stress, 13,* 181–191.

Frank, J. B., Kosten, T. R., Giller, E. L., Jr., Dan, E. (1988). A randomized clinical trial of phenelzine and imipramine for posttraumatic stress disorder. *Archives of General Psychiatry, 145,* 1289–1291.

Frueh, B. C., Hamner, M. B., Cahill, S. P., Gold, P. B., & Hamlin, K. L. (2000). Apparent symptom over-reporting in combat veterans evaluations of PTSD. *Clinical Psychology Review, 20,* 853–885.

Goldstein, A., & Feske, U. (1994). EMDR treatment of panic disorder. *Journal of Anxiety Disorders, 8,* 351–362.

Hertzberg, M. A., Feldman, M. E., Beckham, J. C., Kudler, H. S., & Davidson, J. R. (2000). Lack of efficacy for fluoxetine in PTSD: A placebo controlled trial in combat veterans. *Annals of Clinical Psychiatry, 12,* 101–105.

Krakow, B., Hollifield, M., Johnston, L., Koss, M., Schrader, R., Warner, T. D., Tandberg, D., Lauriellpo, J., McBride, L., Cutchen, L., Cheng, D., Emmons, S., Germain, G. A., Melendrez, D., Sandoval, D., & Prince, H. (2001). Imagery rehearsal therapy for chronic nightmares in sexual assault survivors with post-traumatic stress disorder: A randomized controlled trial. *Journal of the American Medical Association, 286,* 585–588.

Lydiard, R. B., Brawman-Mintzer, O., & Ballenger, J. C. (1996). Recent developments in the psychopharmacology of anxiety disorders. *Journal of Consulting and Clinical Psychology, 64,* 660–668.

Mann, B. J. (1995). The North Carolina Dissociation Index: A measure of dissociation using items from the MMPI. *Journal of Personality Assessment, 64,* 349–359.

Marks, I. (1988). *Cure and care of neuroses: Theory and practice of behavioural psychotherapy.* Washington DC: American Psychiatric Press.

Mayou, R. A., Ehlers, A., & Hobbs, M. (2000). Psychological debriefing for road traffic accident victims. *British Journal of Psychiatry, 117,* 589–593.

Reist, C., Kauffmann, C. D., Haier, R. J., Sangdahl, C., DeMet, E. M., Chiez-DeMet, A., & Nelson, J. N. (1989). A controlled trial of desipramine in 18 men with posttraumatic stress disorder. *American Journal of Psychiatry, 146,* 513–536.

Rosen, C. S., Drescher, K. D., Moos, R. H., Finney, J. W., Murphy, R. T., & Gusman, F. (2000). Six- and ten-item indexes of psychological distress based on the Symptom Checklist-90. *Assessment, 7,* 103–311.

Saxe, G., Stoddard, F., Courtney, D., Cunningham, K., Chawla, N. Sheridan, R., King, D., & King, L. (2001). Relationship between acute morphine and the course of PTSD in children with burns. *Journal of the American Academy of Child and Adolescent Psychiatry, 40,* 915–921.

Schreuder B. J., Kleijn, W. C., & Rooijmans H. G. (2000). Nocturnal re-experiencing more than forty years after war trauma. *Journal of Trauma and Stress, 13,* 453–463.

Shapiro, F. (1989). Eye movement desensitization: A new treatment for post-traumatic stress disorder. *Journal of Behavior Therapy and Experimental Psychiatry, 20,* 211–217.

Shapiro, F. (2001). *Eye movement desensitization and reprocessing: Basic principles, protocols, and procedures* (2nd ed.). New York: Guilford.

Shapiro, F. (2002). EMDR 12 years after its introduction: Past and future. *Journal of Clinical Psychology, 58,* 1–22.

Suzanna, R., Jonathan, B., Simon, W. (2001). Psychological debriefing for preventing post traumatic stress disorder (PTSD). (Cochrane review). *Cochrane Database Systematic Review,* CD000560.

Wang, X., Gao, L., Shinfuku, N., Zhang, H., Zhao, C., & Shen, Y. (2000). Longitudinal study of earthquake-related PTSD in a randomly selected community sample in north China. *American Journal of Psychiatry, 157,* 1260–1266.

Weathers, F. W., Keane, T. M., & Davidson, J. R. (2001). Clinician-administered PTSD scale: A review of the first ten years of research. *Depress Anxiety, 13,* 132–156.

Weisaeth, L. (2001). Acute posttraumatic stress: Nonacceptance of early intervention. *Journal of Clinical Psychiatry, 62,* 35–40.

11 Sexual and Gender Identity Disorders

CHAPTER OVERVIEW

1. The sexual response cycle consists of four phases: desire, excitement, orgasm, and resolution.

2. DSM-IV Sexual Dysfunctions correspond to the first three phases of this cycle in addition to experiences of pain during sexual activity. Thus, there are disorders reflecting a lack of desire (e.g., Sexual Desire Disorder), insufficient sexual arousal (e.g., Male Erectile Dysfunction), and orgasmic difficulties (e.g., Female Orgasmic Disorder, Premature Ejaculation), as well as disorders involving pain during intercourse (e.g., Dyspareunia).

3. Other DSM-IV Sexual and Gender Identity Disorders include Paraphilias, in which a client's object of sexual desire is unusual, and Gender Identity Disorders, in which a client has a strong and persistent identification with the opposite gender.

4. Assessment of Sexual and Gender Identity Disorders may take place through interviews, questionnaires, and physiological measures of sexual functioning, such as plethysmography. Assessment procedures vary greatly in terms of their scope, length, purpose, and context of use. A variety of psychometric measures appear to be both valid and reliable for these applications. The status of physiological measures, however, remains controversial, as they may be subject to faking and fantasizing about material other than the material presented.

5. Sexual and Gender Identity Disorders are relatively common. Approximately one-third of adults living in community settings report these kinds of problems.

6. Treatment for many sexual disorders can be highly effective. Interventions are often based on the early work of Masters and Johnson and may include education, relationship counseling, sensate focus exercises, and behavioral and cognitive-behavioral interventions. A variety of medical interventions, including medications and surgical procedures, may also be employed.

7. The treatment of sexual dysfunction involves several ethical and legal issues. These include ageism, confidentiality, dual relationships, and the protection of minors.

The Human Sexual Response Cycle and Its Relation to Diagnosis

DSM-IV distinguishes four main categories of sexual disorders. First are Sexual Dysfunctions. These are disorders of the normal sexual cycle, which consists of four phases: desire, excitement, orgasm, and resolution (see Table 11.1). Most sexual dysfunctions map directly onto the first three of these phases (few people have problems with resolution) and may be characterized by a lack of interest or aversion to sexual intercourse, an inability to obtain or maintain sufficient sexual excitement, or problems relating to achieving an orgasm. Disorders involving pain during sexual intercourse are included as well. When making a diagnosis of a sexual dysfunction two other disorders are excluded: Sexual Dysfunction Due to a General Medical Condition (e.g., pelvic cancer or spinal injury) and Substance-Induced Sexual Dysfunction (e.g., inability to sustain an erection due to intoxication).

TABLE 11.1   A summary of the human sexual cycle and its relationship to DSM-IV Sexual and Gender Identity Disorders.

Phase	Corresponding DSM-IV diagnoses
Desire: This phase includes fantasies and the desire to engage in sexual behavior.	Sexual Desire Disorders, such as Hypoactive Sexual Desire Disorder and Sexual Aversion Disorder.
Excitement: This phase is characterized by the experience of sexual pleasure and physiological arousal. Includes tumescence and erection in men; includes pelvic vasocongetion, vaginal lubrication, and physiological changes in the external genitalia in women.	Sexual Arousal Disorders, such as Female Sexual Arousal Disorder and Male Erectile Disorder.
Orgasm: Characterized in women by contractions of outer third of the muscles of the vagina and anus. Characterized in men by an inevitable sense of ejaculation. Ejaculation is characterized by release of semen and rhythmic contraction of the muscles of the peritoneum, reproductive organs, and anus. In both genders there is a subjective sense of peak sexual pleasure followed by release of tension.	Orgasmic Disorders, such as Female and Male Orgasmic Disorders and Premature Ejaculation
Resolution: Characterized by a subjective sense of relaxation and well-being. In men there is a refractory period in which erection and orgasm are unlikely. In women further response to stimulation may occur almost immediately.	None.

The second group of sexual disorders is paraphilias, which are characterized by a persistent, debilitating attraction toward unusual objects of sexual desire. Examples of paraphilias include pedophilia and voyeurism. Obviously, there are considerable ethical, personal, and cultural issues involved in deciding whether a person's sexual interest is pathological. DSM-IV *partly* circumvents this issue by requiring that the person's symptoms must cause significant distress or interpersonal problems.

A third group of sexual disorders is Gender Identity Disorders, which are characterized by a strong identification with the opposite gender and a "persistent discomfort with one's assigned sex" (APA, 2000, p. 535). Finally, the fourth category of sexual disorders is Sexual Disorders NOS, which is used to diagnose symptoms of sexual dysfunction that cannot be categorized elsewhere.

Sexual Dysfunctions

Diagnosis

Sexual Desire Disorders.   Sexual desire disorders are characterized by a lack of sexual interest and desire or an outright aversion to sexual activity; that is, these disorders relate to dysfunctions in the desire phase of the human sexual response. A diagnosis of Hyposexual Desire Disorder is assigned if a person exhibits: (1) a deficiency or absence of fantasies or desire for sexual activity; (2) personal distress or interpersonal difficulties; and (3) no medical or drug causes for the problem. Sexual Aversion Disorder is diagnosed when a person exhibits: (1) aversion or avoidance of contact with a partner's genitals; (2) personal distress or interpersonal difficulties associated with the condition; and (3) no medical or drug causes for the symptoms. An occasional loss of sexual arousal that does not cause distress or interpersonal problems for the client does not qualify for these diagnoses.

Sexual Arousal Disorders.   Sexual arousal disorders are characterized by an inability to obtain or maintain sexual arousal through orgasm that causes distress or interpersonal difficulty to the client and that cannot be better accounted for by a general medical condition or drug use. These disorders therefore are disorders of the excitement phase of the human sexual response.

Female Sexual Arousal Disorder, formerly termed "frigidity," is characterized by a persistent or recurrent inability to maintain vaginal lubrication and swelling. Approximately 19 percent of women experience sexual arousal disorder, which may make sexual intercourse uncomfortable or painful (Laumann et al., 1994). Other Axis I disorders (e.g., major depression, obsessive-compulsive disorder, PTSD) and general medical conditions (e.g., postmenopausal reductions in vaginal lubrication, diabetes, radiotherapy) that might account for these symptoms should be excluded. Substance-Induced Sexual Disorder, which is caused by illicit substances or prescribed medications such as antihypertensives, antihistamines, and psychotropic medications, should also be ruled out.

Male Erectile Dysfunction is the corresponding diagnosis in men, experienced by up to 10 percent of men at some point during their lives (Laumann et al., 1994). DSM-IV characterizes this disorder as a *persistent* or *recurrent* inability to obtain or maintain an adequate erection. Occasional erectile difficulties, experienced by many if not most men, do not meet these criteria. General medical conditions, such as diabetes, peripheral neuropathy, and spinal cord injury, and pharmacological agents, such as antihypertensive medication, antidepressants, neuroleptic medications, and illicit drugs, should be ruled out as causes of the client's symptoms. As with female sexual arousal disorder, Axis I diagnoses that might better account for this problem also should be excluded.

Orgasmic Disorders. Female and male Orgasmic Disorders are characterized by an absence or delay in achieving orgasm. Whereas in these disorders a client comfortably experiences sexual desire and excitement, he or she experiences a problem with the orgasm phase of the human sexual response cycle. Approximately 24 percent of women and 8 percent of men experience orgasmic disorders, which are hallmarked by a persistent or recurrent absence or delay in achieving orgasm unusual for the person's age and the adequacy of the stimulation he or she receives (i.e., the clinician must determine that the client's problem does not reflect inadequate performance by the sexual partner). DSM-IV states that men with this disorder may be able to achieve orgasm by masturbation or after prolonged sexual activity, but not during regular sexual intercourse. General medical conditions that directly cause these disorders, such as diabetes, pelvic cancer, or surgical reconstruction, should be excluded, as should substance-induced sexual dysfunctions and other Axis I disorders if they directly cause the presenting problem.

Premature Ejaculation is characterized by a "persistent and recurrent onset of orgasm and ejaculation with minimal stimulation before, on, or shortly after penetration and before the person wishes it" (APA, 1994, p. 509). To qualify for this diagnosis, these symptoms, which are *occasionally* experienced by up to 50 percent of young adult men, must cause marked distress or interpersonal difficulty which, although occurring less frequently, may lead to diagnosis in nearly 30 percent of men (Laumann et al., 1994). As with other sexual dysfunctions, the client's symptoms must not be caused by a general medical condition or, more rarely, by use of a prescribed or illicit substance.

Sexual Pain Disorders. Dyspareunia (Not Due to a General Medical Condition) is characterized by genital pain before, during, or after intercourse and may occur in either women or men. Vaginismus, experienced by women, is characterized by recurrent and persistent involuntary contractions of the muscles of the vagina when penetrated by a penis, fingers, tampon, speculum, or other appropriate object. General medical conditions, substance-related causes, and Axis I disorders should be excluded as causes of these symptoms.

Assessment

Interview. Clinical interviews related to sexual disorders should assess the following areas: specific symptoms of diagnoses described in the preceding section, sexual knowledge, current and previous relationships, and sexual history. In order to meet most DSM-IV diagnoses, evidence of significant personal distress or dysfunction is needed. A detailed history of current and previous medical conditions, including sexually transmitted diseases, is also important. Interviews to assess sexual dysfunctions often are conducted initially by a male and female therapist together (typically with both therapists, the client, and the client's partner present if appropriate). Later, interviews for each client can take place with one therapist, depending on the client's wishes.

Assessment of sexual dysfunction takes place in a number of different contexts. It may take place within highly specialized settings, such as regional forensic services or tertiary services specializing in sexual dysfunctions; in mental health settings as part of a referral for mood disorder, anxiety disorder, or other mental condition; or in a general mental health setting in which the primary referral is for a sexual dysfunction. Primary care physicians, obstetricians and gynecologists, oncologists, surgeons, psychologists, social workers, and counselors may all screen, systematically or otherwise, for sexual dysfunctions.

Psychometric Assessment. There are numerous psychometric measures of sexual dysfunction. Some are intended to serve as broad screening instruments covering all possible diagnoses in great detail. Others are designed to briefly screen large populations for further assessment, if needed. Still other measures are designed to measure change in clients' responses to treatment for sexual dysfunction or to measure change in sexual functioning during the normal course of aging. In addition to screens for the general population, several instruments have been developed to assess sexual dysfunctions associated with more specific contexts, including psychosexual functioning related to general medical conditions (e.g., genitourinary tract infections, cancer, spinal cord injury) and medical treatments, such as radiotherapy or chemotherapy. Measures of sexual functioning also have been developed as part of assessments of psychological disorders such as mood disorders or OCD and their associated psychotropic treatments. Other measures have expanded assessment beyond symptoms to include measures of clients' quality of life (see Rosen 2000a, 2000b).

One example of a general screen for sexual dysfunction is the Golombok-Rust Inventory of Sexual Satisfaction (GRISS; Rust & Golombok, 1985, 1986). The GRISS provides separate scales for male and female sexual functioning, including scales measuring impotence, vaginismus, dissatisfaction, and other specific diagnoses. The scale has high reliability and evidence of validity and is sensitive to change during treatment (Ter Kuile et al., 1999).

When selecting appropriate psychometric measures of sexual function, clinicians must determine whether the primary purpose of the assessment is screening for at-risk clients, diagnosing clients likely to have a DSM-IV condition, identifying target behaviors for change, or evaluating change during the course of a client's treatment. Other important questions relate to the time available for assessment. In some settings, it may be necessary to quickly screen large numbers of clients for many diagnoses. In other contexts it may be helpful to conduct a broad, detailed assessment with many instruments, including one assessing psychosexual dysfunction, or to conduct a detailed assessment focused specifically on these issues. Answers to these questions determine the selection of an instrument appropriate to the purpose and resources at hand.

Assessments themselves range from five- to ten-item questionnaires to comprehensive, time-intensive assessment protocols; they also may employ interviews, self-report measures, diaries, quality-of-life measures, and physiological measures of sexual functioning (Rosen, 2001). In many instances, separate measures have been developed for men and women.

A wide range of assessment procedures, then, is available to the clinician. The following sections will review only a few examples of these procedures.

Interventions

Psychotherapy Interventions.   Therapy for sexual dysfunction was rarely systematically addressed prior to the 1950s. Although various educational and counseling interventions were available to a small number of people prior to this time, few treatments were supported by a good research base. This changed radically with the work of Masters and Johnson (e.g., 1966, 1970), which created an empirically based treatment model on which most current sex therapies have been based.

In addition, the treatment of sexual dysfunction has recently expanded to include therapies outside its initial contexts of young, married heterosexual couples, a problematic cultural restriction for the first three decades of sex therapy interventions. Research and treatment designs now routinely include sexual dysfunction among cancer patients and persons with other medical problems, gay and lesbian sexual partners, older adults, and clients with mental retardation.

Sexual dysfunctions are common among adults in community settings—as many as 40 percent of women and 30 percent of men may suffer from them (Laumann et al., 1994). The most common sexual disorders are hyposexual desire in women and men, sexual arousal disorders in women and men, and orgasmic disorder in women. In addition, approximately 15 percent of women and 5 percent of men experience sexual pain disorders (Rosen, 2000a). Within certain populations, sexual dysfunctions are even more common. For example, Labbate and Lare (2001) found that between 70 and 90 percent of outpatients at a veteran's facility reported sexual dysfunction, as many as half of whom were found to report no sexual functioning at all. Thus, sexual dysfunctions are quite common.

The most commonly referred sexual problems are discrepancies of sexual desire between partners (e.g., one partner enjoying sex less than the other or failing to achieve orgasm when with the other). Practitioners report high success rates, between 50 and 60 percent, with problems such as premature ejaculation, orgasmic dysfunction, and desire discrepancies, although primary erectile dysfunction has had a relatively poor prognosis in the past (Kilman et al., 1986). The basic strategies of sex therapy (described below) have been quite successful.

Current research has focused on such treatment issues as working with people who are not in relationships, bibliotherapy, concomitant sex therapy and relationship therapies, adjunctive cognitive and cognitive-behavioral therapies, and medical and surgical treatments (Hawton, 1995; Rosen & Leiblum, 1995). As mentioned earlier, research has also been extended to include investigations of sex therapy treatment with gay and lesbian couples (Garippa & Sanders, 1997; Igartua, 1998; Usher, 1990). The following sections outline some interventions commonly used in sexual dysfunction treatment. A summary of common elements in psychological treatment of psychosexual problems can be found in Table 11.2.

Education. Educational approaches are often one element of a multicomponent intervention package for sexual dysfunction. Many sexual dysfunction clients

---

TABLE 11.2 Summary of psychological and counseling treatment strategies for Sexual Dysfunctions.

Common elements

Relationship therapy

Psychoeducation

Sensate focus

Treatment elements for specific diagnoses

Erectile Disorder	Rule out medical condition
	Sensate focus
	Medications
Premature Ejaculation	Sensate focus and stopping (squeeze) technique
Female Orgasmic Disorder	Sensate focus and assigned masturbation exercises (e.g., vibrator)
Vaginismus	Sensate focus and assigned graduated dilation exercises

fear they are engaging in abnormal behavior or are unclear about what constitutes typical sexual performance and response patterns. Some clients need information on the effects of drugs, alcohol, fatigue, illness, or aging on sexual performance and how this might apply to their own sexual behavior. Of course, some clients also may need basic sex education.

Other clients may need social-skills training, or information about dating or negotiating sexual behavior with relational partners. One example of the benefits of this approach comes from an evaluation of sex education on primary orgasmic dysfunction in women, in which couples received two two-hour sessions of sex education over the course of a week and reported improvements in their sexual performance, orgasm, and sexual satisfaction (Kilman et al., 1983). However, although for some clients simply providing information and reassurance may be enough to achieve significant gains, education alone is rarely sufficient. Most clients also need more substantive forms of intervention.

Relationship-Based Interventions.   Dissatisfaction with sex often takes place within a context of unhappiness with some aspect of a relationship, either as a causal factor in the development of a sexual disorder or as a direct consequence of it (e.g., Renshaw, 1995). Interventions to improve the quality of relationships include helping clients open communication about aspects of their relationship they find satisfying (as well as dissatisfying), interrupting reciprocal escalations of arguments, and enhancing clients' patience for change while engaging in sexual therapy exercises (see below). Simple skills-training packages often also help distressed couples learn to communicate and resolve conflicts more effectively (e.g., Markman et al., 1993; see Waring et al., 1990, for contrasting findings). Relationship-based interventions often employ homework assignments to help couples learn to negotiate and compromise when disagreements occur in their natural interactions.

Masters and Johnson's Sensate Focus Treatment.   Working with healthy heterosexual couples in the 1950s, Masters and Johnson (e.g., 1966, 1970) observed that their clients' unsatisfactory sexual performance was often intertwined with poor sex education and performance anxiety. Masters and Johnson believed that many clients' equation of sexual performance with the achievement of orgasm led to anxiety (what Albert Ellis once called becoming "scared unstiff") that inhibited their sexual performance and enjoyment. The sensate focus treatment Masters and Johnson developed incorporates a provocative reversal: In the early stages of sex therapy, sex therapy couples are forbidden to engage in sexual intercourse. Instead, they are asked to take turns pleasuring each other with relaxed, sustained attention to nonsexual body parts. Partners also are encouraged to spend beginning sessions communicating about where they enjoy being touched and whether they find specific types of touch pleasurable. As the intervention progresses (e.g., over the course of six to eight weeks), these sensate focus exercises advance to include sexual parts of the body; only at the end of treatment do they permit actual intercourse.

This strategy has several important aspects. First, it encourages partners to communicate and give each other feedback in a nonthreatening and often enjoyable way and removes the pressure to sexually perform by banning actual intercourse. Sensate focus also includes a kind of reciprocal inhibition and desensitization. Pleasurable, relaxing feelings are paired with stimuli that previously evoked anxiety; once both partners enjoy sexual stimulation with one degree of intimacy, they move up the graduated hierarchy to the next degree, progressing to mutual satisfaction.

There is good evidence for the effectiveness of sensate focus and other aspects of Masters and Johnson's approach with uncomplicated sexual dysfunctions in heterosexual couples. In routine services, for example, studies suggest that as many as 65 percent of couples referred for sexual dysfunction may experience significant improvement versus only 2 percent of couples who drop out of therapy (see Sarwer & Durlak, 1997).

Masturbation Exercises.   Masturbatory exercises are often used for orgasmic failure, especially in women with female orgasmic dysfunction. For example, Riley and Riley (1978) evaluated the effectiveness of directed masturbation to treatment primary orgasmic failure in women, in which 90 percent of women in the treatment group were able to achieve orgasm versus 53 percent of women in the control group.

Treatments for Premature Ejaculation and Male Erectile Dysfunction. One of the most commonly used techniques to treat premature ejaculation is the so-called pause/squeeze technique (St. Lawrence & Madakasira, 1992). This treatment is predicated on the observation that men with premature ejaculation have short latencies to ejaculation after sexual arousal. For example, Choi et al. (2000) reported that men referred for treatment for premature ejaculation had latencies of only one and a half minutes. In the pause/squeeze treatment, the man is given assignments to masturbate (or receive sexual stimulation from a partner) to arousal just before the point of orgasm, then squeeze his penis when he feels that he is nearing ejaculation. This position is held (the "pause") for a few seconds until the feeling of inevitability passes, after which sexual stimulation is resumed. The technique may later be repeated during sexual intercourse.

Other psychological treatments for male sexual dysfunctions include biofeedback and cognitive-behavioral therapy. A variety of cognitive and interpersonal interventions for male erectile dysfunction, including education, changes in cognitions, anxiety reduction, modification of personal scripts, conflict resolution, and relapse prevention training, also appear to be effective (Reynolds, 1980; Rosen, Lieblum, & Spector, 1994). Pharmacological treatments for erectile dysfunctions appear particularly promising, especially for men whose symptoms are anxiety-based (see below).

Pharmacological treatments, including setraline, paroxetine, and a number of traditional herbal treatments and topical agents, have also been successfully used for premature ejaculation (Berkovitch, Keresteci & Koren, 1995; Choi,

Seong, & Rha, 1995; Choi et al., 2000; Kim & Paik, 1999; McMahon & Touma, 1996; Rosen, Lane, & Menza, 1999). Although evaluation of these treatments is beyond the scope of this section, clinicians should be aware of their use and should ask clients about their use of these or similar interventions in the past.

Treatment of Vaginismus.   Vaginismus can be successfully treated using desensitization techniques with a series of graduated dildos. Schnyder, Schnyder-Luthi, Ballinari, and Blaser (1998), for instance, found that 97 percent of women assigned these exercises (in which they were assigned to increase the size of insertions during masturbation over the course of several weeks) were able to have intercourse after about six sessions of treatment. One-third also reported an increase in sexual desire. Although surgeries also are sometimes used to treat vaginismus (e.g., physical enlargements of the vagina), these should be explored only after trials of effective psychological and desensitization techniques (Katz & Tabisel, 2001).

Medical and Surgical Treatments

A variety of medical and surgical treatments are commonly used to treat sexual dysfunctions. Medications to treat lack of desire include sildenafil (Viagra), for which extensive research literature supports its effectiveness in the treatment of male erectile disorder (Dinsmore et al., 1999; Marks et al., 1999; Muller et al., 2001). These medications may supplement, or eventually supplant, psychological approaches and other physiological treatments (e.g., vacuum pumps, self-injections, surgically implanted devices). Physicians also have successfully used hormone replacement therapy to increase the sexual functioning of both men and women, and medical treatment of concomitant urinary tract infections and other diseases of the genitourinary tract may be important in other sexual dysfunction cases. Clinicians working with sexual dysfunction clients should make a medical referral both to rule out underlying physiological problems and to consider the appropriateness of medical treatments.

CASE EXAMPLE

Jeremy and Erika

Referral: Jeremy and Erika, a 38-year-old Anglo male and 34-year-old Hispanic female married for seven years, came to a medical center sex therapy clinic after two years of increasingly diminished sexual interactions. An initial interview revealed that Jeremy experienced increasing bouts of erectile dysfunction with Erika. This began after he accidentally viewed a ten-year-old videotape of her intimately, but nonsexually, interacting with a boyfriend of the time at a party. Jeremy reported that he still loved her, but

CASE EXAMPLE   Continued

could not get thoughts about her former boyfriend out of his head when he was with her. Jeremy stated that on several occasions since viewing the video he and Erika had attempted sexual intercourse. However, when the distressing thoughts returned, he lost his erection and sexual activity stopped. After twelve months of these experiences Jeremy stated he avoided sexual contact with Erika and resisted her advances.

Erika and Jeremy both reported they experienced frequent sexual fantasies and privately masturbated regularly. They had not approached each other romantically for the past six months. Erika stated she recently has felt self-conscious around Jeremy and that their lack of sexual interactions had impaired their relationship. Additionally, this had affected their relationship with her family, whom Erika now avoided for fear of revealing the deficit in her sex life with Jeremy.

Immediate concerns: Are there any immediate dangers to the client or other vulnerable persons?

There are no immediate dangers to either client. They should continue to be evaluated throughout treatment for possible depression or other psychological issues that might present a danger to themselves or others.

Short-term goals: What goals need to be achieved in the first two to six sessions?

Sexual dysfunctions are rarely experienced in isolation. Jeremy's sexual dysfunction affected other contexts of his life with Erika, including their relationships with extended family members. In addition, in this case, the erectile dysfunction itself emerged within the context of relationship issues. For these reasons, the relationship-intervention format of traditional sex therapy was especially appropriate.

A thorough history was taken to rule out medical concerns often associated with erectile dysfunction. Individually conducted interviews revealed that both Jeremy and Erika experienced normal patterns of desire, arousal, and orgasm in private masturbation episodes.

Treatment therefore began with three goals in mind. First, sensate focus interventions were employed to broaden Erika and Jeremy's romantic interactions. While heightening their attention to erogenous responses in nongenital body regions, these interventions also reduced Jeremy's pressure to maintain an erection. Eight weeks of sensate focus homework assignments took place. They began at the first week with half an hour of attention to face and shoulder regions. They progressed to sustained penis-vaginal penetration by the eighth week. Jeremy was able to maintain full erections during sexual intercourse with Erika and both were able to climax.

These primarily behavioral interventions were coupled with cognitive interventions that addressed the intrusive thoughts Jeremy experienced during sexual relations with Erika. Jeremy practiced specific alternative self-statements. These included reframing the valence of the intrusive thoughts themselves. Foreboding thoughts of a doomed erection were reframed into being fleeting, if annoying, thoughts of the sort occasionally experienced by many people during sexual intercourse. After three weeks of rehearsing alternative cognitions and continued sensate focus exercises, Jeremy reported that he experienced the intrusive thoughts as only mildly annoying. Three weeks later he reported that he no longer experienced the intrusive thoughts.

(continued)

C A S E   E X A M P L E   Continued

Although these changes themselves improved the comfort of Erika and Jeremy's interactions, interventions were also initiated to focus more directly on improving Erika and Jeremy's relationship. Within-session and homework discussions addressed conflict resolution patterns, strategies for sharing control throughout their relationship. Specific strategies for initiating and negotiating episodes of sexual intimacy were identified. Family systems and cognitive interventions also were used to help Jeremy explore alternative views of Jeremy and Erika's past relationships, including externalizing the symbolic importance of past relational partners.

Long-term goals: What lifestyle changes and other long-term relationship, personal, and career goals need to be achieved?

Long-term management focused on maintaining the positive behavioral changes in Erika and Jeremy's sexual interactions, as well as enhancing the overall quality of their relationship. A plan was developed collaboratively to identify alternatives to Jeremy and Erika's past communication patterns under times of sexual and other relational tensions. Cognitive strategies were used to help them identify other enhancements of their interactions. These included comfortable reengagement with friends and extended family members and building on strengths developed during the initial treatment period. Follow-up sessions were scheduled to reinforce Jeremy and Erika's continued improved sexual interactions and to enhance their reengagement with extended family members and with each other.

Paraphilias

Paraphilias, like the etymology of the word, are characterized by culturally defined "para"-attractions; that is, by recurrent, intense sexual desires directed toward unusual or inappropriate objects such as animals, children, humiliating experiences, or clothing items. DSM-IV lists nine types of paraphilias (see Table 11.3). Whereas many people are sexually attracted to objects or situations that may be regarded as unusual, paraphilia is diagnosed when the person's desires lead to clinically significant distress or impairment in occupational, social, or other important areas of functioning. A gay male client who participates in S&M activities on weekends would not be diagnosed with paraphilia, for instance, unless he suffered clinically significant distress or impairment as a result of his activities and/or fantasies.

Assessment: Photographs and Visual Inspection Time

The Abel Assessment.   One approach to identifying clients' deviant sexual preferences (e.g., among sexual offenders) is the Abel Assessment (Abel et al., 2001). In this assessment a subject observes sixty slides in thirty minutes, includ-

TABLE 11.3   Types of paraphilias described in DSM-IV.

Paraphilia	Object of desire or behavior leading to clinically significant distress or impairment
Exhibitionism	Exposure of genitals to nonconsenting strangers
Fetishism	Restricted or nonliving objects such as underwear, shoes, or feet
Frotteurism	Touching or rubbing against a nonconsenting person
Pedophilia	Prepubescent or similarly aged child (generally 13 years or younger)
Sexual Masochism	Real, not imagined, act of being humiliated, beaten, bound, or made to suffer
Sexual Sadism	Victim made to experience real, not simulated, suffering
Transvestic Fetishism	Cross-dressing
Voyeurism	Observing an unsuspecting person naked or in process of dressing
Paraphilia NOS	Other objects of desire, such as obscene telephone calls, corpses, animals, feces, enemas, or urine

ing pictures of clothed adults, teenagers, and children of both genders. The time taken to observe each slide is used as a measure of sexual preferences.

The Abel Assessment appears to discriminate between offenders against boys and girls and identify those believed to be concealing offenses (Abel et al., 2001). Greater caution should be exercised, however, using the Abel Assessment with adolescent and nonoffending adults (Smith & Fischer, 1999). Some researchers (e.g., Smith & Fischer, 1999) have suggested that the Abel procedure may not be reliable when used with adolescents in residential and day treatments (see Abel, 2000, for contrasting view). Specialized training is needed to conduct this assessment.

Card Sort Procedure.   A technologically less-demanding approach to measuring sexual preferences is a simple card sort task in which clients sort deviant and nondeviant photographic material into piles of preferred and nonpreferred items. Using a sample of 371 male sexual offenders, Holland, Zolondek, Abel, Jordan, and Becker (2000) demonstrated that this relatively simple approach was highly reliable. The information from this task also appeared to correlate well with information gained from more extensive two-hour clinical interviews.

Plethysmography.   Plethysmography is a physiological method of measuring sexual preference in men in which a light strain gauge wire is placed around the shaft of a subject's penis to measure minute changes in its circumference as he is shown various sexual stimuli. The use of plethysmography is controversial. Although it has obvious face validity and some researchers are optimistic about its reliability and validity (e.g., Barker & Howell, 1992), others have objected to the lack of standardization of plethysmograph administration procedures (Simon & Schouten, 1993). Faking arousal by fantasizing about materials others than those presented creates serious validity problems, especially in key populations, such as sexual offenders (Simon & Schouten, 1991, 1993). In addition, some researchers have found that incarcerated rapists and other sexual offenders may not differ from incarcerated nonrapists in their response to plethysmography (Murphy et al., 1984). Although plethysmography has continued to be used with both clinical and supervised populations, its results should be interpreted cautiously.

Treatment: Conditioning and Cognitive Interventions

Masturbatory reconditioning has also been used in both men and women to change the focus of deviant fantasies to acceptable fantasy material. For example, if a person is only able to experience orgasm to deviant fantasy material, he or she may be taught to masturbate initially to deviant fantasy material in order to obtain arousal, before switching to acceptable fantasy material as orgasm approaches. Over time, the amount and early introduction of appropriate materials are increased and the client is asked eventually to refrain from using deviant material altogether. This approach is often used in the treatment of paraphilias.

Cognitive therapies have also been incorporated into treatment of both sexual dysfunctions and paraphilias. Cognitions relating to jealousy, intrusive thoughts or images during sex, and so on may be particularly amenable to change through traditional cognitive therapy. Cognitive therapy may be used to modify both clients' reaction to and evaluation of intrusive thoughts during sexual behavior or to modify offending clients' inappropriate core beliefs, such as a stalker's belief that his or her victim enjoys the attention or a sexual offender's beliefs that women enjoy being forced into sexual activity with a stranger.

CASE EXAMPLE
Roger

Referral: Roger, a 19-year-old male with a history of social isolation, was referred for therapy after his arrest for exhibiting his genitals to a 37-year-old woman and her 9-year-old daughter in a department store. Roger reported he had removed his trousers while standing in a large display of dresses and briefly exposed himself before retreating to the men's restroom to masturbate. A subsequent interview revealed Roger had inappropriately displayed himself in similar situations twice in the past, both during the

CASE EXAMPLE   Continued

previous twelve months. He met the criteria for a DSM-IV diagnosis of Exhibitionism. Roger reported he was very motivated to change his behaviors. He had felt ashamed and unhappy with his past exhibitionist episodes and strongly wanted to avoid future imprisonment.

Immediate concerns: Are there any immediate dangers to the client or other vulnerable persons?

Clinical interview should assess the history and extent of Roger's behavioral patterns as well as related psychological symptoms. Assessment revealed no mood or anxiety symptoms and limited use of alcohol. The limits of confidentiality were clarified with Roger. Informed consent for treatment was also obtained.

There is a risk of harm to others from Roger's exhibitionism and risk of harm to Roger from imprisonment and victimization from committing these crimes. The clinician therefore coordinated treatment with law enforcement and probation enforcement officers in order to minimize the risk that Roger might harm someone else by reoffending. Roger's affective response to his arrest and subsequent embarrassment was evaluated. An assessment of possible suicidal ideation was also made in the first session.

Short-term goals: What goals need to be achieved in the first two to six sessions?

Initial treatment focused on helping Roger reduce his inappropriate sexual fantasies and replacing these with appropriate sexual fantasies and behaviors. Roger stated that his past episodes of exhibitionism were preceded by fantasies, which he tried to fight off before eventually giving in to them. Roger stated he experienced these fantasies as compulsive. They would begin with just a thought or two before building toward masturbation. On occasions he had acted on these fantasies.

Cognitive interventions were used to monitor and interrupt inappropriate fantasies as they emerged and to identify alternative cognitions about their compulsive potency. These interventions were paired with behavioral interventions, including covert sensitization, intended to disassociate his exhibitionist fantasies from sexual arousal. Building on Roger's motivation for defusing the subjective compulsion of his behaviors, homework assignments were used to pair visualizations of exhibitionism with noxious odors. Additionally, in homework sessions and office sessions these fantasies were paired with visualizations of repulsive imagery. Roger kept a journal of fantasies and homework assignments. After eight weeks Roger reported his attraction toward exhibitionist fantasies was significantly abated.

Masturbatory reconditioning assignments were used to increase his sexual arousal and climax with more appropriate fantasies. In this case, images of age-appropriate women were used, which were consistent with Roger's heterosexual orientation. Roger initially was assigned to privately masturbate using existing problematic fantasies but to switch to appropriately targeted fantasies as he neared climax and continue these fantasies through climax. Roger stated he was able to switch successfully after one week. After three weeks the attraction of exhibitionistic fantasies diminished and he was able to masturbate to climax using entirely appropriate fantasies.

Cognitive interventions were used to challenge Roger's distorted thinking patterns. These included his beliefs that his exhibitionistic episodes were not harmful to his victims and in fact may have excited them. In place of these misconceptions, Roger and

(continued)

CASE EXAMPLE   Continued

the clinician explored alternative cognitions affirming the rights of all persons to choose the time and place of their sexual interactions with others. Cognitive interventions also were used to replace Roger's dichotomous views of failure (e.g., succumbing to deviant fantasies while masturbating) with a recognition that many patients' recovery from unwanted behavior patterns include periods of encountering, surmounting, and learning from lapses. Narrative therapy techniques were used to help Roger internalize a strength-based view of himself that included future successful interactions with women to whom he may be romantically and sexually attracted.

Roger kept a daily diary of sexual behaviors and sexual fantasies. After seven weeks of these primarily cognitive-behavioral interventions, Roger reported his deviant sexual fantasies had reduced from twenty per week to zero fantasies per week. Roger also stated he no longer experienced exhibitionist fantasies as compulsive when they did appear. He also no longer was motivated to explore or actualize them.

Long-term goals: What lifestyle changes and other long-term relationship, personal, and career goals need to be achieved?

The clinician helped Roger continue to plan successful moves away from past exhibitionist behavior patterns and to amplify positive changes as they emerge via solution-focused or other theoretically based homework assignments. Cognitive interventions, including narrative therapy interventions, were continued to help Roger internalize a view of himself as a young man in control of his sexual choices. Follow-up sessions were scheduled in concert with the identification of support group resources to insure against the reemergence of inappropriate fantasies or behaviors.

Social-skills training was used to enhance Roger's communication with family members, friends, and potential romantic partners and to improve his self-confidence and comfort with social interactions. Changes in Roger's repertoire of social behaviors were internalized using strategies that build on his continued successes as they appear, gradually, throughout his life. A career counseling referral was also made to help Roger explore his career and educational interests. Finally, follow-up sessions were scheduled to insure that Roger be connected to appropriate resources to pursue his college and vocational interests, as well as to negotiate developmental hurdles associated with life-stage changes as he progresses toward healthy, independent adulthood.

Gender Identity Disorders

According to DSM-IV, Gender Identity Disorder (GID) is a "strong and persistent cross-gender identification[s]" (APA, 2000 p. 581). GID must be distinguished from mere desires to gain the cultural advantages of being perceived as being the opposite gender. GID must also be distinguished from atypical sex role behaviors, Transvestic Fetishism, biological conditions in which the sex of the person is physically unclear, and gender delusions sometimes experienced by schizophrenic clients. A "tomboyish" girl or effeminate boy who doesn't want to be the opposite gender would not be diagnosed with GID. Similarly, by contrast with transvestic fetishism (in which a person is sexually aroused by cross-dressing but retains his or her gender identity), GID clients experience strong and persistent identification with the opposite gender, discomfort with their own gender, and significant distress or occupational or social impairment. Gender disorders that do not meet the exact diagnostic criteria for GID are classified as Gender Disorder Not Otherwise Specified (NOS).

Gender Identity Disorder is often treated by surgical reassignment of gender. Because surgical reassignment is a radical treatment that is difficult to reverse, however, it is typically done only after an extensive period of evaluation, counseling, and education. When performed, surgical reassignment is often successful (Smith, Van Goozen, & Cohen-Kettenis, 2001). Although a minority of clients who undergo this procedure appear to regret it later, poor outcomes may be correlated with lack of family support and lack of a support group of other transsexuals (Landen et al., 1998). Clients undergoing gender reassignment face a host of stressors related to deciding on and waiting for surgery, adjusting to gender reassignment, and vituperative discrimination. An important aspect of their treatment is to ensure they have adequate social support from friends and family or an ongoing transsexual support group. Counseling on safer sexual practices may also be important after surgical reassignment. Some clients may need counseling, skills training, and support during the period of transition from one gender to another and during adjustment to living, often under significant stigmatization, as the opposite gender.

Sexual Disorder Not Otherwise Specified (NOS)

DSM-IV includes a final, general category of Sexual Disorder NOS. This classification is used for clients who do not meet the full criteria of any of the above diagnoses, but who have a significant sexual disorder. Examples may include feelings of inadequacy related to feelings of masculinity or femininity, patterns of multiple sexual partners experienced as objects rather than people, or distress over one's sexual orientation.

Ethical and Professional Issues

The treatment of sexual dysfunctions raises numerous ethical and professional issues. Norms and standards of sexual behaviors change rapidly and vary both between and within cultures. What was illegal and unspoken in polite society fifty years ago is now the hourly fodder of late-night television. Similarly, a mild distraction on the streets of Manhattan or Amsterdam may be a scandalous affront in Muleshoe, Texas. Society regulates sexual behavior in numerous direct and covert ways (including the psychological normalization or abnormalization of sexual behaviors), some of which directly contradict "surface-level" cultural discourses (Foucault, 1954/1978). Laws exist to regulate sexually explicit material, the age of legal sexual behavior, and private behavior in the bedrooms of consenting adults. HIV, incest (by siblings and mothers as well as fathers), treatment for sexual orientation, biological treatments for incarcerated sexual offenders, and treatment of ethnic minorities also continue to challenge both lawyers and clinicians (Banning, 1989; Berlin, 2000; Incenogle, 1994; Schilder et al., 2001). Among the most common challenges clinicians face are HIV-related breaches of confidentiality and ageism related to the diagnosis and treatment of sexual dysfunction.

HIV Status and Confidentiality

As discussions in Chapter 2 underscore, client confidentiality may be breached in a number of circumstances. In the case of HIV-status several circumstances are raised in which practitioners' ethical standards conflict with legal demands.

First, some laws may require certain practitioners, including mental health practitioners such as counselors and psychologists, to report HIV-infected clients. This may conflict directly with the wishes of the therapist and the client; indeed, a client may direct the therapist not to disclose her or his HIV-positive status. In these situations, the clinician's ethical standards may directly conflict with the law. Ultimately, the therapist may be compelled by court order to disclose a client's HIV-status or face legal consequences. Where this may be an issue, clients should be informed early on in therapy that this possibility exists.

A second ethical issue related to HIV status is harm to a specified other person. If an HIV-positive client is having, or intends to have, unprotected sex with a named person, *Tarasoff* laws, which establish a duty to warn and protect potential victims of client harm, may apply. If there is no specific victim, no action may be legally required.

Ageism and Sexuality

Ageism relating to sexual dysfunctions may be a common problem among physicians and mental health professionals. For example, Bouman and Arcelus (2001) found that both psychiatrists and general physicians were more likely to take a sexual history with a middle-aged man than with an elderly man referred for a mood disorder. Elderly men with sexual dysfunctions also were more likely to be referred to a community psychiatric nurse than to a specialized clinic. In part, then, a client's age may inappropriately determine the kinds of assessment and treatment services he or she receives.

CASE EXERCISE

Angela was a 30-year-old Anglo-American woman whose primary complaint was that she did not experience orgasm with her regular boyfriend. Angela reported she could climax alone and had enjoyed orgasms with other boyfriends in the past. She complained that her current problem has caused considerable tension and arguments within the relationship. She was currently miserable with her relationship, but was reluctant to disengage from it, as the prospect of being unattached depressed her. As she looked around at her peers who were married and having children, she felt that life was passing her by and that something must be badly wrong with her.

Study Questions

1. Are there any immediate threats of harm to Angela or others?
2. What DSM-IV diagnoses may apply to Angela's symptoms?
3. Describe how you would conduct an assessment in this case.
4. What are your initial goals for treatment with Angela?
5. What are your long-term goals for treatment with Angela?
6. How would you handle treatment differently if Angela were not in a relationship, but occasionally had sex with men?
7. How would your approach change if Angela were in a lesbian relationship?
8. How would your approach change if an assessment revealed Angela was raped in the past?

REFERENCES

Abel, G. G. (2000). The importance of meeting research standards: A reply to Fisher and Smith's articles on the Abel assessment for sexual interest. *Sex Abuse, 12,* 155–161.

Abel, G. G., Jordan, A., Hand, C. G., Holland, L. A., & Phipps, A. (2001). Classification models of child molesters utilizing the Abel assessment for sexual interest. *Child Abuse and Neglect, 25,* 703–718.

American Psychiatric Association. (1994). *Diagnostic and statistical manual of mental disorders* (4th ed.) *(DSM-IV).* Washington, DC: Author.

Barker, J. G., & Howell, R. J. (1993). The plethysmograph: A review of recent literature. *Bulletin of the American Academy of Psychiatry and the Law, 20,* 505–512.

Banning, A. (1989). Mother-incest: Confronting a prejudice. *Child Abuse and Neglect, 13,* 563–570.

Berkovitch, M., Keresteci, A. G., & Koren, G. (1995). Efficacy of prilocaine-lidocaine cream in the treatment of premature ejaculation. *Journal of Urology, 156,* 1783–1784.

Berlin, F. S. (2000). Treatments to change sexual orientation. *American Journal of Psychiatry, 157,* 786–788.

Bouman, W. P., & Arcelus, J. (2001). Are psychiatrists guilty of "ageism" when it comes to taking a sexual history? *International Journal of Geriatric Psychiatry, 16,* 27–31.

Choi, H. K., Jung, G. W., Moon, K. H., Xin, Z. C., Choi, Y. D., Lee, W. H., Rha, K. H., Choi, Y. K., & Kim, D. K. (2000). Clinical study of SS-cream in patient with lifelong premature ejaculation. *Urology, 55,* 257–261.

Choi, H. K., Seong, D. H., & Rha, K. H. (1995). Clinical efficacy of Koran red ginseng for erectile dysfunction. *International Journal of Impotency Research, 7,* 181–186.

Dinsmore, W. W., Hodges, M., Hargraves, C., Osterloh, I. H., Smith, M. D., & Rosen, R. C. (1999). Sildenafil citrate (Viagra) in erectile dysfunction: Near normalization in men with broad-spectrum erectile dysfunction compared with age-matched healthy control subjects. *Urology, 53,* 800–805.

Foucault, M. (1954/1987). *Mental illness and psychology* (A. Sheridan, trans.). Berkeley: University of California Press. Original work published 1954.

Garippa, P. A., & Sanders, N. (1997). Resolution of erectile dysfunction and inhibited male orgasm in a single homosexual male and transfer of inhibited male orgasm cure to his partner: A case report. *Journal of Sexual and Marital Therapy, 23,* 126–130.

Hawton, K. (1995). Treatment of sexual dysfunction by sex therapy and other approaches. *British Journal of Psychiatry, 167,* 307–314.

Holland, L. A., Zolondek, S. C., Abel, G. G., Jordan, A. D., & Becker, J. V. (2000). Psychometric analysis of the Sexual Interest Card Sort Questionnaire. *Sex Abuse, 12,* 107–122.

Igartua, K. J. (1998). Therapy with lesbian couples: The issues and the interventions. *Canadian Journal of Psychiatry, 43,* 391–396.

Incenogle, D. L. (1994). Sentencing male offenders to the use of biological treatments. A constitutional analysis. *Journal of Legal Medicine, 15,* 274–304.

Katz, D., & Tabisel, R. L. (2001). Is surgery the answer to vaginismus? *Obstetrics and Gynecology, 97, (Suppl. 1),* S27.

Kim, S. W., & Paik, J. S. (1999). Short-term analysis of the effects of as needed use of sertraline at 5 PM for the treatment of premature ejaculation. *Urology, 54,* 544–547.

Kilmann, P. R., Boland, J. P., Norton, S. P., Davidson, E., & Caid, C. (1986). Perspectives of sex therapy outcome: A survey of AASECT providers. *Journal of Sex and Marital Therapy, 12,* 116–138.

Kilman, P. R., Mills, K. H., Bella, B., Caid, C., Davidson, E., Drose, G., & Wanlass, R. (1983). The effects of sex education on women with secondary orgasmic dysfunction. *Journal of Sex and Marital Therapy, 9,* 79–87.

Labatte, L. A., & Lare, S. B. (2001). Sexual dysfunction in male psychiatric outpatients: Validity of the Massachusetts General Hospital sexual functioning questionnaire. *Psychotherapy and Psychosomatics, 70,* 221–225.

Landen, M., Walinder, J., Hambert, G., & Lundstrom, B. (1998). Factors predictive of regret in sex reassignment. *Acta Psychiatrica Scandanavica, 97,* 284–289.

Laumann, E. O., Gagnon, J. H., Michael, R. T., & Michaels, S. (1994). *The social organization of sexuality: Sexual practices in the United States.* Chicago: University of Chicago Press.

Markman, H. J., Renick, M. J., Floyd, F. J., Stanley, S. M., & Clements, M. (1993). Preventing marital distress through communication and conflict management training: A 4- and 5-year follow-up. *Journal of Consulting and Clinical Psychology, 61,* 70–77.

Marks, L. S., Duda, C., Dorey, F. J., Macairan, M. L., & Santos, P. B. (1999). Treatment of erectile dysfunction with sildenafil. *Urology, 53,* 1070–1071.

Masters, W. H., & Johnson, V. E. (1966). *Human sexual response.* Boston: Little, Brown.

Masters, W. H., & Johnson, V. E. (1970). *Human sexual inadequacy.* Boston: Little, Brown.

McMahon, C. G., & Touma, K. (1999). Treatment of premature ejaculation with paroxetine hydrochloride as needed: 1 single-blind placebo controlled crossover studies. *Journal of Urology, 161,* 1826–1830.

Muller, M. J., Ruof, J., Graf-Morgenstern, M., Porst, H., & Benkert, O. (2001). Quality of partnership in patient with erectile dysfunction after sildenafil treatment. *Pharmacopsychiatry, 34,* 91–95.

Murphy, W. D., Kriasak, J. Stagaitis, S., & Anderson, K. (1984). The use of penile tumescence with incarcerated rapists: Further validity issues. *Archives of Sexual Behavior, 13*, 545–554.

Renshaw, D. (1995). *Seven weeks to better sex.* New York: American Medical Association.

Reynolds, B. S. (1980). Biofeedback and facilitation of erections in men with erectile dysfunction. *Archives of Sexual Behavior, 9*, 101–113.

Riley, A. J., & Riley, E. J. (1978) A controlled study to evaluate directed masturbation in the management of primary orgasmic failure in women. *British Journal of Psychiatry, 133*, 404–409.

Rosen, S. C. (2000a). Prevalence and risk factors of sexual dysfunction in men and women. *Current Psychiatry Reports, 2*, 189–195.

Rosen, S. C. (2000b). Quality of life assessment in sexual dysfunction trials. *International Journal of Impotency Research, 10 (Suppl. 2)*, S21–S23.

Rosen, R. C. (2001). Measurement of male and female sexual dysfunction. *Current Psychiatric Reviews, 2*, 182–187.

Rosen, R. C., Lane, R. M., & Menza, M (1999). Effects of sexual dysfunction: A critical review. *Journal of Clinical Psychopharmacology, 19*, 67–85.

Rosen, S. C., & Leiblum, S. R. (1995). Treatment of sexual disorders in the 1990's: An integrated approach. *Journal of Clinical and Consulting Psychology, 63*, 877–890.

Rosen, S. C., Lieblum, S. R., & Spector, I. P. (1994). Psychologically based treatment for male erectile disorder: A cognitive-interpersonal model. *Journal of Sex and Marital Therapy, 20*, 67–85.

Rust, J., & Golumbek, S. (1985). The Golumbek-Rust Inventory of sexual satisfaction (GRISS). *British Journal of Clinical Psychology, 24*, 63–64.

Rust, J., & Golumbek, S. (1986). The GRISS: A psychometric instrument for the assessment of sexual functioning. *British Journal of Clinical Psychology, 25*, 63–64.

Sarwer, D. B., & Durlak, J. A. (1997). A field trial of the effectiveness of behavioral treatment for sexual dysfunctions. *Journal of Sex and Marital Therapy, 23*, 87–97.

Schilder, A. J., Kennedy, C., Goldstone, I. L., Ogden, R. D. Hogg, R. S., & O'Shaughnessy, M. V. (2001). "Being dealt with as a whole person." Care seeking and adherence: The benefits of culturally competent care. *Social Science and Medicine, 52*, 1643–1659.

Schnyder, U., Schnyder-Luthi, C., Ballinari, P., & Blaser, A. (1998). Therapy for vaginismus: In vivo versus in vitro desensitization. *Canadian Journal of Psychiatry, 43*, 941–944.

Simon, W. T., & Schouten, P. G. (1991). Plethysmography in the assessment and treatment of sexual deviance: An overview. *Archives of Sexual Behavior, 20*, 75–91.

Simon, W. T., & Schouten, P. G. (1993). The plethysmograph reconsidered: Comments on Barker and Howell. *Bulletin of the American Academy of Psychiatry and the Law, 21*, 505–512.

Smith, G., & Fischer, L. (1999). Assessment of juvenile sexual offenders: Reliability and validity of the Abel assessment for interest in paraphilias. *Sex Abuse, 11*, 207–216.

Smith, Y. L., Van Goozen, S. H., & Cohen-Kettenis, P. T. (2001). Adolescents with gender identity disorder who were accepted or rejected for sex reassignment surgery: A prospective follow-up study. *Journal of the American Academy of Child Adolescent Psychiatry, 40*, 472–481.

St. Lawrence, J. S., & Madakasira, S. (1992). Evaluation and treatment of premature ejaculation: A critical review. *Journal of International Psychiatry, 22*, 77–97.

Ter Kuile, M. M., Van Lankveld, J. J., Kalkhoven, P., & Van Egmond, M. (1999). The Golombok-Rust Inventory of Sexual Satisfaction (GRISS): Psychometric properties within a Dutch population. *Journal of Sexual and Marital Therapy, 25*, 59–71.

Usher, J. M. (1990). Cognitive behavioral couples therapy with gay men referred for counseling in an AIDS setting: A pilot study. *AIDS Care, 2*, 43–51.

Waring, E. M., Carver, C., Stalker, C. A., Fry, R., & Schefer, B. (1990). A randomized clinical trial of cognitive marital therapy. *Journal of Sexual and Marital Therapy, 16*, 165–180.

12 Personality and Other Disorders

CHAPTER OVERVIEW

1. Personality Disorders are inflexible, maladaptive traits associated with functional impairment or subjective distress. Cluster A Personality Disorders, characterized by eccentric, sometimes psychotic-like personality traits, include Paranoid, Schizoid, and Schizotypal Personality Disorders. Cluster B Personality Disorders, characterized by lack of warmth and empathy, include Antisocial, Borderline, Narcissistic, and Histrionic Personality Disorders. Cluster C Personality Disorders, characterized by anxiety traits, include Avoidant, Dependent, and Obsessive-Compulsive Personality Disorders.

2. Assessment of personality disorders utilizes personality inventories and interviews to establish a history of symptoms tracing at least to the client's adolescence.

3. Treatment of personality disorders should focus on solving specific problems or developing specific coping skills. Dialectic behavior therapy, cognitive therapy, psychodynamic therapies, and token economies are often used with clients with personality disorder.

4. Somatoform Disorders are mental disorders that present in the form of bodily dysfunctions, such as pain or blindness, but which are not under voluntary control. Examples include Somatosization and Conversion Disorders.

5. Factitious Disorders are characterized by deliberate inducement of a physical disorder—for example, by deliberately harming oneself with poisons or medication overdoses in order to adopt a sick role.

6. Dissociative Disorders are characterized by disruptions of consciousness, memory, identity, or perception. Examples include Dissociative Amnesia and Fugue.

7. Sleep Disorders, including Primary Sleep Disorders, are due to underlying dysregulation in the sleep-wake cycle. Primary Sleep Disorders are classified into Dyssomnias, which are problems of the initiation or maintenance of satisfactory sleep, and Parasomnias, which are characterized by abnormal physiological events or disturbing experiences (e.g., nightmares) during sleep. Sleep Disorders are treated using cognitive-behavioral therapies, psychotropic medications, and mechanical devices.

8. Adjustment Disorders are responses to identifiable stressors. They are usually treated, if at all, with a variety of supportive interventions.

9. Additional Conditions That May Be a Focus of Clinical Attention include a wide range of problems not classified elsewhere in DSM-IV. They include Psychological Factors Affecting Medical Conditions, Medication-Induced Movement Disorders, Relational Problems, and Problems Related to Abuse and Neglect.

Personality Disorders

Diagnosis

DSM-IV defines personality traits as "enduring patterns of perceiving, relating to and thinking about the environment and oneself that are exhibited in a wide range of social and personal contexts" (APA, 2000, p. 686). Personality traits that may be described as "disordered" (a strong claim to make about a client's subjective personhood) furthermore must be inflexible, maladaptive, and associated with subjective distress or functional impairment.

To receive a DSM-IV diagnosis of a Personality Disorder, a client must exhibit significant deviation from culturally defined norms of cognition, affect, interpersonal functioning, or impulsivity. The client's personality traits must be inflexible and pervasive (e.g., exhibited not only at home or only among coworkers, but throughout many personal and social situations) and must cause significant impairment in the client's life. Finally, the client's personality traits must be long-standing and stable (e.g., traced to adolescence or earlier) and must not be better accounted for by general medical conditions or other mental disorders.

Unlike Axis I short-term mental illnesses or reactions to specific stressors, personality disorders are relatively permanent conditions. Reflecting this, they are recorded on Axis II of the multiaxial DSM-IV classification system along with other relatively permanent conditions, such as mental retardation. A client may meet diagnostic criteria for more than one personality disorder. If that is the case, *each* diagnosis should be recorded on Axis II, along with specific maladaptive personality traits or persistent defense mechanisms on which the client consistently relies.

Personality disorders are often described as "ego-syntonic," that is, they often are consonant with the person's own view of himself or herself and may not directly (insofar as the client is aware) cause distress or concern. (Avoidant Personality Disorder is a salient exception.) Instead, with most personality disorders it is the client's personality traits that cause distress in *others*, and by so doing, indirectly distress the client himself or herself (e.g., through disrupted interpersonal relationships, poor occupational experiences, or educational difficulties, for which the client may blame others).

Personality disorders are organized into three clusters. Cluster A personality disorders, which include Paranoid, Schizoid, and Schizotypal Personality types, may be thought of crudely as intimations of psychotic personality traits. People with Cluster A disorders may appear to be odd, eccentric, aloof, suspicious, or uncomfortable around other people and typically exude a lack of interpersonal warmth. Cluster B personality disorders, which include Antisocial, Borderline, Histrionic, and Narcissistic Personality Disorders, similarly may be thought of as extreme versions of extroverted personality traits with underlying fragile personality structures (e.g., psychological selfhood) on which to rely when facing stressors. People with Cluster B disorders tend to exhibit dramatic, emotional, or inconsiderate behavior toward others. Finally, Cluster C personality disorders, which include Avoidant, Dependent, and Obsessive-Compulsive Personality Disorders, are characterized by excessively anxious, fearful, and rigid behaviors. Note that Obsessive-Compulsive Personality Disorder is distinct from Obsessive-Compulsive Disorder (see below). These disorders can be thought of as the extremes of anxious or neurotic personality traits.

When making a diagnosis of Personality Disorder, it is helpful to first make a broad decision as to which of the three clusters of personality traits best describe the client. After this assessment, finer distinctions between each diagnosis within that cluster can be examined. Table 12.1 summarizes the personality traits associated with each of the three clusters of personality disorders.

Cluster A Personality Disorders. Paranoid Personality Disorder is characterized by distrust, suspicion, and attribution of malevolent motives to others. People with this diagnosis, who rarely self-refer to psychotherapy, often suspect that others are exploiting, harming, or deceiving them. They may doubt the loyalty of friends or colleagues and may not confide in others out of fear of distrust. They also may bear grudges for a long period of time, misperceive benign interactions as personal attacks, react angrily to ordinary events, or exhibit extreme jealousy of their partners. Like other Cluster A disorders, Paranoid Personality Disorder is more prevalent among males than females.

Schizoid Personality Disorder is characterized by an indifference to warm relationships. Persons with this diagnosis do not want or enjoy friendships or family relationships. Instead they prefer solitude. They typically are disinterested in sex, enjoy few if any activities, and are indifferent to others' praise or criticism. They may be cold, detached, and emotionally flat.

Schizotypal Personality Disorder is characterized by more frankly psychotic traits, including ideas of reference, odd beliefs, magical thinking, and unusual

TABLE 12.1 Personality traits associated with Cluster A, B, and C Personality Disorders.

Cluster A	Cluster B	Cluster C
Psychotic traits	*Extroversion traits*	*Anxiety traits*
Odd	Dramatic	Anxious
Eccentric	Inconsiderate	Fearful
Aloof	Disrespectful of others	Afraid of others
Suspicious		
Uncomfortable around others		
Lack of warmth and comfort with other people		

perceptual thinking. People with this diagnosis may exhibit odd or circumstantial speech, suspiciousness, restricted affect, and diminished interest in friendships or companionship. They also may have continuous social anxieties that do not abate over time. Although hypothesized by some writers to develop into schizophrenia (from which its name, a contraction of the phrase "*schizo*phrenic geno*type*," derives), schizotypal personality disorder may be differentiated from schizophrenia by the latter's more extreme and frank psychotic symptoms, more severe disability, and degenerative course over the lifespan for some adults. Additionally, schizophrenia is hallmarked by sharply diminished functioning, whereas schizotypal persons exhibit consistently poor functioning throughout their lives.

Table 12.1 provides a summary of Cluster A personality disorders that may be helpful in making a differential diagnosis among these related concerns. These disorders can be differentially diagnosed from their related Axis I diagnoses (e.g., PTSD, substance-related disorders) primarily by noting that they are associated with enduring, long-lasting personality characteristics that rarely cause distress to the client.

Cluster B Personality Disorders.   Antisocial Personality Disorder (ASPD) is often conceived as an unrelenting childhood Oppositional Defiant Disorder (ODD) that continues into adolescence as Conduct Disorder and translates into adulthood as ASPD (Hinshaw, 1994). As in conduct disorder, ASPD clients exhibit a consistent pattern of disregard for, and violation of, the rights of others. ASPD clients also exhibit deceitfulness, lying, impulsivity, and irritability and/or aggressiveness and are often reckless, irresponsible, or inconsistent in their home and work lives. Clients with ASPD also typically exhibit a lack of remorse coupled with indifference to, or rationalization of the violation of, others' well-being. Some ASPD clients may be charming and exploitative; others are just exploitative. As many as 3 percent of men and 1 percent of women may have this diagnosis (e.g., Golomb et al., 1995).

Borderline Personality Disorder is characterized by a pattern of unstable relationships, impulsivity, and dramatic concerns over real or imagined abandonment. Most borderline persons are female. Approximately 2 percent of community samples meet criteria for Borderline Personality Disorder (Widiger & Trull, 1993). Interpersonal relationships often vacillate between periods of intense idealization and angry devaluation of others. The person's self-image also is often highly unstable, and he or she may engage in reckless spending, sex, or binge-eating behaviors. Recurrent suicide attempts or gestures and self-mutilation behaviors often are also seen among persons with this disorder. Additionally, they may suffer from chronic feelings of emptiness and transient paranoid states.

Psychodynamic theory suggests that the behaviors of people with borderline personality reflect their attempts to defend themselves by "splitting"; that is, by dichotomously perceiving themselves, others, and the world as either "all good" or "all bad." This may be a consequence of the person's failure to develop a stable self- or other identity (which reflects the integration and internalization of symbolic others) during childhood (Kernberg, 1985, 1996; Kohut, 1977).

Because working with borderline clients can easily exhaust a clinician's time and resilience, clinicians often are advised to accept no more than one or two such clients as part of their caseload. In some settings this may be difficult, given that as many as 8 percent of outpatient clients and 15 percent of inpatient clients may have borderline personalities (Carson, Butcher, & Mineka, 2000).

Histrionic Personality Disorder is also characterized by excess emotion and attention seeking; however, whereas the borderline client seeks attention to avoid abandonment, the histrionic client does so to remain the center of others' focus. In consequence, histrionic clients may be seductive and provocative, drawing attention to themselves through their physical appearance, self-dramatization, and exaggerations of the degree of intimacy they share with others. Histrionic clients also often display shifting, shallow emotions and may be highly suggestible, rendering them vulnerable to manipulations by friends or acquaintances.

Narcissistic Personality Disorder, by contrast, is characterized by grandiosity, an exaggerated sense of self-importance, and a lack of empathy toward others. Whereas most borderline and histrionic personalities are female, most narcissistic persons are male. People with narcissistic personalities often have fantasies of their success and specialness and require excessive admiration to confirm their self-views. Because they possess little empathy, however, they typically are exploitative. They also may exhibit arrogance and a profound sense of entitlement toward those around them.

Differentiating histrionic and narcissistic personality disorders can sometimes be difficult. It may help to recognize that whereas histrionic clients seek attention and concern from others, narcissistic clients seek admiration more than attention and typically are more exploitative than needy.

Cluster C Personality Disorders. Avoidant Personality Disorder is characterized by social inhibition, feelings of inadequacy, and fear of negative evaluation from others. Clients with this disorder avoid activities that might lead to negative social evaluation by others. They also are personally restrained, preoccupied with social criticism, and reluctant to take social risks. Avoidant clients may be socially oriented and desire attention, but because they fear rejection they avoid interpersonal interactions and typically are quite lonely.

Avoidant Personality Disorder can be distinguished from Schizoid Personality Disorder because in Avoidant Personality Disorder the client is *insecure* and hypersensitive to negative social evaluation, whereas in Schizoid Personality Disorder the client is socially *indifferent* rather than socially fearful. Co-morbid diagnoses of Social Phobia or Dependent Personality Disorder are common among clients with avoidant personality disorder. Although few people in community samples have this diagnosis (approximately 0.5 to 1.0 percent; APA, 2000), they are more likely than people with other personality disorders to self-refer for treatment.

Dependent Personality Disorder entails extremely low self-confidence and dependence on others to make decisions. Dependent clients will often undertake activities they find unpleasant in order to ingratiate themselves with others. They typically feel helpless and unable to care for themselves and fear being left on their own.

Obsessive-Compulsive Personality Disorder (OCPD) is characterized by extreme orderliness, perfection, and control. People with OCPD, who almost never self-refer for counseling, are cold, overconscientious, rigid, and stubborn. Psychoanalysts would say they are all superego. They also may be moralistic, parsimonious, overscrupulous, and devoted to work to the exclusion of leisure. OCPD bosses are quickly recognized by employees: They do not delegate tasks, because the tasks would not be performed correctly.

OCPD can be distinguished from OCD on a number of grounds. First, in OCPD clients are not distressed by their problems, since their problematic behaviors are egosyntonic. Rather, they typically fail to understand why others do not share their worldview. In OCD, by contrast, the client is greatly distressed, anxious, and depressed because of rituals and preoccupations (e.g., handwashing, checking, counting). OCPD clients, by contrast, are unlikely to exhibit these patterns. Finally, although some OCD clients exhibit rigid or judgmental personality traits, their dysfunction is more likely to be dated to a specific onset and to fluctuate over time, rather than to be a continuation of personality traits from adolescence.

Personality Disorder Not Otherwise Specified is a diagnosis reserved for clients who clearly have a personality disorder but do not meet the specific criteria of any of the preceding diagnoses (e.g., Depressive Personality Disorder or Passive-Aggressive Personality Disorder; see Appendix B of DSM-IV). This diagnosis should be used carefully. Like other personality disorders, the client must suffer impairment in social or occupation functioning and must present a lifelong history of the personality traits. Other diagnoses also should be ruled out as causes for the client's presenting problems.

Assessment

DSM-IV diagnostic criteria for personality disorders require a long-standing history of the client's problematic traits and display of these problems across many situations. The assessment of personality disorders therefore should include an extensive history and confirmation that the person's problems are displayed across multiple settings.

Psychometric assessment of personality disorders has an extensive literature. Measures such as the MMPI-2 and Millon Clinical Multi-Axial Inventory are often used to assess a wide range of personality disorders (e.g., Hicklin & Widiger, 2000; Lenzenweger, 1999). Merritt, Balogh, and Kok (1998), for instance, suggest that certain profiles on the MMPI may be a good measure of Cluster A Personality Disorders.

Hare's Psychopathy Checklist has been widely used to assess antisocial personality disorder (sometimes termed "psychopathy" in Europe). This scale identifies four traits central to ASPD—emotional detachment, superficial relations, egocentricity, and impulsivity—and has been found to be robustly reliable and valid among several different cultures (Grann et al., 1998; McDermott et al., 2000; Molto, Poy, & Torrubia, 2000; Raine, 1985). One approach to assessing self-harm in clients with Borderline Personality Disorder is the 22-item Self-Harm Inventory (Sansone, Wiederman, & Sansone, 1998), which assesses both obvious (e.g., wrist and arm cutting) and subtle forms of self-defeating behaviors.

Intervention

Almost by definition, the treatment of personality disorders is difficult: Attempts to change a client's personality are unlikely to be successful. Short-term interventions, although often used to target a client's lifestyle, coping skills, or relationship patterns, are less effective for changing long-standing personality traits. A further complication is that many clients with personality disorders are resistant to therapy. Because their problems typically are egosyntonic, personality disorder clients may neither recognize they have a problem nor seek therapy except for clients with borderline, avoidant, or dependent personality disorders. When they do, they often have low motivation for change and high treatment dropout rates. A further treatment complication is that it is difficult to establish working relationships with clients with personality disorder, especially those who are suspicious, aloof, or untrusting.

Although traditional psychotherapy is unlikely to work with personality disorders (and is probably contraindicated for dependent clients), four promising strategies have been identified for some clients with personality disorders: dialectical behavior therapy (Koerner & Linehan, 2000; Linehan, 1993; Linehan et al., 1991; Linehan et al., 1999), cognitive therapy (e.g., Beck & Freeman, 1990), token economies, and psychodynamic psychotherapy (e.g., Kernberg, 1985, 1996).

Linehan's Dialectical Behavior Therapy (DBT).   Linehan (1993; Linehan et al., 1991; Linehan et al., 1999) developed a behavioral model to treat a variety of problems associated with clients with borderline personality disorder, including negative mood, self-harm, and drug use. This treatment model, which has also been applied to other personality disorders, accepts clients as they are while trying to help them change. Emphasis is placed on maintaining a warm accepting relationship while the client is taught a variety of cognitive-behavioral skills (e.g., emotional regulation, interpersonal effectiveness, tolerance for distress, and self-management skills). The focus of treatment, however, is clients' regulation of their negative affect. Dialectical behavior therapy typically combines *structured* individual and group therapy and may include an initial period of inpatient treatment (Linehan et al., 1991).

Several controlled trials of dialectical behavior therapy support its effectiveness with borderline clients. For example, Linehan et al. (1991) evaluated the use of dialectical behavior therapy with chronically parasuicidal borderline personality women. On outcome measures of frequency and severity of parasuicidal attempts, continuation in therapy and inpatient admissions, DBT was superior to alternative treatments throughout the year of the study (there were no differences between the two treatments on measures of mood and hopelessness). In a subsequent investigation, Linehan et al. (1999) evaluated dialectical behavior therapy with borderline personality women who also used illegal drugs. Clients who received DBT were found to use fewer illicit substances and remain in treatment more consistently than clients receiving alternative treatments; they also exhibited better life adjustment. DBT also has been shown to be effective in improving suicidal behavior and psychiatric symptoms (Bohus et al., 2000; Evans et al., 1999) and may be partially implemented by therapists from a variety of theoretical backgrounds (Evans et al., 1999; Hawkins & Sinha, 1998).

Cognitive Therapy.   Cognitive therapy focuses on changing patterns of thinking, attribution, and core beliefs. The therapist helps the client change his or her cognitions through guided exercises and discussions and by offering alternative, adaptive cognitions and behaviors to the client's maladaptive cognitions and attributions. Because personality disorders arguably reflect clients' core beliefs and perceptions, cognitive therapy may be useful for helping clients with these disorders (Ball, 1998; Beck & Freeman, 1990).

Psychodynamic Therapy.   Once the treatment of choice for personality issues, psychodynamic psychotherapy continues to be used for some clients with personality disorders. Specific psychodynamic treatments developed for borderline and other personality disorders appear to be effective with these clients (e.g., Kernberg, 1985, 1996; Kohut, 1977; cf. Bateman & Fonagy, 1999, 2001). More intentional than most psychodynamic models, these treatments in general aim to strengthen the client's developing self by capitalizing on therapeutic recapitulations of the client's early primary relationships (cf. Greenberg & Mitchell, 1983).

Token Economies.   Token economies have been successfully implemented in a variety of controlled environments with personality disorder clients (e.g., inpatient units) (Bloxham et al., 1993; Moyes, Tennent, & Bedford, 1985), although the translation of token-economy treatment gains to clients' outside lives may be questionable. Adolescents with conduct disorders and adult clients with antisocial personality disorder are often the targets of token economies. Well-designed token systems should reinforce clients' positive behaviors by adding to, rather than subtracting from, point tallies clients accrue throughout a relatively brief period, such as a single day. Demerit systems are commonly employed as well, in which a client suffers reductions in point totals for inappropriate behavior. Reinforcements for changes in point levels should be provided as soon as possible after the client's successful accrual of points.

Early Intervention and Prevention. Early interventions targeting at-risk adolescents are often used with groups of adolescents who are susceptible to early oppositional or conduct disorder behaviors. Examples of these interventions include support for depressed mothers, so that they can consistently reinforce their children's prosocial behaviors, and social-skills training to help oppositional children establish positive relationships with peers; social skills and conflict management strategies also may be helpful with adolescent clients (cf. Vera & Gaubatz, 2001). These strategies may be effective even if clients' underlying personality (e.g., lack of empathy or regard for others) is not changed, by expanding their behavioral repertoires to include positive interactions with others. These models may be particularly effective when therapists accept clients' self-reported wants and help them develop more effective strategies to achieve these goals (Glasser, 1965, 2000; Wubbolding, 1988).

CASE EXAMPLE
Angela

Referral: Angela, a 27-year-old Anglo-American woman, presented with concerns that her live-in boyfriend of two years was no longer paying attention to her. An initial consultation revealed a history of brief relationships with similar patterns of disaffection for romantic partners once they no longer swooned over her. Angela also reported a history of covert sexual relationships with other men while dating ostensibly exclusive partners over the past seven years. Intake records reveal Angela attended two years of college before quitting to perform as a topless dancer; she continued this work for two years before meeting her current partner and stated she missed being the center of attention from men and women while dancing. At a recent party at which no one was paying attention to her, Angela removed her blouse and skirt while dancing before her boyfriend intervened. Her presentation during the interview was superficial, with impressionistic speech and flirtatious interactions with the intake clinician (e.g., "You're cute for asking me that").

Immediate concerns: Are there any immediate dangers to the client or other vulnerable persons?

In response to direct questions from her clinician, Angela reported no suicidal ideation or intent and denied thoughts about harming her boyfriend or any other persons. She did not appear to be a threat to herself or others at this time. After ruling out symptoms of Borderline Personality Disorder and Narcissism, Angela was assigned a working diagnosis of Histrionic Personality Disorder.

Short-term goals: What goals need to be achieved in the first two to six sessions?

The clinician's initial treatment plan was to help Angela examine the effectiveness of her attention-seeking behaviors in the context of her own self-identified goals

(*continued*)

CASE EXAMPLE   **Continued**

(cf. Glasser, 1965, 2000). Angela and her clinician identified alternative behaviors to achieve reasonable goals of interacting comfortably, with appropriate levels of attention, with other people in her life. Treatment targeted the enhancement of Angela's social behaviors, including specific interactional skills, coupled with cognitive interventions to help her deal more effectively with the feelings of discomfort she experienced when not receiving attention from others.

To address her underlying cognitions about her expectations for attention from others, Angela rehearsed alternative cognitions/self-statements she could employ when not gaining attention (e.g., "I want the right kind of attention: peaceful and relaxed," "I'm okay when people don't notice me: I like being subtle"). After four to five sessions of in-session rehearsal and journal homework, Angela reported she was increasingly able to identify problematic thought patterns during her social interactions and able to substitute alternative cognitions affirming her well-being in the absence of attention from others.

Small-group and individual therapy sessions targeted enhancements in Angela's social skills. Both formats employed interpersonal feedback and didactic elements to enhance Angela's listening skills and to help her reframe her social identity around the ability (present partly before treatment) to "bounce back" (i.e., reciprocate) discussion topics with conversational partners. Small-group sessions also included in-session rehearsal of specific interactional skills (e.g., turn-taking, reflective listening).

Together, these approaches aimed less at changing Angela's selfhood than at enhancing the quality of, and ultimately, Angela's satisfaction with, her interactions with others. Although Angela's personality did not become so intact as to allow her to produce genuinely empathic responses in most social situations, she developed a social smoothness that produced more satisfying responses from the people with whom she interacted (e.g., increased eye contact, smiles, and the like).

Long-term goals: What lifestyle changes and other long-term relationship, personal, and career goals need to be achieved?

Long-term management should focus on maintaining Angela's positive behavioral changes and help her identify social support resources. Attention also should be given to career planning issues. Whereas some of Angela's psychological reliance on her boyfriend's affections reflected histrionic attempts to maintain a coherent self, for example, other issues were economic: She had no coherent plan for housing or basic material needs outside of her relationship with her boyfriend. Career counseling interventions should help Angela identify both immediate and long-term career interests and help her develop a plan for economic self-reliance should such a need arise. These interventions also might include a referral for career testing and academic counseling if she chooses to return to college.

Long-term work with Angela also might help her identify a solution picture of quality relationships, including relationships with friends, toward which she can work. This picture may emerge from Angela's own views combined with empirical checks (e.g., interviews of friends and family members in long-term relationships) of reasonable expectations for romantic relationships and friendships.

Somatoform Disorders

Somatoform disorders are relatively rare disorders in which a client's presenting symptoms take the form of a general medical condition, such as pain, blindness, or some other physical complaint. Somatoform disorders are not under voluntary control and are not due to a true general medical condition. Because nonmedical somatic symptoms are often associated with anxiety and mood symptoms, it may be difficult to make a differential diagnosis of these conditions from anxiety disorders, panic disorder, and general anxiety disorder. Somatoform disorders can be distinguished from malingering and factitious disorders in that their symptoms are not intentionally produced (although somatoform disorders may coexist with malingering and factitious disorders). A summary of somatoform disorders can be found in Table 12.2.

TABLE 12.2 **Summary of Somatoform Disorders.**

Diagnosis	Description
Somatization Disorder	Formerly known as hysteria. Characterized by presentation of multiple physical symptoms, including multiple pain symptoms, gastrointestinal, sexual and pseudo-neurological symptoms (e.g., conversion symptoms, paralysis, hallucinations, amnesia).
Undifferentiated Somatoform Disorder	A mild version of Somatosization Disorder. One or more symptoms lasts for at least six months.
Conversion Disorder	A voluntary motor or sensory function is affected that suggests a neurological condition. Examples include pseudoseizures without EEG abnormalities, paralysis, or loss of sensory function in which the affected area does not correspond to the underlying neuroanatomy (e.g., glove paralysis).
Pain Disorder	The presenting symptom is pain with a psychological rather than physical origin.
Hypochondriasis	Preoccupation with personal illness due to misperception of bodily functions or symptoms.
Body Dysmorphic Disorder	Preoccupation with imagined or exaggerated abnormalities of physical appearance.
Somatoform Disorder NOS	Other somatoform disorder that does not meet the criteria listed above.

Factitious Disorders

Factitious disorders are characterized by the deliberate inducement of physical or psychological symptoms in order to gain the benefits of a sick role. For example, a person with factitious disorder may repeatedly take medications or directly harm himself or herself in order to induce symptoms of an illness. Malingering (faking a symptom with obvious personal gain, such as avoiding military service) must be ruled out to make this diagnosis. Factitious disorders are relatively rare.

Dissociative Disorders

Dissociative disorders are characterized by disruptions in a person's sense of self, identity, or memory sufficient to cause clinically significant distress or impairment in functioning. Clients diagnosed with dissociative disorders may experience severe memory loss, psychological fugue, or acute symptoms of depersonalization and derealization, although nonsymptomatic people often experience the latter symptoms as well. In making dissociative diagnoses, clinicians should insure that the client's symptoms are not due to medications, substances, or a general medical condition (e.g., temporal lobe epilepsy) and should differentiate between dissociative symptoms and those of Acute Stress Disorder, PTSD, and Somatoform Disorder. Dissociative disorders are quite rare. A summary of dissociative disorders can be found in Table 12.3.

TABLE 12.3   Summary of Dissociative Disorders.

Diagnosis	Description
Dissociative Amnesia	The client cannot recall important personal information. Often follows severe stress or trauma; is not due to everyday forgetfulness.
Dissociative Fugue	The client suddenly and unexpectedly leaves the place of work or residence, cannot recall his or her past or identity, or assumes a new identity.
Dissociative Identity Disorder	Formerly known as Multiple Personality Disorder; characterized by a subjective experience of two or more distinct identities. Client may exhibit an inability to recall important personal information, not due to everyday forgetfulness.
Depersonalization Disorder	A recurrent feeling of detachment from one's body or mental processes.

Sleep Disorders

DSM-IV distinguishes four types of sleep disorders. Primary Sleep Disorders are presumed to be due to an underlying disturbance in the biological mechanisms regulating the sleep-wake cycle. Sleep Disorders Related to Another Mental Disorder code secondary sleep issues that require separate attention, such as a prominent sleep disturbance experienced in the context of a mood or anxiety disorder. Sleep Disorders Due to a General Medical Condition are the direct effects of a general medical condition, such as thyroid dysfunction or chronic pain, and Substance-Induced Sleep Disorder is a sleep disturbance resulting from the direct effects of a substance. The remainder of this section focuses on Primary Sleep Disorders.

Assessment and Diagnosis of Primary Sleep Disorders

Primary Sleep Disorders are classified into two groups of disorders. Dyssomnias are characterized by excessive sleep or problems in initiating or maintaining sleep. Primary Insomnia, in which a client experiences sleep disruptions not due to any other known cause, is an example of a dyssomnia. Parasomnias are characterized by abnormal physiological events, sleep stages, or sleep-wake transitions. Nightmare Disorder is an example of a parasomnia.

Dyssomnias. There are five types of dyssomnias. Primary Insomnia is characterized by difficulty initiating or maintaining sleep or by poor quality of sleep that occurs for at least a month. Primary Hypersomnia is characterized by excessive sleep, either as prolonged sleep or sleeping during the day, that occurs for at least a month. Narcolepsy is characterized by daily attacks of refreshing sleep for at least three months coupled with at least one of two phenomena: (1) episodes of cataplexy, brief losses of muscle tone often associated with intense emotional episodes; or (2) intrusions of REM sleep into the sleep-wake transition, such as sleep paralysis or episodes of intense, dreamlike imagery called hypnogogic or hypnopompic hallucinations (which may be terrifying since the person is unable to move). Breathing-Related Sleep Disorder is characterized by disruptions of sleep due to ventilation problems, such as repeated upper-airway obstructions associated with periods of interrupted breathing and loud snoring. Circadian Rhythm Sleep Disorder is characterized by a disturbance in the timing of sleep and is often associated with sleep cycle disruptions during travel or shift work.

Parasomnias. Parasomnias are disruptive patterns of unusual behavioral or physiological events that take place during sleep, such as nightmares, sleep terrors, and sleep walking. In Nightmare Disorder, the person experiences terrifying nightmares from which he or she wakes oriented and alert and can typically describe the nightmare. Nightmares occur near the end of the sleep cycle. In Night Terror Disorder, by contrast, the person typically wakes with a scream, is physiologically very aroused (e.g., rapid heartbeat, sweating), and is difficult to orient and arouse when he or she wakes. Clients waking from night terror episodes usually cannot remember anything about them, since they occur during the beginning of the sleep cycle. Clients with Sleepwalking Disorder experience repeated episodes of sleepwalking, during which they walk stuporously and from which they awake recalling nothing of their travels.

Treatment of Primary Sleep Disorders

A wide range of psychological and medical treatments is used to treat sleep disorders. Treatment often begins with simple interventions that help some clients, such as restricting caffeine and alcohol intake or other substances or medications that might lead to insomnia during the latter part of the day. Establishing a predictable routine of relaxing activities and avoiding arousing activities (e.g., exercising, studying) prior to bedtime may also be helpful. Reserving the bedroom exclusively for sleeping, a technique called "stimulus control," helps many clients, as do environmental modifications, such as ensuring the bedroom is dark and free of noise and other distractions. Finally, it is important to treat medical conditions that directly cause sleep disorders, such as pain and discomfort.

Cognitive-behavioral therapies, including sleep education, stimulus control, and restricted time in bed, have shown some promise in the treatment of sleep disorders (e.g., Edinger et al., 2001; see Lichstein et al., 2001, for contrasting data). A variety of medical and surgical treatments are also sometimes used. Benzodiazepines, for example, have long been used as a short-term, and, unfortunately, sometimes long-term treatment for sleep disorder symptoms (see Lader, 1999). However, benzodiazepines also produce significant side effects for many, if not most, clients (Holbrook et al., 2000; Lader, 1999). More recently, melatonin (an over-the-counter hormone supplement) has been found to be effective for insomnia, although it also may have significant side effects (Zhdanova et al., 2001). Surgical and mechanical treatments for sleep apnea also appear to be helpful for clients suffering this disorder (Bridgman & Dunn, 2000; Mehta et al., 2001). Practitioners should be aware of these alternatives to psychological treatments and should explore during assessment the medical or other interventions clients may already have attempted.

Impulse Control Disorders

Impulse Control Disorders are characterized by "failure[s] to resist an impulse, drive or temptation that is harmful to the person or to others" (APA, 1994, p. 609). Aggression, stealing, fire setting, gambling, and hair pulling are some specific impulse control disorders recognized by DSM-IV. Clients with these disorders often experience an increase in tension prior to, and a release of tension immediately following, their impulsive acts. When making a diagnosis of an Impulse Control Dis-

TABLE 12.4 **Summary of Impulse Control Disorders.**

Diagnosis	Description
Intermittent Explosive Disorder	Several episodes of failure to resist aggressive impulses, leading to aggression against property or people in which the violence is out of proportion to any provocation and not accounted for by other mental disorders, such as Conduct Disorder or Antisocial Personality Disorder.
Kleptomania	Failure to resist impulses to steal things that are not needed. Not accounted for by other mental disorders, such as Manic Episode.
Pyromania	Fire-setting that is deliberate and purposeful, and preceded by tension or affective arousal, fascination, curiosity, or attraction to fires. Pyromanic fire-setting is not done for personal gain and is not better accounted for by other mental disorders such as Conduct Disorder.
Pathological Gambling	Persistent and maladaptive gambling characterized by preoccupation with gambling, betting increasing amounts of money to gain excitement, unsuccessful efforts to cut back, relief of dysphoric mood when gambling, disruptions of family life, illegal acts, or disruption of relationships or employment, not accounted for by a manic episode.
Trichotillomania	Recurrent hair-pulling resulting in hair loss not accounted for by a physical or other mental disorder.

order, other mental disorders that could account for the behavior, such as Manic Disorder or Borderline Personality Disorder, are excluded, as are medical conditions or substance-related disorders that might better account for the client's symptoms. Similarly, if the client has clear ulterior motives for the behavior, such as stealing in order to gain needed money or goods or setting fires to gain insurance reimbursements, then a diagnosis of Impulse Control Disorder is not made. Examples of specific Impulse Control disorders are contained in Table 12.4. Because impulse control disorders cover a very diverse range of conditions, no general statements can be made about their assessment and treatment here.

Adjustment Disorders

Adjustment Disorders are distressful or impairing conditions that develop in response to identifiable stressors, such as loss of a job, divorce, change in employment, or other significant life event. According to DSM-IV, adjustment symptoms must occur within three months of the onset of the triggering stressor and must discontinue within six months after the termination of the stressor. Additionally, the symptoms must not meet the criteria for another DSM diagnosis (note that uncomplicated bereavement is not considered a DSM-IV disorder). When treated at all, adjustment symptoms may usually be assuaged with a combination of supportive and crisis-counseling interventions intended to help the client marshal (or regain) his or her resources to get through the current stressful situation (e.g., Rosenbluh, 1974).

Additional Conditions That May Be a Focus of Clinical Attention

Additional Conditions That May Be a Focus of Clinical Attention (see Table 12.5) include three kinds of problems: (1) presenting concerns that do not meet diagnostic criteria for another disorder, but that are sufficiently intense to require treatment, (2) presenting concerns that are the focus of clinical attention beyond another unrelated mental disorder, and, (3) problems that are the primary focus of clinical attention beyond a related mental disorder. Although they usually do not qualify for insurance reimbursement, they may be significant issues in clients'

TABLE 12.5 Summary of DSM-IV Additional Conditions That May Be a Focus of Clinical Attention.

Noncompliance with Treatment

Malingering

Adult Antisocial Behavior

Child and Adolescent Antisocial Behavior

Borderline Intellectual Functioning

Age-Related Cognitive Decline

Bereavement

Academic Problem

Occupational Problem

Identity Problem

Religious or Spiritual Problem

Acculturation Problem

Phase of Life Problem

TABLE 12.6   Summary of Medication-Induced Movement Disorders.

Diagnosis	Description
Neuroleptic-Induced Parkinsonism	Parkinsonian tremor, muscular rigidity associated with initiation or dosage increases of neuroleptics.
Neuroleptic Malignant Syndrome	A rare and potentially fatal side effect of neuroleptics, characterized by muscle rigidity, elevated temperature, and so on.
Neuroleptic-Induced Acute Dystonia	Abnormal spasms and posturing of upper body associated with dosage increases of neuroleptics.
Neuroleptic-Induced Acute Akathisia	Subjective complaints of restlessness, pacing, and fidgeting or an inability to sit still.
Neuroleptic-Induced Tardive Dyskinesia	Involuntary movements of the mouth, tongue, and extremities associated with the use of neuroleptics over a period of time.
Medication-Induced Postural Tremor	A fine tremor associated with lithium, antidepressants, and valproate.
Medication-Induced Movement Disorder Not Otherwise Specified	Any other medication-related movement disorder.

lives and frequently are the presenting concerns of clients seen by counselors and counseling psychologists.

DSM-IV identifies six groups of disorders in this category, including Psychological Factors Affecting Medical Condition (e.g., continuing to eat poorly despite receiving a diagnosis of diabetes); Medication-Induced Movement Disorders (e.g., negative side effects of neuroleptics, such as Parkinsonism, Neuroleptic Malignant Syndrome, Dystonia, Akathisia or Tardive Dyskinesia; see Table 12.6); Other Medication-Induced Disorders, a catch-all for other medication-induced negative side effects; Relational Problems; and Problems Related to Abuse and Neglect (see below). A significant proportion of clients seeing counseling psychologists, especially, may present with these conditions.

Problems Related to Abuse or Neglect

Counselors and psychologists encounter problems related to abuse and neglect in many contexts. Current ongoing abuse and neglect may be the primary reason for referral or a component of a broader referral; clients may report a history of abuse and neglect; or clinicians may witness or be told of abuse and neglect during the course of their work. Clinicians also may work with the perpetrators of abuse or neglect.

DSM-IV offers no clear definitions of either abuse or neglect (APA, 1994, p. 682), although it distinguishes physical abuse, sexual abuse, and neglect (DSM-IV also recognizes that both children and adults may be victimized). However, abuse and neglect are defined in a variety of laws, professional ethical standards, and local regulations in agencies where counselors and psychologists work. In these codifications, abuse is usually defined as an act of commission that causes distress or harm to another person, such as verbal or physical threats to harm, physical assault, or a sexual act with another person. Neglect, by contrast, is usually defined as an act of omission, such as failing to prevent a client from harming someone else, leaving vulnerable clients alone who are then harmed or, indeed, failing to report abuse or neglect.

Abuse and neglect vary widely in their impact on a client; they may have no impact or may result in lifelong trauma and dysfunction. Practitioners are cautioned to assess each sufferer of abuse or neglect individually and not assume, for example, that because a client is a victim of sexual assault he or she must suffer extreme psychopathology or dysfunction (although this sometimes occurs).

Assessment of the impact of abuse or neglect may be done through clinical interviews. Assessment also may include screening for mood and anxiety disorders, social dysfunction, or in some cases PTSD. Interventions typically include supportive counseling, helping clients reestablish (and redefine) relationships with perpetrators when appropriate and desirable, prevention of repeat incidents, and treatment of relevant mental health disorders, using methods appropriate to each diagnosis, when these exist. Psychologists and counselors may also work with perpetrators of abuse and neglect to prevent repetition of the offense and improve the client's functioning.

Abuse and neglect frequently give rise to ethical challenges for practitioners. The most common of these include breaching confidentiality and taking actions to protect victims from future reoccurrence of harm. Practitioners are especially vulnerable to charges of neglect, malpractice, or illegal activity if they fail to follow laws and ethical guidelines that require them to report suspected abuse or neglect, as difficult as this may be in particular instances. Practitioners may fail to report because they are unsure if the situation actually constitutes abuse or neglect, because they assume that someone else has already reported the incident, or because they are fearful of the personal repercussions of reporting. Although such fears are understandable and sometimes even well-founded, none of them absolves the practitioner from reporting abuse and neglect. (See Case 12.1.)

CASE 12.1

A Case of Neglect

Trish was a mental health counselor who worked for a small private mental health counseling company with multiple contracts throughout a large metropolitan area. She was reassigned to work with seniors in a nursing home setting on May 1. She mostly worked with clients in the nursing home who did not have severe cognitive impairments, providing bereavement counseling and counseling for depression.

As she walked through the nursing home, she often observed an elderly lady, Mrs. Gonsalva, who was obviously distressed and fearful. She had observed this more or less every day since she started work at the nursing home. On more than one occasion the lady had beckoned Trish over and whispered to her, "You know they beat me every night, don't you?" Being new, Trish was uncertain of what to do. On May 17, over coffee, she asked one of the registered nurses what to do. The nurse remarked, "You know these ladies have dementia. They say all kinds of stuff and not too much of it is reality-based." Trish did not want to ruin her relationship with staff and administrators by making false accusations, so she decided to discuss her concern with her professional supervisor at her next supervision meeting on May 19. Unfortunately, this meeting was canceled because her supervisor had a training workshop.

On May 29, Trish was very cooperative with investigators from the state Department of Human Services who came to interview her about the abuse of Mrs. Gonsalva by two staff members from the night shift. Trish was able to give them a clear and articulate account of what she had seen but was a little more troubled when they asked her why she had failed to report her suspicions. When the investigators asked if she had suspected abuse on May 17 when she spoke with the registered nurse, Trish honestly stated that she had suspected it, but was not sure about the situation or what she should do. When they asked her if she had reported possible abuse between May 17 and May 29, she had to report she had not. The investigators showed Trish pictures of bruising on Mrs. Gonsalva's back and asked if she had ever seen anything like that. Trish correctly said she had not. Trish was surprised when she arrived at work the next day and was asked to step into the facility administrator's office. The administrator told Trish she was now being investigated for neglect because she failed to report possible abuse. The facility administrator was especially concerned because there was evidence that abuse had occurred between May 17 and 29, which could have been prevented had Trish reported her suspicions. The administrator told Trish that in order to protect the facility's clients she could not remain anywhere on the facility grounds until the investigation was completed. Trish returned to her boss's office and explained the situation to her boss. Her boss sent her home until the matter was resolved. Three weeks later she was terminated by her employer for failing to report abuse and was reported to the licensing board for neglect.

CASE EXERCISE

Elisa, an 11-year-old Anglo-American girl you meet in a school setting, presents with multiple symptoms of depression including weight loss, depressed mood, anhedonia, loss of concentration, overwhelming feelings of guilt, and suicidal ideation. An interview with Elisa's teacher reveals that she lives alone with her mother and that their relationship is tense and "extremely upsetting to Elisa." The teacher states that Elisa's mother disciplines Elisa excessively, enforcing rigid, extreme rules that Elisa struggles to conform to. For example, when Elisa missed two problems on a recent homework assignment, her mother berated her in front of classmates and their parents after school. Elisa's mother emphatically stated that Elisa "has to complete every assignment she is given; she has to learn there are no excuses in life."

A phone interview and subsequent school-site visit with Elisa's mother reveals behavior consistent with Obsessive-Compulsive Personality Disorder, including coldness, rigidity, dramatic moralism, and extreme orderliness. As her conversation with you ends, Elisa's mother states emphatically that she doesn't want you meeting with her daughter, in part, she states, because she is concerned that "you will destroy her morality with your liberal, anti-family psychobabble."

Study Questions

1. Given Elisa's mother's prohibitions against working with Elisa, how should you intervene to address her suicidal ideation? How should you handle the situation if Elisa pleads with you to see her (despite her mother's refusal)?

2. How would you conduct treatment if Elisa's mother permits her to see you only under the auspices of improving her attitude toward school (e.g., after consultation between Elisa's mother and her teacher)?

3. How should Elisa's mother be included in treatment if it's clear she is part of the problem? How would you reply to a supervisor who advised you to accept that Elisa's mother's behavior cannot be changed and suggested you simply help Elisa devise a seven-year plan for dealing with her mother?

4. How might your treatment approach change if you learn that Elisa's mother may be prejudiced against you because of your ethnic background? (Assume, for example, that Elisa's mother alluded to racist views when referring to you in her discussions with Elisa's teacher.) How should you handle a conversation with Elisa's mother if she suggests that, as a psychotherapist, you would "distort Elisa's sexual preferences" so that she would engage in sexual relationships with a classmate she recently befriended?

5. Given your constraints in interviewing Elisa, how would you assess for possible physical abuse if she reported to you that her mother spanked her harshly with a belt, leaving a mark on her lower leg? What treatment plan might be arranged to stop this behavior if it were true—and should you be a part of it?

CASE EXERCISE

Ms. Choi is an attractive 23-year-old beautician referred for treatment of an eating disorder. Ms. Choi reports that about once a week she excessively eats high-calorie, sweet foods such as ice cream and candy, then induces vomiting by drinking a glass of water. She states she occasionally smokes marijuana, drinks excessively, and takes various recreational drugs during the weekend or on vacations. Her family is Chinese American and has lived in the United States for over a hundred years.

Ms. Choi is dressed glamorously but provocatively and is wearing somewhat heavy makeup. She stated animatedly in the first interview, "I am a walking, talking, living, DSM doll. You will learn everything from me. I have recovered from half of the stuff that you have never seen before: I have been anorexic; I don't do coke anymore, but I could; I live on antidepressants, because I could not get to therapy without them. I can do the 12-step shuffle faster than you can because I have done that dance twice already. I have done the Jesus thing and recovered from him. So here I am: Fix me."

In the history part of her assessment interview, Ms. Choi reports three past episodes of dysphoric mood characterized by an inability to eat and a general disinterest in life. During these episodes she would often call in sick to work and stay at home drinking. She reported she considered suicide in the past, stating she phoned her boyfriend and threatened to kill herself if he did not come over immediately. She states casually, "Well, I think I was just testing his limits, he was a doll really, not like the dodo I am dating right now." She reports she hates her parents and is jealous of her "freaky-normal, pretty little-bitch sister and her Mr. Porky-Dorky boyfriend." Ms. Choi's sister recently announced she would be getting married in six months.

During the second assessment interview Ms. Choi is quiet, unsmiling, and frequently tearful. She tells you she has episodes of depression that are so bad that she can feel nothing, during which she stays in her bedroom drinking and "praying for it to end." She states that when it gets bad she feels numb and no longer like a real person. The only way she can bring herself out of these episodes, she states, is to cut the bottom of her foot with a piece of glass she keeps in her desk drawer for this purpose. When she experiences pain again, she states, she knows she is alive.

Study Questions

1. Are there any immediate dangers? What actions should you take to prevent them?

2. List the possible DSM-IV diagnoses for Ms. Choi from most to least likely. List the evidence for each diagnosis.

3. Describe the assessment procedures you should use with Ms. Choi.

4. What short-term treatment goals are appropriate for your work with Ms. Choi?

5. What long-term treatment goals are appropriate for your work with Ms. Choi?

6. After two months of therapy, Ms. Choi arrives for her next appointment breezily announcing she has found the root of her problems. The previous weekend, she met a man twenty years her senior, had sex with him, and now she knows she is in love. She states she moved in with this man a couple of days ago and has come to say good-bye to you, since her problems are now resolved. What action should you take?

(continued)

CASE EXERCISE   Continued

7. What difference would it make to your assessment and treatment if Ms. Choi were a recent immigrant from Korea, working in a family grocery store in a predominantly Korean neighborhood?

8. Ms. Choi reports that she cannot pay her bills for therapy, but states that if she does not continue her therapy she knows she will kill herself. She states that she can pay you only a portion of her bill, but could do filing for you or cut your hair in lieu of payment. What action should you take?

9. Ms. Choi phones you at home at 9:00 P.M. on a Friday evening. She is tearful, distraught, and sounds intoxicated. She reports that her boyfriend is seeing another woman and that she is going to kill herself. She has called you to say good-bye and thank you for all your help. What ethical principles are involved in this situation? What action should you take?

REFERENCES

American Psychiatric Association. (1994). *Diagnostic and statistical manual of mental disorders* (4th ed.) *(DSM-IV)*. Washington, DC: Author.

American Psychiatric Association. (2000). *Diagnostic and statistical manual of mental disorders* (4th ed., text revision) *(DSM-IV-TR)*. Washington, DC: Author.

Ball, S. A. (1998). Manualized treatment for substance abusers with personality disorders: Dual focus schema therapy. *Addictive Behaviors, 23*, 883–891.

Bateman, A., & Fonagy, P. (1999). Effectiveness of partial hospitalization in the treatment of borderline personality disorder: a randomized controlled trial. *American Journal of Psychiatry, 156*, 1563–1569.

Bateman, A., & Fonagy, P. (2001). Treatment of borderline personality disorder with psychoanalytically oriented partial hospitalization: An 18 month follow-up. *American Journal of Psychiatry, 158*, 36–42.

Beck, A. T., & Freeman, A. (1990). *Cognitive therapy of personality disorders*. New York: Guilford.

Bloxham, G., Long, C. G., Alderman, N., & Hollin, C. R. (1993). The behavioral treatment of self-starvation and severe self-injury in a patient with borderline personality disorder. *Journal of Behavior Therapy and Experimental Psychiatry, 24*, 261–267.

Bohus, M., Haaf, B. Stigmayr, C., Pohl, U., Bohme, R., & Linehan, M. (2000). Evaluation of inpatient dialectical-behavior therapy for borderline personality disorder: A prospective study. *Behaviour Research and Therapy, 38*, 875–887.

Bridgman, S. A., & Dunn, K. M. (2000). Surgery for obstructive sleep apnoea. *Cochrane Database Review*, CD001004.

Carson, R. C., Butcher, J. N., & Mineka, S. (2000). *Abnormal psychology and modern life* (11th ed.). Boston: Allyn and Bacon.

Edinger, J. D., Wohlgemuth, W. K., Radtke, R. A., Marsh, G. R., & Quillian, R. E. (2001). Cognitive behavioral therapy for treatment of chronic primary insomnia: A randomized controlled trial. *Journal of the American Medical Association, 285*, 1856–1864.

Evans, K., Tryer, P., Catalan, J., Schmidt, U., Davidson, K., Dent, J., Tata, P., Thornton, S., & Thompson, B. J. (1999). Manual-assisted cognitive-behavior therapy (MACT): A randomized controlled trial of a brief intervention with bibliotherapy in the treatment of recurrent deliberate self-harm. *Psychological Medicine, 29,* 19–25.

Glasser, W. (1965). *Reality therapy: A new approach to psychiatry.* New York: Harper & Row.

Glasser, W. (2000). *Reality therapy in action.* New York: HarperCollins.

Golomb, M., Fava, M., Abraham, M., & Rosenbaum, J. F. (1995). Gender differences in personality disorders. *American Journal of Psychiatry, 152,* 579–582.

Grann, M., Langstrom, N., Tebgstrom, A., & Stalenheim, E. G. (1998). Reliability of file-based retrospective ratings of psychopathy with PCL-R. *Journal of Personality Assessment, 70,* 416–426.

Greenberg, J. R., & Mitchell, S. A. (1983). *Object relations in psychoanalytic theory.* Cambridge, MA: Harvard University Press.

Hawkins, K. A., & Sinha, R. (1998). Can line clinicians master the conceptual complexities of dialectical behavior therapy? An evaluation of State Department of Mental Health training program. *Journal of Psychiatric Research, 32,* 379–384.

Hicklin, J., & Widiger, T. A. (2000). Convergent validity of alternative MMPI-2 personality disorder scales. *Journal of Personality Assessment, 75,* 502–518.

Hinshaw, S. P. (1994). Conduct disorder in childhood: Conceptualization, diagnosis, comorbidity, and risk status for antisocial functioning in adulthood. In D. C. Folwes, P. Stuker, & S. H. Goodman (Eds.), *Progress in experimental personality and psychopathology research.* New York: Springer.

Holbrook, A. M., Crowther, R., Lotter, A., Cheng, C., & King, D. (2000). Meta-analysis of benzodiazepines use in the treatment of insomnia. *Canadian Medical Journal, 162,* 225–233.

Kernberg, O. F. (1985). *Borderline conditions and pathological narcissism.* Northvale, NJ: Jason Aronson.

Kernberg, O. F. (1996). *A psychoanalytic theory of personality disorders.* In J. F. Clarkin & M. F. Lenzenweger (Eds.), *Major theories of personality disorder* (pp. 106–140). New York: Guilford.

Koerner, K., & Linehan, M. M. (2000). Research on dialectical behavior therapy for patients with borderline personality disorder. *Psychiatric Clinics of North America, 23,* 151–167.

Kohut, H. (1977). *Restoration of the self.* New York: International Universities Press.

Lader, M. H. (1999). Limitations on the use of benzodiazepines in anxiety and insomnia: Are they justified? *European Journal of Neuropsychopharmacology, 9* (supplement 6), S399–S405.

Lenzenweger, M. F. (1999). Stability and change in personality disorder features: The longitudinal study of personality disorders. *Archives of General Psychiatry, 56,* 1009–1015.

Lichstein, K. L., Riedel, B. W., Wilson, N. M., Lester, K. W., & Aguillard, R. N. (2001). Relaxation and sleep compression for late-life insomnia: A placebo-controlled trial. *Journal of Consulting and Clinical Psychology, 69,* 227–239.

Linehan, M. M. (1993). *Skills-training manual for treatment of borderline personality disorder.* New York: Guilford.

Linehan, M. M., Armstrong, H. E., Suarez, A., Allmon, D., & Heard, H. L. (1991). Cognitive-behavioral treatment of chronically parasuicidal borderline patients. *Archives of General Psychiatry, 48,* 1060–1064.

Linehan, M. M., Schmidt, H., Dimeff, L. A., Craft, J. C., Kanter, J., & Comtois, K. A., (1999). Dialectical behavior therapy for patients with borderline personality disorder and drug-dependence. *American Journal of Addictions, 8,* 279–292.

McDermott, P. A., Alterman, A. I., Cacciola, J. S., Rutherford, M. J., Newman, J. P., & Mulholland, E. M. (2000). Generality of Psychopathy Checklist-revised over prisoners and substance-dependence patients. *Journal of Consulting and Clinical Psychology, 68,* 181–186.

Mehta, A., Qian, J., Petrocz, P. Darendeliler, M. A., & Cistulli, P. A. (2001). A randomized controlled study of a mandibular advancement splint for obstructive sleep apnea. *American Journal of Respiratory Critical Care Medicine, 163,* 1457–1461.

Merrit, R. D., Balogh, D. W., & Kok, C. J. (1998). DSM-IV cluster A personality disorder diagnoses among young adults with a 2-7-8 MMPI profile. *Assessment, 5,* 273–285.

Molto, J., Poy, R., & Torrubia, R. (2000). Standardization of the Hare Psychopathy Checklist I, revised in a Spanish prison population. *Journal of Personality Disorders, 14,* 84–96.

Moyes, T., Tennent, T. G., & Bedford, A. P. (1985). Long-term follow-up of a ward-based behavior modification program of adolescents with acting-out and conduct problems. *British Journal of Psychiatry, 147,* 300–305.

Raine, A. (1985). A psychometric assessment of Hare's checklist for psychopathy in an English prison population. *British Journal of Clinical Psychology, 24,* 247–248.

Rosenbluh, E. S. (1974). *Techniques of crisis intervention.* New York: Behavioral Science Services.

Sansone, R. A., Wiederman, M. W., & Sansone, L. A. (1998). The Self-Harm Inventory (SHI): Development of a scale for identifying self-destructive behaviors and borderline personality disorder. *Journal of Clinical Psychology, 54,* 974–983.

Vera, E. M. & Gaubatz, M. D. (2001). Promoting social competence in school-age children. In C. L. Juntunen & D. R. Atkinson (Eds.), *Counseling across the lifespan: Prevention and treatment* (pp. 57–70). Thousand Oaks, CA: Sage Publications.

Widiger, T., & Trull, T. J. (1993). Borderline and narcissistic personality disorders. In P. B. Sutker & H. E. Adams (Eds.), *Comprehensive handbook of psychopathology* (2nd ed.). New York: Plenum.

Wubbolding, R. E. (1988). *Using reality therapy.* New York: Harper & Row.

Zhdanova, I. V., Wurtman, R. J., Regan, M. M., Taylor, J. A., Shi, J. P., & Leclair, O. U. (2001). *Journal of Clinical Endocrinology and Metabolism, 86,* 4727–4730.

Clinical and
Counseling Practice

INDEX